Administrative Office Management

SHORT COURSE

PATTIE ODGERS, Ed.D.

Coconino Community College

Flagstaff, AZ

THOMSON

SOUTH-WESTERN

Australia · Canada · Mexico · Singapore · Spain · United Kingdom · United States

THOMSON
—★—
SOUTH-WESTERN

Administrative Office Management, Short Course, 13th Edition

Pattie Odgers

VP/Editorial Director:
Jack W. Calhoun

VP/Editor-in-Chief:
Dave Shaut

Senior Publisher:
Karen Schmohe

Acquisitions Editor:
Joseph Vocca

Project Manager:
Penny Shank

Consulting Editor:
Sharon Massen

Production Manager:
Patricia Matthews Boies

Production Editor:
Colleen A. Farmer

VP/Director of Marketing:
Carol Volz

Marketing Manager:
Lori Pegg

Marketing Coordinator:
Georgi Wright

Manufacturing Coordinator:
Kevin Kluck

Cover Designer:
Michael Stratton

Internal Designer:
Michael Stratton

Compositor:
ElectroPub

Printer:
RR Donnelley

Expect More
FROM SOUTH-WESTERN WITH . . .

PROCEDURES & THEORY FOR ADMINISTRATIVE PROFESSIONALS, Fulton-Calkins/Stulz (0-538-72740-3)

The 5th edition of this market-leading text is designed to prepare the office professional for a challenging role in today's workplace. Office topics, procedures, human relations, and technology with online applications are explored.

TECHNOLOGY & PROCEDURES FOR ADMINISTRATIVE PROFESSIONALS, Fulton-Calkins (0-538-72590-7)

This text is designed to develop the knowledge and skills necessary for success in the workplace and to develop communication, human relations, and time and stress management skills.

ONLINE TRAINING FOR ADMINISTRATIVE PROFESSIONALS, Rigby/Jennings/Stulz (0-538-72491-9)

This completely online product is a perfect complement to any office technology course. Content modules include records management, office mail, documents, and reports plus a variety of other office related topics.

RECORDS MANAGEMENT Read-Smith/Ginn/Kallaus (0-538-72466-8)

Thorough coverage of filing and maintenance of paper, automated, micro image, and electronic imaging records are provided in this market-leading text. A practice set is also available for hands-on practice of alphabetic filing rules.

For more information on these and other South-Western products, visit **www.swlearning.com**

THOMSON
SOUTH-WESTERN

Book at a Glance

Part 3

Practicing Leadership and Communication Skills

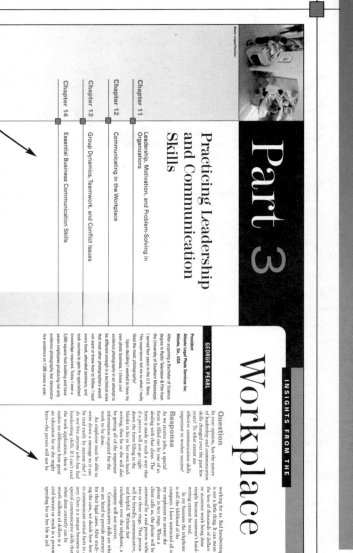

Getty Images/PhotoDisc

Chapter 11	Leadership, Motivation, and Problem-Solving in Organizations
Chapter 12	Communicating in the Workplace
Chapter 13	Group Dynamics, Teamwork, and Conflict Issues
Chapter 14	Essential Business Communication Skills

Management is doing things right; leadership is doing the right things.

—Peter Drucker, management guru

PART OPENER
Provides a two-page spread of key topics and chapters to be covered at a glance

---

INSIGHTS FROM THE WORKPLACE
Offers profiles of managers who describe their jobs and explain methods of solving human and technical problems in the office

---

QUOTATIONS
Offered by historians and other people of fame

NEW

TECHNOLOGY APPLICATIONS IN THE WORKPLACE
Offers a situation in which an issue has taken place or a situation is presenting a difficulty for the manager, employees, or the general public

---

ISSUES TO THINK ABOUT
Questions that relate to the Technology Application in the Workplace

---

INSIGHTS FROM THE

Workplace

President
GEORGE S. PEARL
Atlanta Legal Photo Services Inc.
Atlanta, Ga., USA

Question

In your opinion, has the nature of leadership and communication skills changed over the past few years? To what extent are effective communication skills important to worker success?

Response

As we receive jobs, a special form is filled out by one of us dealing with that client. The information required for the work to be done.

An employee must be able to write down a message so it can be read easily by anyone else. If I can't read a handwriting skills that take place, then it do not hire anyone who had bad handwriting. If I can't read the work application, then it makes no difference how great an education he or she might have—the person will not be

working for us. Bad handwriting is not a little thing. It can mean the loss of thousands of dollars or incorrect work being done simply because someone's handwriting cannot be read.

In my business the telephone is still the lifeblood of the company. I have instructed all of my employees to answer the phone in two rings. When a client calls us, the phone will be answered by a real person within two or three rings. That person will be friendly, communicative, and helpful. Without fast exchanges over the telephone, a company will not survive.

Communication skills are what we are hired to provide attorneys for their legal cases. After studying the case, we decide how best to communicate critical facts to a jury. Ours is a unique business of special communicative skills that when done correctly can be worth millions of dollars in a civil lawsuit or result in a person spending his or her life in jail.

Chapter Eleven

TECHNOLOGY APPLICATIONS IN THE WORKPLACE

The Digital Divide and Leading the Work Force
A major concern of the U.S. government and many citizens around the world is the digital divide. The phrase **digital divide** is used to describe the idea that people of the world can be divided into two distinct groups: (1) those who have access to technology with the ability to use it and (2) those who do not have access to technology or are without the ability to use it.

Society's goal is to narrow the gap, or bridge the divide, between those who have access to technology and those who do not. The National Policy Association's Digital Economic Opportunity Committee recently released its final report, "Building a Digital Workforce—Confronting the Crisis," at a Washington news briefing. The report says that action by Americans to close the information-technology skills gap in the current and future work force is a critical challenge for business, labor, education, government, and the nonprofit sector.

ISSUES TO THINK ABOUT:

1. Do you think the U.S. work force experiences the digital divide phenomenon or is it limited to workers in other countries? Explain.
2. Project ten years from now and forecast the extent to which the digital divide will affect global business, and as a result, the way workers are managed.

TECHNOLOGY APPLICATIONS IN THE WORKPLACE

OBJECTIVES
Focus on expected outcomes from each chapter

ETHICS & CHOICES
Examples of business ethical dilemmas throughout the text which allow students to exercise decision-making skills to determine proper courses of action

TWO-COLUMN LAYOUT
Provides better readability by breaking up long lines of text and providing more white space

MANAGEMENT TIP
Practical suggestions from office managers in today's workplace

---

Chapter 1

The Evolution of Management Practices

OBJECTIVES

After completing this chapter, you will be able to:

1. Define the role of management in the workplace.
2. Identify the five schools of management thought.
3. Define the levels of management and the categories of skills needed by administrative managers.
4. List and describe the traditional management functions.
5. Define the eight principles of management.
6. Reflect on the positive and negative factors in the changing workplace.

In general, the five chapters in Part 1 serve as an introductory overview of administrative office management and the essential elements covered in this textbook. Specifically this chapter explains administrative management and the traditional elements of management and their functions.

Effective information management is at the heart of what most businesses do. Information is recognized today as one of the most strategic resources that an organization possesses. Information must be carefully managed because it is not only the critical basis for sound decision-making but also an essential element in achieving improved productivity over global competitors in business. Because information is produced and transmitted at incredible speed, workplaces and how they are managed are changing. Before studying today's administrative office management practices, let's form a base and look at the origins of traditional management as well as discover how management and administrative management can be defined.

MANAGEMENT TIP
Be a role model. No matter what your job, setting a good example goes a long way in dealing with people.

THE ROLE OF MANAGEMENT IN THE WORKPLACE

We now need to define management in order to highlight the importance, relevance, and necessity of studying it. **Management** is the process of working with and through others to blend together people, materials, money, methods, machines, and morale in an effort to set and to achieve the goals of the organization.

Administrative management is related to the word administration, which describes the performance of, or carrying out of, assigned duties. Administration is also used to refer to a group of persons who execute those duties, such as the governing board of your school or the top-level executives of a corporation. Administration, as you shall see, is essential to every aspect of business operations. To achieve the goals of an organization, a firm must be well managed. Thus, the functions of management involve the planning, organizing, controlling of all resources and the leading or directing of people to attain the goals of a productive, unified organization. You will learn about these later in the chapter.

The functions of management are performed by persons called managers at several levels in any organization. The titles held by managers vary considerably depending on the nature of the work assigned, the responsibilities delegated to the positions, and the type and size of the organization. As you shall see later, many business firms have reduced the number of other managerial levels, which, in turn, provides a "flatter" organizational structure.

In general, what do managers do? Management is much more than the familiar activity of telling employees what to do. Management is a complex and dynamic mixture of systematic techniques and common sense. As with any complex process, the key to learning about management lies in dividing it into readily understood subprocesses. One approach is to focus on managerial roles or behaviors. These roles can be grouped into three major categories: interpersonal, informational, and decisional roles.

- *Interpersonal.* Because of their formal authority and superior status, managers engage in a good deal of interpersonal contact, especially with people who report to them.
- *Informational.* Every manager has a clearinghouse for information relating to the task at hand or issues of relevance.
- *Decisional.* In their decisional roles, managers balance competing interests and make choices. Through decisional roles, strategies are formulated and put into action.

THE ADMINISTRATIVE MANAGER POSITION

The person who heads up the company-wide information management function may have one of several roles, such as administrative manager, office manager, manager of administrative services, information manager or

---

technological challenges and opportunities. Technology trends affect entire organizations, rather than just individual areas.

In the workplace, people use computers, technology devices such as scanners, faxes, copiers, and telecommunication systems to complete vital organizational activities. Using computers, workers create correspondence such as letters, reports, and e-mail messages, calculate payroll, track inventory, and generate invoices. Computers are a primary tool workers use to communicate with others instantly and to access information from all around the globe. Using the advanced computer equipment and network systems that are available, you can not only transmit text, but also voice, sounds, video, and graphics as well.

Workplaces depend on different types of computers and technology systems for a variety of applications. Small companies with fewer than 50 employees, for instance, use several types of specialized communications software on a daily basis and don't think anything about it. Those who work away from the office may take for granted their notebook computers equipped with a modem or other wireless capability as they complete work in other locations. Large businesses use these same applications and provide an automated networked system throughout the company. They also have large databases

ETHICS & CHOICES
An office supply dealer delivers one "free" copy of a new software package to your residence after you, the administrative manager, placed an order for ten copies of that software. Do you keep the software package?

and use high-tech equipment readily accessible to each of their workers.

Many businesses use networks extensively. **Networks** are defined as a collection of computers and devices connected by communications channels that facilitate communication among workers and allow users to share resources with other users. Using a network enables people to communicate efficiently and easily, both outside of and within the organization. Each user on a business network shares hardware, software, data, and information, thereby reducing costs while increasing efficiency and promoting effective information management.

The **Internet**, known as the world's largest network system, is used to send messages to others, obtain information, shop for business-related goods and services, and meet or converse with people around the world. A variety of Internet and online services in the technologically advanced workplace are briefly described below:

- E-mail and the transmission of messages and files are primary methods of rapid communication in the workplace.
- Instant messaging (IM) is a service that notifies you when one or more people are online and then allows you to exchange messages or join in a private chat room.
- A chat is a typed conversation that takes place on a computer in real time through a chat room.
- Internet telephone uses the Internet instead of the telephone to enable workers to talk to other people over the web.

MESSAGE FOR MANAGERS
Concludes each chapter with a final thought and brings together the chapter contents

END-OF-CHAPTER FEATURES
Includes a summary, key terms, review, critical thinking questions, case studies, and an Internet Research Activity

SUMMARY
A quick review for students and teachers

KEY TERMS
Use for review or quiz

NEW

FIGURE 1.4 Responsibility for Management Systems and Activities

Who is responsible for the management of office activities and information systems in organizations?

Only the AOM?

MESSAGE FOR MANAGERS

A concluding comment will help put the historical overview into perspective. Although this chapter provides a useful conceptual framework for students of management, generally it does not carry over to the practice of management. In reality, managers use whatever is ethical, fair, and meets stated objectives. Instead of faithfully adhering to a given school of management thought, one system or functional groupings, successful managers tend to use a "mixed bag" approach. This chapter is, however, a good starting point for you to begin building your own approach to management by blending theory, the experience and advice of others, and your own experience in this technology-driven, global environment. Be ready to put into practice the concepts, principles, and practices that will work for you on the job.

SUMMARY

1. Management is the process of working with and through others to blend people, materials, money, methods, machines, and morale to set and to achieve the goals of the organization.

2. The person responsible for planning, organizing, and controlling the information processing activities and for leading people in attaining the organization's objectives is called the administrative manager or administrative office manager.

3. The five schools of management thought are classical, behavioral, management science, quality management, and systems.

4. The three broad categories of skills needed by AMs are a) conceptual skills, which include analyzing problems and devising solutions and action plans; b) human skills, which allow a manager to identify, comprehend, and solve human problems, and; c) technical skills, which are work-related tasks to a particular field.

5. Most managers perform the major interrelated functions of planning, organizing, leading, and controlling.

6. Planning is choosing organizational objectives and the course of action needed to achieve those objectives. Planning precedes the other three functions of management.

7. Organizing is the multifaceted function that gets things done and involves traditional management concepts such as delegation, authority, responsibility, and accountability.

8. Leading is a critical management function that includes motivating individuals and influencing group activities to accomplish objectives.

9. Controlling means devising ways and means of ensuring that planned performance is actually achieved.

10. The eight principles of management are a) The objectives of an organization and all of its divisions must be clearly defined and understood. b) Responsibility for organizing work exists with managers at all levels. c) All organizations are composed of various functions that must be effectively integrated to achieve their major objectives. d) An organization should utilize specialization to achieve efficiency. e) Authority must be delegated to individuals in keeping with the responsibility assigned them. f) Each employee should receive orders from only one supervisor. g) The number of employees reporting to one supervisor should be limited to a manageable number. h) Centralize managerial authority and responsibility for complex functions, but decentralize for simpler functions.

KEY TERMS

Accountability
Administrative office manager
Authority
Behavioral science approach
Budget
Bureaucracy
Centralized authority
Chain of command
Controlling
Decentralized authority
Delegation
Effectiveness
Efficiency
Hawthorne experiments
Human relations approach
Hygienic factors
Inverted pyramids
Leading
Management
Management by objectives
Management science
Management theory
Motivation-hygiene theory
Motivators
Objectives
Organizing
Planning
Principles
Project
Pyramid
Quality management
Responsibilities
Single-use plans
Span of control
Specialist
Standing plans
Strategic planning process
Theory
Theory Z management
Unity of command

REVIEW

1. Using descriptions in this chapter, briefly describe your interpretation of the word management.
2. List and describe the three roles of administrative managers.
3. What does it mean when we say that management is the science of managing?
4. In the Classical School, what did the early forms of management focus upon?
5. What were the major contributions made by Frederick Taylor, the father of scientific management?
6. In what way are Fayol's concepts related to total entry management?
7. What are the major systems that make up the total system of an organization?
8. What is the purpose of the chain of command as shown on pyramid organizational charts?
9. Name the three types of skills needed by an administrative manager.
10. Briefly explain the purpose of each of the major managerial functions of planning, organizing, leading, and controlling.
11. Distinguish between centralized and decentralized authority in organizations.
12. Of what value are the principles of management to an administrative manager?

CRITICAL THINKING

1. The study of administrative management may lead you to develop a strong belief in management as a science or as an art. In

32 | PART 1 | Identifying Basic Concepts and Trends

your opinion, what is the difference between these views? Which view do you hold now? Once you finish this course, return to this chapter question to assess your beliefs. Will they change? Or will they have been affirmed?

2. Of the five schools of management thought, which two most nearly reflect your personal day-to-day management style? Do you think you will likely change your management style in the future? Why or why not?

3. Describe the behavior and activities performed by two people you know who practice good interpersonal skills. What behavior do they exhibit that led you to think of them?

4. Consider the four functions of management. Which function would an inexperienced administrative manager be likely to spend more time developing and implementing than an administrative manager with two or three years of experience? Which function do you think you will need to spend more time on?

5. Why is the strategic planning process described as comprehensive? Describe an organization you know that has implemented this process. (It may be the school you are attending now or the company where you are working.)

6. Describe five activities administrative managers do that could be measured by either their effectiveness or efficiency.

7. Have you ever had a job wherein you reported to more than one supervisor who assigned and/or checked your work? What issues or concerns arose from this work situation? How did you handle any issues or conflicts that arose?

CASE STUDY 1-1:
PROMOTION TO ADMINISTRATIVE MANAGER

Victor Gomez has served as supervisor of the accounts payable section of his firm for the past ten years. Gomez takes great pains to see that all invoice details are checked twice by his accounting clerks. Unknown to his clerks, Gomez manually spot-checks 10 to 15 percent of their work, which he is required to initial for approval. Other aspects of his supervisory style seem unique. For example, he insists that all employees keep neat desks (which he monitors each week). Also, from 8:50 to 9:10 a.m. each day, Gomez positions himself near the office entrance to check on his workers' punctuality.

None of Gomez's five clerks have objected to his supervisory style. In fact, he is very popular with the group. He keeps records of their birthdays and other important anniversaries in order to remember them in some special way. He also seems to be very sympathetic to their personal needs for time off from work when the occasion demands it.

Gomez's section has an excellent record of productivity. Largely for this reason, he has been chosen to "move up" to the position of administrative manager. In this position, he will be responsible for five sections, each headed by a supervisor who, in turn, is responsible for the work of eight to ten persons, depending on the section involved.

As he starts his new job, Gomez has a good talk with himself in which he looks back approvingly at the success of his work as accounts payable supervisor. Thus, he believes he can effectively manage the entire office using the same leadership style.

The Evolution of Management Practices | **CHAPTER 1** | **33**

that it would be difficult to find a replacement. But, yes, she is kind of sarcastic. I'll just put it off a little longer. Maybe she is having some personal problems at home."

Discussion Questions
1. What is the real problem involved in this case?
2. Did Lowe make the right decision to put off the discussion on the issue with Larson?

Analyze the case and draft brief answers to the questions for a group discussion.

INTERNET RESEARCH ACTIVITY

The U.S. Small Business Administration provides a gold mine of free information for small-business owners and managers. Access the course web site at http://www.swlearning.com and click on the links tab. You'll find several topics of interest. Using your favorite search engine, locate another web site that provides free information for managers. You may try using search words such as business plan, operating a business, managing a business, and so on.

Learning Activity:
1. What was the most useful piece of management information you acquired? Indicate where you found that information.
2. How does what you read relate to topics in Chapter 1 of this text? Be specific.

Prepare a one-page report to share with the class as directed by your instructor.

Discussion Questions
1. What important problem(s) would you anticipate in this case?
2. Considering Gomez's work history, how would you expect him to delegate work? Does it appear that he has applied equally well the principles of management discussed in this chapter?
3. How would you classify his management style? Do you feel that his past style will be effective in his relationship with his new workers? Explain.

Review the case and be prepared to discuss your answers in class.

CASE STUDY 1-2
DEVELOPING A PROBLEM-SOLVING ATTITUDE

Andy Lowe heads up the customer services division of Johnstown Metal Works, a manufacturer of East Coast companies. One of the systems analysts who reports directly to Lowe is Susan Larson, who has been with the firm for ten years. During the past several months, Larson has become irritable and sometimes antagonizes customers. Lowe realizes that he should speak to Larson about her relationship with the customers, but for some reason he has been reluctant to do so.

Today Lowe hears of another "run-in" that Larson had with a customer over the reworking of a large metal work order. He sits back, sighs, and reflects: "I really must sit down and talk with Larson. But I am fearful that she may quit. She handles all this technical measurement so well, and I know

---

OTHER PRODUCT FEATURES

CD-ROM TESTING SOFTWARE

Provides the instructor the ability to create printed tests, Internet tests, and computer-based tests (provided on the Instructor's Resource CD)

PRESENTATION SOFTWARE

Provides chapter-by-chapter PowerPoint® slides correlated to the text (provided on the Instructor's Resource CD)

INTERNET RESEARCH ACTIVITY

Presents an office scenario with questions for the student to research and analyze orally or in writing

http://www.odgers.swlearning.com
COURSE WEB SITE

Preface

In each of its thirteen editions spanning several decades, *Administrative Office Management* has carefully documented the problems and solutions of an expanding office world. It began with the First Edition in the depression years of the 1930s and continued on during the hectic war years, culminating in the present edition. In the 13th Edition, like its predecessors, the author explains *past* office problems, relates them to *current* office conditions and situations, and explains how to ensure *future* effectiveness in office operations.

New thinking has emerged to redefine the office. Instead of a place where secretarial work is performed, now we view the office even more broadly as the *information function* as well as the *information center*—a place where information-related operations occur. The pace of change in information technology, so swift and universal in the 1970s, 1980s, and 1990s, has accelerated even more in the early 2000s. This means that our students preparing for business careers, as well as workers on the job seeking positions in management, need to be on the "cutting edge" of technology and human relations to maximize the use of information tools and procedures in their work.

Administrative Office Management, 13th Edition, still follows the same logical organization plan as its predecessors, but with substantial updating and strengthening of content. It reflects current management thinking based on extensive research in information management, technology,

communications, office systems, and administrative procedures. This multidisciplinary textbook is designed to teach applied systems thinking to students pursuing both administrative support and information management careers.

To compete effectively, the United States needs competent technicians, humanistic supervisors, and highly skilled front-line workers. Our economy—one that is international, information-based, and technology driven—runs on their efforts. As competitors on the global front are thriving, the cultures of organizations in America are readapting to their environments on a daily basis. Still, incredibly and at the same time, businesses are being asked to do more with less. To confront these new, diverse, and multifaceted challenges, administrative office and business professionals need up-to-date knowledge, as well as techniques, to achieve innovative and speedy solutions to problems. Effectively managed administrative office information systems are critical to the success of all organizations and ultimately to the success of our country in the world marketplace. Those with a quality-oriented approach and with an eye to global competition must manage organizations—public or private, domestic or international.

OUR AUDIENCE

Administrative Office Management, 13th Edition, is appropriate for students who have had no experience in an office environment (as an office-oriented supervision text), as well as for those currently on a career track leading toward managing an office. In addition, it can be used as a training tool for future business technology instructors. Moreover, users of this textbook will find it to be an excellent reference source for those in organizations whose responsibility it is to oversee information systems.

Not only does the 13th Edition cover current management principles, concepts, and organizational trends, but also it acknowledges that it is everyone's job to manage office information systems, from the top executive to the receptionist. The text provides a strong, management-based background using a humanistic approach for managing and supervising staff in an office environment. Technological changes in the workplace demand that each employee be computer-oriented with knowledge of efficiency techniques relative to office systems. It is ideal for training and enhancing the productivity of information systems workers at all levels—administrative, managerial, technical, and professional.

THE BOOK AT A GLANCE

Part I

The first part of the text introduces students to the basic management practices, opportunities, and challenges in administrative office management. These basics include discussions of the evolution of management practices, specific administrative management activities in the workplace, emerging elements impacting administrative management practices, and issues surrounding the management of information, technology, and training needs.

Part II

In this part, the critical area of managing human resources in the office is discussed. These resources include staffing and on-the-job employee practices, as well as employee compensation and recognition, health-related, work ethics, and business etiquette issues.

Part III

This part stresses leadership and motivation skills in business environments. It includes working with groups and teams, plus using problem-solving skills when resolving conflict issues.

Part IV

The next part covers managing essential administrative services. These areas include office design, space, and health issues, as well as workplace safety concerns. In addition, other workplace productivity systems are covered such as document management, copying, telephoning, mailing, and accounting.

FEATURES NEW TO THIS EDITION

To update and further strengthen coverage of the office management field, the topics throughout the text are covered in more depth, with an emphasis on the importance of using effective communication techniques and applying state-of-the-art Internet research and technology skills. In addition, the 13th Edition

- Is **extensively researched** by the author and includes new research in excess of 500 publications with 2001-2003 references.

- Introduces a new feature **Technology Applications in the Workplace** that provides an introductory example of how technology is used in the workplace, its impact on business, or a noteworthy situation relative to the chapter content.

- Provides *Key Terms* in the End-of-Chapter Activities as a useful review or a quick quiz to begin the chapter.

- Brings back a *Summary* feature from earlier editions that outlines the key points covered in the chapter for a quick review by the instructor and students.

- *The Management Tips* in each chapter provide practical suggestions from the practices of office managers today.

- *The Ethics and Choices* sections throughout each chapter are examples of office and business ethical dilemmas that allow students to determine their own actions; then discuss them with the entire class.

- A *Message for Managers* feature concludes each chapter with a final thought that brings together the chapter content.

- A *Glossary* concludes the text and contains all definitions of key terms throughout the chapters.

FEATURES RETAINED FROM PREVIOUS EDITION

Many features remain from the prior edition because they have proven to be well received:

- The *personal, informal writing style* that effectively communicates with readers.

- Retention of *general management principles*.

- *Insights from the Workplace* profiles managers who describe their jobs, explain their methods of solving human and technical problems in the office, and provide personal information about their education and work experience. These profiles give students practical information from managers and supervisors currently on the "firing line."

- The *Objectives* section introduces the key concepts students will learn in the chapter.

- A *Quotation* at the start of each chapter introduces the students to a familiar thought from a famous person or historian.

END-OF-CHAPTER ACTIVITIES

At the end of each chapter, you will find more technology-based, Internet-research projects incorporating the following activities following a summary of the key points:

- **Key Terms:** Presents the terms defined in the chapter in bold; useful as a student review or as a quick quiz to start the chapter.

- **Review Questions:** Offered as a review of the key concepts in the chapter.

- **Critical Thinking Questions:** Designed to stretch the reader's thinking, these questions interrelate the content to the reader's philosophy, value system, and work experience.

- **Case Studies:** The two case problems are designed to improve the reader's problem-solving skills by requiring the student to think critically about the problems and develop workable solutions.

- **Internet Research Activity:** This activity is intended for students to surf the web in order to supplement chapter material with the most recently published research about topics, issues, themes, products, or services.

SUPPLEMENTS FOR THIS EDITION

- **Student Workbook with a Data CD** contains the following applied projects for each chapter: Review Activity, Practical Experience Assignments that include field exercises and case studies, Internet Research Assignments, and Hands-on Computer Assignments that include word processing and spreadsheet projects. Many of the projects in the workbook are based on a fictitious company called International Business Services, located in Phoenix, Arizona. The workbook activities give students the opportunity to make decisions based on the information provided and to interpret actions needed. Many projects provide students with forms on the Data CD to make completion easier.

- **Instructor's Resource CD** includes four key resources: an instructor's manual, electronic testing files for each chapter, chapter PowerPoint slides, and chapter solution files for the word processing and spreadsheet computer projects. The instructor's manual section includes an in-depth chapter outline for each chapter, a teaching "snapshot" table showing when to use slides, projects, and activities at each chapter section, and general and specific teaching suggestions for each chapter.

The teaching suggestions provide an overview of each chapter. Key concepts for each major topic in the chapter are presented with points to emphasize specifically. Each key concept section gives tips on how to present the topic, when to use the PowerPoint slides, when and how to assign the cases and/or student workbook activities, along with specific information on how to develop the concept.

Suggested answers are provided for the Ethics & Choices and suggested uses for the Management Tips; solutions to end-of-chapter activities, and solutions to student workbook projects are also included. A minimum of five Microsoft PowerPoint slides per chapter are available for instructor use complete with animations, sound, and transitions. These provide an overview of key concepts presented in each chapter to augment lectures or provide review prior to an exam.

- **Web site** provides links to Internet resources that correlate to the Internet Research Activity in the End-of-Chapter materials. These links can be found by clicking on the link http://odgers. swlearning.com for the particular chapter being studied. When Internet activites are provided in the student workbook projects, students are directed to the web site. In addition, the web site provides additional student activities such as crossword puzzles that review the key terms introduced in the chapters. The web site also includes the electronic test bank. Students and teachers will find that the web site is an excellent way to get updated information.

ACKNOWLEDGMENTS

Creating a textbook is a collaborative venture. Experience, ideas, and advice of instructors, students, researchers, and editors particularly have benefited this 13th Edition of *Administrative Office Management*.

Special thanks to my reviewers, who offered helpful observations for improvements throughout the development and writing processes. The reviewers for this edition included:

Susan Cassidy
York County Community College
Wells, ME

Helen Grattan
Des Moines Area Community College
Ankeny, IA

Loreen W. MacNichol
Andover College
Portland, ME

Dr. Peter F. Meggison
Massasoit Community College
Brockton, MA

Leanne V. Ruff
Blue Ridge Community College
Flat Rock, NC

Candace Schiffer
Mercyhurst College
Erie, PA

Daphne Zito
Katharine Gibbs School
Melville, NY

Thank you for selecting *Administrative Office Management*, 13th Edition. Good luck as you pursue your studies and continue your career in administrative office management. I will appreciate hearing from you and learning how you have used this 13th Edition.

Pattie Odgers, Ed.D.

Contents

Part 1

Identifying Basic Concepts and Trends

Chapter 1

The Evolution of Management Practices

Chapter 2

Handling Administrative Management Challenges

Chapter 3

Administrative Management Activities in the Workplace

Chapter 4

Emerging Elements Impacting Administrative Management Practices

Chapter 5

Managing Information, Technology, and Training in the Workplace

2

Workplace

DORIS YOUNGMAN

Insurance Coordinator, Florida Sports and Orthopedic Medicine, Palm Harbor, Florida

I began my career as a high school instructor in Tampa, Florida, teaching various business courses. Soon I was promoted and became the lead vocational teacher, drawing the attention of a national business and economic publishing company based in Cincinnati, Ohio that offered me a position as a trainer and then years later, a sales representative's position in eastern Tennessee.

Due to a family illness which required care-giving, I left and moved to Florida where a large communications company hired me to be a trainer for their employees in the field of computer programming and software applications. I was promoted to lead trainer within a short amount of time. My current position in the health care industry is in the accounts receivable/billing department where I supervise four employees.

Question

What do you think are some major challenges facing managers in the workplace today and how can students prepare to meet those challenges?

Response

The aging and shrinking workforce adds challenges to the difficulty of finding qualified job applicants. Experience and education are very important, so today's employees need both to be successful. They should take advantage of every training opportunity afforded where they work to help ensure they will not be overlooked when it is time for a promotion.

There is a need for integration of technology without losing the personal touch with customers/patients. At my medical office, for example, employees must be clinical. However, they must never forget that people are human, and compassion and understanding of the client/patient is still an integral part of medical care. Employees should be more interested in the customer/patient than their own agenda.

In addition, companies need employees who can ask probing questions that will help solve problems and trigger new ideas. Employees who can verbalize and solve important problems are in high demand, because they can see the big picture. A manager must communicate carefully to the employee what is desired and give realistic job expectations to today's new employee.

To meet these challenges, students need to learn to be flexible and not always take themselves so seriously. Perhaps a class in speech, debate, and definitely classes in written communication would give a future manager a foundation in communicating ideas persuasively to others.

Students should ask themselves why they want to be a manager. One way to determine if management is for students is to enroll in an internship program early in coursework. Here business and industry can coordinate activities with the local college or university to help students see management realistically.

Chapter 1

The Evolution of Management Practices

In general, the five chapters in Part 1 serve as an introductory overview of administrative office management and the essential elements covered in this chapter. Specifically this chapter explains administrative management and the traditional elements of management and their functions.

Effective information management is at the heart of what most businesses do. Information is recognized today as one of the most strategic resources that an organization possesses. Information must be carefully managed because it is not only the critical basis for sound decision-making but also an essential element in achieving improved productivity over global competitors in business. Because information is produced and transmitted at incredible speed, workplaces and how they are managed are changing. Before studying today's administrative office management practices, let's form a base and look at the origins of traditional management as well as discover how management and administrative management can be defined.

When confused as to how you are doing as a leader, find out how the people you lead are doing. You'll know the answer.

—Larry Bossidy, CEO of AlliedSignal

TECHNOLOGY APPLICATIONS IN THE WORKPLACE

© Getty Images/PhotoDisc

Messaging Habits in the Workplace

According to a recent study on the messaging habits of people in the workplace, professionals have adapted to the overload of electronic devices by assembling a personal "digital toolbox." This toolbox consists of their preferred devices—a desktop, laptop, pager, cell phone, fax machine, overnight mail, postal mail, and even sticky notes—in whatever combination works best for them, along with those features and functions they find useful and easy to learn.[1]

The survey findings offered a revealing snapshot of today's warp speed workweek and workload: The average worker in the study reports sending and receiving 200 messages per day and working on 17 different projects per week across seven different work teams. Those in the study acknowledge that while sometimes technology is a bit much, this whole new communications environment, especially the portability of it, has given them a freedom in their lives they never could have had any other way.

ISSUES TO THINK ABOUT:

1. Have people learned to set limits in their lives around the reach and scope of technology?
2. Are workers in control of their messaging or are the devices managing them and their time?

THE ROLE OF MANAGEMENT IN THE WORKPLACE

We now need to define management in order to highlight the importance, relevance, and necessity of studying it. **Management** is the process of working with and through others to blend together people, materials, money, methods, machines, and morale in an effort to set and to achieve the goals of the organization.

Administrative management is related to the word administration, which describes the performance of, or carrying out of, assigned duties. Administration is also used to refer to a group of persons who execute those duties, such as the governing board of your school or the top-level executives of a corporation. Administration, as you shall see, is essential to every aspect of business operations.

To achieve the goals of an organization, a firm must be well managed. Thus, the functions of management involve the planning, organizing, controlling of all resources and the leading or directing of people to attain the goals of a productive, unified organization. You will learn about these later in the chapter.

The functions of management are performed by persons called managers at several levels in any organization. The titles held by managers vary considerably depending on the nature of the work assigned, the responsibilities delegated to the positions, and the type and size of the organization. As you

shall see later, many business firms have reduced the number of their managerial levels, which, in turn, provides a "flatter" organizational structure.

In general, what do managers do? Management is much more than the familiar activity of telling employees what to do. Management is a complex and dynamic mixture of systematic techniques and common sense. As with any complex process, the key to learning about management lies in dividing it into readily understood subprocesses. One approach is to focus on managerial roles or behaviors. These roles can be grouped into three major categories: interpersonal, informational, and decisional roles.

- *Interpersonal.* Because of their formal authority and superior status, managers engage in a good deal of interpersonal contact, especially with people who report to them.

- *Informational.* Every manager is a clearinghouse for information relating to the task at hand or issues of relevance.

- *Decisional.* In their decisional roles, managers balance competing interests and make choices. Through decisional roles, strategies are formulated and put into action.

THE ADMINISTRATIVE MANAGER POSITION

The person who heads up the company-wide information management function may have one of several titles, such as administrative manager, office manager, manager of administrative services, information manager or

SCHOOLS OF MANAGEMENT THOUGHT

Because of their diverse personal philosophies, administrative managers follow different lines of thinking in managing the information function. For example, some AMs view the management process primarily as the *science* of managing—knowing *what* the principles are and *how* they should work. Others look upon management mainly as an art—knowing *when*, *how*, and *why* to apply a given principle in a particular situation. Like the question, "Which came first—the chicken or the egg?" There is no precise answer to the question of whether management is a science or an art.

Over the years, various functions in the management process have been identified, and attempts have been made to classify the approaches used by management theorists and practitioners. In this discussion, we have divided the divergent streams of management thought into five schools—*classical, behavioral, management science, quality management, and systems.*

Each school of thought emphasizes a somewhat different approach to management and draws separate, though related, conclusions as to the most significant factors in the management process. Although as students of administrative management, you may not find the specific answers you desire in the literature of these schools, the principles will serve as *guidelines* for action. Understanding these general approaches to the theory and practice of management can help you appreciate how management has evolved, where it is today, and where it appears to be headed.

manager of office services. Throughout this textbook, the person responsible for planning, organizing, and controlling the information-processing activities and for leading people in attaining the organization's objectives is called the **administrative office manager.** Because of the high frequency with which this title is used, it will often be abbreviated AOM, or simply AM.

Administrative managers are responsible for managing information, the systems that house information, and the technology and people that maximize productivity. You will learn later that the creative manager needs conceptual, human, and technical skills, all of which are important elements and are interrelated and interconnected with the information and communication systems. The manager must be a skillful innovator to handle the changes that occur in the information-handling activities as well as make insightful decisions.

Management is not for everyone; it requires clear-headed individuals who can envision something better and turn it into reality by working with and through others. How does one learn to manage? One way, and the approach in this book, is to start by studying the beginnings of management thought—to describe the concepts, techniques, principles, and guidelines that have been put into action over the years. Although management activities vary at different organizational levels and within particular organizations, many of the traditional schools of management thought and levels of management activities are still practiced. Let's start our study of management there. Assess your management skills to reveal your approach to management.

The Classical School

In the 18th and early 19th centuries, the Industrial Revolution brought about the mass production of goods and created the modern industrial organization. The new companies with their great potential for production were little understood and the need for knowledge about the management of such firms soon became apparent. The early approaches to the study of management of the newly formed businesses—production. The early theorists emphasized the essential nature of management and its relationship to the production process.

Intertwined in the development of classical management theory were two views toward the management of work and of organizations—scientific management and total entity management. These views and several of the leaders who espoused them are discussed in the following paragraphs.

Scientific Management

Scientific management evolved in order to solve two major problems: how to increase the output of the average worker and how to improve the efficiency of management. What is required in scientific management is a higher order of common sense involving the careful definition of problems and the development of plausible solutions. The scientific method of problem-solving, which characterizes scientific management, involves the use of logical, systematic steps to develop effective solutions to problems. These problem-solving steps are explained fully in Chapter 11.

Frederick W. Taylor is looked upon as the father of scientific management. In the 1880s, using his engineering background, Taylor studied work standards and the relationship of output to wages. He was mainly concerned with the efficiency of workers and managers in actual production. Underlying Taylor's entire approach to scientific management was the conviction that there is one best way of doing everything, whether it be using a shovel or filing a piece of paper.[2]

Taylor saw several new functions emerge for managers: the replacement of rule-of-thumb methods with scientific determination of each element of a person's job; the scientific selection and training of workers; the need for cooperation between management and labor to accomplish work in accordance with the scientific method; and a more equal division of responsibility between managers and workers, with the managers planning and organizing the work.

Frank and Lillian Gilbreth, husband and wife, further developed the scientific management thought. The Gilbreths invented devices and introduced techniques to aid workers in developing to their fullest potential through training, tools, environment, and work methods. Their accomplishments included the use of motion pictures to study and improve motion sequences, the development of charts and diagrams to record work-process and work-flow patterns, the exploration of worker fatigue and its effect on health and productivity, and the application of the principles of management and motion study to self-management.

Max Weber was a German sociologist who developed the concept of an ideal model or pure form of organizational design. The term **bureaucracy** is used to describe Weber's pure form of organization, which is formal, impersonal, and governed by rules rather than by people. Weber's bureaucratic model was identified by features such as:

1. A clear-cut division of labor in which complex jobs are broken down into simple, repetitive operations.

2. A well-defined hierarchy with a fixed chain of command.

3. A system of abstract rules for controlling operations.

4. Administrative acts, decisions, and rules recorded in writing to provide permanent files.

5. Employment and promotion based on technical qualifications.

6. Employee protection against arbitrary dismissal.

William H. Leffingwell, looked upon as the father of office management, was credited with applying the principles of scientific management to office work. He developed the *Five Principles of Effective Work.* Since these principles are related to the proper management of *all* work, they may be applied to managing workplace activities, as shown below:

1. *Plan the work.* Any administrative manager must plan what work must be done; how, when, and where it must be done; and how fast it can be done.

2. *Schedule the work.* By recognizing a total plan of organization and product development, the manager can coordinate the efforts of all workers, machines, and information to formulate a proper work schedule that agrees with the plan.

3. *Execute the work.* Proper operating systems, procedures, record-keeping practices, and methods for executing the work must be developed. The work must be

done skillfully, accurately, rapidly, and without unnecessary effort and delay.

4. *Measure the work.* With the effective development of measurements, standards, and layouts for getting the work done, it must then be measured as to quantity, quality, the workers' potential, and past production records.

5. *Reward the worker.* Perhaps of most importance, the manager must select, train, motivate, compensate, and promote employees to keep their interests and those of the organization at an optimum level.

Total Entity Management The followers of the total entity management concept emphasized an overall approach to the administrative problems of management. Thus, they searched for effective means of directing the business firm as a whole, or as an entity.

Henri Fayol presented his concept of the universal nature of management, developed the first comprehensive theory of management, and stressed the need for teaching management in schools and colleges in his book, *General and Industrial Management.*

Fayol was the first management author to state a series of management principles that would provide guidelines for successful coordination. He looked upon the elements of management as its functions—planning, organizing, commanding, coordinating, and controlling. In his writings, he stressed over and over that these elements apply not only to business but also universally to political, religious, military, philanthropic, and other organizations. Fayol's thesis was that since all enterprises require management, the formulation of a theory of management is necessary to provide for the effective teaching of management.

The classical school functions still represent the most useful way of conceptualizing the manager's job. The functions provide clear and discrete methods of classifying the thousands of different activities that managers carry out and the techniques they use when achieving organizational goals.

Mary Follett was a political philosopher, social reform critic, and creative problem-solver in the field of motivation and group processes. Her work spanned the gap between Taylor's scientific management and the new social psychology of the 1920s that promoted better human relations in industry. In her astute study of human relations, Follett was perhaps the first to promote what she termed "togetherness" and "group thinking."

The Behavioral School

Scientific management is still used as a basis for solving business problems, but coupled with it in the behavioral school is an even greater concern for the human element. There is a clear-cut recognition that workers are interested in more than money. Also of great importance to workers are meeting their social, psychological, and physiological needs.

Having become interested in the human element within the organization, managers began to conceive two main approaches that placed increased emphasis upon the workers in organizations. The early approach to worker behavior—the **human relations approach**—calls attention to the importance of the individual within the organization. The modern approach to worker behavior—

the **behavioral science approach**—cuts across the fields of psychology, anthropology and sociology to emphasize interpersonal relations and democratic actions on the part of workers.

Human Relations Approach to Worker Behavior

In the 1920s and 1930s, the idea emerged that people are important considerations in management since objectives are set and achieved by individuals. Representative of this early approach to the development of human relationship is Elton Mayo, whose Hawthorne experiments are briefly described as follows:

Elton Mayo headed a research team that conducted studies from 1927 to 1932 to study the effects of the physical environment upon worker productivity among a group of women workers at the Hawthorne plant of Western Electric in Chicago. Known as the **Hawthorne experiments**, the studies found that changes in the work environment had little long-term effect upon worker productivity. However, since management had asked for their opinion on working conditions, the workers felt that their relationships with management were no longer impersonal. The workers felt that they had achieved status and some degree of respect.

The Hawthorne experiments proved that the road to more effective worker effort lay in recognizing the emotional as well as the physical well-being of the employees, explaining to them the reasons for management decisions, and making them aware that management appreciated the importance of the work they did. As a result of their concern with improving human relations, a new direction—the behavioral science approach—was given to the study of management.

Behavioral Science Approach to Worker Behavior Early theories of behavior tended to explain all behavior on the basis of a single need, such as the need to assert one's ego. Modern behaviorists, in contrast, typically list several needs ranging from 3 (physical, social, and egoistic) to 15 in number. Different theories about human needs as understood by managers are briefly explained below but will be covered more fully in Chapter 11.

Abraham Maslow, a psychologist who developed a theory of human motivation, came up with one classification of human needs. At the core of his theory is the concept that we are motivated by fulfilling a hierarchy of needs. Maslow's hierarchy of needs shows that as our lower-level needs are satisfied, they are no longer motivating factors. At this point, our higher-level needs become dominant.

Managers must recognize that the needs pattern of each worker is different and should not assume that a single approach can be used to motivate all workers toward the accomplishment of the organization's objectives. Further, managers should be aware that well-satisfied needs do not motivate.

Douglas McGregor explored the human side of organizations and defined the traditional and current views of worker behavior. The nature of people, with all their apparent contradictory feelings and emotions, has long puzzled philosophers. Some see us as having a capacity for tenderness, with little need for external regulation. Others see us as

having tendencies toward cruelty, with the need for close control and regimentation for the good of society. This dual nature of people is the basis of two distinct views on worker behavior. These views, which McGregor labeled Theory X and Theory Y, are explained in Chapter 11.

Frederick Herzberg conducted research in Pittsburgh which resulted in the **motivation-hygiene theory**. According to this theory, we work in an environment where the following two kinds of factors are present:

1. **Motivators** result from experiences that create positive attitudes toward work and arise from the job content itself. Examples of motivators are those incidents associated with the feelings of self-improvement, recognition, achievement, and desire for and acceptance of greater responsibility.

2. **Hygienic** (or maintenance) **factors** are related to productivity on the job but are external to the job itself. Examples of maintenance factors are pay, working conditions (such as heating, lighting, and ventilation), company policies, and quality of supervision.

Herzberg found that when workers feel the hygienic factors are inadequate, they function as dissatisfiers. On the other hand, when the hygienic factors are present, they do not necessarily motivate us to greater productivity; instead, they make it possible for the motivators to function.

Peter F. Drucker introduced the concept of **management by objectives** (MBO). In MBO, objectives are set forth for every area where performance and results directly and vitally affect the survival and prosperity of the organization. Writing about the "knowledge society" in *Managing for the Future: The 1990s and Beyond*, Drucker describes how large business and government organizations operate on the flow of information.

The Management Science School

Management science, also known as *quantitative business methods*, makes use of engineering and mathematical skills to solve complex decision-making problems. Examples of the mathematical techniques for making decisions include: 1) *work sampling*, where a number of random samples are taken in order to supply information for use in setting work standards; 2) *waiting-line, or queuing theory*, in which a study is done on the behavior of persons waiting in line, such as customers lining up at a bank teller's window, and; 3) *forecasting*, which is used to plan capital expenditures for a new plant and equipment. Many mathematical techniques of decision-making use higher-level mathematics and are dependent upon the rapid calculating ability and accuracy of the computer.

The Quality Management School

Quality management, or *total quality management (TQM)*, is both a philosophy and a set of principles used to guide the entire organization in *continuous improvement*. To achieve this goal, TQM uses quantitative methods along with the organization's human and capital resources to improve all processes, performance in every functional area, and the degree to which the organization meets the needs of present and future customers and suppliers. A few of the quality management tools often used include

brainstorming, goal setting, quality circles, statistical measurement, work team techniques, and workflow analysis. In this section, we shall summarize the contributions of two persons mainly concerned with quality improvement programs.

W. Edwards Deming is the leading exponent of quality management and pioneering statistical analysis. During World War II, Deming taught American companies how to improve their production of high-quality goods and services. Following the war, however, most of Deming's lessons were forgotten. During the early 1950s, Deming was invited to Japan to advise its business leaders on quality, a move that sparked Japan's postwar recovery and its subsequent economic rise in global markets. While there, he taught the Japanese how to use statistics to find out what any system would do and then to design improvements that would make the system yield the best results. The basics of Deming's method are contained in a list of objectives that he calls "the 14 points." These objectives are shown in Table 1.1.[3]

In the 1970s, companies in the United States began to "import" and modify certain features of Deming's quality improvement program such as quality circles and employee participation groups.

William Ouchi coined the term Theory Z management. **Theory Z management** is the attitude of Japanese management toward work and workers. Ouchi, a professor, spent years researching Japanese and American companies with Theory Z management styles. We shall further explore the nature and attributes of Theory Z management in Chapter 11.

TABLE 1.1 Deming's 14 Points Explained

Key Point	How it is Applied
1. Create constancy of purpose for improvement of the product and service.	Rather than making money, the goal is to stay in business and provide jobs through innovative research, constant improvement, and maintenance.
2. Adopt a new philosophy about errors.	Make a change in accepting mistakes and negativism; they are unacceptable.
3. Build quality into a product throughout production.	Quality comes from improvement of the process, not inspection.
4. End the practice of awarding business on price tag alone.	Seek the best quality, and work to achieve a long-term relationship with that supplier.
5. Improve constantly and forever the system of production and service.	Improvement is not a one-time effort. Management must continually look for ways to reduce waste and improve quality.
6. Institute training.	All employees need to be trained—quality cannot be left to chance.
7. Institute leadership.	Leading consists of helping people do a better job and of learning (by objective methods) who needs individual help.
8. Drive out fear; create trust.	Encourage employees to ask questions or take a position on issues of concern to them.
9. Break down barriers between departments.	Employees need to work as a team so they can solve or foresee problems.
10. Eliminate slogans and targets for the workforce.	Let people put up their own slogans.
11. Eliminate numerical quotas.	Quotas take into account numbers, not quality or methods.
12. Remove barriers to pride of workmanship.	People are eager to do a good job and distressed when they cannot.
13. Institute a vigorous program of education and retraining.	All people need to be educated in new methods, including teamwork and statistical techniques.
14. Take action to accomplish the transformation by including everyone in the work.	Workers cannot do it on their own, nor can managers. A special top-management team with a plan of action is needed.

Adapted from discussion in W. Edwards Deming, *Out of the Crisis*, 1986, pp. 23-96.

The Systems School

In most modern approaches to the study of the management process, the systems concept is used as a means of describing the total organization. A system is a group of parts that are interrelated in such a manner that they form a unified whole and work together to attain a definite objective. Thus, a business firm—the total system—looks like Figure 1.1 and is made up of the following major systems: sales and marketing, finance, human resources, production, accounting, purchasing, administrative office, and others.

LEVELS AND SKILLS OF MANAGEMENT

Typically, larger organizations have three levels of management—top, middle, and supervisory or operating. The traditional management model has driven a type of organization that is shaped like a **pyramid**.

The pyramid organizational chart demonstrates a clearly defined structure that spells out the chain of command. The **chain of command** is the means of transmitting authority from the top level through successive levels of management to the workers at the lowest operative level. The chain of command shows the authority-responsibility relationships that link superiors and subordinates throughout the entire organization.

The skills required at each managerial level are similar, but are applied differently. Although the purpose of this text is to teach you *all* the skills that managers need to be successful, let's start with three broad categories of skills you will need: conceptual, human, and technical. Although every manager needs all three skills to some degree, middle managers practice human skills the most; whereas, supervisors draw on technical skills most often.

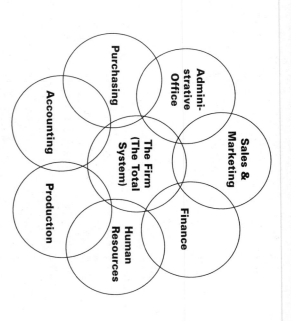

FIGURE 1.1 Major Systems in the Workplace

Administrative Office

Purchasing

Accounting

Sales & Marketing

The Firm (The Total System)

Finance

Production

Human Resources

Conceptual Skill

For a manager, conceptual competence includes analyzing problems, devising solutions and action plans, and anticipating the consequences of decisions. One example of conceptual skill is the ability to view an entity as a whole and see how a change in one of its parts affects all other parts or functions. An administrative office manager is using conceptual skill when evaluating the need to install a centralized automated system for storing major company records. In making that decision, the AOM must question, explore, and probe to see how such a change will affect processing and retrieving of records throughout all departments in the organization.

Human Skill

Human skills, also known as *interpersonal,* *"soft,"* or *people* skills, are skills that allow you to work effectively with others. These skills include a manager's ability to communicate, coach, lead, resolve conflicts, achieve consensus, and motivate workers. The application of such knowledge enables the AM to identify, comprehend, and solve human problems.

Administrative managers exhibit their human skills when leading and directing workers and interrelating with peers and top management. For example, assume that you are appointed to serve as head of a labor-management team that is investigating a change in work schedules. In this role, you exhibit your human skills by being sensitive to the feelings and needs of others and by creating an environment in which workers freely express themselves and offer meaningful suggestions for improvement.

Managers use a multitude of skills when making organizational decisions.

Technical Skill

Technical skills are work-related skills that demonstrate the manager's ability to use the technology, tools, techniques, and procedures specific to a particular field. For example, administrative office managers need to understand and be able to perform such tasks as producing reports, ordering equipment, and generating ideas that streamline document workflow. Of the three skills, technical skills are especially important to technical supervisors, because as the first-line managers, they supervise workers on a one-on-one basis each day. Therefore, as we move down the organization, we see that technical supervisors need more specialized technical skills than conceptual skills, although their human skills would still be very important.

Regardless of the organization, managers with conceptual, human, and technical skills must be able to use those skills to perform the functions of planning, organizing, leading, and controlling human, financial, physical, and informational resources in order to achieve organizational goals.

FUNCTIONS OF MANAGEMENT

Suppose you are a typical manager in today's workplace. What activities would you perform to accomplish the major managerial functions of planning, organizing, leading, and controlling? Let's look at these functions in greater detail.

1. Planning precedes the other three management functions.
2. Planning is most closely related to the controlling function.
3. Effective managers are generally very good planners.

Planning Time-Line Phases Typically, managers make plans according to long-, intermediate-, and short-range time lines. Long-range plans usually cover a time span of three to five years or, in some cases, as many as ten or more years. Intermediate-range plans cover one to three years, and short-range planning covers projects from one day to one year.

Planning at each of the three management levels typically goes like this. Top managers create strategic long-term and intermediate-range plans of one to five years. These types of plans can focus on competitive strategies, new products, and/or capital investments. Middle managers, on the other hand, are concerned with intermediate- and short-range plans of one month to one year in length. This planning activity might outline the tactics to use to improve scheduling and coordination of a critical project.

Supervisors, on the other hand, make short-range plans of one day, one week, or one to six months. These plans can be as simple as how to implement and communicate a new policy or work method or how to assign work. Table 1.2 describes some distinctive characteristics among the three levels of management by offering typical job titles, activities performed within time lines, and information needed by each management level in order to be successful. In the past, traditional managers typically developed

Planning Function

When a person spends little time and energy planning, this can lead to sudden problems, such as unforeseen obstacles and missed deadlines. The result? Usually any time saved is spent "putting out fires." **Planning** is the management function of choosing or generating organizational objectives and then determining the courses of action needed to achieve those objectives. **Objectives** are measurable end results—the goals or targets—that an organization, department, or individual seeks to attain. Two examples of measurable objectives are:

1. By the end of the second week of the spring semester, student enrollment based on headcount will increase by 5 percent.
2. By December 31, 90 percent of all employees will attend and participate in a two-hour customer service workshop presented by an outside consultant.

Some key points about planning that you'll want to remember and apply in the workplace are:

these plans with limited input from subordinates. However, in organizations that are using the strategic planning process, this trend has changed. The strategic planning process will be discussed in the next section.

Strategic Planning Process Many organizations—large and small alike—have undertaken the development of a "comprehensive strategic plan." An effective strategic plan seeks input from all members of the organization. The **strategic planning process** involves defining an organization's mission, setting its objectives, and developing strategies that will enable it to operate successfully

in its internal and external environment.

During this process, members of the organization envision its future and then develop the procedures and operations necessary to achieve that vision. The strategic planning process, in reality, creates the future for that organization. Long-term organizational effectiveness depends, in large part, on the strategic planning process. The strategic planning process, which is described in detail in Table 1.3, usually involves nine phases, beginning with planning and proceeding through implementation of the plan. Each of these phases, as you will note, builds on the previous ones.

TABLE 1.2 Distinctive Characteristics Among Levels of Management

Levels of Management	Typical Job Titles	Activities Performed	Information Needed by Manager
Top	Chief executive officer, president, vice president, superintendent, mayor	Long-range strategic decision-making that sets the tone and vision for the future in terms of new products, new markets, new facilities, etc.	Concise synopsis of interrelated, departmental efficiencies; on-demand reports requested for immediate use
Middle	Department head, branch manager, principal, dean, administrative manager	Intermediate-range tactical decision-making that implements the strategies that have been determined by top management	Summary reports and graphs that show trends and exceptions to norms as related to resource usage spread over a monthly basis
Supervisory	Supervisor, department chair, lead secretary, registrar	Short-range operational decision-making that ensures that specific jobs are performed which meet the objectives of the organization	Detailed, routine information needed to make immediate short-term decisions on a daily basis

TABLE 1.3 Phases in a Typical Strategic Planning Process

Phase	Description
Planning to plan	During this first phase, the organization's leadership decides that planning is necessary. They then determine which organizational units are affected and who should be involved in the planning. From this information, a planning team is formed and decisions are made about how long the process will take, what information is needed, and who will develop the data.
Conducting a values scan	The planning team examines their own, the organization's, and stakeholders' values to determine how those values affect the planning with which they, the planning team, have been tasked. (Stakeholders are those parties who could be impacted by any organizational change.) The team also examines how conflicts among these values can be managed.
Forming a mission statement	The mission statement is written and describes why the organization exists, what functions it performs, how it performs these functions, and for whom they are done. An example of a mission statement is "Coconino Community College provides personalized and accessible opportunities in higher education by offering transfer, career and technical programs, and community interest courses."
Developing strategic business modeling	The planning team conceptualizes specific alternative scenarios or benchmarks toward achieving its mission.
Conducting a performance audit	The planning team evaluates the organization's current performance in order to understand clearly and predict its capacity to achieve the future envisioned for it.
Preparing a gap analysis	As the audit reveals gaps between current and envisioned performance, the reasons for those gaps must be analyzed and understood. Armed with this information, the team can work and rework its modeling scenarios.
Integrating action plans	As certain scenarios take shape and show promise, the team integrates those scenarios and proposed complementary actions into a "grand strategy" or "master business plan." A business plan is a document prepared by a company that specifies the business details, strategies, and structure of the organization.
Planning for contingencies	At this point, "what if" questions must be addressed, such as: "What if the organization loses an 'irreplaceable' staff member?" or "What if a key facility, like a computer room, is destroyed?" Actions are then proposed to deal with contingencies and still meet objectives.
Initiating implementation	All stakeholders are informed of the plan, and it becomes a part of everyday management decisions. At the same time, the organization continues to scan changes that affect it, and the strategic plan is institutionalized as an ongoing process.

At some point in your working future, you may be asked to participate in a company-wide strategic planning process. If you are a manager, for example, you may be asked to formulate strategy as a member of the planning team. If you are a member of the administrative staff, you may be requested to provide information needed for strategic planning purposes. In whatever capacity, your input and efforts will be beneficial, even essential, to the continued well-being and growth of your organization.

Types of Plans There are two types of plans used in organizations—**standing plans** and **single-use plans.** Standing plans are those that remain in effect within the organization. Examples of standing plans include rules, policies, and procedures.

Single-use plans are plans that are developed and used for a certain period of time.

A **budget** is a single-use plan. It is a financial plan for a certain period of time—a fiscal year, an academic year, or a calendar year. Another very popular single-use plan is a **project.** Organizations use a project planning process to achieve objectives. To better explain this process, imagine a group of people getting together to plan an "open house" activity for the company's customers, vendors, and distributors. The time frame for planning is short and the team's objective is clear. How do they proceed?

If the team follows a successful project planning process, they will move to completion of the project by answering the following seven questions:

1. Where are we now?
2. Where are we trying to go?
3. What are our goals and constraints?
4. What are the main steps that we must plan? What is their sequence?
5. When does each step need to be completed? Who is responsible? What will it cost? Will the benefits justify the cost?
6. Exactly what will things look like when we have done a good job?
7. Do we have approval to proceed?

Importance of Planning Successful managers know that the most important step in getting any job done well is the planning step. The presence or absence of planning usually determines how much or how little time will be required to take the job to completion and to take any needed corrective actions. Planning is a critical activity of managers and offers these benefits:

1. *Saves time.* When a plan is conscientiously prepared and then used, errors are significantly reduced, which results in time saved. Scheduling has been completed when the efforts of all parties involved are coordinated effectively to prevent materials, time, and energy waste.

2. *Promotes flexibility.* Planning allows organizations to be highly responsive to change. Because managers have a plan and know basically what needs to be done and how to get there, adjustments are easier to make as the process moves toward completion. Task completion can be monitored and adjusted as group members participate in the implementation of the plan in order to ensure that the goals or targets of the plan are attained.

Organizing Function

Organizing is the multifaceted management function that gets things done. It includes four facets: (1) from the planning phase, determining the resources and activities required to achieve the organization's objectives; (2) combining these resources and activities into a formal structure; (3) assigning responsibility for achieving the activities and; (4) delegating authority (with commensurate responsibility and accountability) to carry out assignments. As such, organizing involves traditional management concepts such as delegation, authority, responsibility, and accountability.

Delegating Process
Delegation is the process by which managers distribute and entrust activities and related authority to subordinates in the organization. Effective delegating is more than just doing out responsibility. It is after you delegate a task that the challenge begins. It is then that you must strike a balance between letting go of a project and guiding it toward completion. Hanging on too tightly, or "micro-managing," can smother motivation and slow progress; whereas, giving up all control could result in chaos.

The three aspects of the delegation process Frederick Herzberg conducted are: (1) delegation of authority to do the job; (2) assignment of responsibility to complete a task and; (3) accountability of the results. How does the process work? In this process, authority is delegated downward while responsibility and accountability flow upward through organizations.

For example, the manager grants or delegates authority and assigns responsibility to

perform certain duties or carry out special assignments, achieve given objectives, and meet stated standards to some person in the organization. That person is accountable to the manager for results, while the manager remains accountable to upper-level management, who in turn remains accountable to even higher levels of managers or owners. Accountability for results resembles an upward spiral effect.

Centralized and Decentralized Authority
Authority is the right to do something, to tell someone else to do it, or to make decisions that affect the reaching of organizational objectives. Authority in the workplace is a tricky matter.

People who don't have authority often want it, while people who have it frequently feel awkward using it. Consequently, those who have authority frequently either underuse it or overuse it.[4] Still, authority is necessary because decisions must be made and difficult issues have to be dealt with. For example, employees need to be hired, coached, disciplined, and, occasionally, they need to be fired.

Authority in an organization is either centralized or decentralized. **Centralized authority** means that the concentration of power and authority is near the top of an organization. Centralized authority is, by its very nature, authoritarian. The upside of centralization is that decisions can be made quickly to react to changing needs. There are, after all, fewer layers of decision-makers with whom to deal. The downside is that centralization of authority leads to a lessened sense of involvement by lower-echelon workers, may lower morale, and can inhibit initiative.

© 2003 Digital Vision

Authority is necessary because business decisions must be made.

Decentralized authority, on the other hand, is in effect when power and decision-making are dispersed to successively lower levels of the organization. Though slower in its movements, decentralized authority usually creates a stronger organization. An added advantage is that customers often find that decentralization speeds up customer service and is more responsive to their complaints or concerns because decisions that affect them directly can be made at a lower level. Top-level executives, therefore, can better use their time by setting policies as well as planning and organizing the firm's goals.

Responsibility and Accountability

Responsibility is the obligation and accountability for properly performing work that is assigned. When a manager shares responsibility with subordinates, however, it does not mean he or she is abandoning responsibility. Managers still have the responsibility to do the following:

- Know what's going on
- Keep abreast of important decisions
- Track the progress of projects (or lack of it)
- Ensure that "derailed" projects get back on track
- Set the direction for subordinates to take
- Make the decisions employees can't
- Offer a guiding hand by opening doors to clear the way, and
- Measure performance.

Accountability involves judging the extent to which employees fulfill their responsibilities. When you delegate, you must also set up benchmarks or controls—controls to

evaluate results and thereby ensure that responsibilities are met. Remember that managers are accountable to others for the results achieved by their subordinates. Such controls can be lumped together under the term *accountability*. The subordinate must be "held accountable" for all of his or her actions if the delegation of authority is to be effective.

Accountability tends to have a negative undertone to it, a perception that many workers would agree is well deserved. To say that you will be "held accountable" may not bring to mind that you will be praised and rewarded, but rather that you will suffer the consequences of any failures. It is problematic, but managers must strive to lessen the negative perceptions of "accountability" held by their subordinates, while at the same time ensuring that the job gets done! Delegation with a positive attitude is essential for all managers.

When differences arise between actual performance and planned performance, corrective action can take the form of coaching, counseling, or correcting mistakes. Consider these eight tactics used by successful managers when delegating activities and tracking important performance outcomes:

1. *Set measurable and specific goals.* Be clear on what you want to accomplish by giving clear, specific instructions. For example, interview all current salespeople within the next two weeks to determine which ones need training on the newest version of Microsoft Outlook, a calendaring software program.

2. *Select the right person.* Before you choose someone, consider each candidate's interest in the assignment, as well as his or her training, ability, and availability.

3. *Schedule progress reviews.* The way to guide an employee is to establish, at the outset, a mutually acceptable schedule of meetings during which objectives are restated and specific steps taken to achieve them are discussed. In this way, problems can be detected quickly and averted.

4. *Establish checkpoints or "milestones" for, and with, subordinates.* Whether taking a trip or completing a project, a large objective is best reached by completing a series of smaller steps and realizing where you are at the end of each step. You can then make adjustments as needed.

5. *Be available as a resource.* If an employee asks for help between checkpoints or requests more frequent progress review meetings, don't turn him or her down. That's your job.

6. *Delegate the entire project, whenever possible.* "Owning" a job—taking it from start to finish—is a great motivator. If an employee is excited about a project, less supervision is generally needed.

7. *Share responsibility and power.* Delegate not only the work but also the appropriate amount of authority over the project. Identifying the limits helps you keep ultimate control. If appropriate, rotate workers during phases of the project so that everyone involved learns the entire process, becomes cross-trained, and, therefore, more effective.

8. *Keep your composure in the face of mistakes.* When the people to whom you delegate tasks make mistakes, offer to work with them, but leave with them the responsibility for solving problems they have caused. Take care not to overreact.[5]

Leading Function

Leading is the management function of motivating individuals and influencing group activities to accomplish objectives. For a manager to lead effectively, he or she must possess personal qualities, a leadership style, and power combined with the abilities to communicate well, motivate enthusiastically, and discipline, if appropriate.

Given the volatility of organizations and the diversity of today's employees, lack of an all-encompassing leadership talent can lead to increased turnover among managers as well as employees. What works in an organization today might not work tomorrow. Because of their importance to success as a manager, leadership, supervisory, and motivational skills are discussed in-depth in Chapter 11.

Controlling Function

Controlling is the management function of devising ways and means of ensuring that planned performance throughout the process is actually achieved. Frequently the terms *effectiveness* and *efficiency* are measurements used to gauge achievement. **Effectiveness** is the ability to get the "right things" accomplished by selecting the most suitable goals and the proper steps, people, and physical resources to achieve them. In contrast, **efficiency** is the ability to "get things right" in a reasonable and timely manner with a minimum expenditure of resources.

The Importance of Control The function of control cannot be overemphasized if a company wants to stay in business. The consequences of poor quality control, for instance, may result in irate customers, loss of business, and loss of reputation, as well as the costs of correcting damage resulting from poor control. Customers have a right to expect good quality in the products and services that they buy. The risk to organizations of not controlling processes effectively can be devastating.

The Control Process The essence of the control process involves four steps, as follows: (1) setting performance standards; (2) measuring actual performance; (3) comparing actual performance with standards and analyzing deviation; and; (4) responding to deviations by taking corrective action, when necessary. Preparing and using a budget is one example of the control process that organizations use every day; the evaluation of employees is another.

The first step in the process, setting performance standards, requires several activities to have already occurred. In other words, you cannot set standards unless overall objectives and plans have been established and communicated first. Measurable standards can be expressed in (1) numbers, such as numbers of items produced; (2) dollars and cents, such as payroll costs or maintenance costs, or; (3) time standards, such as eight-hour document turnaround time. These standards need to be communicated clearly to the workforce who will help attain them.

The second step, measuring actual performance, requires that you answer such questions as *which* specific activities to measure (sales, costs, profits, orders), *when* is the best time to measure, and with *what* frequency should measurements occur in order to produce a fair and accurate result.

If, in the third step, actual performance is identical to the standard you initially established, no further control is necessary at the moment. However, the fourth step would be taken if corrective action were needed. In other words, if actual results do not equal the stated standard for results or performance, then the manager must initiate corrective action. The set of human controls that regulate the performance of managers, supervisors, and workers is probably the most important in ensuring an effective system.

What is the relationship among the four primary management functions? They are all necessary, related, and interrelated with each other as shown in Figure 1.2. But to be effective, the functions must be coordinated and controlled to achieve the optimum level of performance.

FIGURE 1.2 **Relationship Among the Management Functions**

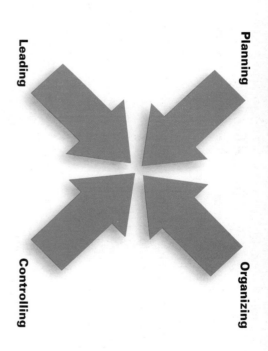

Planning

Organizing

Leading

Controlling

By way of review, Table 1.4 on the next page provides a formal and informal definition of the primary management functions and the key elements of each.

BASIC PRINCIPLES OF MANAGEMENT

Principles are broad, general statements that are considered to be true and that accurately reflect real-world conditions in all walks of life. Thus, in business you find principles of ethics, principles of customer service, and principles of accounting, to name a few. Over the years, new principles are developed. Old principles are questioned and, in some cases, changed or discarded if they no longer serve useful purposes.

When we group sets of principles into a general framework that explains the basic relationships among them, we have created a general framework that explains the basic relationships among them, we have created a **theory**. Thus, the set of eight principles

described below is classified and grouped into a managerial framework and can be thought of as **management theory** that has been practiced for many decades. You will notice as you study these principles that many of their concepts have been introduced earlier in the chapter.

PRINCIPLE 1—Define Objectives

The objectives of an organization and all of its divisions must be clearly defined and understood.

As previously cited, an objective is a desired goal—a target or an aim. A main objective of the administrative management function is to coordinate and communicate the information activities of each of the organization's main divisions so that unit costs of production may be reduced and productivity increased by a specified annual percentage rate.

TABLE 1.4 Management Functions and Key Elements

Function	Formal/Informal Definition	Key Elements
Planning	The management function of choosing or generating organizational objectives and then determining the courses of action needed to achieve those objectives. *In other words*, it answers what to do, how to do it, and when to do it.	*Objectives:* end results, goals, targets. *Strategic planning process:* mission, objectives, strategies to operate successfully.
Organizing	The multifaceted management function that provides the formal structure through which work is defined, subdivided, and coordinated. *In other words*, it gets things done.	*Delegation:* distribute activities and authority to others. *Authority:* the right to make decisions. *Responsibility:* the obligation created when delegation of authority is accepted. *Accountability:* judging the extent to which responsibilities are fulfilled.
Leading	The management function of influencing individual and group activities to accomplish tasks. *In other words*, positive influences increase desired outcomes.	*Involves:* a leader's qualities, style, and power base and the leadership activities of communication, motivation, and discipline.
Controlling	The management function of devising ways and means of ensuring that planned performance is actually achieved. *In other words*, ensuring that what's planned actually gets done.	*Effectiveness:* getting the "right things" accomplished well. *Efficiency:* getting "things right" in a timely manner with minimum expenditure of excess resources.

PRINCIPLE 2—Accept Responsibility

Responsibility for organizing work exists with managers at all levels, beginning with top-level managers and extending to first-line supervisors.

We've discussed that responsibility is the obligation and accountability for properly performing work that is assigned. At the top level, the chief executive officer determines the major work functions and formulates the company's long-range plans. Sound organization is necessary if these plans and objectives are to be achieved. Thus, top management must identify and accept the many responsibilities that accompany such high-level work. In the same way, each succeeding level of management (middle managers and supervisors) must accept their appropriate amount of responsibility as well.

PRINCIPLE 3—Unity of Functions

All organizations are composed of various functions that must be effectively integrated so they can work together as a unit to achieve their major objectives.

The unity-of-functions principle has the following three requirements: (1) The various functions must be in proper balance in keeping with the importance of their contributions to meeting the firm's objectives. (2) A reasonable amount of stability in human resources must be maintained. (3) Flexibility must be ensured to meet operational or economic changes that occur in most businesses.

PRINCIPLE 4—Utilize Specialization

An organization should utilize specialization to achieve efficiency. The more specialized the work assigned to individuals within the limits of human tolerance, the greater the opportunity for efficient performance.

A **specialist** is a person who masters or becomes expert at doing a certain type of work. Usually such expertise comes from extended periods of training, good work experience, or some combination of the two. When people specialize, then the quality of their work is higher, they are usually more accurate, they learn new tasks faster, and they can do more work in a given time period. Hence, such workers are more productive than those without specialized skills.

PRINCIPLE 5—Delegate Authority

Authority must be delegated to individuals in the organization in keeping with the responsibility assigned them so that they can be held accountable for performing their duties properly.

As previously discussed, delegation is a three-part process that involves (1) assigning responsibility to complete a task, which may range from preparing a report to participating actively on a committee; (2) granting authority to do the job, such as giving a department manager the power to hire and fire, and (3) creating accountability to carry out the task assigned.

PRINCIPLE 6—Report to One Supervisor

Each employee should receive orders from, and be responsible to, only one supervisor.

Reporting to one supervisor is often called the **unity of command** principle. When employees receive orders from more than one supervisor, they often do not know from whom they should receive orders or what work should be done first. The result may be confusion among workers and a breakdown in morale and discipline.

PRINCIPLE 7—Limit Span of Control

For effective supervision and leadership, the number of employees reporting to one supervisor should be limited to a manageable number.

Span of control refers to the number of employees who are directly supervised by one person. Many large firms, such as the Motorola Co. and IBM Corp., have reduced their workforce through downsizing by layoffs, attrition, or other means. The resulting effect was to widen the senior managers' spans of control and thus provide "leaner" and "flatter" organizational structures.

PRINCIPLE 8—Centralize or Decentralize Managerial Authority

Wherever possible, centralize managerial authority and responsibility for all highly complex or technical functions in one location and decentralize the responsibility for all simpler functions throughout the organization.

In organizations with centralized authority, similar functions are carried out in one place, and decisions tend to be made at or near the top of the organization. If, on the other hand, much authority is delegated to lower levels in the organization, decentralized authority exists. In a firm with decentralized authority, fewer levels of management exist, and the prevailing philosophy

is that decisions should be made at the lowest levels possible.

THE CHANGING WORKPLACE

Traditionally, the administrative management functions were limited to basic clerical services and to office personnel. However, the role of the traditional administrative secretary, senior executive assistant, or office manager has changed significantly over the past few decades due to corporate downsizing, the economy, and most importantly—technology and telecommunication devices.

The personal computer combined with telecommunication advances has caused a fundamental shift in the traditional corporate pyramid. The computer allows information to be transferred from the highest to lowest members of an organization with lightning speed, replacing the role of middle manager as supplier of information. The reality is that the executive secretary, administrative assistant, or whatever you may call this role has become more critical to businesses.[6] These positions are evolving into managers—*administrative managers* in the workplace.

Management is placing more reliance upon administrative professionals and well-designed work systems as new technology creates greater information-processing power. Administrative professionals have seen their managerial responsibilities increase dramatically over the past decade. The variety of software has allowed these individuals to expand their work roles wider and deeper.[7] As more companies seek ways to increase productivity and decrease operational costs, management will rely more on workplace professionals to increase their knowledge base and take on more management responsibilities.

What changes can managers of workplace activities expect? These new responsibilities will include more direct management of personnel, projects, and budgets, resulting in greater high-level decision-making responsibilities. The "one-department office" concept has given way to a broader, company-wide information or *knowledge management* concept in which the administrative manager, as well as high-level office support workers, has evolved into a *paraprofessional* who is responsible for an expanded area of work in the information age.

As technology becomes more advanced, in many organizations, the "who, what, and how" of managing is pictured best by organizational charts that look like **inverted pyramids,** rather than the traditional upright pyramid as shown in Figure 1.3.

In other cases, management has become more "horizontal." The change from a hierarchical to a horizontal organization can be represented by charts with fewer management levels and more emphasis on using self-managing teams to accomplish an organization's mission and goals.

As the more traditional workplace and its workers with their changing job titles are reengineered and processed differently, a natural question to raise is, "Who, then, is responsible for the management of office activities and information systems in the workplaces of America?" It may be simplistic, but in truth everyone in the organization has a stake in how information is processed and managed, as shown in Figure 1.4. Workers at all levels in an organization are becoming more responsible for decision-making for improving productivity, for making sure that the wants and needs of customers remain paramount, and for ensuring that the customer is continuously well served and satisfied with the quality of service and products. The survival of the information and knowledge-based organization and jobs in America depend on workers taking on more responsibility.

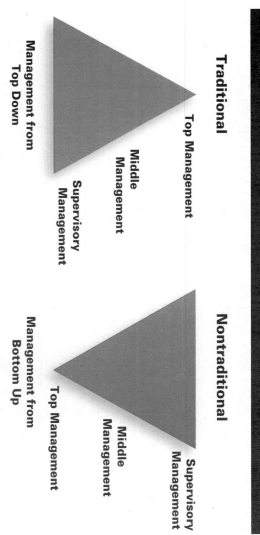

FIGURE 1.3 Traditional Versus Nontraditional Management Organization

Traditional

Top Management
Middle Management
Supervisory Management

Management from Top Down

Nontraditional

Top Management
Middle Management
Supervisory Management

Management from Bottom Up

FIGURE 1.4 Responsibility for Management Systems and Activities

Who is responsible for the management of office activities and information systems in organizations?

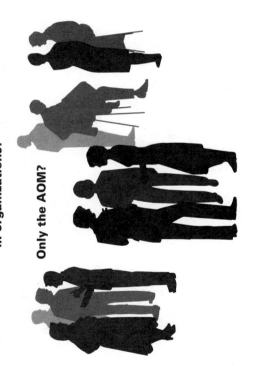

Only the AOM?

MESSAGE FOR MANAGERS

A concluding comment will help put the historical overview into perspective. Although this chapter provides a useful conceptual framework for students of management, generally it does not carry over to the practice of management. In reality, managers use whatever is ethical, fair, and meets stated objectives. Instead of faithfully adhering to a given school of management thought, one system or functional groupings, successful managers tend to use a "mixed bag" approach. This chapter is, however, a good starting point for you to begin building your own approach to management by blending theory, the experience and advice of others, and your own experience in this technology-driven, global environment. Be ready to put into practice the concepts, principles, and practices that will work for you on the job.

Chapter One

S U M M A R Y

1. Management is the process of working with and through others to blend people, materials, money, methods, machines, and morale to set and to achieve the goals of the organization.

2. The person responsible for planning, organizing, and controlling the information-processing activities and for leading people in attaining the organization's objectives is called the administrative manager or administrative office manager.

3. The five schools of management thought are classical, behavioral, management science, quality management, and systems.

4. The three broad categories of skills needed by AMs are a) conceptual skills, which include analyzing problems and devising solutions and action plans; b) human skills, which allow a manager to identify, comprehend, and solve human problems, and; c) technical skills, which are work-related tasks to a particular field.

5. Most managers perform the major interrelated functions of planning, organizing, leading, and controlling.

6. Planning is choosing organizational objectives and the courses of action needed to achieve those objectives. Planning precedes the other three functions of management.

7. Organizing is the multifaceted function that gets things done and involves traditional management concepts such as delegation, authority, responsibility, and accountability.

8. Leading is a critical management function that includes motivating individuals and influencing group activities to accomplish objectives.

9. Controlling means devising ways and means of ensuring that planned performance is actually achieved.

10. The eight principles of management are a) The objectives of an organization and all of its divisions must be clearly defined and understood. b) Responsibility for organizing work exists with managers at all levels. c) All organizations are composed of various functions that must be effectively integrated to achieve their major objectives. d) An organization should utilize specialization to achieve efficiency. e) Authority must be delegated to individuals in keeping with the responsibility assigned them. f) Each employee should receive orders from only one supervisor. g) The number of employees reporting to one supervisor should be limited to a manageable number. h) Centralize managerial authority and responsibility for complex functions, but decentralize for simpler functions.

KEY TERMS

Accountability
Administrative office manager
Authority
Behavioral science approach
Budget
Bureaucracy
Centralized authority
Chain of command
Controlling
Decentralized authority
Delegation
Effectiveness
Efficiency
Hawthorne experiments
Human relations approach
Hygienic factors
Inverted pyramids
Leading
Management
Management by objectives
Management science
Management theory
Motivation-hygiene theory
Motivators
Objectives
Organizing
Planning
Principles
Project
Pyramid
Quality management
Responsibilities
Single-use plans
Span of control
Specialist
Standing plans
Strategic planning process
Theory

Theory Z management
Unity of command

REVIEW

1. Using descriptions in this chapter, briefly describe your interpretation of the word management.

2. List and describe the three roles of administrative managers.

3. What does it mean when we say that management is the science of managing?

4. In the Classical School, what did the early forms of management focus upon?

5. What were the major contributions made by Frederick Taylor, the father of scientific management?

6. In what way are Fayol's concepts related to total entity management?

7. What are the major systems that make up the total system of an organization?

8. What is the purpose of the chain of command as shown on pyramid organizational charts?

9. Name the three types of skills needed by an administrative manager.

10. Briefly explain the purpose of each of the major managerial functions of planning, organizing, leading, and controlling.

11. Distinguish between centralized and decentralized authority in organizations.

12. Of what value are the principles of management to an administrative manager?

CRITICAL THINKING

1. The study of administrative management may lead you to develop a strong belief in management as a science or as an art. In

CASE STUDY 1-1:
PROMOTION TO ADMINISTRATIVE MANAGER

Victor Gomez has served as supervisor of the accounts payable section of his firm for the past ten years. Gomez takes great pains to see that all invoice details are checked twice by his accounting clerks. Unknown to his clerks, Gomez manually spot-checks 10 to 15 percent of their work, which he is required to initial for approval. Other aspects of his supervisory style seem unique. For example, he insists that all employees keep neat desks (which he monitors each week). Also, from 8:50 to 9:10 a.m. each day, Gomez positions himself near the office entrance to check on his workers' punctuality.

None of Gomez's five clerks have objected to his supervisory style. In fact, he is very popular with the group. He keeps records of their birthdays and other important anniversaries in order to remember them in some special way. He also seems to be very sympathetic to their personal needs for time off from work when the occasion demands it.

Gomez's section has an excellent record of productivity. Largely for this reason, he has been chosen to "move up" to the position of administrative manager. In this position, he will be responsible for five sections, each headed by a supervisor who, in turn, is responsible for the work of eight to ten persons, depending on the section involved.

As he starts his new job, Gomez has a good talk with himself in which he looks back approvingly at the success of his work as accounts payable supervisor. Thus, he believes he can effectively manage the entire office using the same leadership style.

---

your opinion, what is the difference between these views? Which view do you hold now? Once you finish this course, return to this chapter question to assess your beliefs. Will they change? Or will they have been affirmed?

2. Of the five schools of management thought, which two most nearly reflect your personal day-to-day management style? Do you think you will likely change your management style in the future? Why or why not?

3. Describe the behavior and activities performed by two people you know who practice good interpersonal skills. What behavior do they exhibit that led you to think of them?

4. Consider the four functions of management. Which function would an inexperienced administrative manager be likely to spend more time developing and implementing than an administrative manager with two or three years of experience? Which function do you think you will need to spend more time on?

5. Why is the strategic planning process described as comprehensive? Describe an organization you know that has implemented this process. (It may be the school you are attending now or the company where you are working.)

6. Describe five activities administrative managers do that could be measured by either their effectiveness or efficiency.

7. Have you ever had a job wherein you reported to more than one supervisor who assigned and/or checked your work? What issues or concerns arose from this work situation? How did you handle any issues or conflicts that arose?

Discussion Questions

1. What important problem(s) would you anticipate in this case?

2. Considering Gomez's work history, how would you expect him to delegate work? Does it appear that he has applied equally well the principles of management discussed in this chapter?

3. How would you classify his management style? Do you feel that his past style will be effective in his relationship with his new workers? Explain.

Review the case and be prepared to discuss your answers in class.

CASE STUDY 1-2
DEVELOPING A PROBLEM-SOLVING ATTITUDE

Andy Lowe heads up the customer services division of Johnstown Metal Works, a manufacturer that processes materials for hundreds of East Coast companies. One of the systems analysts who reports directly to Lowe is Susan Larson, who has been with the firm for ten years. During the past several months, Larson has become irritable and sometimes antagonizes customers. Lowe realizes that he should speak to Larson about her relationship with the customers, but for some reason he has been reluctant to do so.

Today Lowe hears of another "run-in" that Larson had with a customer over the reworking of a large metal work order. He sits back, sighs, and reflects: "I really must sit down and talk with Larson. But I am fearful that she may quit. She handles all this technical measurement so well, and I know

that it would be difficult to find a replacement. But, yes, she is kind of sarcastic. I'll just put it off a little longer. Maybe she is having some personal problems at home."

Discussion Questions

1. What is the real problem involved in this case?

2. Did Lowe make the right decision to put off the discussion on the issue with Larson?

Analyze the case and draft brief answers to the questions for a group discussion.

INTERNET RESEARCH ACTIVITY

The U.S. Small Business Administration provides a gold mine of free information for small-business owners and managers. Access the course web site at http://www.swlearning.com and click on the links tab. You'll find several topics of interest. Using your favorite search engine, locate another web site that provides free information for managers. You may try using search words such as business plan, operating a business, managing a business, and so on.

Learning Activity:

1. What was the most useful piece of management information you acquired? Indicate where you found that information.

2. How does what you read relate to topics in Chapter 1 of this text? Be specific.

Prepare a one-page report to share with the class as directed by your instructor.

Chapter 2

Handling Administrative Management Challenges

OBJECTIVES

After completing this chapter, you will be able to:

1. Identify and describe four challenges in the business world that most affect the ways in which administrative managers direct activities in the workplace and office environment.

2. Discuss the concept of the "Infotech" worker as it is applied to managing workplace activities.

3. List actions an administrative manager can take to stay challenged in a job position and career.

The focus of this chapter is on what administrative managers do, whom they manage, and how they grow professionally. This chapter will:

- Provide a realistic look into the challenges that affect the way administrative managers do their jobs

- Spotlight those activities the administrative manager performs when managing the "Infotech" worker

- Discuss ways the administrative manager can personally stay challenged and grow through career development and participation in professional activities.

It is our attitude, more than anything else that will affect a successful outcome. —*William James*

TECHNOLOGY APPLICATIONS IN THE WORKPLACE

© Brand X Pictures

The Internet's Legal Minefield – Workplace Misuse Issues

The Internet and e-mail have brought with them countless business advantages—and, not surprisingly, a goodly amount of trouble spots. They can put a company on the legal defensive (discriminatory or harassing e-mails that return to haunt) or the offensive (employees blasting management on Internet chat rooms). What is the most pervasive problem in this area? There are situations in which people use e-mail inappropriately—to harass somebody or to tell off-color jokes.

Increasingly, e-mail is playing a role in what would otherwise be a run-of-the-mill employment-law case. Say, for example, that someone was terminated for poor performance, and you have a manager who was sending inappropriate e-mails about that person, which of course should not have happened. It complicates what would have been a very straightforward case. The issue about e-mail is it's never gone—you think it's gone—you deleted it, he deleted it, she deleted it—but it's not gone.

ISSUES TO THINK ABOUT:

1. Have you ever sent a less-than-thoughtful e-mail and then regretted doing so? How did it make you feel? Did any problems result from having sent the message?
2. Whose responsibility is it to inform employees of the legal risks involved in misusing business e-mail or Internet services?

CHALLENGES THAT AFFECT ADMINISTRATIVE MANAGERS

Four challenges or conditions in the business world that most influence how administrative managers direct activities in the workplace and office environment are (1) the growth in the information sector; 2) the focus on and increasing concerns about ethical business behavior; 3) the significance of corporate culture to the practice of effective management, and; 4) the increasing workloads of employees and issues surrounding their work/life boundaries. Let's take each of these conditions, analyze them, and try to determine how and where each impacts an administrative manager's performance.

Growth in the Information Sector

Careers in the information sector of the economy—in particular, those careers that administrative managers oversee—are in a growth stage. These information careers involve collecting, analyzing, synthesizing, storing, and retrieving data. In the last couple of decades, a vast array of electronic information technologies have melded, and access to information has become so immediate that it has changed the way we work, play, learn, and live.

The "big four" information technologies—computer networks, image processing, data storage, and artificial intelligence—have affected ways that workers retrieve, process, and output information. Increasingly, these key technologies are reshaping occupations that use these vital tools.

1. *Networks* are indispensable in companies for sharing data and communicating information with anyone, anywhere, anytime. By using a network, people can communicate efficiently and easily via e-mail, instant messaging, chat rooms, video telephone calls, and videoconferencing.

2. *Image processing*, which consists of capturing, storing, analyzing, displaying, printing, and manipulating images, allows users to convert paper documents such as reports, memos, and procedures manuals into electronic images. An image processing system is similar to an electronic filing cabinet that provides access to exact reproductions of the original documents.

3. *Data storage systems*, sometimes referred to as enterprise storage systems, handle information and store it electronically in readily accessible and concise formats. Not only do these storage systems focus on availability of data anytime and anywhere, but they also protect, organize, and backup documents, critical data, and information in a company.

4. *Artificial intelligence systems*, including expert systems, "knowbots," and agent software, are partnering with workers in doing routine office tasks. **Artificial intelligence** is the application of human intelligence to computers. This technology senses a person's actions, and based on logical assumptions and prior experience, takes the appropriate action to complete the task. One example of artificial intelligence in the workplace is speech recognition through software programs that allow users to input data, access the web, and process activities by voice alone.

As a result of growth in the information sector and increased use of these information technologies, today's workplace looks like this:

1. *"Virtual" organizations have replaced traditional companies with collaborative networks.* By integrating computer, information, and communications technologies, corporations have created collaborative networks linking thousands of people at separate locations around the globe.

2. *"Road warriors," the new ultra-mobile workforce, increasingly work out of "briefcase offices."* A single computerized palmtop unit, for example, now can serve as a communication tool, Internet browser, mailbox, fax machine, notebook, and much more.

3. *Businesses are outsourcing more functions to stay flexible and still profitable in times of rapid change.* Computerized training and support systems enable temporary and part-time workers to keep pace with core employees and provide just-in-time skills and services needed by organizations.

4. *Lifetime jobs are a thing of the past.* Creating a strategy for one's career is requiring new, more portable skills that can be marketed to a variety of potential employers on an as-needed basis. For example, an individual worker can expect to work as a temp at one place and as a consultant at another within the same month, provided they are not competitors.

Coping with changes of this magnitude will test an administrative manager's flexibility and foresight—the *flexibility* to change and the *foresight* to anticipate the changes and prepare for new ways of doing what must be done. These changes are also producing specialists in the workplace with new job titles and responsibilities. Table 2.1 shows examples of administrative career job titles as they have evolved from then to now.

TABLE 2.1 Technology Has Allowed for More Specialists in the Office

ADMINISTRATIVE CAREER JOB TITLES	
Then	**Now**
Clerk Typist	Administrative Assistant/Executive Assistant
Executive Secretary	Administrative Information Specialist
Office Manager	Administrative Manager
Receptionist	Administrative Receptionist
Clerical Worker	Desktop Publishing/Graphics Specialist
Secretary	Help Desk Specialist

The Focus on Ethical Business Behavior

Has corporate America acquired a bottom-line management style with a "win at all costs" mentality? Or is there room in the corner office for a little integrity? According to the American Management Association's 2002 Corporate Values survey, 76 percent of member respondents reported that ethics and integrity are listed among their companies' corporate values. To stand behind that claim, 71 percent of the companies surveyed actually state their values in the employee's handbook while 67 percent list them in company brochures, and 50 percent post them on their web sites.[1]

The importance of a good business reputation ranks high in the business world. It is invaluable. **Reputation** means what people think of the way you do business and how they assess your character as a businessperson. In other words: Do you compete fairly? Do you run a nice, clean operation? Do you treat your employees well? Do you go around bad-mouthing other companies in the industries, or do you speak about them with respect?[2] These factors help to shape your business reputation. In turn, they affect your ability to hire people, attract and retain customers, get financing, make deals, and do everything else that goes into building a successful company.

Related directly to a company's reputation are the ethics it practices on a day-to-day basis. **Ethics** are the moral guidelines involving right versus wrong. Business ethics is a hot topic these days because of Enron, Martha Stewart, and other companies and their executives being questioned on their ethical and legal practices. With everything from **insider trading** (use of information unavailable to the public) to employee theft on the rise, it is no wonder that businesses are beginning to focus on the impact of ethical leadership. But along with this new focus comes a lot of "gray area." Many times, managers are forced to decide on issues where there are arguments on both sides—a problem that makes ethical decision making very difficult.

According to Kenneth Blanchard and Norman Vincent Peale, authors of *The Power of Ethical Management*, there are three questions you should ask yourself when you are faced with an ethical dilemma:

1. *Is it legal?* In other words, will you be violating any criminal laws, civil laws, or company policies by engaging in this activity?

2. *Is it balanced?* Is it fair to all parties concerned, both in the short-term as well as the long-term? Is this a win-win situation for those directly, as well as indirectly, involved?

3. *Is it right?* Most of us know the difference between right and wrong, but when it comes down to it, how does this decision make you feel about yourself? Are you proud of yourself for making this decision? Would you like to explain your involvement in this issue on a 6 o'clock news show? Would you like others to know you made the decision you did?[3]

A well-defined ethics policy, along with an outline of related standards of conduct, provides the framework for ethical and moral behavior within organizations. Ethics come from the top. Without setting an example at the top, it is difficult, if not impossible, to convince employees that they, too, should be ethical in their business dealings.

As ethics policies are developed, focus should be placed on the bigger picture of how the organization relates to society as a whole and what its responsibility is to the greater good. Of course, in these days of downsizing and unending change, some may argue that these ideals are unrealistic. The bottom line is "what goes around comes around." If you treat your employees with disrespect and distrust, chances are they will do the same toward your customers.

What should go into a sound ethical policy? According to Blanchard and Peale, you can base an ethical policy on the following five fundamental principles:

1. *Purpose.* The purpose of an ethics policy combines both the vision and the values you would like to see upheld in your business. It comes from the top and outlines specifically what is considered acceptable, as well as unacceptable, in terms of conduct in your business.

2. *Pride.* Pride builds dignity and self-respect. If employees are proud of where they work and what they are doing, they are more apt to act in an ethical and professional manner.

3. *Patience.* Since ethics focus on long-term versus short-term results, you must develop a certain degree of **patience** or the ability of being able to wait for results without complaint or anxiety. Without it, you will become too frustrated and will be more tempted to choose unethical alternatives as a short-term solution to a problem.

4. *Persistence.* **Persistence** means continuing steadfastly and being committed. In the case of ethics, if you are not committed to the principled stance you have taken, then your ethics are of no value. Standing by your word is fundamental, and an ethical person will stay the course because it's the right thing to do.

5. *Perspective.* In a world where there is never enough time to do everything we need or want to do, it is often difficult to maintain perspective. A person's **perspective** can be defined as his or her broad view of an event or idea. It is advisable from time to time to stop and reflect on where your business is headed, why you are headed that way, and how you are going to get there. This allows you to recognize that change happens when it's least expected and to make the best decisions both in the short term as well as the long term.[4]

An excellent way to introduce a new ethics policy is to complete the honesty test in Table 2.2. This self-test was developed by Dr. Denis Waitley. In his book, *Empires of the Mind*, Dr. Waitley outlines ten questions to test a person's honesty and sincerity level.[5] The questions address both work and personal life situations. Since the questions are self-testing, no one but you has to see the results. As you reflect on your answers to each statement, think about why you answered the way you did. Are there any statements on which you feel you should try to improve in your score?

To some degree, an organization's reputation and ethical conduct are reflected in its corporate culture. We'll show that relationship now and why corporate culture is a major factor that contributes to successful companies.

Significance of Corporate Culture

Several factors affect the definition of a corporation's culture. Corporate culture is that invisible driving force that reflects the collective values and behaviors of those associated with the organization. It is how things get done in a company. Though based on belief, culture is manifested in behaviors. In other words, culture is how people behave when no one is watching them. As companies grow and hire more workers, managing the culture becomes more important.[6]

T A B L E   2 . 2   How Honest Are You?

Instructions: Read each statement and rank them using a 5-point scale, with 1 indicating strongly disagree and 5 indicating strongly agree.

Rank	Statement
1 2 3 4 5	I don't give in to the temptation to pad my expense account.
1 2 3 4 5	I do a full day's work for a full day's pay.
1 2 3 4 5	I never take office items, even small ones.
1 2 3 4 5	If my colleagues were as honest as I, our company would never have to worry about white-collar crime.
1 2 3 4 5	Those who know me consider my word my bond.
1 2 3 4 5	"Loyal and faithful friend" is one way my friends would describe me.
1 2 3 4 5	Recognizing how readily we influence the behavior of others, I strive to set a good example in all my endeavors.
1 2 3 4 5	Each day I work at remaining honest in all interactions, both in and out of the office.
1 2 3 4 5	If my spouse/significant other's emotional and physical fidelity were equal to mine, I would be satisfied.
1 2 3 4 5	In general, my approach toward others, both at home and away from home, is to treat them the way I would like to be treated.

From *Empires of the Mind*, Copyright © 1995 by Denis Waitley. Reprinted by permission of Harper Collins Publishers Inc.

Culture greatly influences job fulfillment, productivity, quality, customer service, creativity, and even profitability. Progressive leaders do not leave formation of culture to chance; instead, they deliberately act to shape it. They take actions to create a compelling purpose, engage the passion of their employees, and ultimately experience performance results that they've forecast they would achieve. Employees who work for companies with values closely matching their own tend to stay in jobs longer and have greater job satisfaction.

According to an article in the April 2003 issue of *HR Magazine*, three organizational cultures generally emerge in corporate America's workplaces. According to the article, you can often identify the presence of a particular culture by looking into the eyes of employees and using that as an analogy for understanding their differences. While all three employee groups discussed below often exist within a given company, a dominant group typically influences and defines the overall culture. Here is what you will likely see and experience in most organizations. See if you can identify with any of these or know someone who does.

- *The Glazed Eye Group.* About 54 percent of employees fall into this category. The members of this disengaged group are characterized by their lack of spirit and vitality. They are quick to explain why something cannot be done and frequently offer excuses. They look to other people to fix the situation and seldom share creative ideas. They feel discounted, unappreciated, and insignificant. You are likely to hear such statements as "Nobody listens to me," and "It's not my job."

Members of this group avoid risk-taking at almost all costs, do the absolute minimum they can to get by, and tend to watch the clock very closely. This group will slowly drain the vitality out of an organization when it becomes the dominating force. Curiously, and in spite of their low productivity, people in this group tend to leave work exhausted.

- *The Beady Eye Group.* Members of this actively disengaged group represent about 17 percent of the corporate workforce, but dealing with their negative energy often consumes a disproportionate amount of time and talent from organizations. These people work against the organization and go out of their way to seek out and find flaws. They focus on problems and even resist attempted solutions. They feel angry, frustrated, and highly disconnected. As they are blaming, moaning, and whining, you will likely hear them say things like "My boss is a jerk," and "This place is the pits." Even though they may be relatively small in number, their relentless negative energy drags others down. Moreover, their high-stress levels contribute to the stress of others. In some respects, they take some degree of pleasure when the leader fails or even when the organization itself fails.

- *The Bright Eye Group.* This "dream team" represents about 29 percent of the employee population in corporate America. Bright eye employees feel energized, recognized, appreciated, and encouraged to do their best. A "can-do"

MANAGEMENT TIP

Those organizations that do not shape their culture will ultimately be shaped by it.

attitude characterizes their behavior because they go the extra mile of giving and doing their best. They function in a spirit of partnership. These people have a clear understanding and are personally accountable and tend to look to themselves first for resources and solutions. Instead of fixing blame, they fix the problems. These star employees embrace change and look for ways to reinvent themselves while continuing to provide high value. They work hard, yet seem to be energized by the quality and significance of their work. They take great pride in their accomplishments and speak well of their company. You will likely hear such statements from them as "I love my job," and "This is a great place to work." You will see large groups of bright eye employees at places like Southwest Airlines, Disneyland, the Ritz-Carlton Hotels, and other organizations with aware leadership.[7]

See Table 2.3 for some strategies organizations can use to create a winning culture dream team. Strategies such as hiring well, clearing a worker's path, motivating, and coaching for growth are shown in the chart. Some of the problems associated with corporate culture challenges administrative managers and manifest often in an employee's ability to set and control personal and work boundaries. Creating and sustaining a "Bright Eye" culture of excellence requires the AM to take deliberate and sustained efforts and steps to take talent to the top. As an AM, look around and determine what "eyes" you see in your organization. Ask yourself, "Do I see results or consequences?"

Workloads and Work/Life Boundaries

From the increased use of temps, to the reclassification of hourly workers into salaried employees ineligible for overtime pay, to the rise in variable pay that puts part of a worker's paycheck at risk, companies are now able to get more work out of employees while concurrently offering employees less.[8] Still whatever the numbers say, there's no doubt that right now employees feel they have little choice but to accept the grueling workloads handed down by managers.

Managers are beginning to recognize what workers have known all along—that many workers have too much work and too little time in which to do it. According to a recent Office Team survey, 70 percent of the managers responding in a nationwide poll said that the average worker is at least somewhat overburdened. Ten percent said that the workload was significantly heavy.[9]

Job cuts are no longer a last resort in hard times, but are becoming an ongoing tool for matching supply with demand. Companies are looking first to bring in contract workers that they can quickly use and let go without paying any benefits or severance. In fact, the temporary workers have been the fastest-growing sector of employment over recent years. This trend is expected to continue over time.

As a result, companies are able to pare down staff without reducing workloads. They are also making employees work harder to create new business revenues. What's more, pay is increasingly tied to company performance, which further saves money when profits evaporate.[10]

TABLE 2.3 Strategies to Use to Create a Winning Culture in Organizations

Hire winners	Take the time to hire well. This is often one of the most important decisions. Consider applicants': Attitude—Do they have the right spirit for this job? Aptitude—Do they have the right talent for this job? Alignment—Are they the right fit with the company's mission and values?
Engage their spirit	Find out what turns workers on about their job and do more of that; conversely, find out what turns people off about their job and do less of that.
Coach for success	**Coaching** is an ongoing, collaborative process intended to clarify performance targets, reinforce strengths, and encourage individuals to stretch to even higher levels of performance.
Focus on deliverables	Celebrate successes and look for the lessons learned when mistakes are made.
Clear their path	Create an environment for workers to excel and then get out of their way.
Commit to renewal	Maintaining the status quo in a competitive environment is not a viable option. Since most employees want to learn and grow on the job, let them.

Reprinted with the permission of *HR Magazine* published by the Society for Human Resource Management (www.shrm.org), Alexandria, Va. Adapted from "The Eyes Have It" by Eric Allenbaugh in *HR Magazine*, April 2003, pp. 101-102.

All of these events, changes, and pressures of increased workloads among workers have brought about a new and trendy concept in the workplace—work/life boundaries. **Work/life boundaries** can be defined as the goal of workers to perfectly balance responsibilities on the job with responsibilities at home. But this is not always easy. The lines between work and home are being blurred with the increased availability and use of laptops, pagers, and cell phones. Employees are bringing their work home, and taking their home to work. Taking home to work is a new concept that means employees do home-related activities while at work. (Examples will be given shortly.) Why? Every day employees are faced with the challenge to maintain this delicate balance between their careers and home lives, and it is difficult to do so well without employing some time-saving techniques.

Experts agree that helping employees balance their professional and personal lives is not only good policy—but also it is a smart business move. The companies that help employees juggle the demands of work and family will be the biggest winners in the competition for good employees. Because happiness is fundamental to an employee's productivity, respecting his or her time and being flexible relative to reasonable work arrangements are strongly advised accommodations to make.

According to the November 2000 Xylo Report on Shifts in Work and Home Life Boundaries, the national survey on work/life issues reveals that 17 percent of workers put in overtime or take work home everyday, and 19 percent of men report working overtime every day, compared to 14 percent of women. Furthermore, people with incomes between $30,000 and $60,000 per year are more than three times as likely to work extra hours on a daily basis as people making less than $30,000 annually.[11]

Equally, it is reported that workers today are bringing "home" to work. Of those surveyed, 75 percent indicated they take care of personal responsibilities while on the job. Those personal responsibilities can include banking or bill paying responsibilities, making personal phone calls, taking care of child-care concerns, doing grocery shopping, conducting medical research, and making appointments. Although currently not all companies approve of such actions on the job, it is clear that more flexible working arrangements and methods of managing Infotech workers are obligatory in today's business world. Increasingly, family-friendly policies are realigning with the need for a greater work/life balance for workers.

MANAGING THE "INFOTECH" WORKER

Restructuring the organization around information is something that, of necessity, all businesses have done. Employees today are known as "Infotech" or IT workers. **Information technology**, or Infotech, consists primarily of computing, combined with telecommunications and networking. Primarily, Infotech will affect workers on two levels:

1. It is an important tool that allows workers to do more of their jobs through an intermediary or telecommunication device, such as a personal computer, PDA, database storage system, or other information devices.

2. It changes the nature of jobs because organizations have designed computer-based jobs to take advantage of telecommunications and networking.

No one is exempt from the effects of information technology. In general, today's workers' primary activities are gathering, creating, manipulating, storing, and distributing information—related to products, services, and customer needs.

Infotech workers present administrative managers with a major challenge—using computers to monitor employees' work habits and productivity, personal behavior, their electronic communications, and use of the Internet.

ETHICS & CHOICES

Through a computer error, your department has overcharged a regular customer for consulting services. When you confront the billing manager, she tells you to mind your own business. You believe she will not correct the error. What should you do?

Employee Monitoring

Workplace monitoring is nothing new—it's as old as employer-employee relationships. The main difference today is that so much of the monitoring is from information that is gathered in secret, thanks to technology. Employees may think their privacy is protected by the Fourth Amendment, which protects against unreasonable searches and seizures; but courts have ruled that the Constitution doesn't apply to employees of private firms. And while some states have passed privacy legislation, the protections are not consistently applied in all 50 states.

According to the American Management Association, the nation's largest management development and training organization, more than one-third of its members surveyed indicated they tape phone conversations, videotape employees, review voice mail, and check computer files and e-mail.[12] What is more, personal behavior is no longer off-limits. Some firms have adopted rules that limit coworkers' dating. Others ban off-the-clock smoking and drinking. Many companies regularly test for drugs. While companies say they collect information on their employees to comply with the law and protect their business interests, many feel it goes beyond that and consider all of these measures an invasion of their privacy.

One way to help ease employees' apprehension about monitoring and at the same time set up some fair boundaries for workplace surveillance is for companies to create a formal privacy policy. A good **privacy policy** articulates the reason for monitoring, specifies when, where, and how employees will be monitored, and outlines how any surveillance data will be used.

Computer and Internet Usage Monitoring

The words "computer monitoring" sound threatening to most workers, but it is possible for computer monitoring to become a worker's friend. **Computer monitoring** involves using computers to observe, record, and review an individual's use of the computer, including communications such as e-mail, keyboard activity (to measure productivity), and Internet sites visited. For example, a computer that counts keystrokes and identifies errors might not result in a reprimand but instead suggest that the worker take a short breather. Other monitors could act as prompters, reminding the worker of special details when talking with customers, or as coaches, giving tips on improving performance.

As more and more businesses provide high-speed dial-up Internet access to their employees, they seek to avoid employees accessing pornography or games or doing personal business through the web or e-mail. A 2001 study found that 14 million employees in the United States—more than one-third of 40 million employees online—have their Internet or e-mail use at work under continuous watch. Worldwide, the number of employees under surveillance is estimated at 27 million, according to the Privacy Foundation study.[13]

Employees need to understand that it is the employer's right to protect its business communication vehicles from abuse, including situations that could prove to be liable or even embarrassing to the company. Employers, likewise, need to understand that expectations need to be set and met and that an appropriate balance needs to be achieved between total trust of employees and total lack of trust. The law protecting both the rights of employers and employees in this area is still in its infancy. Until there is more clarity, employers will have to "fend for themselves" in designing enforceable e-mail and Internet use policies that will limit their exposure to lawsuits.

Companies need to create a sound policy on electronic usage so that employees understand what is or isn't acceptable in their use of electronic communications. Here is an example of a good computer communications policy:

Computer communications at XYZ Corporation must be consistent with conventional standards of ethical and proper conduct, behavior, and manners and are not to be used to create, forward, or display any offensive or disruptive messages, including photographs, graphics, and audio materials.

Table 2.4 shows the types and extent of worker activities that employers monitor, according to a June 2002 article in *Communications and the Law*.[14] Although at first blush there appears to be much concern over employee monitoring, there are both pros and cons to the practice.

Pros of Monitoring Monitoring can be done in a humane fashion if employees are guaranteed several rights—including access to all information gathered through monitoring. In fact, some argue that it might be motivational to give employees personal access to this information. Information given to the supervisor often is feared by the employee, but when it goes directly to the worker, it can become a positive motivator.

TABLE 2.4 Types of Worker Activities that Employers Monitor	
Activity	**Percentage**
Internet Use	54.7%
Telephone Use	44.0%
E-Mail Messages	38.1%
Computer Files	30.8%
Computer Use	19.4%
Job Performance — Use of video cameras	14.6%
Telephone Conversations	11.5%
Voice Mail Messages	6.8%

During productivity monitoring, for instance, advanced computer systems are able to make suggestions based on information that the employee enters. Not only do these computers keep closer tabs on employees, but based on this added information, the computer also may help employees do their jobs more effectively. Overall, the use of prompts can be positive because employees will not have to worry as much about remembering and recording countless details.

For the administrative manager, information gathered via computer monitoring can be used to coach employees. Currently, many organizations use the information gathered as a basis for criticism. Companies are realizing, however, that it is more motivating for employees to be coached rather than reproached.

Cons of Monitoring As a result of connecting employees to the World Wide Web, management is painfully aware that these workers have access to everything from marketing data to porn sites. To exercise a little control over just what Internet waves employees surf, a software program that allows managers to monitor Internet usage patterns is now on the market and is called spyware. **Spyware** is used for the sole purpose of tracking and recording computer actions.

Those who favor spyware say monitoring Internet usage makes workers more productive, conserves network resources, and helps limit legal liability by discouraging workers from downloading objectionable material to company computers. On the other hand, critics say the practice is unnecessary and misguided.

As more technology has invaded the workplace and employees have gained access to e-mail and the Internet on employer-owned computers, questions have arisen as to an employer's right to monitor personal use of these devices in the workplace. Cases indicate that an employee uses e-mail and the Internet for personal purposes at his or her peril. Despite the fact that most employers tell their employees that they are being monitored and share written policies with workers spelling out appropriate business usage of the Internet and e-mail, many employees let their guards down and find themselves the object of disciplinary action.

In the hierarchy of employee privacy rights, most protected are employees' own person and bodily fluids as well as the employees' personal belongings such as a car, briefcase, or purse. Fewer protections, however, are afforded to employer-provided items for employees' personal use such as the desk, locker, and mail. Further, minimal protection is afforded to employer-provided items that are shared by a number of employees such as an office, files, and e-mail. Because e-mail is among the least protected of employee privacy rights and employers have access to numerous monitoring devices on the market today, an employee's major workplace concern should be that a manager might say, "You've got inappropriate e-mail." Knowing and abiding by company policies should be standard procedures throughout the organization.

STAYING CHALLENGED AS AN ADMINISTRATIVE MANAGER

Any job has its good and not-so-good days. To stay challenged, administrative managers must do several things. They must 1) take charge of their careers by setting goals and managing career changing issues on a regular basis (not just on not-so-good days); 2) understand the stages of career development, and; 3) be open to participating in professional development and growth opportunities, which are plentiful.

Goal Setting and Career Management Issues

In the workplace, each individual is responsible for managing his or her own career. Although there are probably as many individual career goals as there are people working in the world, the process of career management has two fundamental objectives. There is an internal dimension, or what the process can do for people psychologically and emotionally. Then there is an external dimension, which relates to an individual's employability. Balancing the emotional with the practical is the goal of successful career management.[15]

Career development cannot be taken for granted. In other words, it will not take care of itself. Your career must be planned and managed in such a way that your personal and professional goals are frequently adjusted as circumstances change and new events occur. Once you have identified your personal and professional goals, mapping out a career strategy should be easy.

A career **strategy**, or detailed plan, should be flexible and based on your own personal experience and values. Here are some sample questions you should ask yourself and steps you should take follow.

1. What *might* you do? Identify your opportunities.

2. What do you *want* to do? Clarify your ambitions and hopes.

3. What *can* you do? Inventory your competencies and resources.

4. What *should* you do? Acknowledge your obligations.

5. What are you *willing* or *not willing* to do? Recognize your personal values.

6. How *will* you proceed? Develop a clearly defined plan of action with time lines for completion.

By helping employees understand what it means to manage their careers successfully, companies may in fact be implementing a **retention strategy** (techniques to retain workers). For example, if employees recognize that their career satisfaction is important to the company, they may be more inclined to realize through their self-assessment that they are in the right place—jobwise—because their values are aligned with the organization's values. When employees know this, their job satisfaction increases. Therefore, retention rates often go up.

Most people can expect to have six to seven employers and perhaps three to four careers during their lifetime, so careful self-management of careers is critical. Begin the self-management process by asking, "What will give my life meaning?" Be honest with yourself regarding your **values**, or those things that are important to you. In other words, what gives your life meaning?

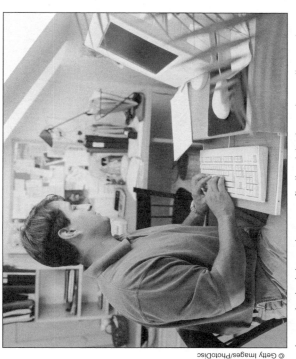

© Getty Images/PhotoDisc

When should you be concerned with setting career goals? A good recommendation is to reevaluate your career goals soon after you have experienced any significant life change, such as obtaining a higher level of education, getting married, separated, or divorced, having a child, moving to another city or state, or being a part of a company's downsizing. Do not wait for others to "develop" you; it is up to you to create and seek out your own developmental opportunities. In that way, when timing and luck seek you out, you will be ready to launch yourself into your next job.

Using on-line career resources and developing a professional portfolio are two ways to manage your career.

Online Job Searches Job seekers are finding lots of help when using the Internet for job searches. It is possible using the Internet to search for job openings with companies around the world and to apply for positions by electronically transmitting your resume for consideration. It has been estimated that there are 80,000 web job sites. Further, there are thousands of other sites that have job openings—company web sites, professional association web sites, Chamber of Commerce web sites, college alumni web sites, etc. That's more options than you could probably use in a lifetime.[16]

The Internet is an overwhelming information job source, but think of it only as a "tool" in your search toolbox. Remember, you will be hired by a *person* who will probably want to meet you and talk with you before offering you a job. So, use the Internet's vast resources to help you, but don't limit your efforts to this on-line world.

Increasingly, job seekers are finding jobs by going online and completing a job search.

It's a lot of work to find a new job. There are very few true short cuts, but the Internet has improved the process considerably while also adding some new complications (like protecting your privacy). It's so much easier to find thousands of job openings and to research companies, industries, and opportunities. It's also easier to find help. Take some time now to review various web sites that have an employment link to become familiar with the process of online hiring. For instance, go to a corporate power like IBM (ibm.com) or Microsoft (microsoft.com) or to the FBI (fbi.gov) and click on the employment or jobs link button. See what you find to use in your job search.

Portfolios One way career-minded business professionals manage their careers is by putting together one of the most important books a prospective employer will read about you—your portfolio. A **portfolio** contains a collection of items in book form that documents and chronicles the accomplishments that can give your career a boost. This book can offer unparalleled benefits during evaluations and job searches because it enables your current bosses or prospective employers to see your documented achievements.

One way to organize your portfolio is according to projects you have completed, training you have had, and skills you have developed and can perform. Here is an overview of each of those categories and the materials and information you may want to include in each part.

1. *Projects.* Include copies or templates for such forms as inventory, billing, time-sheets, style books, and manuals you helped create; include your time- and money-saving ideas that the company adopted. Of course, be careful never to violate the confidentiality of a current or past employer when selecting items to include in your portfolio.

2. *Training.* Include copies of certificates, academic degrees, courses, and seminars, as well as documentation of self-directed computer training you have completed and used on the job.

3. *Skills.* Create three subcategories such as management, computer, and interpersonal skills.

- Under management, include samples of management responsibilities such as communication, multi-project management, problem-solving, mentoring, and delegating.

- Under computer, include how you helped your coworkers or subordinates improve their computer skills. Also

include any technical skills you have learned, such as troubleshooting and solving software problems and making minor hardware repair.

- Under interpersonal, document situations that demonstrate you are a team player, showing your flexibility and adaptability in the workplace.

Stages of Career Development

Workers who are on a career track realize that there are stages to career development that can be expected at particular ages. For example, most of us spend the years between ages 1 and 25 preparing for work. Between ages 18 and 25, we find our first job and enter the world of work. After age 25 through approximately age 40, we focus on our career and usually make some significant career accomplishments. Then, from ages 40 through 55, we continue to progress and, in some cases, advance to higher levels in an organization. Finally, from age 55 to retirement, we begin to make some late career choices to phase out the present job. Table 2.5 lists some major tasks at each of the five career stages.

When preparing for or furthering a career, keep the following suggestions in mind:

1. *Be flexible.* Administrators, accountants, information systems technicians, and administrative support personnel are in demand in almost every field from medicine, insurance, and education to law enforcement.

2. *Develop communication and people skills.* Employers say over and over that they want employees who can speak and write well and who can interact and accomplish

TABLE 2.5 Stages of Career Development

STAGE	AGE RANGE	MAJOR ACTIVITIES
Preparing for Work	1–25	Develop occupational self-image, evaluate alternative occupations, develop initial occupational choice, and pursue necessary education.
Selecting Job Opportunities	18–25	Secure job offer(s) from desired organization(s), select suitable job based on accurate information.
Making Early Career Choices	25–40	Learn job responsibilities, learn organizational rules and norms, fit into chosen occupation and organization, increase competence, pursue goals.
Making Mid-Career Choices	40–55	Reappraise early career and early adulthood, reaffirm or adjust goals, make choices appropriate to middle adult years, remain productive in work.
Making Late Career Choices	55–retirement	Remain productive in work, maintain self-esteem, and prepare for active retirement.

tasks with and through others. Employers say that communication skills are the number one requirement for most jobs.

3. *Think globally.* Trade barriers are dropping, meaning more and more companies are competing internationally. As a result, opportunities will increase. To be marketable to such companies, you may need to learn another language, gain knowledge about other cultures, and study how business is conducted in other countries.

4. *Advance your knowledge about technology and communication devices.* Stay on top of new technologies, software packages, and operating systems. Get comfortable with using all types of modern communication devices. Be open

to going back to school or attending workshops to upgrade and become current on these skills. Many companies will reimburse for courses that upgrade skills for use on the job.

5. *Get an edge on your competitors.* Any extra skill, knowledge, or ability that will help you stand out from other applicants—computer skills, an extra degree, an industry-recognized certification, or a foreign language, for example—can be the plus that makes you the person chosen for the job.

6. *Keep learning.* Once you're employed, make learning a lifelong endeavor by attending seminars, conferences, in-house training programs, and pursuing college classes, certificates, and degrees.

© Digital Vision

Professional organizations are a great way for administrative managers to stay current.

Professional Growth Opportunities

Seeking opportunities to grow in a career is not always an easy task, depending on where you live and work and other family and personal obligations you might have. Many successful workers, however, have used several sources to help them. They have joined professional associations, have attained professionally recognized certifications, and have developed a mentoring relationship with others.

Professional Organizations and Associations

Joining a professional association is only one way that people pursue career development. In an association, people with similar career interests share information and help each other. By joining a professional association, you become an "insider." Attending professional meetings as a guest or student member provides an excellent opportunity to learn about the management profession and to meet and talk with professionals in the field.

Professional associations offer the following features and benefits:

- Monthly or quarterly meetings
- Workshops, seminars, and conventions
- Publications, including magazines, journals, and books that help professionals negotiate career challenges
- Programs to help with continuing education needs

You can learn about the concerns of the people in the profession and observe the strategies that successful people use to get ahead at meetings or by reading association publications. Through professional organizations, members are provided opportunities to acquire skills and professional credentials, to find or become a mentor, or simply to enjoy the networking aspects with others.

Table 2.6 provides a limited list containing information on some major professional associations available to administrative managers and office professionals.

Although this list is not complete, each association listed has some relevance for administrative managers. Contact any of those listed for details about membership and activities each sponsors. Add information to this list as you learn about other associations.

T A B L E   2 . 6   Professional Associations of Interest to Administrative Managers

Professional Association	Purpose and Description
National Virtual Assistants Society (NVAS) Telephone: (480) 515-5055 E-mail: info@nvas.org	A professional organization for virtual assistants. The goal is to provide networking, workshops, special events, tips and tricks, newsletters, resources, and advertising options. NVAS is open to any virtual assistant interested in networking, education, and information to help support their efforts.
Health Care Executive Assistants (HCEA) Chicago, IL 60606 Telephone: (312) 422-3851 E-mail: hcea@aha.org	A not-for-profit health care organization dedicated to executive assistants, administrative assistants, and other professionals reporting to health care management. HCEA is the largest professional membership organization committed exclusively to health care executive assistants.
International Virtual Assistants Association (IVAA) 11024 Balboa Blvd., Ste. 315 Los Angeles, CA 91344 Telephone: (877) 440.2750 www.ivaa.org	A non-profit organization dedicated to the professional education and development of members of the virtual assistance profession, and to educating the public on the role and function of the virtual assistant. The IVAA offers the Certified Virtual Assistant (CVA) exam, recognized internationally as the standard that virtual assistants strive to attain.
American Management Association (AMA) 1601 Broadway New York, NY 10019 Telephone: (212) 586-8100 www.amanet.org	The world's leading membership-based management development organization. AMA offers a full range of business education and management development programs for individuals and organizations in Europe, the Americas, and Asia.
International Association of Administrative Professionals (IAAP) Telephone: (816) 891-6600 E-mail: service@iaap-hq.org	The world's largest association for administrative support staff, with nearly 700 chapters and 40,000 members and affiliates worldwide. IAPP provides up-to-date research on office trends, publications, seminars and conferences, and superior resources to help administrative professionals.
National Association of Executive Secretaries and Administrative Assistants (NAESAA) 900 S. Washington St., G-13, Falls Church, VA 22046 Telephone: (703) 237-8616 http://www.naesaa.com	An association dedicated to promoting the professional stature of the administrative profession. NAESAA endeavors to accomplish this goal through the continuing education of its members and the development of valuable benefits designed to enhance the personal and professional lives of its many satisfied members.

Adapted from web site *http://www.adminprof.com/associations.htm.* (©2003.)

Professional Certifications What is certification? Certification is a way for employers to ensure a level of competency, skills, or quality in a particular area. Companies are looking for certified professionals with the knowledge and skills to work with others and direct organizations. A sponsoring organization develops and administers each certification. Some companies reimburse the costs of certification.

Professional certification via IAAP's Certified Administrative Professional (CAP) and Certified Professional Secretary (CPS) examination programs, shows employers, clients, and associates your commitment to your profession. IAAP suggests the following benefits of CPS and CAP certification:

- Job Advancement. Certification gives you a competitive edge for hiring and promotion.
- Professional Skills. You will learn more about office operations and build your skills by taking the CPS or CAP exam.
- Esteem. Attaining certification demonstrates to your employer and yourself that you are committed as a professional.
- Salary. Studies show that CPS holders earn an average of $2,228 more per year than those who do not have certification.[17]

The CPS examination is a one-day exam with three parts. The CAP exam is a one-and-one-half-day exam with four parts. The exams are administered each May and November at more than 250 locations across the United States, Canada, and other countries. Recertification is required every five years. For more information, visit www.iaap-hq.org.

The Microsoft Office Specialist program is a Microsoft certification designed to measure and validate users' skills within these areas of Microsoft Office: Word, Excel, PowerPoint, Access, and Outlook. Core and expert certification levels exist for most Office releases. Requirements to become certified are as follows:

1. Register for an exam of your chosen area of expertise and certification level.
2. Take the hands-on computer-based performance exam and pass with a score of 80 percent or better.

For more information about Microsoft certification, visit http://microsoft.com/traincert.

Mentoring Relationships As you strive to make progress in your career, you will at times encounter obstacles. Some barriers to career progress, such as the lack of a particular skill, are obvious. But sometimes you may find yourself confused and discouraged by your unexplained lack of progress. At these times, having someone to advise, teach, and encourage you could make the difference between being on a temporary plateau or finding your career at a permanent standstill.

A **mentor** is an adviser, teacher, sounding board, cheerleader, and critic, all rolled into one. A mentoring relationship gives you someone with whom you can freely talk through problems, analyze and learn from your mistakes, and celebrate your successes.

MANAGEMENT TIP

Look for opportunities to grow and learn through on-the-job experiences. Be open to coaching, understudy assignment, job rotation, lateral promotion, project management opportunities, and committee assignments.

You quickly learn things you might normally find out only through the long process of trial and error.

Some organizations provide formal mentoring programs. However, in many cases, mentor/protégé relationships evolve spontaneously and exist informally. In any case, when you choose a mentor, look for someone in a position you aspire to, who is a role model, and who possesses skills you wish to develop. The ideal mentor will have navigated some of the same paths you hope to travel and can alert you to potential pitfalls.

ETHICS & CHOICES

Suppose a married executive in your company is mentoring an administrative assistant. The gossip is they are also having an affair. Would you promote the gossip or say nothing?

MESSAGE FOR MANAGERS

Focus on your career because very few companies feel they owe or should guarantee anyone pay increases, promotions, a job, or a future. Success in life is not accidental; it requires detailed planning, meticulous preparation, and excruciating effort. Without dreams, life can be difficult, meaningless, and without direction. If you operate on the theory of hit or miss, expect a miss. To succeed, you need a plan. Think about what you need to do to achieve your life's goals and dreams. Make a list of these skills and competencies and how you can best attain them.

Chapter Two

S U M M A R Y

1. Several challenges or conditions in today's workplace affect administrative managers and how they do their work such as a) the growth in the information sector; b) the focus on ethical business behavior; c) the significance of corporate culture and; d) the increasing workloads of employees and issues surrounding worker work/life boundaries.

2. Work/life boundaries can be defined as the goal to perfectly balance our responsibilities on the job with our responsibilities at home. It becomes even more challenging to do so with the increased use of laptops, pagers, and cell phones.

3. Restructuring the organization around information has produced a new employee known as an Infotech worker, who performs his or her duties using computing, telecommunications, and networking technologies.

4. As more technology has invaded the workplace and employees have gained access to e-mail and the Internet through employer-owned computers, employee monitoring is on the increase and can include monitoring an employee's Internet use, telephone use, e-mail messages, computer files, computer keyboard activity, and voice mail messages.

5. Workers who are on a career track realize that there are stages to career development that can be expected at particular ages. In today's workplace, each individual is responsible for managing his or her own career and developing career strategies.

6. A portfolio is a collection of items in book form that documents and chronicles the accomplishments that can give a career a boost. Portfolios can be organized according to projects completed, training received, and skills possessed.

7. Professional growth opportunities are important to engage in. Whether it is joining professional associations, attaining professionally-recognized certifications, or developing mentoring relationships with others, it is a wise career move to continue growing professionally.

8. To stay challenged, administrative managers should a) take charge of their careers by setting goals and managing career changing issues; b) understand the stages of career development, and; c) be open to participating in professional growth opportunities that can include joining professional associations, attaining certifications, and developing a mentoring relationship.

KEY TERMS

Artificial intelligence
Certification
Coaching
Computer monitoring
Corporate culture
Ethics
Information technology
Insider trading
Mentor
Patience
Persistence
Perspective
Portfolio
Privacy policy
Reputation
Retention strategy
Spyware
Strategy
Values
Work/life boundaries

REVIEW

1. What are the four information technologies that are used today that affect how administrative professionals retrieve, process, and output information on the job?

2. How have virtual organizations replaced traditional companies?

3. Offer three questions you should ask yourself when you are faced with an ethical dilemma.

4. Define corporate culture. Using your job or your school as an example, briefly describe your perceptions of its corporate culture.

5. Name three reasons why you think setting work/life boundaries is becoming a critical concern when workers choose to work for a particular company.

6. What are some major workplace activities that are monitored by organizations?

7. Why is it necessary for administrative managers to set career goals?

8. What are the stages of career development described in the chapter?

9. List several advantages of joining professional organizations for administrative managers.

10. What are three certifications administrative managers can attain?

CRITICAL THINKING

1. Of the four conditions in the business world that will most affect how AMs direct activities, which two do you think will affect your life most? Why?

2. Describe someone you know who is struggling with setting reasonable work/life boundaries at work and at home. In your opinion, to what extent is it a difficult or easy process?

3. In your opinion, if a person does not want to be monitored on the job by a computer, should that person have a choice in the matter?

4. Do you believe you would feel comfortable in a mentor-protégé relationship as a means of getting ahead on the job? Why or why not?

CASE STUDY 2-1

PLAYING FAVORITES WITH A NEW WORKING ARRANGEMENT

Shortly after being hired as an administrative assistant, Michelle Alpert decided she would give up her lunch hours in order to cover the receptionist's desk. In fact, Alpert made an agreement with Jennifer Fleming, the administrative manager, whereby she would be allowed to quit work each day at 3:30 p.m. in exchange for giving up her lunch hour. Alpert saw this move as an excellent way to solve her problem of having someone home with her children when her husband left for night school at 5 p.m. In turn, Fleming was pleased to have someone on hand to receive incoming calls and thus assure customers their calls would be answered by a person during the entire workday.

One afternoon after Alpert had left at 3:30 p.m., several of her coworkers came into Fleming's office to air their complaints about the favoritism being shown Alpert. One of the executive secretaries, Gail Irwin, remarked, "All of us have agreed to give up our lunch hours, too, so we can leave early every day. You know, Jennifer, more and more firms are allowing their employees to do this sort of thing."

Fleming patiently listened and then made this statement in support of her feeling that the request was out of the question: "This company can't afford to shut down the entire office every day at 3:30 p.m. We'd be out of business in six months!"

Fleming went on to say she was surprised by the employees' request, for she felt they all knew about Alpert's problems at home—her husband's attending school and the need for someone to care for their children. The

workers said that they understood Alpert's problems and sympathized with her. However, they indicated that they, too, had personal problems—picking up children at the day-care center, avoiding traffic tie-ups during rush hours, being at home when the children got out of school, and so on. Irwin wrapped up the discussion by saying, "What's fair for Michelle should be fair for all of us. Think about it, won't you, Jennifer? It really isn't fair to play favorites."

Discussion Questions

Assuming the role of the administrative manager, Fleming:

1. How would you answer the complaints made by the employees who met with you?

2. What alternative courses of action are available to you in order to achieve the company's goals and still satisfy your workers' needs?

Analyze the case. Be ready to present your viewpoint in a class discussion.

CASE STUDY 2-2

IMPRESSIONS AND PROMOTIONS

Estelle Lopez has been on her new office job for about 15 weeks. She likes the job very much and eagerly continues to learn as much as she can about it. You, as her supervisor, consider Estelle an excellent employee because of her enthusiasm and her willingness to take on new responsibilities.

Though Estelle tries to do her best in all areas of her employment, she has a problem with grooming. She doesn't realize it, but the clothes she wears are more appropriate for an outside rock concert than an office setting.

You call Estelle in for her three-month evaluation and praise her for her excellent working habits, her punctuality, and her dependability.

Then you ask her about her career goals. Estelle responds that she eagerly looks forward to advancement and more responsibility. In fact, she says that someday she would like to become an administrative manager, just like you. You look surprised and tell Estelle that you thought she was more of a fun-loving gal than a serious career-minded woman. Estelle is very surprised, and a little hurt; her attitude about the job is still good though.

Discussion Questions

1. What would you do as the AM at this point, assuming Estelle wants to change her image as quickly as possible and have you regard her more seriously?

2. In your opinion, is this a realistic "dress and grooming" situation that occurs in offices today on a regular basis?

Analyze this case from both sides. Do you think the administrative manager responded appropriately? Be prepared to discuss the case in class and defend your stand.

INTERNET RESEARCH ACTIVITY

One of *Fortune* magazine's annual features is its list of "America's Most Admired Companies." Our purpose here is to learn more about the reputations of the current top ten on the list. What makes them stand out from the others? To find out, do a keyword search to locate *Fortune's* web site. Navigate through the site to locate the list of

America's Most Admired Companies. For a direct link to this site, go to odgers.swlearning.com and click on the Links tab. Then locate Chapter 2, "Internet Research Activity."

Pick one of the top ten companies, either at random or based on your interests, and do a web search for more information on that company. Be sure to make notes of the company's social responsibility, ethics initiatives, and the like. Record the web site address of each company you searched.

Learning Activity:

1. What are the top ten most admired companies?

2. Which one did you pick? Why?

3. What does this company do to earn its top ranking?

4. Does its high ranking in this category make you want to work for the company? Why or why not?

5. Define reputation in relation to this company. Do you see any evidence on the site to verify the reputation of the company? Ask a few of your friends their opinions of this company and how they would rank the company for reputation among consumers and/or for employment opportunities.

Complete the research for this project. Develop a report from the information that provides answers to the above questions. Analyze the information and compare it with another company you may be interested in for possible employment. Your instructor may ask that you submit the report for grading.

Chapter 3

Administrative Management Activities in the Workplace

OBJECTIVES

After completing this chapter, you will be able to:

1. Discuss results from recent surveys describing the ways in which the administrative professional's job has changed.

2. Within the scope of an administrative manager's skill set, describe the four literacy skills managers and workers alike should acquire and use in the workplace.

3. Explain the significance to organizations of each of the four major areas of management study in this textbook.

It is projected that in ten years, an administrative assistant will have progressed to the point of taking on most dealings for management. As such, managers will be involved mostly with marketing their products and services while administrative assistants, who are assuming more managerial responsibilities, will attend to the day-to-day activities.[1]

Over the past decade, technology has not only reshaped the administrative worker's workday with PCs, the Internet, e-mail, cell phones, and personal digital assistants (such as Palm Pilots) but also has transformed the way companies think of administrative professionals, elevating them from helpful assistants to resourceful team players and promoting many into leadership roles.

Research has found that every person can do at least one thing better than any other 10,000 people. There are, in fact, a great many hidden talents in every employee.

—David Spitzer, Motivational Consultant

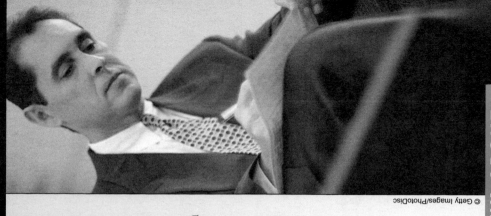

© Getty Images/PhotoDisc

TECHNOLOGY APPLICATIONS IN THE WORKPLACE

Information Sharing Basics – Paper vs. Electronic

Sharing information is more than copying a phone list for someone. Sharing information is making as much relevant knowledge available as possible to all those who need it. How and how well you distribute information to superiors, employees, and others is a reflection of you, your company, and even your ability to perform your job well.

Computers and their networks will likely make paper information sharing decline for three reasons. First, paper is dated the moment the ink hits it; therefore, it is no longer current. Second, paper is expensive and time-consuming to use. The third reason paper use between parties will shrink is that to share it, you have to physically transport it to the other party, which often takes longer and costs more than sharing electronic files.

ISSUES TO THINK ABOUT:

1. Does electronic information sharing enhance a company's ability to be competitive?
2. Predict what you think electronic information sharing for managers will be like in three to five years.

THE CHANGING ROLE OF THE ADMINISTRATIVE PROFESSIONAL

Today administrative professionals are stepping into more proactive roles as project managers, presentation designers, and valued members of teams and committees. Professional organizations, such as the International Association of Administrative Professionals (IAAP), are recognizing that their group's members have more college education and more certifications than in the past. Moreover, employers are looking more intently at the credentials workers have because the job description of the administrative professional or administrative manager (AM) requires knowledge, drive, and staying composed under pressure.

Administrative managers most often rise from the ranks of office professionals in organizations. Their job titles could be executive assistant, administrative assistant, or office manager.

According to a May 2002 article in *Essential Assistant*, office professionals make up one of the largest occupations in the United States.[2]

Scope of the Administrative Management Position

Administrative managers work in organizations that vary widely, such as public or private, domestic or international. They also have varied responsibilities, experience, earnings, and education. Because of the substantial supply of competent, experienced

workers seeking managerial positions, companies hiring AMs are in a great position to select from among the best applicants.

In the fall of 2002, the American Management Association administered the Administrative Professionals Survey to administrative professionals across the United States. According to results of that survey, administrative professionals have increasingly assumed more responsibility, are doing more work, and have taken on more of a leadership role than ever before.[3] As a result, administrative assistants say they need more training in additional areas of management and leadership skills to improve their performance on the job. Here is a snapshot of other key survey findings:

- Seventy-six percent of the respondents say they had more responsibilities over the past year and 65 percent believe they have more work in their in-basket than before. In the previous year's survey, only 48 percent of administrative professionals thought their workload had increased.

- The effect of 9/11 is evident in the workday of administrative professionals. About 41 percent say that security has tightened and 17 percent report that mailing procedures have changed. In addition, more than one-third indicate they feel more stress while at the job than before.

- Fifty-six percent of respondents believe that more training is the most important step they can take to improve their job performance. Other notable improvements that, if made, would advance their job performance are access to additional information, better work processes, and more clarity as to job responsibilities.

- Respondents surveyed believe the ability to plan a project and then begin to systematically work that plan is the most important skill they need to succeed in their job. Four other skills that ranked high in importance are professional behavior, critical thinking, diplomacy, and flexibility. These topics will be discussed in later chapters.

- Administrative assistants reported they spend much of their time coordinating travel and meeting arrangements and executing correspondence. Two-thirds cited managing the department and boss's calendars as one of the top five tasks on which they spend their time, just ahead of correspondence, and meeting and event organization.

- In general, administrative professionals consider themselves secure in their jobs with 53 percent rating their jobs very secure. If an administrative professional's immediate manager were laid off, two-thirds believe they would still remain in their current role. Noting the companies that have downsized in your community, have you seen this happening?

Administrative managers aren't CEOs, but today's AMs are performing their jobs more like managers, as they manage everything from the processes by which their own tasks are performed to complex projects that previously would have been tackled exclusively by executives. The most important reason companies are moving their AMs into more management-oriented roles is simple economics— organizations are looking for leaders who help drive business and act as a business partner. Although each of these skills will be covered in more depth in the

chapters that follow, we'll introduce six key skills that administrative managers especially need in today's fast-paced business environment. Presented briefly in Table 3.1, these workplace skills are leadership; a problem-solving, solution-driven approach; project management; team building; multi-tasking; and communication and public speaking.

With the need for these critical skills in the workplace, what does the job outlook and nature of work for administrative managers look like?

Where do you see yourself in administrative management as you start your business career? Make a note of job opportunities you would like to pursue.

Job Outlook and Nature of Work

Employment of administrative managers is expected to grow about as fast as the average for all occupations through 2010. Many additional job openings will stem from the need to replace workers who transfer to other jobs, retire, or stop working for other reasons.

Office, or administrative, professionals are employed in every type of organization or industry. Nearly three out of five administrative assistants are employed in firms that provide services, ranging from education and health to legal and business services.

TABLE 3.1 Critical Administrative Management Workplace Skills

Leadership	As more administrative managers are leading workplace teams and committees, as well as organizing meetings and conferences, employers prefer administrative managers with some previous supervisory experience.
A problem-solving, solution-driven approach	Businesses need administrative managers who can not only define specific problems but also offer viable and creative solutions as well.
Project management	Administrative managers need the skills to manage a project from start to finish. Strong organizational skills have always been an asset for administrative managers; but in project management, these skills become essential. They are essential to be able to organize a staff, schedule projects, coordinate daily duties, and keep an up-to-date list of tasks not yet completed.
Team building	The core quality here is building consensus. Team building is a natural extension of leadership. A team, based around task relevance, might include workers from marketing, manufacturing, human resources, and administration. Team members would share information and ideas continuously when planning and completing an assignment.
Multitasking	Administrative managers need to switch gears at the drop of a hat and be prepared for and unafraid of change. While not a management skill per se, multitasking and flexibility are key to keeping up in today's fast-paced work environment where executives are not looking for someone who is comfortable with routines, but need someone who can perform superbly in unusual circumstances.
Communication and public speaking	Executives increasingly want their administrative managers to be their right hand as well as an extension of their voice and presence. For that reason, administrative managers need to be able to engage comfortably in public speaking to both small and large audiences. When attending seminars, meetings, and networking functions, administrative managers are acting as ambassadors for their companies and must act accordingly. Moreover, they must be knowledgeable about their companies and answer all questions with tact and diplomacy, while always accentuating the positive.

Adapted from Anya Martin, "Management Skills that Matter," *OfficePro*, April 2002, p. 10.

Others work for manufacturing, construction, wholesale and retail trade, transportation, and communications firms. Banks, insurance companies, investment firms, and real estate firms are also important employers of office professionals, as are federal, state, and local government agencies.

The administrative professional is no longer "just" a team member, but at times must be a team coach, team supervisor, team recruiter, and all-around team leader. To be successful, administrative professionals are being told to "think like a manager," but what does that really mean? It requires seeing the big picture and having a vision that inspires passion and commitment. It requires performing activities on the job similar to those performed by managers shown in Table 3.2.

According to the most recent data from the U.S. Department of Labor, Bureau of Labor Statistics, administrative managers held about 362,000 jobs in 2000. About half worked in service industries, including engineering and management, business, educational, social, and health services.[4]

TABLE 3.2 Take Actions to "Think like a Manager"

- Effectively delegate tasks and projects—what to do, what to avoid, and how to follow up without looking over shoulders
- Determine where your efforts are needed and say no without guilt or remorse
- Maximize your influence and reach your goals, even when you are not in charge
- Deal effectively with the people who try to put roadblocks in front of you and sabotage your efforts
- Turn interruptions and unreasonable demands into "teaching moments" to modify behavior
- Break free of restraining thoughts and embrace possibilities—and calculate the odds and the consequences of a win, place, or show outcome
- Present a commanding and credible image in meetings and social events to stand out from the crowd and the competitions
- Think smarter when tackling workplace challenges
- Tap into your natural creativity and come up with innovative options for real-world situations
- Discover the best routes—avoid the roadblocks, carve out new trails
- Proactively fine-tune your decision-making abilities
- More effectively persuade others to buy into your ideas
- Focus across departmental lines to optimize big-picture goals
- Carve out a personal career path that uses all your strengths to do the best job you can and to get ahead in life

A virtual coordinator often works from a home office.

© Corbis

productivity and customer service, define the responsibilities of first-line managers, and may be involved in the hiring and dismissal of employees.

With many executives on the road 90 percent of the time and so much communication via cell phones and e-mail, administrative managers may well be thought of as a "virtual coordinator." The new **virtual coordinator (VC)** is someone who can adapt quickly and without hesitation; step in when needed, and be able to access information immediately—whether it's electronically retrieved from the company's data storage system or researched on the Internet.[5] The virtual coordinator will be the connection point where many lines intersect. That is to say, a VC will perform many of the following coordinating tasks for several different units within the organization:

- Confirm or reschedule appointments with participants

- Send out the agenda for the virtual meeting along with any documents participants may need during the meeting

- Schedule the videoconferencing rooms and needed equipment such as fax machines, copiers, and projection systems for the meeting rooms at all locations

- Verify that conference participants have notepads, flip charts, markers, and other such supplies. Verify with the facilitator that any equipment training has been scheduled as needed.

- Arrange meeting times and locations while checking participants' availability by using a calendaring software package, such as Microsoft Outlook

As previously noted, administrative managers perform a broad range of duties in virtually every sector of the economy. They coordinate and direct the support activities that allow organizations to operate efficiently, such as secretarial and reception, administration, payroll, conference planning and travel, information and data processing, mail, materials scheduling and distribution, printing and reproduction, records management, telecommunications management, security, parking, personal property procurement, supply, and disposal. Administrative managers are organized and able to handle multiple priorities, but still are able to answer phones with a caring and concerned voice.

It should be noted that specific duties for these managers vary by degree of responsibility and authority. For example, first-line administrative managers directly supervise a staff that performs various support services. Mid-level managers, on the other hand, develop departmental plans, set goals and deadlines, implement procedures to improve

Training, Other Qualifications, and Advancement

Staying current with job skills is critical for an administrative manager. Educational requirements for AMs vary widely, depending on the size and complexity of the organization. In small organizations, for example, experience may be the only requirement to enter a position as office manager. Specific requirements vary also by job responsibility. For first-line administrative managers of secretarial, mailroom, and related support activities, many employers prefer an associate degree in business or management, although a high school diploma may suffice when combined with appropriate experience.[6]

Managers of highly complex services, such as those involved in negotiating contracts for services, generally need at least a bachelor's degree in business, human resources, or finance. Regardless of major, the curriculum should include courses in office technology, accounting, business mathematics, computer applications, human resources, and business law.[7]

Persons interested in becoming administrative managers should have good communication skills and be able to establish effective working relationships with many different people, ranging from managers and supervisors to clerks and blue-collar workers. They should be analytical, detail-oriented, flexible, and decisive. Further, they must be able to coordinate several activities at once, quickly analyze and resolve specific problems, and cope with deadlines.

Changes in the administrative profession are spurring administrative managers to acquire certifications because of the increasing importance of knowing a person's credibility when employers scan resumes or evaluate their current work force. Gaining in popularity as ways to promote a manager's improved skill levels are several certifications that include the International Association of Administrative Professionals' Certified Administrative Professional (CAP) certification, the Certified Administrative Manager (CAM) designation offered by the Institute of Certified Professional Managers, and certifications in specific software programs, such as the Microsoft Office Specialist.

Earnings and Working Conditions

Earnings of administrative managers vary greatly depending on the employer and the geographic area. The most recent figures from the Bureau of Labor Statistics (BLS) in 2003 indicate that the median annual earnings of administrative managers in 2000 were \$47,080 with the low and high at \$32,550 and \$67,630, respectively. Median annual earnings in the industries employing the largest numbers of administrative managers across the United States, according to the BLS, are shown in the chart below:

Computer and data processing services	\$54,700
Colleges and universities	\$51,470
Local government	\$48,470
Management and public relations	\$44,420
State government	\$43,710

Administrative managers generally work in comfortable offices. Yet new technology has increased the number of managers who telecommute from home or other offices, and teleconferencing has reduced the need

Literacy Skills that Managers in a Diverse Work Force Need

In the continuing economic and global expansion of today's workplace, recruiting and retaining a diverse work force has become a more difficult challenge for employers. The task calls for the need to identify and hire workers with a more comprehensive literacy skill set as well as to update the administrative manager's literacy skill set, as needed. This four-prong literacy skill set encompasses information literacy, workplace literacy, global literacy, and cultural literacy. These are briefly discussed below.

Information Literacy Information literacy is the ability to use computers and technology to find, analyze, and use information in a meaningful way. Technology is helping to shape the way employees work and managers function. Rather than technology being a starting point in completing any workplace task, technology, as a resource, should be available *wherever* and *whenever* we need it. The ability to store, retrieve, analyze, and use information can make the difference between a business that succeeds and a business that fails.[9] Knowledge, in the form of information, is different from all other resources. It makes itself constantly obsolete, so today's advanced knowledge is tomorrow's ignorance.

Knowledge makes resources mobile. That is to say, knowledge workers, unlike manual workers in manufacturing, own the means of production. The knowledge that an administrative manager possesses is critical to organizations because his or her daily interaction with the company's files and data

---

for in-state and out-of-state travel. According to the BLS, most administrative managers work a standard 40-hour week. However, uncompensated overtime frequently is required to resolve problems and meet deadlines. Because of frequent deadlines and the challenges of managing staff and resources, the work of AMs can be stressful at times. What do you think are the major skills needed by an AM?

SCOPE OF ADMINISTRATIVE MANAGER'S SKILL SET

Imagine a classified advertisement for an administrative manager's position 10 years from now. It might look something like this:

The successful candidate will be a project management expert, apply creative problem-solving to ambiguous issues and situations, integrate and train employees, demonstrate expertise in software applications and technology, be a role model of professional ethical conduct, build team morale, provide superstar external and internal customer service, and perform job activities more efficiently and effectively by utilizing online tools and continually updating his or her skill set.[8]

These skill areas are not that far off-base, even now. When combined with the new literacy skills required in our culturally rich workplaces, the applicant would be an extraordinary candidate with a more complete skill set to offer.

results in creating, manipulating, and storing information. Should an AM leave his or her job, then companies lose a lot of history and useful knowledge that cannot be recaptured. AMs carry that knowledge in their heads and can, therefore, take it with them. What this means is that managers and organizations alike must value the worker as never before because in some cases, knowledge that leaves an organization may not be recaptured fully or used effectively again. Developing a procedures manual may be helpful.

Workplace Literacy A major concern for managers is the difficulty in locating and hiring a person who is literate; specifically, one who can demonstrate literacy while performing routine workplace activities. **Workplace literacy** is the aspect of functional, or day-to-day literacy, that is related to employability and skill requirements for particular jobs.

The basis of workplace literacy is literacy in a broad sense—that is, a combination of traditional literacy, which is the ability to read, write, and do basic math, and the ability to pull together the information obtained from reading and calculations and *apply* it in real-life situations. The application of workplace literacy requires information processing, logical reasoning, and critical-thinking capabilities together with basic reading, writing, and mathematics skills.

How much reading, writing, and mathematics skills do organizations seek in administrative managers and workers today? In addition to these basics, managers also need other types of skills as noted.

- *Reading Skills*. All managers and workers must be able to read well enough to understand correspondence, reports, records, equipment manuals, charts and graphs. On the job, reading is the primary method used to locate information needed to make decisions, recommend courses of action, or complete a task.
- *Writing Skills*. Composition and grammar skills become more critical as additional writing responsibilities are assumed by workers in the workplace. Creating professional e-mail messages or being given the authorization to directly correspond with customers involve writing skills that all persons in the organization need to perform very well.
- *Mathematics Skills*. The ability to do basic mathematical calculations is important in almost every job. In some positions, advanced math or accounting skills are necessary.

Communicating with customers both in person and by telephone, explaining schedules and procedures, relaying messages accurately, working as a team player, teaching others, solving problems, and reasoning logically are also needed skills.

Global Literacy Global literacy is the newest leadership skill required for business success. To be **globally literate** means seeing, thinking, and acting in culturally mindful ways. It's the sum of the attitudes, beliefs, knowledge, skills, and behaviors needed for success in a multicultural, global economy. For example, it means understanding, respecting, and accepting the attitudes, beliefs, and behaviors of other people and cultures without compromising your own.

In the current borderless economy, all business is global. Because competition comes from everywhere, businesses of all sizes are required to develop a global perspective, strategy, and skill base.[10] International competition, the global war for talent, joint ventures and alliances, and pressures for greater productivity are demands that managers are dealing with more often than not.

Cultural Literacy

A multicultural workforce creates unanticipated problems that require delicate handling to keep valuable employees happy. When diversity issues such as discrimination and cultural alienation arise, they affect productivity. **Cultural literacy** is not just about race and religion; it's about global etiquette, helping people feel comfortable in the workplace, and understanding other cultures.

A culturally-diverse employee wants what *all* employees want from their employer— fair treatment, a sense of belonging, understanding and acceptance, and a feeling that they are making a contribution. The bottom line for employees is how they feel about coming to work every day. Is it a horrible thing? Or do they feel that they are able to contribute? Steps taken to overcome diversity difficulties can stumble if they are inadequately supported, weak, or undersold. Unfortunately, some diversity efforts are little more than window dressing that result in wasting the organization's time and resources and frustrating employees. Employees are quick to recognize any efforts that are not really in the interests of developing better understanding and a more accepting work force.

Table 3.3 summarizes key elements in understanding cultural diversity. Specifically, it defines and cites examples of primary and secondary issues in cultural diversity. In addition, the table points out the benefits of valuing, as well as the disadvantage of not valuing cultural diversity.

As you can see from the table, statements can be hurtful, even if made in jest or without malice. Being in tune with the people you work with and for is the fair way to avoid promoting insensitivity to cultural diversity.

With the recognition that literacy is multifaceted and affects how managers manage, this awareness will help as we next introduce the major areas of study for administrative managers.

Administrative Management— Major Areas of Study

Today's managers face a complex web of difficult and exciting challenges. The challenge for administrative managers is to guide large or small, profit or nonprofit, organizations into the 21st century in a way that allocates and uses society's precious human, material, financial, and informational resources in the best way.

All too often, new managers are hired or promoted and then forgotten. Putting new or untrained supervisors into uncharted waters can be devastating without a first-rate understanding of certain managerial skills at the outset. Effective training in major areas of management study is clearly necessary because untrained supervisors may make potentially costly mistakes. Just consider the detrimental effect of letting the supervisor learn to supervise by making mistakes. We would probably see fewer expected results,

TABLE 3.3 **Cultural Diversity**

What Issues Define Examples of Cultural Diversity?	Examples of Belittling Comments
Primary Issues	
Age	"Shouldn't you be retiring soon?"
Ethnicity	"Those people are too traditional to understand computers."
Gender	"Shouldn't she wait for a man to do that?"
Physical abilities	"Why don't we all get larger monitors?"
Sexual orientation	"Did you hear that now he can get health insurance for the guy he lives with?"
Secondary Issues	
Education	"He couldn't even make it through high school."
Income	"I don't think she can afford good clothes."
Marital status	"What makes you think anyone could put up with him!"
Military experience	"He thinks he's still giving orders in the Army."
Parental status	"Poor thing, she grew up in a foster home."
Religious beliefs	"She's one of the 'born again' people."
Advantages of Valuing Diversity	**Disadvantages of *Not* Valuing Diversity**
Full utilization of the work force	High turnover among employees
Reduced interpersonal conflict	Low employee morale
Enhanced work relationships	Limited innovation
Shared organizational vision	Lagging productivity
Increased commitment among diverse employees	Legal matters
Greater innovation and flexibility	Increased inability to recruit the most talented new workers

confused directions leading to lower productivity, poorly executed work assignments of inferior quality, problems recognized but ignored, or solutions applied to symptoms instead of root causes.[11]

Although there is no real formula for success as a manager, acquiring the theory of management (definitions, relevant facts, concepts, techniques, guidelines) and then using that theory in practical application (on-the-job, case studies, and role playing in training situations) helps tremendously.

By studying the four major areas of management study as shown in Figure 3.1, new managers will be on the right track. The four areas are: human resources management, leadership and communication skills, essential administrative services, and workplace systems and technology.

A brief introduction of each major area of study is presented below.

FIGURE 3.1 Major Areas of Management Study

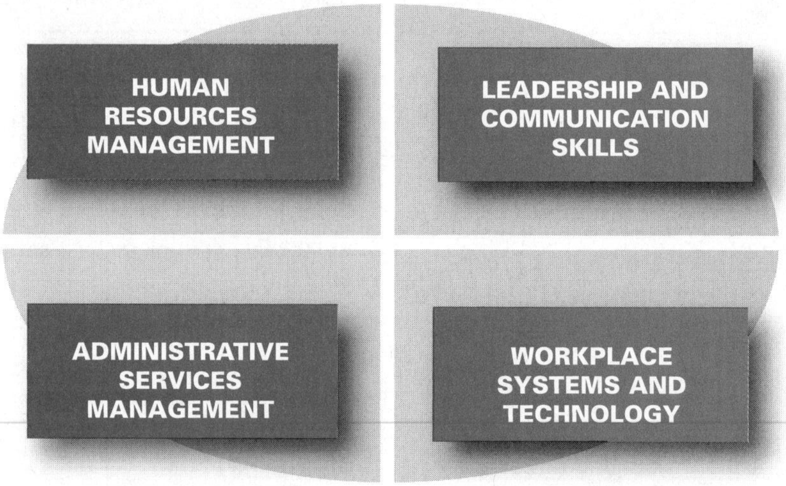

Human Resources Management With varying degrees of involvement, administrative managers perform personnel, or human resources, activities on a daily basis. Human resources management involves work force planning, acquisition, and development. We have moved from an industrial society, where the primary source of wealth was machinery, to a knowledge society, where the primary source of wealth is human capital. A company's **human capital** is the collective sum of the attributes, life experience, knowledge, inventiveness, energy, and enthusiasm that its people choose to invest in work. In the closing years of the 20th century, management came to accept that people, not cash, buildings, or equipment, are the critical differentiators of a business enterprise. That acceptance is considerable because in principle up to 70 percent of a company's expenses are related to human capital.[12]

Administrative managers have a critical role in the wise use and understanding of human capital. Its characteristics include that it can be developed and cultivated, but it (as the company's employees) can also decide to leave the organization, become sick, disheartened, and even influence others to behave in a way that may not be to the advantage of the organization. Unlike raw materials or equipment, human capital cannot be simply bought and used. Human capital must be contributed *voluntarily* by the employee.

That is why human capital is arguably the most valuable asset held by any organization today. It is, however, the most challenging asset to manage for a variety of reasons. Surprisingly, human capital is not the people in an organization per se. That's because people exercise control over their human capital and are free to invest it as they see fit in different aspects of their lives such as family, community interest groups, physical fitness pursuits, or work.

Why should a manager know about the best use of human capital? In a knowledge-based society, competitive advantage will depend to a large extent on the caliber of the people working in the organization. Individuals who are highly skilled and/or who possess highly transferable competencies are not tied to *any* organization. Their skills are in demand and as a result, they can choose for whom and how to work.

To build and maintain human capital investment in organizations, AMs must support workplace training programs that enhance core activities by focusing on the development of people as a major source of obtaining and maintaining a competitive advantage. Core activities of an organization

Critical skills needed by administrative managers are varied and broad.

are its operations, and include the creation, selling, and support of the products and services that the company produces. Continuing education and training programs designed to promote core activities should be developed with as many technology-based learning tools as possible. These tools, such as audiocasts, webcasts, computer-based learning software, and simulated job training models enhance the opportunity for individual and group learning in remote settings.

If we believe that people are a company's greatest asset, then we must also believe that organizations compete for business through the people they employ. If this is the case, then it is to the organization's advantage to ensure that its greatest asset, albeit its most elusive one, human capital, is utilized to its best and greatest use. This cannot and will not happen of its own accord. That is why a major area of study for any administrator is human resources management. A manager can do much to retain human assets.

Leadership and Communication Skills

Merely placing people together does not guarantee success in organizations that are composed of individuals with diverse backgrounds and perceptions. The real challenge comes in effectively leading and motivating people and solving problems as they arise. Leadership has many definitions. In administrative management, the definition offered is that **leadership** is the human process of influencing people to work willingly and enthusiastically to attain organizational objectives. Leadership skills involve providing direction, giving positive and negative feedback, motivating subordinates, communicating effectively, and resolving conflicts.

To effectively lead, managers need a working understanding of how groups function because groups are the basic building blocks in organizations. **Groups** are made up of two or more freely interacting individuals who have a common identity and purpose. Teams are becoming the structural format of choice for groups in the workplace. Today's employees, however, generally have better technical skills than team skills. Trust, honesty, and dependability are key components of effective teamwork. Managers and team members alike can build on these key components through support, respect, fairness, predictability, competence, and communication with others inside and outside the organization.

Communication is the process by which

information and human attitudes are exchanged with others. The communication process involves the transfer of information and understanding. Modern technology has made communicating easier and less costly, with the unintended side effect of information overload. Managers at all levels are challenged to manage information and to improve the effectiveness of their communication because it is at the core of everything they do.

Listening at all levels of the organization does not get sufficient attention as a communication skill. Active, cooperative listening is to be encouraged. Writing skills are no less important in the computer age. Written messages need to be specific, simply worded, and concise.

New managers need training in another area as well—delegating tasks. Delegating tasks is difficult to do for different reasons, but one reason seems to stand out as being the most common. High-performance workers often get promoted to manager positions; however, their instincts are to roll up their sleeves, push people out of the way, and say, "Let me handle this one." But this consistent pattern of action from a manager sends the message to subordinates that says, "I don't trust you. You are not capable."

The result is that the best and brightest (under this manager) will quit or at the very least become disillusioned with their jobs. The rest of the employee population will learn they can sit back on their heels and do little or nothing. New managers need to learn how to delegate. Delegation is a behavior learned through practice and learning the basics of how to delegate from training seminars, books, and mostly, on-the-job experiences.

Administrative Services Management

Managing the workplace environment consists of several actions on an administrative manager's part. For example, it not only deals with the most efficient office design and space concerns, but also has to do with safety and other health-related issues as well. Workplaces that are designed with an eye toward managing the efficient flow of work and maximizing the use of space increases worker productivity, and lessens the incidence of absenteeism and worker turnover. Ultimately a well-designed workplace should increase the profitability of the organization.

Office Design and Space Issues

An office environment is made up of several interdependent systems: people, floor plans, furniture, equipment, lighting, color, air quality, temperature, and acoustics. These interdependent systems are constantly changing; and for that reason, offices should be designed with the capability to adapt to changing needs. **Ergonomics**, also known as human engineering, is an applied science devoted to incorporating comfort, efficiency, and safety into the design of items in the workplace to satisfy the physical and psychological needs of workers.

Health, Safety, and Security Issues

Four primary sources of frequent physical problems in offices are air, chairs, lighting, and computers. Though these four health factors abound in offices, they can be controlled in several ways by administrative managers. Business crises come in many forms and can occur any time without notice. So,

whether it is an accident, a scandal, an act of nature, or a malicious act, organizations recognize that they need to be prepared.

Threats to employee safety in the workplace are increasing in frequency and severity and, contrary to most thinking, are not limited to big cities or high-profile companies. In certain cities across America, frequent news reports reaffirm that holdups, homicides, hostage-taking, rape, and other acts of violence are being committed where people work.

People are not the only workplace element at risk. Computers are too! A **computer security risk** is any event or action that could cause a loss of or damage to computer hardware, software, data, information, or processing capability. Computer security risks include computer viruses, unauthorized access and use, hardware theft, software theft, information theft, and system failure. Safeguards are protective measures that can be taken to minimize or prevent the consequences of computer security risks. For example, an **anti-virus program** protects computers against viruses by identifying, removing, or quarantining any computer viruses found in memory, on storage media, or on incoming files.

Workplace Systems and Technology

Technology has seeped into practically every aspect of organizational life, affecting everything from processes to people. Technology paves the way for new possibilities that, until now, were thought only possible in science-fiction movies. This means that administrative managers must understand and anticipate these technological challenges and opportunities. Technology trends affect entire organizations, rather than just individual areas.

In the workplace, people use computers, technology devices such as scanners, faxes, copiers, and telecommunication systems to complete vital organizational activities. Using computers, workers create correspondence such as letters, reports, and e-mail messages, calculate payroll, track inventory, and generate invoices. Computers are a primary tool workers use to communicate with others instantly and to access information from all around the globe. Using the advanced computer equipment and network systems that are available, you can not only transmit text, but also voice, sounds, video, and graphics as well.

Workplaces depend on different types of computers and technology systems for a variety of applications. Small companies with fewer than 50 employees, for instance, use several types of specialized communications software on a daily basis and don't think anything about it. Those who work away from the office may take for granted their notebook computers equipped with a modem or other wireless capability as they complete work in other locations. Large businesses use these same applications and provide an automated networked system throughout the company. They also have large databases

and use high-tech equipment readily accessible to each of their workers.

Many businesses use networks extensively. **Networks** are defined as a collection of computers and devices connected by communications channels that facilitate communication among workers and allow users to share resources with other users. Using a network enables people to communicate efficiently and easily, both outside of and within the organization. Each user on a business network shares hardware, software, data, and information, thereby reducing costs while increasing efficiency and promoting effective information management.

The **Internet,** known as the world's largest network system, is used to send messages to others, obtain information, shop for business-related goods and services, and meet or converse with people around the world. A variety of Internet and online services in the technologically advanced workplace are briefly described below:

• E-mail and the transmission of messages and files are primary methods of rapid communication in the workplace.

• FTP (File Transfer Protocol) is an Internet standard that allows workers to upload and download files with other computers.

• A chat is a typed conversation that takes place on a computer in real time through a chat room.

• Instant messaging (IM) is a service that notifies you when one or more people are online and then allows you to exchange messages or join in a private chat room.

• Internet telephone uses the Internet instead of the telephone to enable workers to talk to other people over the web.

ETHICS & CHOICES

An office supply dealer delivers one "free" copy of a new software package to your residence after you, the administrative manager, placed an order for ten copies of that software. Do you keep the software package?

- Videoconferencing uses video and computer technology to conduct a meeting among participants at geographically separate locations.

Company **intranets**, as opposed to the Internet, generally make company information accessible to employees via the organization's computer server and networked systems, usually via a password. Simple intranet services and applications that businesses make available to employees are telephone directories, event calendars, procedures manuals, employee benefits information, and job postings.

MESSAGE FOR MANAGERS

With the trend toward more managerial tasks for administrative professionals, administrative managers have a tremendous opportunity for increased job satisfaction, increased accomplishments, and if desired, career progression within a company. A decade or more ago, companies looked for administrative workers and managers who had very strong technical computer skills, who were fast typists, and who had knowledge of whatever particular software the company had or was planning to use. Though they are still important, companies today put considerably less importance on those hard skills.[13] Here's why.

The resumes that will likely get noticed today are the ones that list actual accomplishments as opposed to simply job duties or skills. For example, a resume that states the applicant actually developed a policy manual on in- and out-of-state travel procedures or that he or she saved the company money through a particular suggestion he or she made is highly desired. In other words, past examples of applied management skills and initiative rather than simply following orders and routines is a top qualification for administrative managers in today's marketplace.

Other key qualifications are flexibility in the face of change, and the ability to be a true multitasker who eagerly takes on the challenge of doing whatever it takes to do a job and to do it well. The person who views his or her job as "nothing is below me, nothing is above me; no task is too small, no challenge is too large" will become successful.[14]

Chapter **Three**

S U M M A R Y

1. Administrative professionals are stepping into more proactive roles as project managers, presentation designers, and valued members of teams and committees.

2. Administrative managers work in organizations that are wide-ranging, such as public or private, domestic or international, and have varied responsibilities, experience, earnings, and education.

3. The six general skills administrative managers need in fast-paced business environments are leadership; a problem-solving, solutions-driven approach; project management; team building; multitasking; and communication and public speaking.

4. Administrative managers most often rise from the ranks of office professionals in organizations. Their job titles could be executive assistant, administrative assistant, or office manager.

5. Administrative managers perform a broad range of duties in virtually every sector of the economy as they direct and coordinate workplace services, such as secretarial and reception, administration, payroll, conference planning and travel, among others.

6. Because of frequent deadlines and the

challenges of managing staff and resources, the work of administrative managers can be stressful at times.

7. Recruiting and retaining a diverse work force has become more complex for organizations because administrative managers and workers need four additional literacy skills to be successful—information literacy, workplace literacy, global literacy, and cultural literacy.

8. Information literacy is the ability to use computers and technology to find, analyze, and use information in a meaningful way. Workplace literacy, on the other hand, is the aspect of functional, or day-to-day, literacy acts in culturally mindful ways. A culturally commas that is related to employability and skill requirements for particular jobs.

9. A globally literate person sees, thinks, and acts in culturally mindful ways. A culturally literate person understands other cultures and practices global etiquette.

10. Four major areas of management study that managers of all levels need to learn and carry out well are human resources management, leadership and communication skills, administrative services management, and workplace systems and technology.

KEY TERMS

Anti-virus program

Communication

Computer security risk

Core activities

Cultural literacy

Ergonomics

Globally literate

Groups

Human capital

Information literacy

Internet

Intranets

Leadership

Networks

Virtual coordinator (VC)

Workplace literacy

REVIEW

1. List six critical administrative management workplace skills.

2. What are some actions administrative professionals can take "to think like a manager"?

3. What is the job outlook for administrative managers according to recent studies presented in the text?

4. Define the term virtual coordinator and list several tasks this person does in an organization.

5. Define each of the following terms: information literacy, workplace literacy, global literacy, and cultural literacy.

6. Identify the four major areas of management study.

7. Describe what is meant by the term a "company's human capital."

8. Name the major activities an administrative manager oversees in the area of administrative services.

9. Make a distinction between the two terms the Internet and a company's intranet.

10. List four Internet and online services available to AMs in the technologically advanced workplace.

CRITICAL THINKING

1. According to the American Management Association, in what ways has the administrative professional's job changed over the past few years and have these changes been for the better in your opinion?

2. Of the critical workplace skills presented in Table 3.1 that administrative managers must have to be successful, select the top three skills you feel are most important to have in the workplace and explain why you chose the three you did. Which of these do you feel that you can perform with a high degree of proficiency?

3. Based on current information provided by the Bureau of Labor Statistics, is the job outlook for administrative managers stronger or weaker than what you thought it would be? In what way?

4. Of the four literacy skills covered in the chapter, which ones do you think are most important for workers to use in today's economy?

5. In addition to those management areas of study mentioned in this chapter, can you think of additional skill areas that administrative managers should be familiar with? Talk about your reasoning.

CASE STUDY 3-1
HIRING A CHURCH OFFICE ASSISTANT

Sarah Jordan, an associate pastor of a large church in Florida, was asked to make arrangements to hire an office assistant. She put the advertisement in the paper and selected three candidates to interview from those applications received.

The interviewing team was composed of Pastor Jordan, the office manager, and a member of the staff parish committee. Two of the applicants were so highly qualified, that it ended up they did not want the job after coming in for the interview. The third candidate, Betty, was asked to use the church computer to prepare a portion of the church bulletin. (The other two applicants were asked to do the same.) The hands-on document looked fairly good so they decided to hire Betty.

Within the next few weeks, however, they noticed that Betty was using just a few of her fingers to key material into documents she prepared. After asking a few questions, they learned that she could not type. Now, keying the bulletin and other materials would require keyboarding and getting the work completed rather quickly. Betty admitted that she looked at the keys, but said she felt her typing skills were pretty good.

The senior pastor stopped by the associate's and the office manager's office and said: "Do you know that Betty can't type? I saw her using her hunt-and-pick method when she was taking the production test during the interview."

The office manager has brought in her old keyboarding textbook and suggested that Betty start learning to type and that she also

buy an inexpensive "learn to type" software program for her own computer to teach her to type as well.

Discussion Questions

1. How could this situation have been prevented? What do you think the office manager and/or the associate pastor should do about this situation?

2. Should the senior pastor have said anything about what he observed before they hired her?

   Reflect on the facts in the case. Be prepared to share your observations and recommendations in a class discussion.

CASE STUDY 3-2
ASSESSING THE POTENTIAL OF A MINORITY EMPLOYEE

Shortly after migrating to the United States from Haiti six months ago, Ana Ramos joined your sales office staff. Her duties involve typing correspondence and reports and serving as a backup receptionist to assist in handling the many customers coming to the office. Ramos has excellent writing skills stemming from seven years of English language study in her homeland; however, owing to lack of practice, her oral language skills are not yet well developed. This has created problems, because the longer she is on the job, the more she is expected to answer the telephone and help in receiving customers, which requires making introductions and giving extensive verbal instructions and directions.

Coupled with this problem is Ramos' personality. Although she is very pleasant and well-liked, she is unusually shy, making her reluctant to speak out and gain the speaking experience she needs. As time goes on, her typing work improves, but she has "gone into a shell," as the supervisor, Helen Masters, mentions.

Masters has discussed the problem with you, her assistant, and the other office supervisors, who feel that Ramos is making progress and that in time she will overcome the language barrier. Masters, on the other hand, does not agree, indicating that she is strongly considering terminating Ramos's employment because of her inability to perform the job for which she was hired. Only because of a physical handicap (Ramos lost the use of one leg in a childhood accident) has Masters delayed making a decision earlier.

Discussion Questions

1. Define the problem in this case.
2. What alternate solutions would you recommend to Masters?
3. How would you defend your opinion about Ramos' work to Masters, seeing that she has taken a tough stand?

Review the facts in this case. Determine if any employment laws have been or will likely be violated. Are there any laws to protect workers with disabilities? Be prepared to discuss the case in a group or class discussion.

INTERNET RESEARCH ACTIVITY

The U.S. Department of Labor, Bureau of Labor Statistics Occupational Outlook Handbook provides free, factual, and up-to-date information for thousands of jobs. For each job, you'll find information on the nature of the work, working conditions, employment training, other qualifications, and advancement, job outlook, earnings, related occupations and sources of additional information. Access the course web site http://odgers.swlearning.com to locate links to research two occupations related to the administrative manager's description. Also note any changes and updates you find to the information for the administrative manager position as described in the textbook.

Learning Activity:

1. Were there updates to the information covered in the text relative to the administrative management position?
2. What other management related occupations did you research and what information did you find that was interesting about those occupations?

Draft a one-page report on your findings. Your instructor may ask you to discuss your findings in class and/or submit the report for a grade.

Chapter 4

Emerging Elements Impacting Administrative Management Practices

As we discussed earlier, in today's business climate the operative word is change. Traditionally, dealing with changes at work was merely a matter of learning new skills, which were generally just added onto the existing ones. None of it was easy, but it did not require that we completely retool the most basic element in the workplace—ourselves. The new organizational structure can create confusion and disorientation at all levels of management and operations. Business as usual cannot be counted upon as technology changes the way we do business. New practices, attitudes, and actions are already evident in the workplace. The workers must continually change to accommodate the changes thrust upon them. In addition they must also effect change as situations demand.

Experience is not what happens to a man, it is what a man does with what happens to him. —*Aldous Huxley*

© Getty Images/PhotoDisc

TECHNOLOGY APPLICATIONS IN THE WORKPLACE

Increasing Use of Cell Phones at Work

A cellular phone is a type of telephone device that uses high-frequency radio waves to transmit voice and digital data messages. Using a cell phone from a car or a park bench, some mobile users regularly access the Web to send and receive e-mail, enter a chat room, or connect to an office while away from a standard telephone line.

The use of cell phones in business and personal life is skyrocketing. According to a September 2002 article in *Essential Assistant*, nearly half of adult Americans who subscribe to wireless phone service are now using their cell phone at work for personal calls, and significantly more women than men are making the calls.[1] With companies cutting back on and monitoring employee telephone use, wireless subscribers are finding a way around the system. They are taking a "cell phone break" while at work. No longer considered a business tool only to stay connected to the office 24/7, the cell phone has become a work/life tool as ever-present as an office voice mail system.

ISSUES TO THINK ABOUT:

1. How do cell phones assist to balance work/life issues?
2. Predict what you think the next generation of cellular communications will look like in three to five years.

WORKPLACE TRENDS

In the March 2001 issue of *The Futurist*, an article titled, "Trends Now Changing the World: Technology, The Workplace, Management, and Institutions," projected several trends that are now changing the world.[2] Below are some of those significant trends broken down into two areas that affect administrative management—new technology and new managerial approaches with a diverse work force.

New Technology

New technology will continue to transform the way we live and work because technology increasingly dominates and influences both our economy and society. Because advanced technologies present dozens of new opportunities to create businesses and jobs, technology literacy is a requirement for all workers in the workplace. Staying ahead of these new technologies and using them effectively often require a higher level of education and more technical training.

The Internet has become so important as a communications and research tool that virtually all major corporate offices, and many smaller offices, are now wired with high-speed lines that can transmit multiple signals simultaneously. Moreover, with wireless modems, portable computers give us access to networked data *wherever* we go. Increasingly, satellite-based telephone systems and Internet connections and other wireless links will allow mobile workers to work wherever and whenever they must.

Some predict, however, that the downside of new technology is that employees will find themselves increasingly isolated by these new tools. As voice mail and other technologies replace face-to-face exchanges, the ability to interact directly with others or to participate in a team environment may suffer.

This concern is worth noting as the rise in computer addiction is a growing health concern in our society. **Computer addiction** occurs when computer use consumes someone's entire social life. Users addicted to the Internet are said to have **Internet addiction disorder.** As with other addictions, computer addiction is a treatable illness through therapy and support groups.[3]

New Management Approaches with a Diverse Work Force

Decision processes, management structures, and modes of work are being transformed as businesses learn to use information generated by computers. For one thing, computers and information management systems have stretched the manager's effective span of control from 6 to 21 subordinates. For another, analysis of information now flows with greater degrees of freedom from front-line workers, who directly interact with customers, to higher management. Thus, fewer mid-level managers are needed, flattening the "corporate pyramid."

A growing trend is for top management to set performance expectations for the organization, its specialists, and teams rather than to give detailed orders. As a result, employees will gain new power with the authority to make decisions based on the data they develop. Managers still need to oversee the process, provide training, and supply the feedback necessary to determine whether results have met expectations.

Several trends are evident in the makeup of today's work force and in corporate day-to-day attitudes:

- To begin with, service organizations are the fastest-growing sector of the global economy. By 2010, it is predicted that close to 10 million jobs will open up for professionals, executives, and technicians in the highly skilled service occupations. However, many of these positions may be for part-time workers. In other words, for hundreds of tasks, corporations will turn to and use specialists in the form of contracted consultants rather than hiring full-time, benefit-eligible, employees.

- The new generation of workers cannot simply be hired and ignored. Some feel they must be made to feel appreciated and paid well. Managers will have to find innovative ways to motivate and reward new generation employees and to earn their respect. People from Generations X and dot-coms thrive on challenge, opportunity, and training. They will do whatever is necessary to better prepare themselves for their next career move. These generations have a powerful urge to do things their way.

- Between 1996 and 2006, the number of women employed in the United States will grow from 61.8 million to 70.6 million, an increase of 14 percent. In 75 percent of households, both partners will work full time by the year 2005, up from 63 percent in 1992. Therefore, demand for on-the-job child care, extended parental leave, and other family-oriented benefits can only grow. Further, there are significant areas that organizations will have to

manage because of stress-related problems that affect employee morale and health. Because of this, companies more than ever before are recognizing their responsibility to help employees balance their time at work with their family lives and need for leisure.

- Hispanics will be the largest minority group in the United States by 2004, while other ethnic and racial minority populations will exceed that of Caucasian. The work force will also see baby boomers retire in droves in the coming years, which will create a hole in the U.S. work force, leaving behind a smaller work force to replace them.

- Both management and employees must get used to the idea of lifelong learning because it will become a significant part of work life at all levels. Much of this will be carried out by current employers, who have come to view employee training as a good investment, rather than an expense. Motorola, for example, estimates that it reaps $30 in profits for each dollar it spends on training. IBM and Xerox put their profits at $20 to $25 per dollar of training.[4]

Forces of Change and Their Outcomes

The trends just mentioned are changing the social contract between the individual and the organization. Here are some possible outcomes predicted in 2001. You can readily see that many of these predictions are already in place or moving quickly to be the norm in the workplace. How many predictions do you recognize already?

- Labor will continue to flow freely around the world, as our world economy and telecommuting permit workers to seek opportunities anywhere. Telecommuting lifts the geographical constraints that once tied workers to their corporate offices in cities. As air transportation and Internet technology continue to expand, people will move about the globe both in reality and virtually.

- Voice-recognition software programs will soon make keyboards obsolete for many and put computers into the hands of the masses.

- U.S. companies now utilize a flexible employment system consisting of numerous temporaries, contractors, and consultants. A segment of the blue-collar work force is now "permanently temporary" and project-based. When downturns hit, companies can immediately cut costs by eliminating temporaries, overtime, perks, and various other soft benefits put in place to attract the best workers in times of expansion.

- Employees and workers must view their careers in terms of what skills they can offer to any company—whether in person or virtually, whether for a week or for a year or more. As individual identity has become uncoupled from a particular company, people have focused on functional career areas and are becoming more specialized in those fields.

- Perhaps the most positive change in the allocation of human capital arises from how employers are using their most experienced workers. Retirement at age 65 in the United States is disappearing.

- Companies are creating work arrangements that allow seniors to work into their 70s and 80s. Part-time, contingency, and consulting work arrangements allow seniors to rebalance work and personal life needs.[5]

One of the most important charges for administrative managers is to have the resilience to manage a multitude of changes in the workplace, which we will discuss now.

MANAGING CHANGES IN THE WORKPLACE

Most persons would agree that no single company could be best for every kind of employee. They would further agree that even if you are managing to get it right today, you can be sure your success will not last—at least, not as currently constructed. Things will change, and swiftly. Competitors will come and go; the economy will boom or bust; fortune will smile on you or frown. Employees—experiencing it all—will change their minds about what they need, want, or think they deserve.

A reputation for being a great place to work must be earned anew every day—which requires that managers must do a lot of juggling. Issues like job security, the work environment, increased focus on collaboration and self-managed teams, and the compensation and benefits program are all part of the whole, and no single part dominates. All of these issues will be discussed as the course continues.

In reality, of course, one element sometimes will take over. Then you have to work to bring everything back into balance. That

MANAGEMENT TIP

When you "fight" change, you use up valuable energy that could be better spent celebrating the change or understanding its positive results. Learn to use your abilities better by being flexible and adaptable.

is what leadership is all about—continually managing that balance—not just ensuring greater productivity for the company and its stockholders.

Many of the faces of change have long been predicted: the wireless office, increased electronic 24/7 communications, the increasingly diverse work force, management by teams, and managing a different employee—the *knowledge worker*. But until expanding global competition made them a necessity for survival, most managers resisted these changes.

Changes in the workplace require managers to be prepared to *manage challenges* rather than to *manage solutions*. At all levels and in all types of enterprises, those who succeed in times of chaos are those who can turn a situation "inside out" and find some personal advantage in it. In other words, look for the good in situations, rather than focusing only on the bad aspects of change. Those are the most sought-after employees for tomorrow's business success. Employees who can adapt to change generally maintain an upbeat, energetic attitude while others border in a state of virtual collapse.

People who like to deal with **ambiguity** (uncertainty) and those who do not need structure or a well-defined job are in high demand. Organizations need people who can survive change and still enjoy their work. So, managers and employees who work at companies that embrace and manage change in a positive way can consider themselves fortunate.

The distinction among administrative managers may well be determined by how well they manage change; that is, how well the manager can coordinate resources that

help workers adapt to change. Wonderful people placed in no-win situations generally make, at best, ineffective employees. Examples abound. One that comes to mind, in relation to today's work environment, is that of equipping the office with all the latest in information processing hardware and software but not providing the necessary resources to train office staffs how to use technology. Workers who are allowed to feel incompetent, ineffective, or "obsolete" will probably leave their job. Then, unfortunately, no one wins.

The Pros and Cons of Change

It is human nature to resist change. As a result, almost everyone feels afraid when asked to change. It's what you do with the fear that counts. A technique called "reframing" can be profoundly effective. **Reframing** refers to looking for evidence of a more positive, less catastrophic, view of some change. By reframing the concern, issue, or problem, most of us can usually find the energy to take the next step. In other words, even though change usually involves some loss, the flexible worker views change as opening up new opportunities for gain. For example, let's say a worker is already stretching himself to complete the current work assignments. His supervisor, however, approaches him and asks him to begin assuming some managerial tasks because he is seen as a very organized and capable employee. Rather than the employee becoming angry and outright refusing the "extra" assignments, he reframes the situation as a positive. He accepts the added work because he sees it as a way to learn and grow in his position and to do a better job.

To be inclusive, the opposing view of change must be stated. As changes (sometimes seen as inconvenient choices and disruptions at work) continue to mount, this constant state of "red alert" takes its toll on many workers. Workers begin to experience fatigue, apathy, and irritability. Poor decision-making, reduced trust, decreased honesty, and a tendency to vent job frustrations at home are common side effects resulting from work-related stress. As the stakes rise and confusion grows, these stress symptoms can include such severe dysfunctional reactions as malicious compliance (doing only what is absolutely necessary), chronic depression, addictive behaviors, and overt, as well as covert, undermining of the company. Change is indeed troublesome but must still be managed. Thus, when events cause changes, administrative managers should listen and help workers reframe changes in more positive ways.

Table 4.1 recaps and compares the upside and downside of change on organizations and workers. Change and how it is approached, the possible physical and mental outcomes that change manifests, and what effects those outcomes have on the organization are presented.

TABLE 4.1 The Upside and Downside of Change on Organizations and Their Workers

UPSIDE OF CHANGE	DOWNSIDE OF CHANGE
If change is approached as a necessity, then	*If change is approached as an inconvenience, then:*
Change results in the following physical and mental outcomes on workers:	Change results in the following physical and mental outcomes on workers:
Renewed energy and enthusiasm	Fatigue
New goals to reach for	Apathy
Reason to stay on the job and be challenged	Irritability
With the following *effects* on the organization:	With the following *effects* on the organization:
New approaches to and resources for effective decision-making	Poor decision-making
Better suited to challenges and future problem-solving	Reduced trust and possible sabotage
Can manage change and meet the unknown with confidence	Decreased honesty and directness that they can readily find replacement workers who are already trained

What is happening in this high-tech and networked business world of ongoing change is that many people and corporations are going through paradigm shifts, where the accepted "reality" of their world is shifting.

Paradigm Shifts

A **paradigm** is defined as a set of assumptions or a frame of reference. One definition of **paradigm shift** is a fundamental change in the assumptions we make about a certain body of knowledge. Simply put, this concept means that people will go for years believing one thing—for example, it is not necessary to learn to use the e-mail, search features, and electronic commerce activities available on the Internet—despite mounting evidence to the contrary. Then all of a sudden, they notice the conflicting evidence and change their minds and wonder why they continued to believe otherwise. In this instance, a paradigm shift occurred. Some businesses make the transition required of these paradigm shifts; others do not and are simply out of the race.

Paradigm shifts, then, are not simply a matter of buying into the latest innovations. Businesses are beginning to recognize this shortsightedness. Paradigm shifts, if recognized and embraced by management and workers alike, can keep organizations abreast of change and ahead of the competition. Organizations usually end up in a better place as a result of the unanticipated shifts in thinking.

Let's take, for example, the tremendous growth in the e-commerce retail market where Amazon.com rules. **E-commerce,** or electronic commerce, is a financial business transaction that occurs over an electronic network. With the elimination of the barriers of time and distance that slow down traditional business dealings, transactions can occur instantaneously and globally. E-commerce has produced a paradigm shift in the way people and businesses buy and sell products and services. Many companies like Sears or Wal-Mart no longer have merely a physical location but an online presence too.

THE LOOK OF CURRENT ORGANIZATIONS

In Jim Clemmer's book titled *Pathways to Performance,* the Canadian author and organizational expert states that high-performing organizations are thriving in today's chaotic world as they adapt and pioneer a wide variety of highly decentralized structures. These organizations are giving up control of people so that people can control their own and their organization's destiny.[6]

The look and feel of organizations have matured in a more humane manner. Organizations now include a stronger commitment to customer service and worker empowerment, fewer management levels, and companies that are transforming into learning organizations as discussed in the next sections.

Customer Service and Worker Empowerment

In a world-class organization, everybody in the company has to be empowered to think

Empowering workers solves customer problems when they occur.

© Getty Images/PhotoDisc

every day about ways to make the business better in quality, output, costs, sales, and customer satisfaction. We need to get away from the old workplace adage that bosses think, managers manage, and workers work. Instead, we must commit to a new work style, which says that bosses, managers, and workers alike will think, manage, and work.

Increasingly, the customer service function is a critical element in the success and future of all businesses competing in today's economy. With global markets more crowded than ever, it is a major challenge for organizations to attract and retain customers because more companies are competing for the same customers. The result appears to be that the secret in getting and keeping loyal customers today comes in creating new business and a common-sense approach for serving customers.[7]

Successful organizations are emerging with a common focus—customers. Further, these thriving organizations live the mantra that every member in the organization is

involved in delivering exemplary customer service. As Sam Walton, founder and former CEO of Wal-Mart, so fittingly put it, "There is only one boss—the customer. And he can terminate everybody in the company, from the chairman on down, simply by spending his [sic] money somewhere else."

Good customer service starts with empowering employees. Empowering is the chief motivational tool used by the forward-thinking managers and a means of providing exceptional customer service. **Empowerment** is defined as a set of practices designed to authorize, drive, and enable day-to-day decision-making at lower levels within an organization. In the past, engineers or professionals charged with that responsibility defined a "one best way"—the opposite of empowerment. It may have been successful then, but not in today's fast-moving competitive marketplace.

Empowerment is founded on the belief that the person doing the job knows better than anyone else the best way to do the job and how to improve job performance. As a result, empowerment utilizes a worker's abilities and potential to a much greater extent, while cutting costs and serving customers better. This eliminates the need for customers to be shifted from one employee to another, speeds decision-making, and decreases mistakes because fewer people are involved in solving the customer's concern.

People who feel they have a stake in an organization's success will have an enhanced sense of involvement in achieving the successful outcome. All employees—from top executive to receptionist—are stakeholders in a company's success. This sense of total involvement and commitment must be encouraged from the top to the bottom of the company. For empowerment to truly work, managers must allow workers to make final decisions; otherwise, the concept is only words with no meaning. It is worth mentioning that the act of empowering workers more often than not leads to fewer management levels in an organization.

Fewer Management Levels

Entrenched bureaucracy, meaning a company where workers are more concerned with their bosses rather than with customers, can be seen in the typical vertical organization. And even after these companies undergo all the cutting, downsizing, and delayering designed to streamline such a company's operations, too many layers of management still slow decision-making and lead to high coordination costs.

In the quest for greater efficiency and productivity, corporate America's biggest names have redrawn their hierarchical organizational charts. The trend is toward flatter **horizontal organizations** in which managing "across" has become more critical than managing "up and down" in a top-heavy hierarchy. In its purest state, the horizontal organization might boast a skeleton group of senior executives at the top in such traditional support functions as finance and human resources. Virtually everyone else in the organization, however, would work together in cross-functional teams. A **cross-functional team** is a group staffed with a mix of specialists focused on a common objective, problem, or goal. They are becoming more commonplace and typically are tasked with developing products or generating increased sales as discussed next.

Teams are highly autonomous and decentralized. For example, suppose the organization wanted to develop a new product line or new service. With cross-functional teams, workers from marketing, manufacturing, human resources, finance, and administration would share information and ideas and follow this new idea from start to finish. Over a decade ago, Saturn focused on creating a different kind of company, one dedicated to finding better ways for people (Saturn employees) to work together to design, build, and sell cars.

Team performance objectives, as described by the Saturn difference, are linked to customer satisfaction rather than profitability or shareholder value. Moreover, many workers are now rewarded not only for individual performance but also for the development of their skills and for team performance. Gaining quantum leaps in performance requires rethinking the way work gets done.

Companies Transforming into Learning Organizations

As more organizations become knowledge-based, they realize how important continuous or lifelong learning is to their overall success. It is, therefore, essential that companies promote and capture learning at the individual, team, and organizational levels. That need has fueled considerable interest in the concept of the learning organization.

ETHICS & CHOICES

You inadvertently saw a confidential paper while at the copy machine and noticed your friend is on the list to be "downsized" with a year's severance pay. Do you tell her?

Within a **learning organization**, training is central to actual work. That is to say, learning is emerging as a *byproduct* of work rather than something done in isolation. In a learning organization, learning is the daily responsibility of line managers and work teams; the work itself becomes the primary learning process. A learning organization has these characteristics:

- A climate that encourages, rewards, and enhances individual and collective learning.
- A view that believes mistakes and failures are learning opportunities.
- A widely available and unlimited access to information and resources.
- A desire for continuous improvement and renewal.
- An environment where learning is integrated into everyday work.
- An opportunity for open dialogue and inquiry.[8]

As organizations are taking on a new look, organizational charts are similarly taking on new shapes.

RESHAPING THE ORGANIZATIONAL CHART

The familiar management hierarchy is depicted on organizational charts as a pyramid. The hierarchical chart shows the upper management at the peak. As the chart flows downward, it broadens to show the levels of management and workers. This traditional organizational chart illustrates how work is divided and, most importantly, who reports to whom. But that mentality, which worked so beautifully a century ago, has come under scrutiny of late.

For example, few business leaders really foresaw the changes that occurred in the early 1990s, such as the cutthroat competition, the emergence of a more skilled and educated work force, and fancy technologies that do everything faster and smarter. As a result, a paradigm shift occurring in work places today involves reorganizing the organizational chart. The pyramid as we have known it for many years is passé; inverted pyramids, clusters, wheels, virtual organization, hourglasses, and the like are increasing in popularity.

Because of these changes to the scope of management, many organizations are reshaping the traditional pyramid organization. As Figure 4.1 illustrates, some of the imaginative alternatives to the pyramid style of organization are:

- *Inverted Pyramid Organization.* Created by the retailer Nordstrom, the inverted pyramid literally turns the traditional organizational structure upside down. This organizational structure is relatively flat. There are only a few levels, with salespeople and sales support people on top, making the key decisions. In fact, there is only one formal rule at Nordstrom—use your own best judgment at all times. The company believes that salespeople should pay more attention to their customers' needs than to their bosses' needs.

- *Cluster Organization.* The cluster organization brings groups of people from different disciplines together to work on a semi-permanent basis. In a cluster organization, groups are arranged like bunches

FIGURE 4 . 1 Five Alternatives to the Traditional Pyramid Organization

Nontraditional Organizational Structures

Inverted Pyramid	Cluster	Wagon Wheel	Virtual	Hourglass

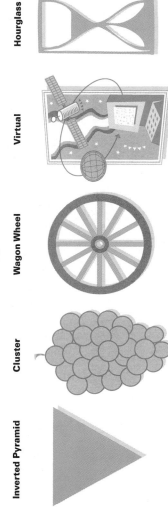

of grapes on a corporate vine. The vine is the vision that connects one group—a bunch of people working together—to another. W.L. Gore & Associates Inc., the makers of Gore-Tex, is similar to the cluster organization.

- *Wagon Wheel Organization.* This organization has three main parts—the hub; a series of spokes that radiate from the hub; and the outer rim. Customers are the hub. The spokes could be the business functions such as finance, marketing, or engineering or they could be teams dedicated to working on new product development or customer satisfaction. The chief executive and board are on the outer rim keeping it all together and making sure everyone has what they need to serve the customer. In this organizational design, managers are coaches and supporters, not authoritarian whip-crackers.

- *Virtual organizations.* Customers today can get exactly what they want, at a good price, and fast. Virtual organizations are

gaining in popularity with new-start companies, in particular. They are flexible and linked networks that easily use the Internet, e-mail, fax machines, and multiple communication devices when conducting business. Cross-functional teams are the norm and job reassignments are frequent, so this type of work life is often hectic because everything moves at Internet speed, and change and learning are constant.

- *Hourglass Organization.* Typically this organization consists of three layers, with the middle layer constricted. The top part of the hourglass represents those who formulate a vision for the organization and see to it that the vision becomes reality. The middle layer carries out a coordinating function for diverse lower-level activities. At the bottom of the hourglass is a broad layer of technical specialists who act as their own supervisors much of the time. At this level, the distinction between supervisors and the rank-and-file worker is blurred. Management's task is to keep them motivated with challenging work assignments, lateral transfers, skill-training opportunities, and pay-for-performance arrangements.

Each of these newfangled organizational types has its cadre of supporters, those who claim that their design is the once-and-for-all cure for all that ails a company. Not true. Without the right mind-set, supporting measures, rewards, and management (and sometimes the absence of management), any type of organization is doomed. If you do it right, redesigning an organization can be very effective in harnessing the intelligence that resides within it. Redrawing relationships is not the same as reorganizing, delayering, or flattening the organization, although it may, in fact, produce a flatter organization.

DEVELOPING CHANGE MANAGEMENT SKILLS

When people, functions, and activities are reorganized, leaders must be equipped with change management skills. Successful organizations, managers, and workers recognize the difficulties presented by change. Figure 4.2 lists reasons each of us has given from time to time when resisting change.

Change Management Skills

There will always be emerging trends and new ideas that will require each of us to alter our thinking and behavior and to develop change management skills. **Change management** involves managing the changes organizations are experiencing. This new focus on the skill of management requires proficiency in three areas:

1. Leadership development — to get people to believe in you

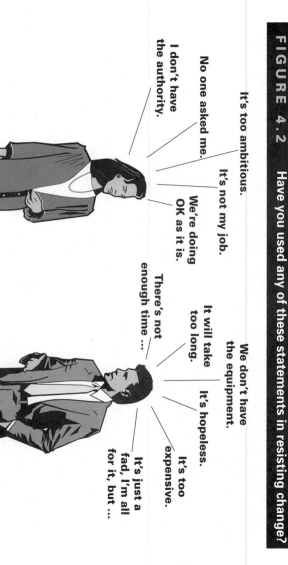

FIGURE 4.2 Have you used any of these statements in resisting change?

I don't have the authority.

No one asked me.

It's too ambitious.

It's not my job.

We're doing OK as it is.

We don't have the equipment.

It will take too long.

There's not enough time …

It's hopeless.

It's too expensive.

It's just a fad, I'm all for it, but …

2. Marketing and sales abilities — to promote your case for change, and
3. Communication skills — to help build support for the decision to change.[9]

Leadership Development The first thing you will want to focus on when developing change management skills is your leadership ability. Companies continue to make the mistake of focusing too much on business processes and not enough on good, strong examples of leadership. To be an effective leader in the change management process, it helps if managers focus on the following:

- *Set an example.* As a leader, others look to you for direction, not only in terms of business needs but also in terms of behavior, ethics, and standards. If you want others in your business to change, you must set an example for them to follow.

- *Eliminate perks.* Perks suggest division and hierarchical thought processes. By reducing your own perks, you show your desire to level the playing field and be fair with employees.

- *Walk around and talk to people.* The old school of business management promoted the idea that leaders are off-limits. Leaders of today interact more with their employees. Many manage by walking around and getting to know their employees and learning about the problems they are facing on a day-to-day basis.

- *Be genuine.* As a leader of change, it is important to be as real and honest as possible in your interactions with others. Let others get to know you. Being a leader

doesn't mean hiding your emotions. By interacting with employees on a one-to-one human basis, you will build rapport and trust.

- *Have passion.* To be a strong leader, you must have passion around your vision. Without it, you will soon find yourself facing burnout. Leadership is tiring and saps energy at a very high rate so make sure you are passionate about what you do.

Marketing and Sales Abilities Building your ability as a leader is the first step in the change management process; yet, once employees believe in you and trust what you're doing, you can then begin your marketing campaign for change. Your campaign for change should target the different "groups" within your business and outline for each the reasons why a change is necessary. For instance, the board of directors will want to know what the long-term effects of the change will be. Similarly, your employees will want to know how they will be personally affected by the changes you are proposing.

Communication Skills Once a change occurs, it is very important to communicate on a regular basis with all who will be affected. Let employees know what is happening. If your communication skills are weak or you don't have a formal way of informing your employees what is happening, set one up before you hit this stage of the change process. By keeping everyone informed, you reduce the chances of low productivity and low morale that often accompany unaccepted change.

Phases for Dealing with Change

It is important to realize that although you can use techniques to smooth the change transition process, you will never be able to completely jump from one way of doing something to another without experiencing at least some resistance. Why is this? Well, people adjust to change at different rates. It's just part of human nature. To reduce your frustration with this process, it helps to know the six phases people go through whenever they are experiencing any type of change—personal or professional. The six phases shown in Table 4-2 are anticipation, confrontation, realization, depression, acceptance, and enlightenment.[10]

Interestingly, people proceed through the six stages at different rates of speed. One person may require two months to reach Phase 6 while another may require twelve.

To make things even more complex, the cycle of change is not linear. In other words, a person does not necessarily complete Phases 1 through 6 in order. It is more common for people to jump around. One person may go from Phase 4 to Phase 5 and then back to Phase 2 again. That is why there is no easy way to determine how long an organizational change will take to implement.

As every organization looks to manage change, an employee's outlook on change

TABLE 4.2 Six Phases Workers Experience when Dealing with a Change

Anticipation	People in Phase 1 are in the waiting stage. They really don't know what to expect so they wait, anticipating what the future holds for a manager.
Confrontation	At some point, people reach Phase 2 and begin to confront reality. At this stage, they are beginning to realize that the change is really going to happen or is happening.
Realization	Once the change has happened, people will usually reach Phase 3 - the stage where they realize that nothing is ever going to be as it once was. Often times, this realization will plunge them into Phase 4.
Depression	Phase 4 is a necessary step in the change process. This is the stage where people mourn the past. Not only have they realized the change intellectually, but now they are beginning to comprehend it emotionally as well.
Acceptance	Phase 5 marks the point where people begin to accept the change emotionally. Although they may still have reservations, they are not fighting the change at this stage. Usually, they are beginning to see some of the benefits even if they are not completely convinced.
Enlightenment	In phase 6, people completely accept the new change. In fact, many wonder how they ever managed the "old" way. Overall, they feel good about the change and accept it as the status quo from here forward.

can either hamper or promote those efforts. The traditionalist, maintainer, adapter, and innovator are four titles given to attitudes about change that workers and managers typically display on the job.

1. The *traditionalist* tends to be an overt and vocal resister of change.

2. The *maintainer* also resists change but more subtly; i.e., stating an interest in learning new skills but not putting in appropriate energy.

3. The *adapter* recognizes learning as crucial to career mobility and future.

4. The *innovator* leads the way, adopting change early, but sometimes earning the resentment of coworkers.

Forward-looking adapters and innovators will flourish in the digital office, while traditionalists and maintainers are likely to fall by the wayside.[11] As opportunities open up for workers to create unique working arrangements for themselves, the more adaptive and innovative workers are frequently those who choose to set up flexible work arrangements.

ALTERNATIVE WORK STYLES

Advances in technology affect our culture and work arrangements. Changes in how information is produced and exchanged will allow for more flexible working styles and schedules. Many employers are finding that in order to get and keep good workers, they have to adopt alternative employment patterns. Success with alternative work patterns requires certain qualities that are desirable but not always found in all administrative workers. For example, telecommuters must be self-starters who can work without supervision, and job sharers should combine a flexible attitude with good communication skills.

New policies covering flextime workdays, compressed workweeks, job sharing, independent contracting, part-time employment, and telecommuting have emerged. The law has had to struggle to keep up with all these changes, and questions include who is entitled to benefits, what constitutes a workplace, and how the employer-employee relationship is defined.

Flexible Work Arrangements

Flexible work arrangements send the message that there is no one right way to get work done. To be consistent with definitions, consider the following brief explanations:

- Flextime—core hours with flexible start/stop times
- Compressed work schedule—working a full schedule in fewer days
- Job share—two people share one job
- Telecommuting—working from another location or from home

Flextime Workday Flextime in its most simple form is where workers are required to report for work on each working day and work a given number of hours. However, the times at which they arrive and leave are flexible as long as they are present during certain core times. For example, employees might be permitted to begin their day anytime after 6:30 a.m. and work as late as 6:30 p.m., as long as they put in eight hours and are present during the core times of 9 a.m. until noon and 2 p.m. until 4:30 p.m.

Flexible scheduling, long considered a grudgingly given perk for working mothers, is turning out to be a strategic business solution that reduces turnover, improves morale, and draws hard-to-get talent in a painfully tight job market. However, as flextime grows in popularity, companies are realizing that informal schedule changes can create communication problems and hostility among employees.[12] To combat this problem, more organizations are implementing formal policies that require workers to present solid business cases for going with flextime, including how it will benefit their clients and how they plan to communicate effectively with team members and supervisors.

Compressed Workweek The compressed workweek condenses the hours worked each week into fewer days. The most common compressed workweek is the 4-40 system, in which employees work four ten-hour days each week rather than the traditional five eight-hour days. To better serve customers

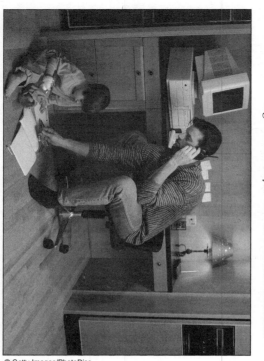

© Getty Images/PhotoDisc

Telecommuting is considered a family-friendly flexible work arrangement.

with enough staff coverage, some organizations lengthen their workday by staggering hours among work groups. For example, certain employees begin and end their workday two hours earlier than other groups.

Job Sharing Job sharing allows two people to share the duties—and prorate the salaries and benefits—of one full-time position. Teaming up for job sharing is an innovative approach that is gaining popularity, especially among working parents. To ensure success, job sharing requires that day-to-day tasks be clearly spelled out in writing for each member of the job-share arrangement and commensurate responsibilities defined and agreed upon.

Telecommuting Telecommuting, also known as teleworking, is on the rise. **Telecommuting** is a work arrangement in which employees work away from a company's standard workplace, and often communicate with the office using telecommunications and computer technology. By the year 2010, more than half of American wage earners will spend more than two days a week working outside the office, reports the Sulzer Infrastructure Services firm in London.[13]

At the home office, telecommuters are connected to office database and information systems through the screens of their personal computers. The problems of physical commuting, pollution, and the changing family and work force have brought greater pressure from employees and employers alike to substitute phone lines for traffic lanes.

As a result, more companies are turning to telecommuting to solve some very tough problems. Some employers are driven by the need to shrink real estate budgets. Others want another option available to comply with new laws such as the Americans with Disabilities Act and the Family and Medical Leave Act, which will be covered in detail in Chapter 6. Still other employers are using telecommuting as a way to meet worker demands for a better balance between work and family. The advantages of telecommuting to the employee and employer plus the benefits to society are shown in Table 4.3. Technology makes working at home possible and can give the smallest home office the illusion of a fully supported main office. A well-equipped telecommuter has up-to-date communication technology. Advanced equipment requirements vary with the job and could include any of the following: a personal or laptop portable computer, phone, modem, voice mail, electronic mail, fax machine, and printer. Equipment that makes it possible to teleconference is a real plus.

Telecommuters and their managers are unanimous in what telecommuting requires from both sides—trust. To manage telecommuters effectively, managers have to change their thinking from keeping tabs on people from 9 to 5 to the quality and quantity of output produced. To make telecommuting work, jobs must be able to be measured by some kind of results, filled by people who are self-starters, and managed by managers who can adapt and support this arrangement.

TABLE 4.3	**Advantages of Telecommuting**
To the Employee	Provides flexibility for disabled employees and working parents.
	Schedules work projects within 24-hour period, rather than 8-hour workday.
	Takes advantage of self-motivation and self-directed behavior toward task completion.
	Reduces costs associated with office dress and gasoline required for commuting to work.
To the Employer	Stretches the usage of existing office space.
	Increases productivity because it appears telecommuters do more and better work with better on-time performance.
	Hires someone it especially wants, but who will not, or cannot, relocate.
To Society	Reduces transportation and energy requirements.
	Encourages greater community stability since employees don't have to move every time they change jobs.
	Deepens the emotional relationships in the home and the neighborhood.

In the final analysis, the essence of telecommuting is a manager's ability to feel comfortable with a person being away from the office. It is worth repeating that managers of telecommuters must change their focus from observing activity to managing for results.

Not everyone agrees that telecommuting and working at home really work. They argue that the office gives discipline, structure, and social interaction to the job. A further concern is that, in time, telecommuting may not be so voluntary. To ensure success, a telecommuting arrangement should begin with a formal agreement covering the work expectancies of the supervisor, employee, and organization. There should be no surprises for anyone. A formal telecommuting agreement should include these elements:

1. Makes sure performance matches the mission statement and all parties agree with the statement of performance.
2. Identifies equipment needs and costs ahead of time.
3. Establishes a start time and tries to project why, when, and how the telecommuting arrangement might end.
4. Establishes times and frequency of face-to-face meetings at the office.
5. Makes training available to the telecommuter, especially on unfamiliar telecommunications equipment.
6. Explains clearly the effects and/or changes this new arrangement may have on compensation and benefits.
7. Details the relationship with the supervisor, particularly how often employee and supervisor must communicate.
8. Spells out performance standards.
9. Works out exactly how the employee will be involved in departmental meetings.
10. States how often performance will be reviewed.
11. Establishes terms of eligibility for bonuses and salary increases.

In summary, telecommuting makes good business sense to organizations. In addition to the advantages already mentioned, it allows many companies to create a "shared workspace," whereby one desk can serve 6 or 8 people. Companies are hopeful that office efficiencies, such as telecommuting, will account for about half their real estate savings.

Telecommuting offers potential benefits for employers and employees. Companies may save money, and employees may experience a more desirable work site. In addition to the wear and tear of getting to and from work, the noise, the interruptions, and the endless meetings at work decrease productivity. As a growth industry, telecommuting has such a strong appeal that many people are giving up fast-track careers for the chance to work at home.

Temporary Employees

As permanent jobs become more and more temporary, temporary jobs are becoming more and more permanent. Organizations no longer use temps, or temporary workers, just to fill in for vacationing receptionists. Now, temporary workers are found in a variety of businesses, including those in need of unskilled labor and seasonal employees, and in companies where work flow and talent demands vary.

Many companies recognize now that small numbers of versatile, sometimes temporary, workers can get jobs done as well or better than larger conventional full-time work forces. Companies save money by using these temporary employees because, in most cases, there are no recruiting costs incurred or benefits provided. In addition, no company can afford to staff all the people for all of the things it needs to do.

A multiskilled adaptable worker who can do two or more different types of jobs (e.g., desktop publishing and project management activities) has an edge on becoming and staying employed. Temporary employees bring with them knowledge and experience. They are usually self-starters and focus on completing the project. In addition, when they are no longer needed, they can be dismissed without emotional trauma.

Keep in mind that many workers are temporarily employed by choice. They enjoy moving from company to company and taking on new challenges. By treating them well, an organization reaps the benefits of having flexibility in its work force as well as a constant stream of new ideas.

Conventional wisdom dictates that using temporary staff, especially that provided through temporary-staffing agencies, allows companies to save on recruiting, training, and payroll costs, particularly when it comes to staffing high-turnover and seasonal job categories. The fact that Manpower Inc., the Milwaukee-based staffing firm, is now one of the largest employers in the United States attests to the popularity of the demands by businesses for temporary employees.

When deciding on whether to bring on a full-time hire or temp, companies should ask themselves:

- Does this project have a start and stop date?
- Can the work be completed within a six-month period?
- Is this a revenue item with questionable longevity?
- Is the organization looking for elasticity?[14]

If companies respond with yes to any of these questions, then temporary workers might be in their future. Hiring temporary employees gives companies the opportunity to evaluate people prior to putting them on the payroll.

Years of corporate downsizing and the high-tech labor shortages have forced companies to rely heavily on temporary workers. However, with the move toward so-called **permatemps**, or long-term temporary employees, many employees feel the permatemp system creates a stratified work force composed of permanent and temporary employees. This situation makes it hard for employees to work effectively as a team. Though temporary employees offer tremendous benefits in today's fast-moving, redefining organization, there are increasing challenges ahead—many of which are only beginning to surface—that will demand the administrative manager's full attention.

MANAGEMENT TIP

Temporary employees are used to taking direction—the best ones insist on detailed instructions, as to avoid misunderstanding later.

The newest types of working arrangements—in addition to those just mentioned—

that are gaining popularity include transactional employment and outsourcing as an external employment arrangement.

The transactional employment environment of today is one where employees continuously develop their skills to allow them to move from one employer to another. We see resumes that show people holding jobs for one or two years. Depending on the industry and discipline, we frequently accept it when candidates explain this as tactical moves to obtain diverse skill sets and enhance competencies. With the movement toward employees *owning* their careers, it is a priority for employees to maintain their professional skills in the best way they see fit.

Outsourcing

The company of the future will be a lean organization drawing on a network of external relationships. The trend toward outsourcing will have an even broader effect. Managing those relationships will be key. **Outsourcing** is a management strategy by which an organization utilizes specialized, efficient service providers to perform major, noncore functions. Examples of **noncore functions** are security, information technology, and human resources.

The job will be made easier when organizations truly understand their **core competencies** and then determine which noncore functions to outsource. Core competencies are the primary functions of a business that directly makes money for the company. A company handles core functions internally, as opposed to noncore functions or support systems that are handled externally through outsourcing.

Double-digit growth is expected in the multibillion-dollar outsourcing market, gobbling up traditional human resources tasks and significantly altering people management. Companies spent $61.2 billion worldwide in 2002 on human resources management outsourcing, an amount expected to jump 11 percent annually, to $103.3 billion by 2007.[15]

Businesses consider outsourcing noncore business functions because it:

1. Gives access to world-class capabilities from workers across the globe.
2. Eliminates difficult-to-manage functional departments, such as security, human relations, and information technology.
3. Frees up capital funds and reduces operating costs.
4. Provides access to resources not available internally.[16]

Outsourcing usually saves time and money—but sometimes it goes terribly wrong. Problems with outsourcing can include the inability of those companies providing the outsourcing services to answer employee questions, provide correct information, or furnish service reports.

Rather than a Band-Aid solution, outsourcing needs to be viewed as a long-term strategy. Because of its importance, consider these factors when choosing an outsourcing vendor:

- *Strong client base.* Look to see whether the vendor has long-term relationships or repeat clients. Ask for references before signing any contract.

- *Personal integrity.* This may seem obvious, but one of the things a reliable outsource firm will quickly tell you is whether your company is *ready* for outsourcing.

- *Avoid generic solutions.* A firm worthy of assuming responsibility for your work must be flexible and skilled enough to provide innovative and customized approaches to problem-solving.

- *Focus on outcomes.* Collaborate in advance to identify specific outcomes and specific accountability for achieving them.

- *Cultural Fit.* It is important that the culture of the vendor fit the culture of the organization so they can behave as partners.[17]

MESSAGE FOR MANAGERS

To manage workplace information systems effectively in today's business environment, administrative professionals must approach the task as one that is multifaceted and interrelated.

What is emerging is a requirement that all support professionals be visionaries. That is to say, they must regularly use their "change" skills more readily in customer-oriented, worker-empowered environments. It is almost as if administrative professionals today are painting new identities for themselves as they reinvent their roles each day in the workplace.

The new leadership is similar to a shifting mosaic that changes every day. There is a powerful lineup of social, political, and economic forces that are systematically shattering these traditional notions of leadership. The reality of modern business is that power is shifting, and in many cases has already shifted, from the system to the empowered worker.

Successful companies do what unsuccessful companies are unwilling to do. Successful companies live outside of their comfort zone—they "think outside the box." Successful companies find opportunities. We can also say that for successful people and leaders. Organizations and leaders that focus on fulfilling real human needs and helping people to find meaningful and productive work are, without question, living outside their comfort zone. They are positioning themselves to seize new opportunities and create a brave new forward-thinking organization.

S U M M A R Y

1. Technology literacy is a requirement for everyone throughout the workplace; however, new technologies often require a higher level of education and training.

2. Decision processes, management structures, and modes of work are being transformed as businesses learn to use information generated by computers.

3. Changes in the workplace require managers to be prepared to manage challenges rather than to manage solutions.

4. A growing trend for top management is to set performance expectations for the organization, its specialists, and teams rather than to give detailed orders.

5. People who like to deal with uncertainty and those who do not need structure or a well-defined job are in high demand.

6. A paradigm shift is a fundamental change in the assumptions, or frame of reference, we make about a certain body of knowledge.

7. In a world-class organization, everybody in the company has to be empowered to

think every day about ways to make the business better in quality, output, costs, sales, and customer satisfaction.

8. Empowerment is a set of practices designed to authorize, drive, and enable day-to-day decision-making at lower levels within an organization.

9. As more organizations become knowledge-based, they realize how important continuous or lifelong learning can be to their overall success.

10. Many organizations are reshaping the traditional pyramid, or hierarchical, organization to some imaginative alternatives, such as the inverted pyramid, cluster, wagon wheel, virtual, or hourglass.

11. Change management skills include leadership development, marketing and sales abilities, and communication skills.

12. Alternative work styles include flexible work arrangements, temporary employees, and outsourcing relationships. New policies covering these alternatives have emerged.

KEY TERMS

Ambiguity

Change management

Compressed workweek

Computer addiction

Core competencies

Cross-functional team

E-commerce

Empowerment

Entrenched bureaucracy

Flextime

Horizontal organizations

Internet addiction disorder

Job sharing

Learning organization

Noncore functions

Outsourcing

Paradigm

Paradigm shift

Permatemps

Reframing

Telecommuting

Transactional employment

REVIEW

1. How does the process of reframing deal positively with change?

2. How are paradigm shifts different from just changing your mind about something?

3. What basic belief is empowerment centered around?

4. Why are companies becoming learning organizations in today's fast-paced business world?

5. List several alternatives to the pyramid style of organizations.

6. Identify the six phases workers experience when dealing with an organizational change.

7. Cite some examples of flexible work arrangements.

8. In what ways is telecommuting advantageous to society?

9. Relate the concept of outsourcing to core competencies.

CRITICAL THINKING

1. Of the two trends that affect the ways in which workplaces function, which one do you think is the most influential relative to its importance to administrative management?

2. Describe an example of a paradigm shift that you've experienced over the past few years.

3. What is the relationship between providing exemplary customer service and empowering workers?

4. Of the key elements of horizontal corporations described in this chapter, which in your opinion, is the most difficult to implement?

5. Of the five alternatives to the traditional pyramid organizational chart, which type of organization would best fit you as a worker? As an administrative manager?

6. Why, in your opinion, are there so many flexible work arrangements in use in organizations today? Do you think there are too many choices? Do you think there should be more choices?

7. If you were managing an organization, how would you use outsourcing to save time and money?

CASE STUDY 4-1
PLANNING WITH DEMOGRAPHICS IN MIND

Jerry Chambers, the human resource specialist for the Cap Company, which manufactures baseball caps in Des Moines, Iowa, just returned from a luncheon where a speaker from the university presented current data on demographic trends in his city.

Jerry is concerned about what he just learned. The university professor said that the older worker would make up the largest majority of the work force within the next 10 years. On the drive back to the office, Jerry is thinking of all the positives and negatives involved in future hiring decisions. He mentally computes the number of older workers on the staff. He realizes that he does have several who do a good job and that perhaps hiring others would be a great idea. In fact, there are several openings that he anticipates in the next couple of weeks. He decides to talk to you, the administrative manager, to get your ideas about how this might work.

Discussion Questions

1. As the AM, in your opinion, what are some benefits of employing the older worker in the workplace?

2. What are some drawbacks to employing the older worker? Explain your reasons for describing these drawbacks.

3. Do you feel companies need to plan in any special way for the older worker? If so, what type of planning should occur?

Be ready to participate in a group discussion in which you respond to the questions.

Be prepared to justify your answers from your research or personal experience.

CASE STUDY 4-2
JUST-IN-TIME HIRING POLICY

Mr. Larry Kuban, human resources director of a software testing company, just got off the phone with an insurance representative who informed him the company's health and accident premiums would be going up 30 percent next year. This is alarming news to him, since top management is in a state of transition in the firm and decisions need to be made.

The president, Mr. Kuban, and the newly hired vice president for business services, Ms. Jerica Hatch meet, and it is clear that two decidedly different points of view exist. Ms. Hatch recommends laying off workers and implementing just-in-time hiring to meet the increased cost of benefits premiums. She said it makes good financial sense in the long run.

On the other hand, Mr. Kuban (who was a founding employee of the company ten years ago) promptly said, "We can't treat our loyal employees that way—just calling them in when we need them, without any security or benefits. In my opinion, it's just not right or the fair thing to do."

Discussion Questions

1. If you were the president, which point of view would you support given the reality that insurance premiums are increasing dramatically?

2. Describe any other options or compromises that might work in this situation.

Be prepared to voice your opinion as to which view you would support and why. Research insurance policies to determine any other options available or other options the company may use. Prepare a brief report of your findings to submit, if requested by your instructor.

INTERNET RESEARCH ACTIVITY

Given that the workplace and the way workers perform their jobs are increasingly more and more affected by flexible work arrangements, visit web sites of your choice that provide up-to-date information on flexible work arrangements. In addition, access the course web site at http://odgers.swlearning.com to locate links to other sites for more information.

Learning Activity:

1. In this constantly changing world of work, research and report on new information regarding telecommuting, temporary workers, independent contractors, and flexible work arrangements in general. You may find some interesting information if you search on the key words "free-lance workers" and "cottage industries."

2. In your research, which web sites that you visited provided information for the worker and which web sites were geared more toward providing information for organizations and the management team?

3. From your research, which work option is more commonly used in your town or city? Explain why you think this work option is more popular with the work force you are familiar with in your area. Do you have a preference of work options?

Prepare a one-page report in which you summarize the information that you learned from this research. Be prepared to discuss your findings in class before you submit your report to the instructor if directed.

Chapter 5

Managing Information, Technology, and Training in the Workplace

OBJECTIVES

After completing this chapter, you will be able to:

1. Describe a computer system in an office or workplace environment.
2. Discuss the advantages and use of networks in a virtual business environment.
3. Relate how technology is affecting the need for varied approaches to and topics for work force training.

Technology is changing the way people work, learn, and interact with each other at school, at work, and in everyday living.

Using computer networking, organizations benefit from time efficiencies and cost savings because files, information, devices, and programs are shared among employees. Because of the sophistication of today's business network systems, staying ahead of these new technologies and providing adequate and ongoing training for workers on the job are becoming recognized as critical activities for companies of all sizes.

You can't escape the responsibility of tomorrow by evading it today.

—Abraham Lincoln

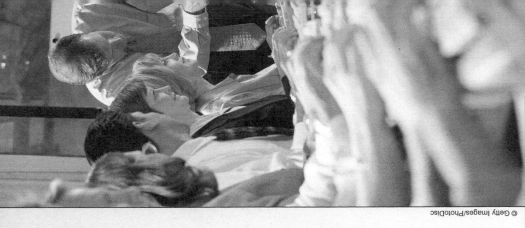

© Getty Images/PhotoDisc

TECHNOLOGY APPLICATIONS IN THE WORKPLACE

Etiquette Tips for Workers On the Move

Regardless of how organizations handle flexible work arrangements, simply tracking down people may become difficult. Judy Voss of Haworth's Ideation Team offers etiquette tips to handle the comings and goings of workers who are tied to their offices by way of technologies.[1]

1. Always use sign-out boards—electronic, if possible—to allow coworkers to quickly and easily locate each other.

2. Have a predetermined method of notifying other group members if a person decides to work at home. For each worker, find out how to notify, whom to notify, when to notify, and any other contact information.

3. Coordinate set work times for your administrative support person(s) to be available to a team or work group.

4. The way you present yourself away from the office, as a representative of your company, is very important. Find out if your company/organization has a dress code, and, if so, follow it.

5. Don't abuse the system or become unavailable. If this way of working doesn't produce results or causes work-group problems, everybody suffers and formality will return.

ISSUES TO THINK ABOUT:

1. Why do you think workers need to be reminded of etiquette tips when working in a flexible work arrangement?

2. Predict what you think the next stage of flexible work arrangements will look like in three to five years.

NETWORKED SYSTEMS IN THE OFFICE

Through computers and telecommunications devices, society and businesses have access to networked information from all around the globe. Instantaneously, you can find local and national news, weather reports, stock prices, and countless forms of educational materials. With a click of your finger or with a voice command, you can send messages to others or take a course online. To be clear on terminology, let's first define what we mean when we refer to *systems* and their relationship to *networks*.

Systems

A **system** is a group of parts that are interrelated in such a manner that they form a unified whole and work together to meet a defined need. Systems have evolved because we no longer enjoy the ease of using just one piece of equipment, for example, to create a business document. Tasks are more complex. For instance, some years ago a typewriter served as the input device, processor, and output device to complete a three-page report. Today, a computer system can complete the activity with professional-quality results, error-free, in a fraction of the time.

A **computer system**, such as that shown in Figure 5.1, is a group of computer devices that are connected, coordinated, and linked in such a way that they work as one to complete a task. These hardware components work together with software to perform calculations, organize data, and communicate with other computers. In the workplace, people use computers to create correspondence, such as letters and memos; calculate

payroll; track inventory; generate invoices; and update web sites.

With a computer system, the three-page report referred to earlier would be input using a computer keyboard or voice recognition software, processed using the editing, formatting, and other features of a word processing software program, and then output to a printer. In addition to the computer and its related systems in the workplace, you will also find other information processing systems. These systems may be electronic telecommunications and mailing systems, accounting and records management systems, inventory, or copier systems.

Networks

The development of communications channels and devices makes possible the widespread use of workplace networks. A **network** is a body of computers and devices connected together via communications device, and media. A popular communications device, the **modem**, enables computers to communicate, usually via telephone lines or cable. Here are some examples of **communications media**: cables, telephone lines, cellular radio, and satellites. Terminals and central processing units (CPUs) may be either geographically dispersed throughout a city, state, or country, or they may be situated within the physical constraints of a single office building as a local area network.

When computers and other devices are connected as a seamless network they allow users to share resources, which results in organizations saving substantial amounts of time, energy, and money. Although the

FIGURE 5.1 A computer system works as one integrated group to provide its services.

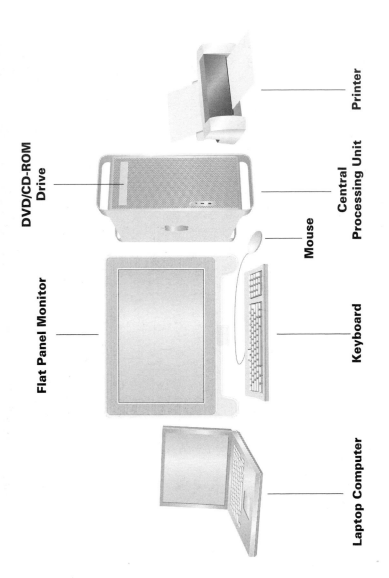

Flat Panel Monitor

DVD/CD-ROM Drive

Laptop Computer

Keyboard

Mouse

Central Processing Unit

Printer

administrative manager usually does not directly troubleshoot problems regarding networking operations, he or she must be able to understand the abilities and functionality of the company's network system. Most companies employ a **network administrator** to provide upgrades and assistance with networking difficulties. The administrative manager coordinates any technology difficulties with the network administrator. The network administrator is also responsible for network security and for being alert to any outside threats to information on the network.

Network technologies promote the virtual workplace. They affect not only how information systems in the workplace are managed, but also those employees who use them. Administrative managers who oversee networked technologies are presented with an unprecedented challenge—the absent (from view), but working, employee. More and more, managers are working within a virtual organization with a staff of virtual workers. This staff may work at other locations a distance away from the traditional office setting.

NETWORKS AND THE VIRTUAL BUSINESS ENVIRONMENT

Virtual organizations are collaborative networks that make it possible to draw on vital resources as needed, regardless of *where they are located physically* and regardless of *who "owns" them*—supplier, worker, or customer. According to a study by consulting firm Access Markets International Partners, a revolution is underway in the U.S. workplace. The study predicts 67 million people—more than half of the U.S. domestic work force—will be working virtually, remotely, or by telecommuting by 2006.[2]

Let's look at three elements that comprise the virtual business environment that AMs must effectively manage—the virtual workplace, the virtual work force, and the virtual assistant.

The Virtual Workplace

A **virtual company** or **workplace** is where work is performed outside of a defined place. **Virtual work** is primarily the manufacture, retail, and distribution of *intellectual property*, or work that is produced with the mind. Some of that intellectual property can lead to a product, as in the case of document creation using software, or to web site development.

Link Resources, a New York-based research firm, reports the most common arrangement for the virtual workplace is for employees to work at home a few days a week and report to the office the remainder of the time.[3] According to Kinetic Workplace, a provider of virtual officing solutions, companies with telecommuting work arrangements have saved $12,000

annually per telecommuter by reducing their real estate costs by 40 percent to 60 percent. Survey findings also indicate that one-third of workers say that they would switch jobs to gain the ability to telecommute. With more than 62 percent of Fortune 1000 companies and 87 percent of the "100 best companies to work for" using such programs, telecommuting is more than an office alternative—it's a competitive business requirement.[4]

You may be asking how the customer is served in the workplace by these new "virtual" concepts. One scenario is that of a customer calling to place an order or to get information about a product or service. When the call is received, all information about that customer flashes on the computer screen of the distant worker, wherever he or she is located. To customers, the process is transparent, such that they are unaware of where, how, or by whom they are being served. Those widely scattered workers can operate as if they were all at company headquarters because whatever is needed to serve the customer is literally at their fingertips.

The main factor driving businesses toward virtual organizations is the pace of business operations. As author Alvin Toffler predicted more than a few decades ago, businesses now run at warp speeds and provide immediate responses—anywhere, anytime. Today, it is survival of the fastest, not the fittest. Organizations are under pressure to cut drastically the time it takes to deliver a product from the engineer's workbench to the showroom floor or Internet Web page. If they cannot deliver, organizations will lose millions of dollars in investments to a faster global competitor who can deliver with an equal or better quality product.

The virtual workplace offers benefits to organizations such as the opportunity to reduce costs, increase productivity, and attract and retain employees. These benefits are attractive in the face of keen global business competition. The geographical and time flexibility factors are attractive in that employees may no longer need to commute daily to a conventional office; thanks to technology they are able to send their work along electronic highways. However, companies are aware that there are concerns, issues, problems, and costs to virtual workplaces.[5]

For example there are often few, if any, established policies or practices to guide virtual workplace decisions. Virtual companies have to rewrite a lot of the traditional rules and make many of them up as they go along.[6] Oftentimes, flexible work can be as difficult as (if not more difficult than) a regular 9-to-5 job. Workers need to be disciplined if they are working from home. They need to make themselves available for calls and meetings with coworkers, or virtual workers may come to be viewed as colleagues that other workers cannot count on. However, if workers handle themselves in a professional manner and are willing to put in the time and effort, a flexible work arrangement can be the ticket to the best of both worlds—a more balanced work and home life.

A Virtual Work Force

As some have observed, the work force composed totally of traditional workers is quickly becoming a thing of the past. The **virtual work force** is taking its place. One aspect fueling this change is technology. With the advent of small laptops, handheld PDAs, and tiny cell phones, employees can literally work anywhere—and do. The local library, the park, a hotel room, the airport, a conference center, home, a vacation house—equipped with the right high-tech equipment, are all potential offices.

We are an unwired but wired society. It is the age of emancipation. Time and space have collapsed; the barriers to communication have fallen away. Workers are truly connected—linked to one another by an invisible web of communications networks and intelligent, integrated appliances. Traditional offices have shrunk to mere "landing sites," where workers dock for an hour or so at a communal electronic desk. Here, workers plug in their personal communicator and download all the data they have collected into a single electronic unit.

This new flexibility reduces commuting time and increases family time for employees, which means there should be less stress. These new work options particularly benefit workers facing child-rearing and elder-care responsibilities as well as workers with disabilities. Companies may have to offer the latest technology to employees in order to accommodate mobility, but the benefits may outweigh those financial obligations. The Midwest Institute of Telecommuting Education, based in

© Getty Images/PhotoDisc

The Virtual Assistant

One of the newest opportunities with a slight twist from temporary employment allows office support workers to perform administrative tasks in their own homes. They call themselves virtual assistants (VAs).

Essentially, virtual assistants are what were formerly known as home secretarial businesses, but they are connected to their clients electronically rather than, as before, by automobile. A **virtual assistant** is an independent entrepreneur who offers business support services in a virtual environment.

The history of the virtual assistant profession is quite short—no more than a few years old—and bound up with a number of emerging factors. These factors include the growth of the Internet, changing demographics, corporate downsizing, and the evolution of telecommuting relationships. These factors have made the use of virtual assistants a very productive concept.

Communication between a company and its VA is accomplished using phone, fax, e-mail, diskette transfer, cassette tape, overnight mail, and instant messaging.

Among other activities, virtual assistants perform information processing, Internet research, bill-paying services, mail and e-mail services, event planning, and assist in making travel arrangements for virtual employers. Educational levels of VAs vary but overall, they are normally well-educated and have a multitude of hard skills and practical experience in office management and computer systems and software. They are, in essence, small-business owners who, like any other business owner, define their success by customer satisfaction.[8]

Workers are connected by an invisible web of communication and intelligent devices.

Minneapolis, cites these benefits to businesses that offer a virtual work environment to its workers:

- *Increased productivity.* A company can realistically expect productivity gains of 15 percent to 25 percent from employees.

- *Decreased turnover.* Offering flexibility can be one way to retain skilled workers in jobs with high turnover rates.

- *Less overhead.* If enough people begin working off-site, fewer physical offices will be needed. Parking needs might also decrease drastically, reducing expensive parking fees in large cities.[7]

At first glance, virtual offices may seem like a great way to work, but not everyone possesses the traits to work effectively in such a flexible situation. Table 5.1 shows some common traits managers look for in employees who are offered a chance to work off-site.

TABLE 5.1 **Desirable Traits for Successful Virtual Workers**

- Trustworthy
- Reliable
- Independent
- Cooperative
- Capable of separating personal life from work life
- Self-motivated
- Organized
- Knowledgeable about all aspects of the job
- Able to solve problems as they arise

Source: Deena C. Knight, "Employee Mobility is Changing the Face of Today's Workplace," *OfficeSolutions*, September 2001, p. 14.

TECHNOLOGY AND UPDATING WORKPLACE TRAINING NEEDS

The effect of technology is evident in every aspect of society because it is a driving force in creating, using, and storing information in a knowledge-based society. In a broad sense, **technology** can be viewed as an aid to making a task easier by using equipment and procedures to create, process, and output information. Technology's effect is also evident in the changing job market.

Employers will hire and pay good wages to employees who can demonstrate an ability to use technology effectively to harness and create meaningful and useful information.

Therefore, all workers essentially must know how to use electronic information and communication technologies. These electronic information technologies can be integrated in the workplace to manipulate text, numerics, graphics, voice, video, and sensory data.

Today's workers need to locate, assess, and apply information more often than they need to remember things, because content changes and new information replaces old information at an alarming rate. Unfortunately, workers often lack skills for processing new information and integrating the new information with what they already know. Those processing and integrating skills are vital in the fast-changing business world we work in today.

Technology has lowered the skill levels of some jobs or eliminated them altogether, while raising the skill levels of other jobs. Technology also influences areas of training development and delivery most needed by today's changing organizations. To take advantage of technology, however, workers first must be literate in the workplace.

Workplace Literacy and Other Skill Areas

There is a national literacy crisis, and it is costing business money—big money. The U.S. Department of Labor estimates that illiteracy accounts for about $225 billion each year in lost productivity.[9] Literacy at work, unlike in school, is seldom a matter of understanding or writing whole paragraphs. Rather, it involves sets of words that relate in a restrictive way to the organization and its particular work. **Workplace literacy** involves the ability to use words clearly and communicate with brevity and accuracy in the context of a given job.

In similar fashion, the specialized language of the workplace is not academic in style; over time, workers tend to develop a highly specialized vocabulary, a language apart from the one learned in school.

Though writing well is an important communication skill, researchers estimate that the typical U.S. worker spends only about 9 percent of the workday writing and about 13 percent of it reading. An additional 23 percent of a worker's day is spent in speaking and a significant 55 percent in listening.[10]

In addition to literate workers, employers need employees who are capable in two other areas. Workers need to:

- Know "how to learn" so they can quickly apply strategies and tactics for learning new tasks.

- Develop skills that are portable. To possess **portable skills** means you are able to transfer what you already know to slightly new situations. Smart workers need to recognize when a problem is enough like something they have done before that they can risk using skills and previous experience to solve the new problem.

Employers must value their workers' knowledge and skills, while at the same time offer training or other career enhancements. Administrative managers are involved in the whole effort of retraining the existing work force to include giving input to developing and delivering training programs through several modalities.

Retraining the Existing Work Force

In addition to employees who are entering the job market from school, there are many employees currently on the job who need retraining and skills upgrading to keep their jobs. Why are companies choosing to invest so much in workers with clearly deficient skills? Why not replace them with workers who have better skills? Loyalty and access to fewer skilled workers are two reasons for this decision.

1. *Loyalty.* Companies realize that most of the people have been loyal employees for a number of years. In fact, they have performed their jobs competently, doing what organizations have asked them to do. For years, unfortunately, American industry has been intentionally modifying the structure of work to accommodate workers with diminishing levels of proficiency in the basic skills. Now, because companies are consciously changing the nature of that work, they feel responsible for providing workers with an opportunity to develop new skills.

2. *Few skilled workers.* Depending on the job, the option of replacing these employees with ones who are more highly skilled is not possible. There simply are not enough skilled workers in the labor pool to meet the demand. Though companies cannot quantify the cumulative costs of all the instances where a lack of basic skills led to defects in products, productivity loss, or other problems, they have, to some extent, quantified the improvements in quality and productivity that result from having a work force that possesses basic workplace skills.

- Better trained and skilled workers can adapt faster and more efficiently to change and are better at implementing new work practices and products. They can help a firm update its practices and products at the rate demanded by rapidly changing markets and technical advances, making the firm more flexible and productive.

- Similarly, people are also found to be more effective if they are trained to understand *what* they are doing and *why*, and *how* they can contribute to their organization's objectives.

- Training typically fosters a common culture within firms and helps to keep staff motivated. A highly motivated staff simply performs better.

- There is a link between training, qualifications, employment and wages, with higher levels of training and qualifications associated with higher earnings and greater employability.

Training efforts and plans need to go hand in hand with other human resources policies as well as the wider strategic policies of the organization. When training policies are linked to the strategic plans of the organization, this should ensure that all areas of the business are working toward the same goals.

The benefits from training are multifaceted, and training cannot be thought of as an end in itself, or as a stand-alone policy.

Developing Workplace Training Programs

One of the most compelling economic reasons for investing in training is because of the positive effects it has on worker productivity and performance.

MANAGEMENT TIP

One reason training is purposeful is because people often don't know exactly what they know and how to apply that knowledge until training makes it clear.

While research has shown that "training works," this should not be a one-size-fits-all solution. Training needs differ among organizations and among individuals within the organization.

Innovative organizations are teaming with third-party providers like SkillPath Seminars and Fred Pryor Seminars, as well as with community colleges, to deliver much of the retraining today's workers need. Table 5.2 lists workplace training topics such as those promoted through mailings of training brochures or advertisements on Internet web sites. Successful companies are changing their attitudes and putting more people and financial resources into training at *all* levels.

To improve the quality of the work force, organizations must provide an atmosphere where ongoing training and continuous learning are valued.

As an AM, when developing workplace training programs, keep these tips in mind:

- Design a learner-friendly environment and put the learner in control.

T A B L E 5 . 2 Training Topics in the Workplace

- Managing Multiple Projects, Objectives, and Deadlines

- Project Management

- Leadership for Nonmanagers

- Global Issues for the Quality Workplace

- Network Training and Certification

- Computer Usage and Network Applications

- Writing for Results

- Coaching and Team-building Skills

- Business Ethics

- Delivering Exemplary Customer Service

- Essentials of Credibility, Composure, and Confidence

- Conflict Management Skills

- Computer Skills In Microsoft® Word, Excel, Access, PowerPoint®, and Outlook

- Develop interactive outlines of key skills needed for advancement.
- Provide learners with skill-assessment tools to evaluate strengths and weaknesses that they must address in order to advance.
- Provide a number of programs that are geared to various learning styles to make it easier for people to work through the training.
- Provide incentives by rewarding learners with salary increases, promotions, or credits toward degree programs.[11]

Once the training program is developed, the next step is to choose how best to deliver the training. Knowing the options available is important in selecting the best delivery method.

Delivering Training Programs

According to an online survey and interviews with more than 200 training and HR professionals conducted by Fairfield Research Inc., third-party training as offered through professional seminar and workshop organizations leads training expenditures, with 36 percent of training funds devoted to those activities. In second place was staff-led training, followed by tuition reimbursements for training at colleges and universities.[12] Other trends when delivering training include corporate training programs delivered in person as well as virtually through e-learning approaches. These methods will be discussed in the next section.

Corporate Training Programs To meet the demands of a complex and fast-changing business world as described in earlier chapters, more and more corporations have taken

a new approach to retooling their own work forces. They've created their own universities to do the job. Sears, Motorola, Saturn, Intel, and hundreds more have taken the plunge, making corporate universities perhaps one of the fastest-expanding segments of higher education.

The purpose of **corporate universities** is to perpetuate the organization. By definition, a corporate university isn't a "university" at all because it does not grant a degree. It is instead a centralized, proactive entity that is responsible for all training and education at a given company. Its focus is far narrower than that of a traditional university. Ideally, the courses offered at a corporate university are in-depth, customized, and closely linked to the company's strategic mission.

Some corporate universities have their own brick-and-mortar campuses, but many have no central location at all. They are virtual universities, which rely heavily on the Internet, company intranets, satellite TV, and other e-training technologies to transmit knowledge and skills. The faculty is often a blend of full-time employees of the corporate university, instructors borrowed from nearby community colleges or universities, and employees of various vendors or other companies.

Traditionally, most corporate universities have concentrated their curricula on training

MANAGEMENT TIP

Periodically visit your local Chamber of Commerce web site to learn what training sessions it sponsors for its members. By doing this, you can usually get an up-to-date idea of new trends, procedures, and hot training topics in business in less than five minutes.

junior and midlevel employees. However, a recent trend toward in-house executive education has led some companies to include a new emphasis on leadership development in their programs.[13] In fact, many companies send their promotable, fast-track employees to school to learn basic etiquette, dining, and social behavior to prepare them for executive or leadership positions. Speech courses and proper English usage are often included in this training.

Whatever form they take, corporate universities have the goal of producing highly skilled, knowledgeable, and adaptable workers who are invaluable in today's burgeoning "knowledge economy." For example, Motorola University, which began operations in 1981, has an annual operating budget in excess of $200 million. All Motorola employees worldwide must complete at least 40 hours of job-related training annually in such areas as technology education, software design, executive education,

© Mark Peterson/CORBIS

Entrance to McDonalds' Hamburger University in Oak Brook, Illinois.

quality control, and competencies in marketing, sales, and distribution.[14]

E-Learning Training The cost efficiencies of e-learning are becoming more apparent every day. E-learning can take many forms, but it essentially means that a person is learning at his or her own pace using computers and telecommunication devices. According to the results of a survey by *HRfocus* publisher American Management Association, it is reported that e-learning is a leading cost-saver among training options. One of the main reasons is the cost-savings advantage that comes primarily from eliminating travel costs and reducing time away from work to attend training courses.

E-learning can be a flexible and cost-effective alternative to classroom training, but it can also be a colossal waste of time and money if not implemented correctly. The reasons why some e-learning projects are unsuccessful while others flourish are varied. There are those who attribute the problems to lack of employee motivation. Others point to poor course marketing, or training time restrictions, or the individual's fear of being placed in an unfamiliar learning environment.

When e-learning initiatives fail, it is often because managers have provided no connection between learning and the company's defined business needs. To be successful, training must be tied directly to tangible outcomes and workers need to know why a class or seminar is important to attend. The content of the learning must be measurable and performance-based. People have to know going in what they are expected to learn, how they are expected to apply that on the job, and how the experience will benefit them and the company.

When training in a virtual environment, here are some common e-learning mistakes to avoid:

1. *"Trendy" e-learning.* Senior executives may request e-learning, even in situations where it's inappropriate and unlikely to work. Managers must argue for e-learning when it's the best method—over others—to use.

2. *Learning styles.* The "one-solution-fits-all" approach rarely works—different people learn best in different ways. Making everyone take identical online learning classes means that some will fail. Give employees choices of several ways to learn.

3. *Technology.* Take time before buying e-learning software. Start with the goals and design of your educational program, and then buy the software that will meet the training needs.

4. *Interactivity.* Instead of a written test at the end of the course, present a simulation and ask learners to solve the problem or to take appropriate action.[15] By providing some interaction during the learning process, concepts presented are reinforced more fully.

MESSAGE FOR MANAGERS

By using integrated computer and communication technologies, successful organizations will increasingly be defined not by concrete walls or physical space but by collaborative electronic networks linking hundreds, thousands, or even tens of thousands of people worldwide. Virtual organizations are becoming business ecosystems characterized by flexible relationships that are formed electronically within seconds.

If you step back and look at the big picture, there is a learning revolution at work. Organizations are valuing the brainpower and diversity of their work force as never before. You see management structures changing, barriers coming down, and technology available to *all* workers through networked systems. Moreover, the AM's job is in the process of *becoming.* Supervisors are becoming mentors and coaches—not taskmasters. As a result, workers are being asked to play roles as communicators, problem-solvers, and decision-makers—roles that are new to them but critical to their overall success as an administrative manager.

Chapter Five

S U M M A R Y

1. Through computers and telecommunication devices, society and businesses have access to networked information from all around the globe. With a click of your finger or with a voice command, you can send messages to others or take a course online.

2. A network is a body of computers and devices connected via communication devices, such as a modem, and media that can include cables, telephone lines, cellular radio, and satellites. Most companies employ a network administrator to provide upgrades and assistance with networking difficulties.

3. The pace of business operations is driving more companies to be virtual, meaning that work is performed outside of a defined location, such as an office or corporate headquarters.

4. Virtual offices are not for everyone because it takes special traits to effectively work in such a flexible situation. These traits include being trustworthy, reliable, independent, cooperative, capable of separating personal life from work life, self-motivated, organized, knowledgeable about all aspects of the job, and able to solve problems as they arise.

5. Several factors that created the virtual assistant include the growth of the Internet, changing demographics, corporate down-

sizing, and the evolution of telecommuting relationships. These factors have made the use of virtual assistants a productive concept.

6. Workers now most often need to use technology for the purpose of locating, assessing, and applying information as opposed to remembering things.

7. Workplace literacy involves the ability to use words clearly and communicate with brevity and accuracy in the context of a given job.

8. Loyalty and access to fewer skilled workers are two reasons companies decide to allocate money to retrain their existing work force.

9. One of the most compelling economic reasons for investing in training is because of the positive effects it has on worker productivity and performance.

10. Corporate universities are linked to the company's strategic mission and designed to perpetuate the organization.

11. The cost-saving advantages of e-learning training come primarily from eliminating travel costs, reducing time away from work to attend training courses, and promoting the ease and convenience of upgrading skills and information.

KEY TERMS

Communications media
Computer system
Corporate universities
E-learning
Modem
Network administrator
Portable skills
System
Technology
Virtual assistant
Virtual company (workplace)
Virtual organizations
Virtual work
Virtual work force
Workplace literacy

REVIEW

1. How do you define a computer system?
2. What are the advantages of using networks in organizations?
3. List three benefits of the virtual workplace to organizations and employees. Why have virtual companies had to rewrite a lot of traditional rules?
4. Identify several desirable traits for successful virtual workers.
5. Explain why a virtual assistant is considered an independent entrepreneur.
6. Define the term workplace literacy.
7. What are two reasons businesses choose to retrain their existing work force?
8. List several training topics offered by training institutions and providers that are popular for the work force. Why do workers find these topics valuable and how do companies offer them?

9. Why are organizations using e-learning as a method for delivering training programs?
10. What would you suggest that administrative managers do to ensure a successful e-learning experience for workers?

CRITICAL THINKING

1. In your own words, describe your understanding of a computer networked system in an office or workplace environment.
2. Describe your understanding of a virtual organization. Include in your description the tasks performed in a virtual organization.
3. Using examples, compare workplace literacy to functional literacy.
4. Describe what kind of training or retraining workers are receiving and from whom.
5. Discuss which new workplace skills are valued by employers and why.
6. From an employee's perspective, describe the pros and cons of an organization training its employees using e-learning methods.
7. What are the goals that corporate universities seek to attain?

CASE STUDY 5-1
PLANNING A TRAINING PROGRAM FOR HELP-DESK PERSONNEL

Paul Jordan has just graduated from high school and has accepted the job of help desk specialist in the home office of the Durand Oil Co. As a customer service representative at the help desk, Paul answers customer questions by phone, fax, e-mail, and web-based technologies. Software is provided to assist help desk specialists in quickly finding answers to commonly asked questions about particular products and services.

It is your plan, as administrative manager, to have each worker, such as Paul, properly trained before actual employment begins. Your budget allows you to pay all new workers an hourly wage of $9.50 during the initial training period. After having successfully completed the entry-level training program, the new workers will be placed on an annual salary of $20,000 to $21,750 during the three-month probationary period.

Outline a complete plan for training the entry-level office workers in your department to include the particular areas of training and methods that can be used for each area of training.

Discussion Questions

1. How will you determine where employees are in their skill level so that you can make an evaluation of the training needed?

2. What plans do you need in place to assess the training program to find out if it is doing what it needs to be doing for the new workers?

3. If workers feel they are competent when they arrive on the job, how will you convince them to take the training you are offering? Or will you?

Submit your plan to your instructor and be prepared to participate in a class discussion. Your instructor will provide directions for submitting the plan and/or participating in class discussions.

CASE STUDY 5-2
VOLUNTEERING AT INNOVATIVE PRODUCTS

David Sutton and Melissa Dodgers work together in administrative services at a small company called Innovative Products Inc., in Seattle, Wash. Though Melissa respects David's work and regards him highly, lately she has been having some problems with his attitude. For starters, when Melissa was asked by the cooperative education coordinator at North Seattle Community College to mentor a graduating student in a 20-hour work internship project, David belittled Melissa and said she would get behind in her work. Further, he hinted that she was doing it just to "show off" and make points with the bosses.

On another recent occasion, when Innovative Products networked the six PCs in their department, David volunteered Melissa to be the interim network administrator by saying "she has plenty of time and seems to know everything." Melissa normally would not have minded taking on this extra task because learning has always been important to her, but she thinks David's two actions are motivated by anger, jealousy, or both. As a result, Melissa is beginning to resent David and is starting to avoid him. He appears to be hurt. He often avoids her even at lunch.

Discussion Questions

1. Is there a perceived problem as far as Melissa is concerned? As far as David is concerned? If so, what is/are the precise problem(s)?

2. Evaluate David's behavior. Is Melissa overreacting?

3. Evaluate Melissa's reaction.

4. If this relationship continues as it is now, what do you think will be the possible immediate outcomes?

5. What recommendations would you make to resolve the apparent conflict?

Prepare a one-page report incorporating your answers to the discussion questions. Your instructor will provide directions for submitting the report and/or participating in class discussions.

INTERNET RESEARCH ACTIVITY

Let's assume that you might be interested in becoming a virtual assistant and want more information to make an informed decision.

As you know, searching the Internet can provide you with lots of information on almost any topic you can think of to research. For example, you might use the search words virtual assistant, free-lance worker, starting a business as a virtual assistant, telecommuting, cottage industries, and web-based industries.

You may use other search terms that you have learned in the chapters in this text.

You may also go to the web site for this course, *http://odgers.swlearning.com*, to find additional links to web sites that may give you current information on this topic.

Learning Activity:

1. From your research, do you think that becoming an entrepreneur as a virtual assistant would be a career you would want to pursue?

2. Do you have the necessary skills to be successful or do you feel you could acquire them with some study?

3. Are the start-up costs for this type of business prohibitive? From your research, what have you found your expenditures will be to set up this type of business?

This Internet Activity will provide you with a large amount of information. Summarize your findings and be prepared to participate in a group discussion.

Part 2

Managing Human Resources in the Workplace

Workplace

JANIE D. JUDE-ASKEW

Benefits Manager
Vorys, Sater, Seymour & Pease LLP

I began my career as a file clerk in an accounting department of a law firm in Columbus, Ohio about 16 years ago. Since that first job, I have worked at two different law firms, in both the Accounting and Human Resources Departments. I have always been described as a people person and HR seems to be a natural environment for me to work within.

I received my Bachelor of Science degree, with a major in Business Administration and a minor in Human Resources, from Franklin University, in Columbus, Ohio. I completed my Master of Business Administration at Franklin University in January 2003. My career has completely been shaped due to my education. I have a tremendously supportive family both at home and at VSSP LLP. Without their support and encouragement to attain my goals, I would not be where I am today in my career.

Question

What is the role of administrative managers in the human relations arena today and how has your job changed over the past few years?

Response

Managing human resources on a day-to-day basis is vital in today's workplace. With the speed in which change occurs in today's environment and with the rapid globalization that is occurring in our world, you must be knowledgeable, adaptive, and proactive in managing your most important asset—your employees. You must constantly be innovative in all aspects of retention, evaluation, motivation, compensation, and strategic planning.

Administrative managers in the human resource arena wear many hats; we can analyze the current or annual HR budget, we can be a shoulder to cry on, instrumental in changing an employee's career path or we can just be an unbiased person who listens. To many, we are seen as the keepers of discipline, when that is not our primary function at all. Our primary function is to create and maintain a positive environment that is user-friendly. We want to have workers who are happy and successful in their positions.

A few years ago, a typical job was completed on site from 9 a.m. to 5 p.m., with a basic benefit package. That is not the case in today's job market. Some of the predominate trends in HR today involve flextime (working an adapted time schedule), telecommuting (working from your home or another site other than your employer's site), and requests for more in-depth employee benefit packages (elder care, 125 cafeteria packages, and pretax parking). Adapting and accepting the changes necessary to make your company more attractive requires constant diligence and research. Surveying other companies in your specific fields is vital in order to stay competitive.

Chapter 6

Staffing Practices: Employment Laws and Job Analysis

OBJECTIVES

After completing this chapter, you will be able to:

1. Describe major legislation that affects the employment process administrative managers must administer in organizations.

2. Identify the discriminatory practices that are prohibited in the workplace.

3. Describe the purpose of a job analysis.

4. List the steps required to perform a job analysis process.

People and their complex behavior patterns are the lifeblood of any organization. The next five chapters contain essential information every administrative manager must know to manage people and human resource activities effectively. We start our study of this subject in Chapter 6 to get a better understanding of the laws that affect human resources management and the job analysis process. Chapter 7 covers on-the-job practices, specifically employee recruitment and the selection process, as well as employee orientation, training, counseling, and appraisals. Chapter 8 examines employee recognition and compensation plans, while Chapter 9 covers health-related and other workplace issues. Finally, Chapter 10 examines work ethics and business etiquette issues—stateside and abroad.

Let's begin with an introduction to the laws that affect human resources management in the workplace.

If men cannot agree on how to rule themselves, someone else must rule them.

—*Theodore H. White*

TECHNOLOGY APPLICATIONS IN THE WORKPLACE

©Getty Images/PhotoDisc

Workplace-Related Assistive Technologies

Technology has continued to make advances in helping people with disabilities be even more effective employees in a wide range of jobs. From powerful screen readers to accessible web sites and online forms, companies are creating and using innovative technologies. Simply stated, assistive technology works with a computer or operating system to accommodate specific disabilities.

Apart from Microsoft XP's latest advances on the operating system front, they are improving technologies that allow the disabled to be even more productive in the workplace.

- *Visually Impaired.* Considered by many experts as the toughest workplace challenge, people who are either blind or visually impaired have several options open to them. Devices include screen readers/magnifiers, voice input, on-screen keyboards, and keyboard switches.

- *Upper Body Disabilities.* The ergonomic computer keyboard avoids the hand, finger, and arm stress associated with work on the traditional flat keyboard.[1]

ISSUES TO THINK ABOUT:

1. Does assistive technology level the playing field for disabled workers?
2. In what other ways have you seen organizations accommodate workers who have disabilities?

LAWS AFFECTING HUMAN RESOURCES MANAGEMENT

The administrative manager's responsibility to manage human resources is a challenge. It requires an administrative manager who understands legal issues, handles change, anticipates trends, and moves calmly and quickly to reach effective solutions. During the past four decades, federal legislation has changed the rules for employers by granting employees specific rights. Failure to comply with these laws subjects employers not only to the risk of litigation, but also to negative public attitudes and poor employee morale.

Among the most important legislation that influences how people are managed are the Equal Pay Act of 1963, the Civil Rights Act of 1964 (and its numerous subsequent amendments), the Americans with Disabilities Act of 1990, and the Family and Medical Leave Act of 1993.

Equal Pay Act of 1963

One of the first equal employment requirements resulting in a mandate to employers was the **Equal Pay Act of 1963**. The Equal Pay Act prohibits discrimination on the basis of sex in the payment of wages or benefits, where men and women perform work of similar skill, effort, and responsibility for the same employer under similar working conditions.

The concept of comparable worth applies to jobs that are valued similarly in the organization, whether or not they are the same. **Comparable worth** implies that jobs with comparable levels of knowledge, skill, and ability should be paid similarly even if actual duties differ significantly.

Civil Rights Act of 1964

Beginning with the Civil Rights Act of 1964 and specifically with its Title VII, known as Equal Employment Opportunity, employment practices in organizations were put on notice to be nonbiased, consistent, and fair in the treatment of *all* employees. The agency authorized under Title VII to oversee compliance with the Civil Rights Act is the **Equal Employment Opportunity Commission (EEOC)**. This agency handles complaints relative to race, color, religion, and national origin, plus age and disability discrimination and compensation charges.

The primary functions of the EEOC are to investigate and mediate equal employment opportunity complaints. Normally, most complaints are either settled privately or litigated in the courts. The EEOC has the legitimate power, however, to issue an injunction in an attempt to mediate and remedy the complaint. An **injunction** is a court order requiring a person or corporation to do or to refrain from doing a particular act.

Significant amendments have been made to the Civil Rights Act. Enacted in part to reverse several Supreme Court decisions that limited the rights of persons protected by these laws, the Civil Rights Act also provides additional protections. For example, it authorizes compensatory and punitive damages in cases of intentional discrimination and provides for attorneys' fees and the possibility of jury trials.

These amendments have affected employment practices in the United States and changed the way managers manage. The following paragraphs discuss four significant mandates that affect employment practices and with which managers must comply.

Age Discrimination in Employment Act of 1967 (ADEA)

Originally, the age discrimination legislation prohibited mandatory retirement before age 65 for most employees. However, with longer productive years predicted among older workers, this mandatory retirement age was raised to age 70 in the late 1970s. In 1986, the ADEA was amended again, this time prohibiting mandatory retirement at *any* age for almost all employees.

At a time of cutting jobs and clipping resources, the workplace can be particularly cruel to older people. There is a misperception that older workers are slow to learn new technology, can't be trained, and can't keep up with the workload. Reporting data from the EEOC show that allegations of discrimination based on age is a category of charges filed with the agency against private employers that is increasing.[2] However, age limits are applied in federal and military positions. The law does not prohibit the government from establishing restrictions for service entrance.

The ADEA's broad ban against age discrimination most notably prohibits:

- Statements or specifications in job notices or advertisements of age preference and limitations. An age limit may only be specified in the rare circumstance where age has been proven to be a bona fide occupational qualification (BFOQ).
- Denial of benefits to older employees. An employer may reduce benefits based on age only if the cost of providing the reduced benefits to older workers is the same as the cost of providing benefits to younger workers.

Equal Employment Opportunity Act of 1972

Title VII of the Civil Rights Act was amended in 1972. Its effects were sweeping because the act applied to virtually all forms of job discrimination, such as discriminatory treatment in hiring, promoting, testing, training opportunities, evaluating, compensating, disciplining, and terminating employees. This amendment became known as the **Equal Employment Opportunity Act.** It forbids discrimination on the basis of race, color, sex, religion, or national origin.

Equal employment opportunity is not only a legal issue, it is also an emotional issue. Perhaps no other regulatory agency has so thoroughly affected human resource management as has the EEOC. For example, if an employer behaves as described in the employment situations listed in Table 6.1, he or she may be in violation of the Equal Employment Opportunity Act. If found in violation, penalties against the company would likely be assessed and remedies provided the employee.

Pregnancy Discrimination Act of 1978

Discrimination on the basis of pregnancy, childbirth, or related medical conditions constitutes unlawful sex discrimination under Title VII of the Civil Rights Act of 1964. Women affected by pregnancy or related conditions must receive the same treatment as other applicants or employees with similar abilities or limitations.

MANAGEMENT TIP

By hiring people who "break the mold" of your usual hires, you can provide a different perspective—in work experience, age, cultural background, etc.—to your work force.

TABLE 6.1 Equal Employment Opportunity Act of 1972

Examples of Discrimination Based on Race, Color, Sex, Religion, National Origin, Age, or Disability

Employment Practice	Discrimination Examples
Hiring	"I don't care if he is the right person for the job, I think we are going overboard in this company by hiring so many minorities."
Promotions	"Perhaps we can have dinner some evening after work and discuss your future with the company."
Testing	"We are going to have to change our entire testing procedure to accommodate him (applicant has a disability)."
Evaluations	"I have a problem with anyone who cannot look me in the eyes when I give them an evaluation—even though I realize certain ethnic groups are that way."
Compensation	"We can get by paying Mr. Ziede minimum wage because he has lots of retirement income coming in."
Discipline	"Women always cry when they receive a reprimand!"
Termination	"I'm afraid if she gets fired, I'll have her entire church congregation in my office tomorrow. You know how they stick together."

The Pregnancy Discrimination Act states that an employer cannot refuse to hire a woman because of her pregnancy-related condition as long as she is able to perform the major functions of her job. Further, once on the job, an employer may not single out pregnancy-related conditions for special procedures to determine an employee's ability to work. However, an employer may use any procedure used to screen other employees' ability to work. For example, if an employer requires its employees to submit a doctor's statement concerning their inability to work before granting leave or paying sick benefits,

the employer may require employees affected by pregnancy-related conditions to submit such statements.

If an employee is temporarily unable to perform her job due to pregnancy, the employer must treat her the same as any other temporarily disabled employee; for example, by providing modified tasks, alternative assignments, disability leave, or leave without pay.

Pregnant employees must be permitted to work as long as they are able to perform their jobs. If an employee has been absent from work as a result of a pregnancy-related condition and recovers, her employer may not require her to remain on leave until the baby's birth. An employer may not have a rule which prohibits an employee from returning to work for a predetermined length of time after childbirth. Employers must hold open a job for a pregnancy-related absence the same length of time jobs are held open for employees on sick or disability leave.

Any health insurance provided by an employer must cover expenses for pregnancy-related conditions on the same basis as costs for other medical conditions. Health insurance for expenses arising from abortion is not required, except where the life of the mother is endangered. Employees with pregnancy-related disabilities must be treated the same as other temporarily disabled employees for accrual and crediting of seniority, vacation calculation, pay increases, and temporary disability benefits.

Sexual Harassment Law of 1991 The sexual harassment law also has its roots in Title VII of the Civil Rights Act of 1964, which prohibits discrimination on the basis of sex. Beginning in 1991, however, events such as the Anita Hill–Justice Clarence Thomas harrassment allegations and the U.S. Navy "Tailhook" scandal involving sexual harassment of women attending a convention of naval aviators led not only to an increase in legal action but also to major shifts in the way people think about sexual harassment at work.

As a practical matter, the Supreme Court's most recent sexual harassment rulings in the summer of 1998 required companies of any size to have:

- A written policy outlawing all forms of sexual harassment.
- Sexual harassment training for supervisors.
- A strategy for responding to sexual harassment complaints.

Organizations are committed to maintaining a work environment free of discriminatory intimidation and sexual harassment and typically have a policy covering these actions. In addition to defining prohibited behavior, a written sexual harassment policy should also provide as follows:

- Make clear that the company won't tolerate misbehavior from anyone, including supervisors and customers.
- Encourage harassed employees to complain to their supervisor—or, if the supervisor is the accused harasser, to some other designated person.
- Assure employees of confidentiality.
- Assure employees that retaliation will not be tolerated.

Sexual harassment is broadly defined as unwelcome sexual advances, requests for sexual favors, and other verbal or physical conduct of a sexual nature that creates an intimidating, offensive, or hostile work environment. There are two kinds of harassment that the courts have recognized—quid pro quo and hostile work environment.

ETHICS & CHOICES

When news of a sexual harassment complaint reached a recently promoted top manager, he dismissed it with a wisecrack about "those nutty feminists." As a new administrative manager who overheard his comment, what would you say?

The first, *quid pro quo*—a Latin term meaning "this for that"—forbids a supervisor from telling a subordinate he or she must have sex with the supervisor or else suffer adverse consequences on the job, such as a promotion, a raise, or benefits. The other is **hostile work environment**, where supervisors or coworkers do things that make the work atmosphere more difficult for people based on their gender.

Hostile work environment harassment really isn't about sexual exploitation. It's about exclusion—one person or group trying to make the work atmosphere more difficult for another because they would really rather not have the person or group around. Sometimes it is sex, but sometimes other means are used to make someone appear less serious, less capable, different, and out of place on the job.

A hostile environment is determined by the circumstances of each case. However, four factors that contribute to a hostile environment are: (1) frequency of the discriminatory conduct; (2) the severity of the conduct; (3) whether the conduct is physically threatening, humiliating, or an offensive utterance; and (4) if the conduct interferes with an employee's work performance.

Harassment can be prevented if informal actions are taken before incidents escalate into full-blown problems. This strategy puts a stop to the harassing behavior at the lowest level possible, which requires addressing the situation *before* it becomes a formal complaint. Formal complaints are more difficult to handle because they are often confrontational and unpleasant.

Informal options available to employers are:

• Appointing an ombudsman who is designated as neutral and usually reports directly to the president or chief executive officer of the organization.

• Planning an intervention whereby the manager or human resources representative sits down with all parties to review the issue.

• Hiring a professional to mediate who is an impartial expert and who guides the disputing parties through a process that encourages open discussion of the problem, listening, and empathizing.

• Fact-finding and an investigation are used with situations that are more complex.

Table 6.2 outlines steps a company can take to reduce the risk of sexual harassment on the job. The challenge for employers and managers is to find a resolution to sexual harassment charges that is fair to all parties involved.

Americans with Disabilities Act of 1990

Many people feel that the **Americans with Disabilities Act** (ADA) of 1990 is the single most important piece of anti-discrimination legislation to be enacted since the Civil Rights Act of 1964. Title I of the ADA, which took effect in July 1992, prohibits private employers, state and local governments, employment agencies, and labor unions from discriminating against qualified individuals with disabilities in job application procedures, hiring, firing, advancement, compensation, job training, and other terms, conditions, and privileges of employment.

TABLE 6.2 **Sexual Harassment on the Job**

Steps to Reduce the Risk

Create a company policy with procedures covering sexual harassment.	Ensure that the policy is explained to and understood by all employees.
Educate managers and employees.	All employees must understand what sexual harassment is so they can avoid it or so they can recognize it if they become targets.
Treat complaints seriously.	Investigate complaints as soon as possible, and take appropriate action while respecting your employees' rights to confidentiality.
Recognize that harassment is not just a crime of men against women.	While their numbers are still relatively small, cases involving same-sex harassment or females harassing males are on the rise.
Consider mediation if a complaint is made.	*Mediation* is always less expensive than a lawsuit. In **mediation** an impartial third party tries to bring both sides to a point of common agreement.
Be prepared to take action against third-party harassment.	Remember that harassers can come from the ranks of vendors, clients, customers, and other outsiders.
Consider purchasing Employee Practices Liability Insurance (EPLI).	EPLI protects employers against claims such as discrimination and sexual harassment.

An individual with a disability is a person who:

- Has a physical or mental impairment that substantially limits one or more major life activity;
- Has a record of such an impairment; or
- Is regarded as having such an impairment.

A qualified employee or applicant with a disability is an individual who, with or without reasonable accommodation, can perform the essential functions of the job in question. **Reasonable accommodation** may include, but is not limited to:

- Making existing facilities used by employees readily accessible to and usable by persons with disabilities;
- Job restructuring, modifying work schedules, reassignment to a vacant position;
- Acquiring or modifying equipment or devices, adjusting or modifying

The Americans with Disabilities Act prevents discrimination against disabled workers.

© Getty Images/PhotoDisc

examinations, training materials, or policies, and providing qualified readers or interpreters.

Reasonable accommodation may be necessary to apply for a job, to perform job functions, or to receive the benefits and privileges of employment that are enjoyed by people without disabilities. An employer is not required to lower production standards to make an accommodation. Nor is an employer obligated to provide personal use items, such as eyeglasses or hearing aids.

An employer is required, however, to make an accommodation to the known disability of a qualified applicant or employee if it would not impose an "undue hardship" on the operation of the employer's business. **Undue hardship** is defined as an action requiring significant difficulty or expense when considered in light of factors such as an employer's size, financial resources, and the nature and structure of its operation.

Employers may not ask job applicants about the existence, nature, or severity of a disability. Applicants may be asked about their ability to perform specific job functions. A job offer may be conditioned on the results of a medical examination, but only if the examination is required for all entering employees in similar jobs. Medical examinations of employees must be job-related and consistent with the employer's business needs.

Employees and applicants engaging in the illegal use of drugs are not covered by the ADA, when an employer acts on the basis of such use. Tests for illegal drugs are not subject to the ADA's restrictions on medical examinations. Employers may hold illegal drug users and alcoholics to the same performance standards as other employees.

At the time the EEOC issued regulations to enforce the provisions of Title I of the ADA in July 1991, the provisions covered employers with 25 or more employees. However, in July 1994, the threshold dropped to include employers with 15 or more employees.

In a 2001 survey regarding workplace hiring and accommodation of people with disabilities, 1,042 human resources managers, who are members of the Society for Human Resource Management, responded in this way. Eighty-two percent have modified facilities to make them accessible; 79 percent have been flexible in applying human resources policies; 79 percent have restructured jobs or modified work hours; and 80 percent have changed the questions they ask during interviews and have made interview locations and restrooms accessible.[3]

Given that there is so much legislation directing employment practices by administrative managers, Table 6.3 is presented to summarize the discriminating practices that are prohibited in the workplace.

Family and Medical Leave Act of 1993

The U.S. Department of Labor's Employment Standards Administration, Wage and Hour Division, administers and enforces the **Family and Medical Leave Act (FMLA)** for all private, state and local government employees, and some federal employees.

FMLA became effective in August 1993 for most employers. FMLA entitles eligible employees to take up to twelve weeks of unpaid, job-protected leave in a twelve month period for specified family and medical reasons.

The law contains provisions on employer coverage; employee eligibility for the law's benefits; entitlement to leave, maintenance of health benefits during leave, and job restoration after leave; notice and certification of the need for FMLA leave; and protection for employees who request or take FMLA leave. The law also requires employers to keep certain records.

FMLA applies to all public agencies, including state, local and federal employers, local education agencies (schools), private-sector employers that employ 50 or more employees in 20 or more workweeks in the current or preceding calendar year and who are engaged in commerce or in any industry or activity affecting commerce—including joint employers and successors of covered employers.

To be eligible for FMLA benefits, an employee must:

© South-Western/Deanna Ettinger

Employers must post notices advising employees of their rights under the laws the EEOC enforces.

1. Work for a covered employer and have worked for that employer for a total of 12 months.
2. Have worked at least 1,250 hours during the previous 12 months; and
3. Work at a location in the United States or in any territory or possession of the United States where there are at least 50 employees.

A covered employer must grant an eligible employee up to a total of 12 workweeks of unpaid leave during any 12-month period for one or more of the following reasons:

- For the birth or adoption and care of the newborn child of the employee;
- For placement with the employee of a child for adoption or foster care;
- To care for an immediate family member (spouse, child, or parent) with a serious health condition; or
- When the employee is unable to work because of a serious health condition.

T A B L E 6 . 3 **What Discriminatory Practices Are Prohibited in the Workplace?**

It Is Illegal To Discriminate In Any Aspect Of Employment, Including:	Discriminatory Practices Under These Laws Also Include:
• hiring and firing	• harassment on the basis of race, color, religion, sex, national origin, disability, or age
• compensation, assignment, or classification of employees	
• transfer, promotion, layoff, or recall	• retaliation against an individual for filing a charge of discrimination, participating in an investigation, or opposing discriminatory practices
• job advertisements	
• recruitment	
• testing	• employment decisions based on stereotypes or assumptions about the abilities, traits, or performance of individuals of a certain sex, race, age, religion, or ethnic group, or individuals with disabilities; and
• use of company facilities	
• training and apprenticeship program	
• fringe benefits	• denying employment opportunities to a person because of marriage to, or association with, an individual of a particular race, religion, national origin, or an individual with a disability.
• pay, retirement plans, and disability leave	
• other terms and conditions of employment	

Employers are required to post notices to all employees advising them of their rights under the laws the EEOC enforces and their right to be free from retaliation. Such notices must be accessible, as needed, to persons with visual or other disabilities that affect reading.

Serious health condition means an illness, injury, impairment, or physical or mental condition that involves either:

• Any period of incapacity or treatment connected with inpatient care (i.e., an overnight stay) in a hospital, hospice, or residential medical-care facility, and any period of incapacity or subsequent treatment in connection with such inpatient care; or

• Continuing treatment by a health-care provider that includes any period of incapacity (i.e., inability to work, attend school or perform other regular daily activities) due to:

  • A health condition lasting more than three consecutive days, and any subsequent treatment or period of incapacity relating to the same condition;

  • Pregnancy or prenatal care;

- A chronic serious health condition which continues over an extended period of time, requires periodic visits to a health-care provider, and may involve occasional episodes of incapacity (e.g., asthma, diabetes);

- A permanent or long-term condition for which treatment may not be effective (e.g., Alzheimer's, a severe stroke, terminal cancer);

- Any absences to receive multiple treatments for restorative surgery.

A covered employer is required to maintain group health insurance coverage for an employee on FMLA leave whenever such insurance was provided before the leave was taken and on the same terms as if the employee had continued to work. If applicable, arrangements will need to be made for employees to pay their share of health insurance premiums while on leave. In some instances, the employer may recover premiums it paid to maintain health coverage for an employee who fails to return to work from FMLA leave.

Upon return from FMLA leave, an employee must be restored to the employee's original job, or to an equivalent job with equivalent pay, benefits, and other terms and conditions of employment.

Employees seeking to use FMLA leave are required to provide 30-day advance notice of the need to take FMLA leave when the need is foreseeable and such notice is practicable. Employers may also require employees to provide:

- Medical certification supporting the need for leave due to a serious health condition affecting the employee or an immediate family member;

- Second or third medical opinions (at the employer's expense) and periodic recertification; and

- Periodic reports during FMLA leave regarding the employee's status and intent to return to work.

When intermittent leave is needed to care for an immediate family member or the employee's own illness, and is for planned medical treatment, the employee must try to schedule treatment so as not to unduly disrupt the employer's operation.

Applying Employment Laws and Remedies for Violations

How do organizations go about achieving fairness in the application of equal employment opportunity? As an administrative manager, you can do the following:

1. Eliminate irrelevant job requirements.

2. Open job and promotion opportunities to the handicapped, minorities, and women.

3. Facilitate child care through flexible job arrangements, such as job sharing, a compressed workweek, and telecommuting opportunities.

4. Provide equal pay for equal work.

5. Provide training in EEO requirements.

6. Offer sensitivity training to employees to better understand minority and disabled persons' needs.

7. Modify employee benefits to meet the needs of women, minorities, and working families.

What remedies are available to workers when discrimination is found? The "relief" or remedies available for employment discrimination, whether caused by intentional acts or by practices that have a discriminatory effect, may include back pay, hiring, promotion, reinstatement, reasonable accommodation, or other actions that will make an individual "whole" (in the condition she or he would have been but for the discrimination). Remedies also may include payment of attorneys' fees, expert witness fees, and court costs.

Under most EEOC-enforced laws, compensatory and punitive damages also may be available where intentional discrimination is found. **Compensatory damages** may be available to pay for actual monetary losses, for future monetary losses, and for mental anguish and inconvenience.

Punitive damages also may be available if an employer acted with malice or reckless indifference.

In cases concerning reasonable accommodation under the ADA, compensatory or punitive damages may not be awarded to the charging party if an employer can demonstrate that "good faith" efforts were made to provide reasonable accommodation. In case an employer must prove "good faith" efforts were taken, it is important that the employer provide thorough records.

An employer may be required to post notices to all employees addressing any violations with which the employer has been charged and advising the employees of their

> **MANAGEMENT TIP**
>
> Never look through or talk around people with disabilities. They are not invisible. Treat them with the fullest degree of dignity and respect.

rights under the laws that the EEOC enforces and their right to be free from retaliation. Such notices must be accessible, as needed, to persons with visual or other disabilities that affect reading.

Other Employment Laws and Executive Orders

In addition to the laws already mentioned, there are other EEO laws and executive orders that are applicable to agencies of and contractors with the federal government. Table 6.4 describes the general provisions of four mandates.

The legal and ethical foundation of the staffing function in companies is the job analysis, which will be covered in the next section.

JOB ANALYSIS

Job analysis is the process of collecting and organizing information about jobs performed in the organization and the principle elements involved in performing them. Specifically, it is a systematic way to gather and analyze information about the content of the jobs, specific human requirements, and the context of jobs.

It is essential for organizations to perform job analysis because the information gathered is used throughout the selection process. In fact, time spent developing a complete list of essential qualifications for a particular job results in significant time savings throughout the employee selection process. If companies fail to complete this essential step, they can expect delays, increased turnover, and potential problems when trying to defend their selection process against grievances or legal actions.

TABLE 6.4 **EEO Laws and Executive Orders Applicable to Agencies of and Contractors with the Federal Government**

General Provisions	
Laws	
Vocational Rehabilitation Act of 1973	• Prohibits discrimination against disabled individuals.
	• Requires development of an affirmative action plan.
Vietnam Era Veterans Readjustment Assistance Act of 1974	• Prohibits discrimination against Vietnam-era veterans.
	• Mandates affirmative action to employ and advance disabled and qualified veterans.
Executive Orders	
EO #1246 (1965) As amended by Executive Order 11375 (1967)	• Prohibits employment discrimination based on race, color, religion, sex, or national origin.
	• Requires development of affirmative action plans.
	• Established Office of Federal Contract Compliance Programs.
EO #1478 (1969)	• Requires the federal government to ensure that all personnel actions regarding employment be free from discrimination based on race, color, religion, sex, and national origin.

The core of a job analysis is the distinction that is made among jobs in an organization relative to these seven criteria:

1. Work activity and behaviors
2. Interactions with others
3. Performance standards
4. Machines and equipment used
5. Working conditions
6. Supervision given and received, and
7. Knowledge, skills, and abilities needed.

Without a job analysis, it would be difficult to develop complete, accurate, and effective job descriptions and job specifications. As previously mentioned, it would also be difficult to comply with the Americans with Disabilities Act mandate to list essential skills if you had not given thought to what those skills are. Administrative managers or others who do a job analysis can benefit by asking workers to list the skills used in particular areas of their job, or they can simply observe the job being performed.

The Job Analysis Process

Who typically performs the job analysis and what steps are usually followed? First, a job analysis can be conducted by someone inside the organization or by an outside human resources consultant. If the job analysis is performed internally, a human resources department specialist or you, as an administrative manager, may be assigned the task.

Job analysis information serves a wide variety of purposes; such as recruitment and selection, followed closely by the setting of equitable wage and salary levels. Although the steps can vary from organization to organization, a job analysis typically follows these customary steps:

1. Identify the job that will be studied.
2. Determine how to collect details about the jobs tasks, responsibilities, and skill requirements.
3. Identify who in the organization—employees and/or managers—has this information.
4. Inform employees and managers alike as to the purpose and procedures that will be followed during this analysis as an effort to calm any fears and to obtain their cooperation.
5. Gather all pertinent data that exists about those jobs, such as job descriptions, organization charts, and other industry-related resources.
6. Conduct the job analysis by gathering complete information through interviews, questionnaires, records, and observations.
7. Evaluate and verify the accuracy of the data collected with other employees and managers.
8. Prepare job descriptions and job specifications with input from employees and managers.

A **job description** defines in written form the tasks, duties, and responsibilities of a particular job; the **job specification** goes further and clarifies the knowledge, degree, skills, and abilities a worker needs in order to do the job competently. The job specification explains the minimum job requirements in relation to the job factors (skill, effort, responsibility, and working conditions).

Job Description When preparing a typical job description, the administrative manager should make sure certain factors are considered. For instance, a job description needs as many of the following items listed as possible: job title, department, code, salary range, and supervisor. In addition, this description should include the following information:

1. Physical demands of the job and minimum physical requirements needed;
2. Working conditions, including responsibilities for other people, money and equipment, and relationships with others;
3. Duties and responsibilities of the job;
4. Days and hours of work; and
5. Machines, tools, and equipment used.

Job Specifications After the job description is written, the specifications of the job need to be detailed. Consider such employee characteristics for the job as these:

1. Educational background and knowledge, skills and techniques, and training and experience required to perform the job, as well as any special training needed; and
2. Personal characteristics such as sociability, and organizational and communication skills.

An example of a completed job description and job specification for an administrative assistant is shown in Figure 6.1. Review the document to learn how and in what order information is presented.

FIGURE 6.1 **A job description and specifications for an administrative assistant position.**

INTERNATIONAL BUSINESS SERVICES
JOB DESCRIPTION AND SPECIFICATIONS

JOB TITLE: ADMINISTRATIVE ASSISTANT
POSITION SUMMARY: Reporting to the administrative office manager, this 30-hour position is primarily responsible for providing secretarial support.

Essential Job Functions:

1. Receives and screens telephone calls and visitors and assists visitors or callers by answering questions or providing information regarding company procedures.

2. Keys, formats, and proofreads material such as forms, newsletters, advertisements, and corrects grammatical, punctuation, and spelling errors.

3. Organizes, establishes, and maintains recordkeeping systems for records, sets up files and records, and follows up on missing information.

4. Records and tracks account expenditures, creates worksheets on computer or in a manual system, prepares periodic reports, and submits data to supervisors.

5. Assembles and distributes or mails general information requested by employees, visitors, and customers.

6. Initiates responses to customer inquiries and requests for information by composing correspondence of a nontechnical nature, such as explanation of established procedure.

7. Performs other duties as assigned.

Knowledge, Skills, and Abilities:

1. Knowledge of general office practices and procedures.

2. Knowledge of written communication formats, business terminology, and composition.

3. Skill in use of personal computers with word processing, spreadsheet, and database software.

4. Skill in both oral and written communication.

5. Skill in operating various office equipment, such as ten-key adding machine, calculator, copy machine, facsimile machine, postage scale, and telephone system.

6. Ability to communicate with employees and other business contacts in a courteous and professional manner.

7. Ability to work on your own with minimal supervision.

8. Ability to lift up to fifteen pounds on a frequent basis.

Table 6.5 describes the nature of job analysis. In addition, it shows how elements are related and become the basis for other actions an administrative manager may take during the employment process.

Final Thoughts on Job Analysis

Many faulty hiring decisions are the result of incorrectly identified essential qualifications, such as inflated, inaccurate, nonessential, vague, or missing qualifications. This happens sometimes when job analysis is perceived as too difficult, cumbersome, and time-consuming, or when managers try to reinvent the wheel when they analyze a job or update a job description. Without a thorough list of the essential qualifications, managers often change the requirements of the job as the selection process continues. When this occurs, it is not only unfair to applicants, but also a legal mine field for the organization.

TABLE 6.5 Nature of the Job Analysis

How Job Analysis, Job Description, and Job Specification Can be Used by the Administrative Office Manager

Job Analysis describes	and is the basis for determining
· what the employee does	· job requirements
· how and why the employee does it	· compliance with ADA relative to essential skills required for the job

Job Description presents	and is the basis for:
· a summary statement of the job	· employee orientation
· a list of duties and responsibilities	· employee instruction
	· supervision and control
	· disciplinary action
	· grievance handling

Job Specification lists	and is the basis for:
· the personal qualifications required in terms of skills, education, experience	· recruitment
	· selection
· the working conditions affecting health, safety, and comfort	· development
	· job evaluation and wage determination
	· health and safety programs

External evidence of faulty job analysis can be seen in online and newspaper recruitment advertisements. Many are vague, poorly put together, and loaded with irrelevant information. When these ads omit qualifications essential for the job, unqualified job seekers apply. Screening these applicants takes time. When you recruit candidates for openings, take time to study

the job analysis to write an effective job advertisement.

Internal evidence of faulty job analysis can readily be seen in the tests and interview questions used to hire applicants. It is almost impossible to get a top performer unless you ask the right questions. And to do so, you need to fully understand the requirements of the job in question.

MESSAGE FOR MANAGERS

Human resources managers often use the expression "the right fit" or "firm fit" when referring to having selected the *right* person for the *right* job in the *right* firm at the *right* time. This chapter details for the AM pertinent facts, options, and processes involved in getting that "right fit." As a manager on the job,

refer to the tables for critical steps to be followed in staffing practices.

To a large extent, Chapter 6 is similar to planning any project, trip, or event. If it's done right from the beginning, you can expect fewer problems, complications, or delays as you progress, and the entire process will not

take as long and be safer for employers and employees by following the dictates of the law. Administering staffing practices in today's workplace is critical to the success of any organization because employees are not only an organization's most valued asset but also its most expensive one.

Chapter Six

SUMMARY

1. Federal legislation has changed the rules for employers by granting employees specific rights. Failure to comply with these laws subjects employers not only to the risk of litigation, but it also invites negative public attitudes and can damage employee morale.

2. Among the most important legislation that influences how people are managed are the Equal Pay Act of 1963, the Civil Rights Act of 1964 (and its numerous subsequent amendments), the Americans with Disabilities Act of 1990, and the Family and Medical Leave Act of 1993.

3. Additional mandates that evolved as a result of the Civil Rights Act of 1964 that affect employment practices in the work force are the Age Discrimination in Employment Act of 1967, the Equal Employment Opportunity Act of 1972, the Pregnancy Discrimination Act of 1978, and the Sexual Harassment Law of 1991.

4. Title VII of the Civil Rights Act of 1964 requires that employment practices in organizations be nonbiased, consistent, and fair in the treatment of all employees relative to race, sex, color, religion, and national origin, plus age and disability discrimination and compensation charges.

5. The Pregnancy Discrimination Act states that an employer cannot refuse to hire a woman because of her pregnancy-related condition as long as she is able to perform the major functions of her job.

6. Sexual harassment is broadly defined as unwelcome sexual advances, requests for sexual favors, and other verbal or physical conduct of a sexual nature that creates an intimidating, offensive, or hostile work environment.

7. The Americans with Disabilities Act of 1990 prohibits employers from discriminating against qualified individuals with disabilities in job application procedures, hiring, firing, advancement, compensation, job training, and other terms, conditions, and privileges of employment.

8. The Family and Medical Leave Act of 1993 entitles eligible employees to take up to twelve weeks of unpaid, job-protected leave in a twelve-month period for specified family and medical reasons.

9. The relief or remedies available for employment discrimination, may include back pay, hiring, promotion, reinstatement, reasonable accommodations, or other actions that will make an individual in the condition he or she would have been but for the discrimination.

10. Job analysis is the process of collecting and organizing information about jobs performed in the organizations, relative to the jobs' content, specific human requirements, and context.

11. As a result of conducting a job analysis, an organization is able to write an effective job description and job specification.

KEY TERMS

Americans with Disabilities Act

Comparable worth

Compensatory damages

Equal Employment Opportunity Act

Equal Employment Opportunity Commission

Equal Pay Act of 1963

Family and Medical Leave Act

Hostile work environment

Injunction

Job analysis

Job description

Job specification

Mediation

Pregnancy Discrimination Act

Punitive damages

Reasonable accommodation

Serious health condition

Sexual harassment

Undue hardship

REVIEW

1. What are the provisions of the Equal Pay Act of 1963?

2. What types of complaints does the Equal Employment Opportunity Commission handle?

3. List four significant pieces of legislation that evolved from the Civil Rights Act of 1964.

4. Describe the two kinds of sexual harassment that the courts have recognized.

5. Relative to the Americans with Disabilities Act of 1990, interpret the terms *reasonable accommodation* and *undue hardship*.

6. Who is eligible for leave under the Family and Medical Leave Act of 1993?

7. What remedies are available to workers when discrimination is found?

8. State the seven criteria around which a job analysis is performed.

9. Distinguish between the terms *job description* and *job specification*.

CRITICAL THINKING

1. Of the major legislation described in this chapter that affects the employment process, which two do you think are the most challenging to administer and why?

2. Using Table 6.3 that describes the discriminatory practices that are prohibited in the workplace, describe a situation you know of personally in which someone was discriminated against on the job.

3. Why should organizations perform a job analysis of positions if it takes so much time?

4. Critique the job description and job specification shown in Figure 6.1. In other words, are they complete and accurate? Suggest improvements, as needed.

CASE STUDY 6-1
DISCRIMINATING ON THE BASIS OF ACCENT

As part of her pre-employment screening, Tien Ho scored in the top 2 percent on the two-hour battery of tests. In fact, Tien's skill and performance on the mathematical skills tests yielded the best score in the history of the Colony Finance Co. However, during her interview with Mark Lariman, assistant controller, she found herself facing a brick wall. The interview ended something like this:

Lariman: I congratulate you, Tien, on your outstanding scores on all the written tests. You surely have a fine grasp of mathematics.

Ho: You are very kind. Thank you, Mr. Lariman.

Lariman: (struggling to understand Ho's words) What's that? Oh yes. As you know, Tien, this job requires you to work closely with clients on a one-to-one basis every day. And these people come from all walks of life. I'm afraid that, like me, most of our clients will not be able to understand your accent. During our interview, I found it hard to understand you sometimes, and we can't have that. So, Tien, we shall be unable to hire you. I do thank you for thinking of us…

Ho left the office, feeling that Colony Finance just did not want a foreigner on the job and that the company rejected her application solely because of her accent.

Discussion Questions

1. Has Colony Finance illegally discriminated in its rejection of Tien's application for employment?

2. Would your answer be the same if Tien had applied for a "behind-the-scenes" job such as data-entry clerk?

Analyze the case; determine if any employment laws were violated. Be ready to participate in a group discussion as directed by your instructor or to submit a case analysis if requested.

CASE STUDY 6-2
SEXUAL HARASSMENT ISSUE OR NOT?

Keith had just been recognized by his advertising agency for preparing an exemplary ad campaign presentation book for the agency's top client by using desktop publishing software. Keith is studying to be a graphic artist in night school, and he had prepared a "model" document that could be used with all future clients. Annette, an advertising executive, asked Keith to join her at lunch to celebrate and to discuss his "future in advertising."

During the course of the meal, the conversation took an unexpected turn. Annette began commenting on how attractive and sexy she thought Keith was and expressed a desire to spend more time with him. Keith refused her advances and felt embarrassed. However, Annette continued to make uncomfortable statements and to remind him how the agency could advance an "attractive" employee like him.

The working relationship between Keith and Annette deteriorated after this luncheon. Unwelcome suggestions became common, and Annette seemed to wind up around his work area. When they were alone, she playfully winked at him and touched his arm or shoulder. Although Keith was certain he was being subjected to sexual harassment, he was hesitant to pursue it any further with his supervisor, the agency's administrative office manager. Keith believes that the AM actually saw Annette "coming on to him" when she recently walked up on them at the water cooler.

Discussion Questions

1. Does this scenario constitute grounds for sexual harassment? If so, discuss what action you think Keith should take.

2. If you were the AM and saw the scene at the water cooler, what would you do?

3. Would the situation be any different if the advances had been made by a man to a woman? Explain.

Research the issues involved in this case. Determine how you would react if you were Keith. What should the administrative manager do once apprised of this situation? How can an administrative manager keep such issues from becoming a problem?

Prepare a brief analysis of the case to use in a class discussion or to submit if requested by your instructor.

INTERNET RESEARCH ACTIVITY

A great way to stay informed in human resources is to go to the course web site *http://odgers.swlearning.com.* There you will find a number of links to various human resources articles or other materials. You may also enter search key words in your Internet browser to search for articles on human resources. Such keywords may be words such as the following: discrimination; employment laws; job analysis; job description; job specification; Equal Employment Opportunity Commission; sex harassment; human resources associations; management associations; and/or media-tion.

You'll find a rich supply of recent full-text articles on all key human resources topics.

Learning Activity:

1. What are some current issues discussed in any of the articles that you located that links to the material covered in Chapter 6?

2. What are the advantages to administrative managers of joining professional associations such as human relations or management organizations or attending seminars sponsored by these types of associations?

Write a one-page report to summarize your findings. Be prepared to participate in a discussion of your findings.

Chapter 7

On-the-Job Employee Practices

After completing this chapter, you will be able to:

1. **List several sources that are used for internal and external recruitment of employees.**

2. **Describe the seven steps that companies follow when completing a typical employee selection process.**

3. **Describe the content of a new employee orientation session as conducted by an administrative manager.**

4. **Discuss the concepts behind the systems approach to training.**

5. **Distinguish among the three categories of discipline problems.**

6. **Describe the importance of the performance appraisal process to the employer, administrative manager, and employee.**

7. **Identify reasons employees leave their jobs and what managers can do to prevent excessive turnover.**

In this chapter, we begin our study of other practices in managing human resources as they relate to the AM's role in employee recruitment, selection, orientation, training, counseling, and performance appraisals. More and more, employees are looking to their companies to hire the right people, train them correctly, and develop their potential. Some suggestions on how to select, train, and develop employees include:

- Screen and select for the skills that are needed: both hard skills (such as problem-solving, math, and reading) and soft skills (such as attitudes, motivation, and communication skills).

- Use behavior-based questions during the job interview.

- Provide training that enhances and upgrades the skills of employees.

- Unify organizations around shared values and manage corporate culture on a daily basis.

Chapter Seven

Communicate everything to your associates. The more they know, the more they care. —Sam Walton, founder of Wal-Mart

TECHNOLOGY APPLICATIONS IN THE WORKPLACE

© Brand X Pictures

E-Learning Helps Busy Workers Stay Ahead

Learning needs to be a tactical process that enables employees to get information in a just-in-time, just-enough, and just-for-me format. To that end, the instructional approach called e-learning (computer-ized electronic learning online) helps workers learn and retain information as quickly, conveniently, and effectively as possible. Those workers who stand to benefit from an e-learning are:

1. *Unserved users.* Despite recent events, employees in many compa-nies still travel to traditional classroom training that takes place in a few centralized locations. Workers who experience a major disruption involving extensive time and travel benefit from e-learning.

2. *Time-challenged users.* The idea of being away from the office for a few days is inconsistent with most people's job requirements. E-learning becomes far less event-based and more of a continuous process that opens up training to people who can't leave work.

ISSUES TO THINK ABOUT:

1. What are your personal feelings about e-learning? Does the concept make you feel comfortable or anxious?
2. Predict what you think the business world will do with e-learning over the next three to five years.

EMPLOYEE RECRUITMENT

Employee recruitment is the process of generating a pool of qualified applicants for organizational job vacancies. This process should take into account the current and projected needs for employees in various job categories. Before starting any recruiting efforts, however, an administrative manager needs to take some preliminary steps. To begin, if the company has an HR department, the AM must recommend to that department the number of people needed, any special skills and experience required of the candidates, and possible recruitment

sources to use to find the best job candidates. In smaller companies that do not have an HR department, the AM would determine and carry out those decisions alone. Qualified employees can be a company's most valuable assets (human assets), while hiring the wrong candidates can prove detrimental to business in the short and long run, costing the company time and money.

Consider all recruitment sources when vacancies occur in organizations. Generally, these sources fall into two major categories: internal sources and external sources.

Internal Sources

When recruiting internally, vacancies are advertised only within the organization, usually on a job-posting bulletin board. Interested applicants generally come from

current employees, former employees, and previous applicants who might regularly check the bulletin board postings.

When job vacancies arise, many companies use internal sources for upgrading and transferring positions and for promoting to new positions within the organization. Companies also find internal recruiting advantageous because it:

1. Costs less to fill vacancies internally;
2. Provides a worker whose strengths and weaknesses are already known;
3. Ensures continuity of employment and corporate knowledge;
4. Promotes loyalty to the organization
5. Builds morale; and
6. Motivates employees to achieve better performance.

Disadvantages to this method include not having new employees entering the work force, playing favorites for promotions, and possible stagnation of ideas.

External Sources

Various external recruiting sources are available. These sources include computerized online job announcements, private and public employment agencies, temporary employment services, college placement centers, and job fairs, as well as media advertisements in newspapers and magazines and on television, radio, and billboards. Job web sites may also be a good source.

Why is recruiting externally a good step for companies to consider?

- Qualified employees within the organization may be unwilling to apply for a position or they may lack the skills needed;

- The different perspectives and varied experiences of new hires can rejuvenate and bring new ideas into an organization; and

- Sometimes develops complacency among current employees, which stymies growth.

Figure 7.1 shows the relationship among these various recruiting sources for office workers.

Disadvantages of recruiting externally include the increase in time and the additional cost of interviewing new prospects to find the skills and attributes needed for the positions available. Many companies are finding that online recruiting, a rather recent method of recruiting externally, may cut the time and cost of locating candidates who meet the skills and attributes required by the organization.

Online Recruitment

More than just a convenience, online recruiting can be a money-saving hiring tool that can bring better candidates into companies. And its use, whether on third-party sites or on organizations' own web sites, continues to grow.

According to results of the 2002 Recruiter Budget/Cost Survey from the Society for Human Resources Management, the Internet has proven to be a cost-effective tool for recruiting that complements newspaper advertising and other techniques. Of the survey's respondents, 82 percent said they use online advertising to fill open positions. In fact, Internet recruiting is now second only to newspaper advertising in terms of volume of applicants generated, and is third in terms of quality of candidates (after newspaper advertisements and referrals).

FIGURE 7.1   Consider all recruitment sources when filling job vacancies.

EXTERNAL
Private and Public Employment Agencies

INTERNAL
- Employee Requests
- Temporary Assignments
- Transfers
- Promotions

Temporary Employment Agencies

College Placement Centers

Professional Organizations

Job Fairs

Want Ads (newspapers, radio, TV, billboards)

Internet

This survey's respondents noted that Internet ads allow them to penetrate new markets and broaden their range of qualified applicants.[1]

What we see now is new technology options that were unthinkable a few years ago. The way job seekers and employers connect has been forever changed. Many job seekers are turning to the Internet for information and resources. Job searches can now be conducted 24 hours a day, seven days a week. A job seeker can e-mail a resume and expect it to reach its destination within seconds.

The main drawback to conducting electronic searches for potential job candidates based on keyword searches is not having the appropriate terminology or buzz words. In other words, if the resume is not formatted correctly, it is invisible to the company seeking job candidates through its Internet site. Computers also cannot evaluate intangible but important human factors like motivation, interpersonal skills, creativity, a positive attitude, or sense of humor. These factors would need to be evaluated by the AM in a personal meeting (face-to-face) at some point.

EMPLOYEE SELECTION

Employee selection is the process of choosing individuals who have relevant qualifications to fill jobs in an organization. Although each organization adapts the process to its own needs, the seven steps described on the following pages are normally followed in a typical selection process.

1. *Forward position requisition.* To begin the process, the administrative manager completes a position approval form. The **position approval form** identifies the position title and related classification information, essential functions of the position, and the duties, experience, education, and training needed to perform the duties. For an example of a position approval form, see Figure 7.2. This form may be sent to HR for writing the advertisement and initial screening of applicants, to the person in charge of the company if no HR department exists, or it may be used solely by the AM to recruit for the position.

2. *Complete application form.* Each applicant completes an **employment application form,** which will serve as the basis for initial screening of minimum qualifications and become the basis for any subsequent interview. Many applicants submit resumes, but employers still require completion of an application. Why? Legally, the same information must be collected on all applicants, and the application form is used for that purpose. Figure 7.3 shows an example of a two-page employment application form. Note that specific questions related to marital status, age, number of dependents, information on spouse, height and weight of the applicant, or any other personal information questions do not appear on the application because they are illegal to ask. The Equal Employment Opportunity Commission requires that data requested on application forms not be of a personal nature, but job-related.

You may ask an applicant for his or her telephone number, address, and Social Security number.

FIGURE 7.2   Example of a position approval form

INTERNATIONAL BUSINESS SERVICES
REQUEST FOR POSITION APPROVAL

☐ NEW POSITION ☐ EXISTING POSITION ☐ FULL-TIME ☐ PART-TIME/TEMPORARY
☐ EXEMPT ☐ NONEXEMPT ☐ BUDGETED ☐ NOT BUDGETED

Proposed Position Title _____ Department _____ Location _____

Proposed Position Reports To _____ (Title) Position Implementation Date _____

Position Classification _____ Salary Range _____ Funding Source: Account Number _____

Describe Funding Source: _____

Primary Purpose of the Position: _____

ESSENTIAL FUNCTIONS OF THE POSITION:

_____

_____

_____

_____

_____

_____

_____

Minimum Amount and Kind, if any, of Education REQUIRED to Perform These Duties. _____

Minimum Amount of Experience (Years and Kind) REQUIRED to Perform These Duties. _____

Licenses, Certification, or Registration REQUIRED, if any. _____

Does This Position Supervise Anyone? If So, List Name and Title. _____

Is Anyone Currently Performing These or Similar Duties? If So, Explain. _____

JUSTIFICATION OF NEED FOR THE POSITION (Why the position is needed). _____

BUDGET IMPLEMENTATION
Acct. Name/# _____

EXPLANATION OF ANY EXCEPTIONS TO BUDGET ALLOCATIONS: _____

_____

Request Approval: _____   _____
                  Initiator's Signature Date   Department Head Signature Date

Financial Department Approval: _____
                               Signature Date

Human Resources Department Approval: _____   President Approval: _____

          Signature Date   Signature Date
DISTRIBUTION: White Human Resources   Yellow Payroll   Pink Department

FIGURE 7.3 Example of an employment application form

INTERNATIONAL BUSINESS SERVICES
4050 West Company Way
Phoenix, AZ 85008

APPLICATION FOR EMPLOYMENT

It is necessary to answer each question as completely as possible even if you attached a resume.

A separate application is required for each position for which you apply (copies acceptable)

POSITION APPLYING FOR _____

JOB NUMBER _____ DEPARTMENT _____

PERSONAL INFORMATION

Social Security Number _____   Application Date _____

Applicant Name _____ _____ _____
                (Last)   (First)   (Middle)

Address _____ _____ _____ _____
        (Current Address) (City)   (State)   (Zip Code)

Residence Phone Number _____   Message Phone Number _____

NOTICE TO APPLICANT
Please read carefully

International Business Services reaffirms its commitment to the policy of equal opportunity in employment regardless of race, color, religion, creed, age, gender, national origin, physical or mental disability, or veteran status in accordance with applicable federal and state statutes and regulations.

All information given by me in this application is true. I understand that false information (misrepresentation or omission of information) will disqualify me for employment or cause my subsequent dismissal. I authorize investigation of all statements contained herein. I also authorize the employers and/or references listed (exceptions noted under Employment History) to release any and all information concerning my previous employment and any pertinent information they may have and release all parties from any liability for any damages that may result from furnishing such information.

Signature of Applicant _____   Date _____

EDUCATIONAL HISTORY

Circle last grade completed in elementary or high school   Name and Location (City/State) of Last High School _____

1 2 3 4 5 6 7 8 9 10 11 12 ☐ GED

SCHOOL NAME/LOCATION	Dates Attended		Credit Hours Completed	Type of Degree Earned	Curriculum	
	From	To			Major	Minor
College or University:						
College or University:						
Other Training (Business, Vocational, or Technical School)						

Have you taken any additional courses or attended any seminars which have a bearing on the job for which you are applying? _____

OTHER IMPORTANT INFORMATION

Specify office machines that you can operate and years of experience (if applicable to position for which you are applying).

	Shorthand	Typing
	WPM	WPM
	W/Processing	Data Entry
	WPM	WPM

Specify word processing or computer equipment you can operate and years of experience (if applicable to position for which you are applying).

Specify computer software you can use (if applicable to position for which you are applying).

Specify other equipment you can operate and years of experience (if applicable to position for which you are applying).

Have you ever been convicted of anything other than minor traffic violations?   ☐ NO ☐ YES

Have you ever been warned about, disciplined, or discharged for sexual harassment, fighting, assault, or related offenses?   ☐ NO ☐ YES

Have you ever been warned about, disciplined, or discharged for violating safety rules?   ☐ NO ☐ YES

If you answered yes to any of the above, please explain on a separate sheet of paper.

Note: A conviction will not necessarily bar you from employment. Each conviction will be judged on its own merits with respect to time, circumstance, and seriousness.

FIGURE 7.3 Example of an employment application form (*continued*)

RECORD OF EMPLOYMENT

Fill in completely, beginning with current or last position held.
THIS SECTION MUST BE COMPLETED EVEN IF A RESUME IS ATTACHED.

Name of current or last employer & address (include city and state)

☐ Full-Time ☐ Part-Time

Hours worked per week

Type of Business/Name of Supervisor		Starting Date	Leaving Date
Job Title	Phone Number	Starting Pay	Ending Pay

Reason for Leaving

Description of Work and Responsibilities

Name of next previous employer & address (include city and state)

☐ Full-Time ☐ Part-Time

Hours worked per week

Type of Business/Name of Supervisor		Starting Date	Leaving Date
Job Title	Phone Number	Starting Pay	Ending Pay

Reason for Leaving

Description of Work and Responsibilities

MAY WE CONTACT ALL EMPLOYERS/SUPERVISORS LISTED? ☐ YES ☐ NO

Indicate exceptions: _____

REFERENCES

Please provide the names of three additional references.

1. _____ Name _____ Address/Telephone No. _____ Position

2. _____ Name _____ Address/Telephone No. _____ Position

3. _____ Name _____ Address/Telephone No. _____ Position

ADDITIONAL INFORMATION

Please give any additional information which may more fully describe your qualifications, skills, experience, education, background, and interests.

If more space is needed, please attach additional sheets

3. **Complete preliminary screening.** The preliminary manual screening of the application ensures that minimum requirements as specified on the position approval form have been met by each candidate. Normally, a human resources specialist performs this step. The purpose of the screening process is to eliminate any applicants early in the process who do not meet the minimum requirements as stated in the position approval form, which will save time and which could facilitate the process.

4. **Administer employment tests.** Employers are relying more on aptitude tests and personality tests to ensure that new employees have the necessary skills and personality for the job. However, managers must be careful in using these tests because of possible litigation based on Title VII of the Civil Rights Act of 1964, and as amended in 1972, which forbids discrimination due to race, color, religion, sex, or national origin. Further, the Civil Rights Act of 1991 also explicitly made the use of test scores for discrimination purposes illegal. If the applicant meets minimum qualifications for the job, a variety of tests may be administered to assess the applicant's job-related aptitudes and skills. Aptitude, ability, and work sample tests are three of the more common testing instruments used to screen applicants.

- *Aptitude test.* This is a paper-and-pencil or computer-generated test that measures general ability to learn or to acquire a skill. Example: Sales or marketing aptitude test.

- *Ability test.* This is also a paper-and-pencil or computer-generated test that assesses the skills the candidate has learned. Example: English or math ability.

- *Work sample test.* This performance-based test requires an applicant to perform a simulated job task that the position requires the applicant to be able to do on the job. Example: Using a computer to produce a form letter, a financial statement, a multiple-row table, or a simple brochure. Currently, employers test for quantifiable skills (such as computer knowledge and clerical skills) and personal qualities (such as honesty or emotional intelligence).

    As pre-employment tests become more common—and shift from a paper-and-pencil method to online computerized exams—employers may have to work with the following issues to ensure that their tests are both equitable and effective. Problems such as technology glitches or security issues also may surface in completing online applications or testing.

- *Age and Education.* Age and education levels often are significant determinants when it comes to comfort with technology. As the population ages, employers may need to structure computer- or online-based testing around the needs of an aging work force. The same may be true regarding education levels of applicants with respect to technology know-how.

- *Technological glitches.* Unlike a paper and pencil test, if a company server crashes while the applicant is taking an online test from a remote location, the applicant most likely will have no proof that the computer lost his or her test. Sometimes the computer will end the test if the applicant makes certain keying errors or strikes the "back key." This could create problems for the testee as well as the company.

- *Security.* As long as there have been tests, unfortunately, there has been cheating. And as more testing is offered online, and applicants are able to take tests from anywhere, the security of the testing situation becomes that much more critical. Finding a way to ensure that the person testing is the applicant may present technology or security problems for the organization.

- *Cost.* Cost savings is usually one of the advantages of any new technology. But people often forget that most savings occur over time. Computer- and online-based testing may be much more expensive in the short-term start-up costs than paper-and-pencil tests.[2]

5. **Conduct job interview.** An interview is designed to assess job-related knowledge, skills, and abilities and to clarify information from other sources. Table 7.1 lists nine hints administrative managers should keep in mind when conducting the employment interview. As an AM, you may choose to select other colleagues to serve with you as part of an interview team, or you may choose to conduct the interview yourself. Whichever approach you take, you will need to prepare your interview questions ahead of time. Moreover, to be fair and legal according to Equal Employment Opportunity Commission rulings, the same set of interview questions must be used during each job candidate's interview. Standardized questions are fair to all candidates, and the responses are more easily compared. Three types of interview questions commonly used are **structured, situational,** and **behavioral.** These questions may be open-ended (requiring a longer answer) or closed-ended (requiring a yes or no or a brief answer to the question). Descriptions and examples of interview questions for each type are shown below.

- *Structured interview questions.* These questions are typically asked of each applicant:

  - How does your experience qualify you for this job?

  - Please take a few minutes and tell us about yourself. Conclude your response with a statement summarizing your preparation for this job.

- *Situational interview questions.* These questions are related to the job requirements and knowledge, training, and education needed for the position that is being advertised:

  - Are you proficient in Microsoft Word applications?

TABLE 7.1 Hints for the Employment Interviewer

- Establish the objectives and scope of each interview.

- Establish and maintain rapport with each candidate.

- Pay attention to body language and nonverbal cues given by the candidate in his or her responses to questions. Nervousness is natural, but a candidate who is overly shaken or lacking in composure may indicate that he or she is not qualified for the position.

- Provide information about the job and company as accurately and honestly as possible when asked. Candidates may ask about promotional opportunities or rumors that have circulated in the community if the company is being considered for sale or bankruptcy.

- Control the course of the interview to ensure all objectives are met.

- Separate facts from inferences as candidates respond to questions.

- Use questions effectively and consistently with all candidates.

- Keep careful notes to refer to before selecting the best applicant. Note taking may make the candidate nervous. Develop a method of taking notes that is easily done, such as having a checklist or other type of form that can be used effectively and quickly. Don't make any notes about an applicant's gender, sex, race, religion, color, or national origin, even if the candidate volunteers such information. These notes could be used in a lawsuit if you were ever accused of discriminatory hiring practices. In addition, for the same reasons, don't make any notes about the applicant's dress or personal appearance.

- End the interview effectively by asking the candidate if he/she has any questions and telling the candidate when the hiring decision will be made.

- Can you operate a scanner?

- Suppose you worked for two bosses, and both came to you with a rush project that had to be completed in the next two hours. How would you proceed if you only had time to do one of the projects?

- If you were required to take minutes at evening meetings (not to exceed three nights per month), would this job requirement give you concern?

- *Behavioral interview questions.* These questions usually elicit a response detailing how the applicant did a job in the past or performed a particular task. Sample questions include:

- Describe a work situation where you took a project from start to finish and were complimented on the results.

- Have you ever had an ethical dilemma on the job? If so, describe the nature of the dilemma and how you dealt with it. What was the result of this dilemma?

The **Affirmative Action Program** provides guidelines to eliminate discrimination in the employment selection process. As such, the job interview must avoid areas that could inadvertently be the source of legal violations. Unless the information you seek is directly related to job performance, questions in certain areas are viewed as an abridgement of equal employment opportunity and have legal consequences for the institution. The Equal Employment Opportunity Commission considers 14 areas of discussion particularly sensitive and unacceptable as shown in Table 7.2.

6. ***Check references and verify prior employment.*** Before extending a job offer to the top candidate, attempt to conduct background checks on prior employment and references. A background check may be conducted by HR or a service agency may be hired. Private investigators and others in similar businesses often perform background checks for a fee. The reference checks are usually very good sources of information and can help confirm or question any impressions you have formed about the candidate. Typically, the

manager that the successful candidate reports to will check references. This can be accomplished through a telephone conversation or by sending a request for a reference by mail. Some companies have a special form to be sent to request reference information. This information must relate only to information that is nondiscriminatory about the potential candidate. Any discriminatory information must be ignored.

7. ***Give physical exams.*** If applicable and depending on the nature of the job, a medical examination and/or drug test may be appropriate parts of the selection process for the top candidate before final acceptance or rejection of the job offer by either party. For example, a school district might require a drug test for school bus drivers to safeguard children who are being transported from home to school. The AM, of course, does not give this exam but may help the applicant secure an appointment with the company doctor if one is provided or suggest another doctor in the community.

Finally, with any job selection process it is a good idea to take some time to review all information about the top candidate before extending any job offer. By the end of this seven-step process, you have collected substantial data on each of the candidates from many sources. Remember to recheck the

TABLE 7.2 Legal Considerations During Job Interviews

Questions Regarding	Avoid
Age	All questions designed to discover age. The only permissible question is whether the applicant is over the state minimum legal employment age of 18 (special regulations apply to minors under age 18).
Arrest Record	All questions relating to arrests.
Citizenship/National Origin	All questions relating to citizenship, lineage, ancestry, national origin, descent, birthplace, mother tongue.
Education	All questions relating to a degree when a degree is not necessary for the job.
Financial/Credit Status	All questions about financial condition/credit rating. May ask about minimum salary requirements.
Gender or Sex-linked Information/Sexual Orientation	All comments about gender. If you would not ask a question of a man, do not ask it of a woman, and vice versa.
Health/Disability	All questions about health not related to specific job requirements; disabilities and nature/severity of disabilities.
Marital/Family Status/ Child Care Needs	All questions about whether the applicant is married, single, divorced, number and age of children, child care needs, or spouse's job.
Military/Veteran Status	All questions about type or condition of discharge.
Organizations	All questions relating to organizations whose names or character may indicate economic or social class, race, sex, marital status, religion.
Pregnancy	All questions about pregnancy or medical history concerning pregnancy.
Race or Color	All questions about race or color.
Religion	All questions to indicate or identify religious denomination or customs.
Residence	All questions regarding renting or owning a home.

Digital Vision

information on the application forms, transcripts of courses taken or degrees and certificates received, interviews, tests, reference checks, and medical exam. Selecting the right employee is critical to your success as the manager, to the organization, and to the person you hire. Once employees have been selected and report for work, provide a series of orientation activities to ensure the success of the employee and the organization.

EMPLOYEE ORIENTATION

Orientation is a meeting or the formal activity that specifically prepares employees for working in a particular organization and working environment. An orientation meeting can be formal, with several new hires in a conference room, or it can be informal, with the supervisor or another employee on a one-on-one basis. Regardless of the method, however, an orientation meeting is a necessary first step for every new employee.

In general, a good orientation should provide information about the physical workplace, policies, procedures, and expected performance, as well as routine information such as payroll arrangements, breaks, benefits, and working hours. Some orientations also prepare the new hire with a review of policy and procedures manuals, an introduction to other employees, a review of emergency procedures relative to safety or weather conditions, and a preview of upcoming training programs.

In many organizations, the responsibility for new employee orientation is shared between the human resources department and the administrative manager. When this occurs, it is important to clarify what topic

The success of an employee's first week on the job is as important to the company as it is to the employee.

each person will discuss. Table 7.3 provides a checklist to follow when conducting an orientation. This checklist is divided according to the items covered by the human resources department and those normally covered by the AM.

Normally, the human resources department explains the conditions of employment, security requirements, and how pay and benefits will be dispensed. A human resources specialist also may provide a tour of the facilities and give each new hire an orientation packet containing necessary forms to complete and other information new employees need to know. To get some idea of what is included in an orientation packet, an example of a cover transmittal memorandum describing the contents of the orientation packet is shown in Figure 7.4.

When the human resources department is finished with its portion of the employee orientation, the AM discusses with the new employee the job duties, hours of work, and how overtime, sick leave, absences, and

TABLE 7.3 Employee Orientation Checklist

Human Resources Department	Administrative Manager
First Day of Work:	**First Day of Work:**
Ask employee to fill out the following forms (if applicable in your state):	Introduce to coworkers.
• I-9 employment eligibility verification	Tour department and show around work area (coat closet, restroom, break room, copy and fax machines, etc.).
• W-4 federal income tax withholding form	Discuss specific working hours relative to lunch, breaks, starting and stopping the workday, and overtime.
• A-4 state income tax withholding form	Clarify parking and dress issues.
• Employee information sheet; employment contract, if any	Discuss use of electronic equipment, e-mail, and how infractions are handled.
• Loyalty oath or confidentiality agreements	**Second Day of Work:**
• Retirement enrollment form	Introduce to "buddy" who will then mentor new employee.
• Group insurance enrollment and other benefit forms	Discuss training programs.
Discuss the following:	Clarify questions regarding job duties or contents of employment contract.
• Time cards	Discuss emergency contingency plans (medical, power failure, fire, personal safety, etc.).
• Pay dates	**Second Week of Work:**
• Direct deposit availability	Discuss any questions the new employee has relative to the content in the employee handbook.
• Attendance policies	
Distribute employee handbook; new employees sign form showing receipt.	
Give tour of facilities and discuss emergency evacuation procedures.	

FIGURE 7.4 Some orientation items must be signed and returned promptly.

INTERNATIONAL BUSINESS SERVICES
MEMORANDUM

To: New Employee

From: Human Resources Department

Welcome to International Business Services and best of luck in your new position! The enclosed information and forms have been gathered together to provide you with a practical introduction to the employment environment at IBS, and also to ensure a timely collection of necessary paperwork to initiate your official status as an employee. If you have any questions, please feel free to contact us any time during business hours at (602) 555-8314.

The following items must be completed and on file with the Human Resources office within 3 days after your starting date:

_____ I-9 Employment Eligibility Verification
         (You must present your social security card and a photo ID in person at the Human Resources
         office to properly complete this form.)

_____ W-4 Federal Income Tax Withholding form

_____ A-4 Arizona State Income Tax Withholding form

_____ IBS Employee Information Sheet

_____ Selective Service Certification Statement

_____ Loyalty Oath

_____ Group Insurance Enrollment Forms

These following items are provided for your information and convenience:

_____ Direct Department Authorization

_____ Most Recent *Human Resources Update*

_____ Benefits Summary Sheet

_____ List of Paydays and Holidays

_____ Essential Policy Information
         (Affirmative Action, Drug-Free Workplace, Sexual Harassment)

_____ Pamphlets on Vision Care, Prescription Options, and Managed Care

_____ Medical and Dental Insurance Certificate Booklets and ID Cards

tardiness will be handled. Usually, it is at this time that the new employee is introduced to current employees and is shown workplace facilities including his or her desk area, the break room, and the restroom.

A popular practice in some organizations is to use a buddy system to supplement the new employee orientation process. The **buddy system** matches a new employee with an experienced employee who maintains close contact with the new employee and lends support by answering routine questions. This system could be set up to cover the first few weeks of employment or for a longer period of time, based on the needs of the new employee. Psychologically, this system is believed to have significant advantages for new employees by relieving anxiety and stimulating the feeling of belonging. In general, many new employees seem more comfortable asking a peer questions rather than an immediate supervisor. The seasoned employee chosen for this buddy system should also feel honored to participate in the system. Being so chosen is based on being good at one's job. Publicity for the buddy system should emphasize that this is a system acknowledging the worker's expertise, not just extra work. Some additional compensation or item (such as a plaque, dinner) can be presented to the participants at a company or departmental meeting.

Regardless of whether a company uses a follow-up "buddy" system approach or whether a second orientation session with new employees is scheduled, a systematic orientation program should have some follow-up to clarify questions the new employee may have after spending some time on the job. Orientation should be seen as a continuous process because organizations are constantly undergoing changes and employees need to be informed of new processes that will affect their attitude and success on the job.

First impressions count. When you bring a new player on board, Day One counts, possibly more than any other day does. Administrative managers should have a detailed plan for the first day of each new hire's employment. During this brief window of time, a manager either ignites the new hires' imagination and motivation or sets them on an uncertain path. Experiences on the first day of work often determine whether new hires will become productive employees or revolving-door memories.

For new employees to connect with the company, they need to bond with their manager. When managers take these seven steps before new hires arrive, they increase the odds that the candidates will feel they made the right career choice.

1. *Alert Existing Staff to the Start Date and Its Role.* Make sure current employees know the new hire's start date, responsibilities, title, and qualifications summary. Ask the new employee's peers what would make the first days easier, and have them create a calendar of events for the new person, detailing each employee's role. Determine who will make introductions, who will give a tour of the department and greater organization—preferably you with another employee—and who will walk the new employee through his/her job.

2. *Set a Positive Tone of Anticipation.* When someone new is being added, each staff member wonders, "What's in it for me?" Talk to your staff to set the stage for positive relationships and to ensure any questions are answered. Having information about the new employee may help current employees welcome the new staff member.

3. *Send Paperwork for Completion in Advance.* Even if you have to pay the new employee for time taken, sending him/her payroll and insurance enrollment forms before the first day will help establish your organization's professional tone. The positive first impression is worth the extra effort and dollars.

4. *Enable Access in Advance.* If security badges, parking stickers, or copier or computer system access are required, greet the new hire with everything he or she needs. Tell the information technology department and security about the new hire, and ask the receptionist to welcome him/her and alert you upon arrival.

5. *Set up the Work Area.* Ensure the new hire's work area, including keyboard and desk, is clean. Remove irrelevant files and provide paper clips, scissors, pens, and folders. A clean, well-stocked workstation says, "We're ready. Are you?"

6. *Schedule Necessary Skills Training.* Most employees need training in sexual harassment prevention, computer database access rights, voice-mail procedures, e-mail and online calendaring systems, along with a review of how to operate other equipment. If it is essential for job success, schedule the new hire's training early.

7. *Be there.* New hires should be welcomed by their new manager. This is a big day for the new person, and you're his or her new boss. Not being there sends the wrong message. The first day is one of the most negotiable items during the hiring process. So if necessary, delay the start date until required appointments in your schedule are cleared.[3]

Once oriented on the job, most employees need to upgrade skills periodically to stay current. Successful administrative managers understand their role in training as critical to the success of the organizations. Providing adequate training is another way to develop and motivate employees.

EMPLOYEE TRAINING

Training is intended to improve individual work performance by equipping people with the knowledge, skills, and attitudes they must possess to be successful in their work.[4] Familiarity with the systems approach to training and the various methods available for training is important for success on the job for both an administrative manager and the employee.

The Systems Approach to Training

Before meaningful training can occur, the organization needs to assess what the training needs are and then develop, design, and make arrangements for delivering educational programs for employees at *all* levels. How is this best done? The **systems approach to training** emphasizes formulating instructional objectives, developing learning activities to meet those objectives, establishing performance criteria to be met, and evaluating the results of training. Table 7.4 shows the necessary activities involved in each phase of planning and assessing training needs, developing training plans and instructional delivery, and evaluating training according to this formalized systems approach. The administrative manager would be assisted by members of the human resources department in developing each phase of the process. Coordination of each phase of training is important.

TABLE 7.4 Systems Approach to Training

Emphasis of Systems Approach to Training

- To formulate instructional objectives.
- To develop learning experiences that achieve those objectives.
- To establish performance criteria to be met.
- To obtain evaluative information.

Phase I Assessment of Training	Phase II Training and Development	Phase III Evaluation of Training
Steps:	Steps:	Steps:
Analyze organizational needs (who requires what, any problem areas, etc.).	Develop the training environment to effectively achieve the objectives.	Evaluate based on the objectives of the training.
Analyze the tasks of the job (difficulty of learning, how performed, etc.).	Determine what methods and interactive media will be most effective in delivering the instruction.	Give trainees a pre-test and a post-test and compare the results.
Analyze what characteristics, skills, knowledge, and attitudes are needed in the person doing the specific job.	Deliver the training or development program.	Ask for feedback from trainees at the end of the program and again in three to six months to determine if training objectives were met.
Develop instructional objectives.	Critique the effectiveness of the training and what improvements are needed and how they will be put into practice.	Compare performance with supervisors' evaluation of employees on appraisal forms.

Methods of Training

The companies that train best deliver instruction when and where the employee needs it—sometimes training is in a classroom, sometimes by satellite TV, or sometimes on the worker's personal computer from a training CD or online training subscription. It should be noted that one of the downsides of computer-based classes is the absence of a human instructor, who responds spontaneously to student questions, tailors classes to specific situations, and adjusts the class to the students' best pace.[5] Regardless, however, the most effective training is concise and interactive, interspersed with group projects, role-playing, and hands-on experiences. In general, AMs can train employees on the job or use a wide selection of outside training sources. Locating inside and outside training resources takes time, but it is a necessary part of a manager's job in some companies.

On-the-Job Training (OJT) This training is best described as "learning by doing." Organizations provide a variety of in-house training programs, such as one-on-one supervisor training, job rotation, computer-assisted instruction, special projects or assignments, and mentoring.

The two main advantages of OJT are that production is carried on while the employee is being trained and OJT results in low out-of-pocket costs. On the other hand, the major disadvantages of OJT are the poor learning environment, which can be one of interruptions and other working distractions, and the awareness by the employee that work still has to get done—after training or after hours—or a backlog will occur.

To realize maximum performance, most workers expect OJT coaching on how to do their jobs well. As an effective manager, you will want to recognize an employee's need for effective performance feedback and systematically follow through in providing it. Giving feedback helps employees understand what training may be needed and how the training may benefit them and their jobs. When effective job-skill training is conducted, some of the time-tested coaching steps used by a manager or trainer include:

1. Explain the purpose and importance of what you are trying to teach.
2. Explain the process you will use.
3. Show how the process is done.
4. Observe while the person practices the process.
5. Provide immediate and specific feedback.
6. Express confidence in the person's ability to be successful.
7. Agree on follow-up actions.

Many companies have brought their training activities in-house as a result of downsizing and cost reductions. In doing so, these companies utilize other employee experts to train other employees on a wide range of issues. Peer experts are often more effective because of their personal knowledge of a particular company's job processes. In addition, companies find that a colleague's presence and availability to others help build stronger working relationships. To support effective in-house training, many companies offer **train-the-trainer workshops**. These workshops teach peer experts how to teach using interactive and instructional skills and can be conducted by trainers within the organization or by contracting with an outside training source to provide this training.

Outside Training

Outside training occurs when learners are sent to some outside source, such as a school, college, professional workshop or seminar, or equipment manufacturer to learn or upgrade aspects of the job. For instance, learning the graphics program CorelDRAW® at a community college is an example of outside training.

Because organizations realize how important training is to their eventual success, many companies provide total or partial educational benefits, such as payments for tuition, fees, and books to defray costs associated with employees attending off-site training. Moreover, if the training is directly applicable to work, it is cost-effective for companies to release employees during the workday to attend job-related classes.

COUNSELING AND DISCIPLINING EMPLOYEES

Counseling and, if necessary, disciplining employees are actions administrative managers will perform. However, it should be noted that good leadership and motivational skills (which will be covered later in the book) on the AM's part tend to have a minimizing effect on the need to counsel and discipline in the workplace.

Counseling Employees

As an AM, you may need to perform employee counseling in a number of areas. Primary counseling occasions include consultations about job performance, career

planning, safety, layoffs, termination, and retirement. Other areas of a more personal nature are counseling about physical, mental, or emotional illness, substance abuse problems, hygiene, dress codes, and use of company property. Since most AMs are not qualified to counsel on many of these topics, a list of referral agencies is always a good idea to have available.

Critical to on-the-job counseling is centering the dialogue *only* on job performance. Do not get personal. Give specific counseling comments, rather than general ones. For example, instead of saying, "You have to do more work," say instead, "Your work output must increase 20 percent to reach minimum standards." Or, instead of saying, "You have got to do a better job of communicating with me," say instead, "You must notify me in advance when you cannot keep an appointment or are going to be late."

If you are counseling a troubled employee who needs more than you can offer, point out to him/her the availability of internal or external counseling services and further explain that only the employee can decide whether to seek assistance. Emphasize the confidentiality of your conversation, but do not leave until you get a commitment from the employee to meet specific work criteria that will be monitored in line with a plan for improvement based on work performance.

To make counseling more effective, act natural and listen attentively. The benefits of effective job counseling, you should see these changes in the worker:

- A reduction in anxiety, fear, and distrust,
- More cooperation, and

- A sense of direction that stimulates personal growth, often expressed by employees as one of their goals.

Handling Discipline Problems

When performance problems are ignored, they don't go away. They turn into bigger problems—for you and your organization. The cost of unsatisfactory job performance is staggering—and often comes in ways that are hard to measure. Performance is sometimes hindered by procrastination. To avoid this outcome, the employees and managers should look at the consequences of poor quality work or missed deadlines, review carefully reasons or explanations given by employees for loss of a customer or a missed deadline, and know that losing face is something that no one likes to experience. Delegate and give pep talks before productivity begins to drop. [6]

Generally, problem employees are those with bad attitudes, those who are unskilled, or those who are simply misdirected. These three exhibit the following set of behaviors:

- *The bad attitudes.* Employees with bad attitudes complain constantly, and their dismal outlook negatively affects others. Often they have the skills to do their work well, but they fall short when it comes to enthusiasm, energy, and commitment.

- *The unskilled.* These workers just don't have the skills they need. Maybe their jobs have outgrown them. Maybe they never had the skills, and it's becoming more and more apparent. Or perhaps the main skill they're lacking is good judgment.

- *The misdirected.* These employees aren't really problem employees at all. They work hard and demonstrate their commitment. Unfortunately, they're confused about what you expect. Or they've gotten distracted from their goals. They'll be happy to perform if you can help them find the way. Simplify the problem with clear standards, realistic action plans, and progressive discipline. [7]

Every organization's objective should be to reduce the need for discipline, but if discipline becomes necessary, it should be administered immediately after the infraction in a fair, consistent, impersonal manner and only after advance warning has been given to the employee. Once discipline has been administered, follow up is necessary to ensure improvement is taking place or to ensure that the discipline has been followed through correctly and enforced. Making a calendar note to check on the worker's progress is often helpful.

Categories of Discipline Problems

Organizations generally classify discipline problems according to their severity. In other words, AMs must first determine whether the behavior is a minor infraction, a major violation, or an intolerable offense. AMs must determine whether a verbal discussion or written charge is needed and whether it must be noted in the employee's files. In the majority of cases, a written note in the file is necessary.

- *Minor Infractions.* These instances do little harm but may become serious when they happen frequently. Some examples include absenteeism and tardiness.

- *Major Violations.* These actions are disciplinary problems that substantially interfere with orderly operation of a business; for example, major violations include violating safety rules, stealing, failure to carry out an order, and lying.

- *Intolerable Offenses.* These misconducts are disciplinary problems of such drastic, dangerous, or illegal nature that they endanger employment relationships. Possession of deadly weapons and use of drugs on the job are examples of intolerable offenses.

Progressive Discipline Discipline should be dispensed in a progressive way. Figure 7.5 shows that before an employee can be discharged, a sequence of steps must take place. These could be one or more warnings, a written reprimand, or a suspension. Care must be taken to follow due process in any disciplinary action. Table 7.5 provides some factors to consider when determining whether due process was followed.

FIGURE 7.5   An AM must follow procedures before discharging an employee.

Progressive Discipline

PERFORMANCE APPRAISALS

Performance appraisals have the potential to advance or derail careers. As a supervisor, you will notice your employees' attitudes, their performances, and their work habits nearly every day. That is your job. Eventually, you will use these observations as a basis for employee performance appraisals.

Annual performance reviews of employees are an effective and necessary management tool. Reviews should document employee shortcomings as legal protection in case of a dismissal. Fairness and consistency are key requirements when conducting reviews. When conducting performance appraisals, AMs need to understand what the objectives of an appraisal are, how to prepare for and conduct review activities, and what outcomes to expect at the conclusion of the appraisal process. Employees also need to be aware of the appraisal process and understand its objectives.

T A B L E   7 . 5   Was Due Process Followed?

When handling disciplinary problems, consider these factors and ask yourself if due process was followed:

Did the employee have prior warning that his or her conduct would result in disciplinary action, including possible discharge?

Was the misconduct related to the safe, efficient, and orderly operation of the organization?

Was an investigation held?

Was the investigation fair and objective?

Did the investigation obtain circumstantial evidence that the employee was guilty?

Was the disciplinary action nondiscriminatory?

Was the disciplinary action reasonably related to the seriousness of the offense and the employee's record with the organization?

Note: YES answers to these questions indicate that due process was followed.

Objectives of an Appraisal

The objectives of a performance appraisal are to:

1. Recognize subordinates for outstanding performance;
2. Help subordinates improve performance;
3. Change behavior; and
4. Provide data for making personnel decisions involving compensation, promotion, training and development, and discipline or termination.

Certain conditions must be present for an employee to feel he or she has been given a fair performance appraisal. The manager must adequately observe the employee, understand the job requirements, and have a fair and appropriate point of view. Most importantly, a performance appraisal should

never surprise the employee. Never save criticism or compliments for the once-a-year review. Constantly and consistently counsel or praise the employee throughout the year. Neither should employees be surprised as to the timing of the appraisals. A set time for each appraisal should be made, communicated to the employees, and adhered to. Copies of the last appraisal should be available as part of the appraisal process.

Conducting an Appraisal

Imagine you are going to be giving a performance appraisal tomorrow morning. What steps might you take to prepare?

1. You might first want to prepare for the appraisal by completing the performance appraisal form and by anticipating the

© Getty Images/PhotoDisc

The setting for an appraisal should put the employee at ease.

tone of the conference (friendly, stressful, or otherwise) as well as what you want to accomplish for the good of the company and employee when the appraisal is over. Figure 7.6 shows an example of a performance appraisal form.

2. Then, you could make performance and development of the employee your major concern. In other words, think ahead and reflect on the employee's past job performance. Be prepared with specific examples that will clarify the reasons for your ratings should the employee question your evaluative judgments.

3. Finally, anticipate and decide on the specific steps that you will suggest the employee take to improve performance on the job. Set a convenient time and date with the employee to review performance within the next week or so.

Delivering constructive criticism during a performance evaluation requires a tactful

approach and is generally difficult for most managers to do. You must, however, present any problems you have observed strongly enough to elicit a desired change in behavior. Yet, you do not want to spark resentment or undermine your employee's confidence by being too harsh. Practice and a caring approach are required in order to create a sensitive balance.

How do you meet this challenge? Most managers find it helpful to start by giving positive feedback about the employee's work before bringing up the negatives. By planning ahead and organizing the sequence and timing of your comments, your delivery of the appraisal will be clearer and better received.

If your criticism is accepted as justified, reiterate your confidence in the employee by scheduling a meeting within a few weeks or a month to review his or her progress. If, on the other hand, the employee denies that there is a problem or gets angry, try to get beyond the reflexive response. Provide specific examples of the performance problem and ask about any obstacles that may

have stood in the employee's way of being successful on the job. Active participation by the employee is necessary for a performance evaluation to be objective and useful.

Outcomes of Appraisals

A positive performance evaluation allows an employee to capitalize on the moment by asking for additional responsibilities that could lead to a promotion or a substantial raise. If, on the other hand, an employee had an "off" year, it is smart to lessen the damage by demonstrating how a program of improvement will begin.

FIGURE 7.6 Administrative support performance appraisal form

INTERNATIONAL BUSINESS SERVICES
PERFORMANCE APPRAISAL
Administrative Support

NAME: _____ POSITION: _____

PLEASE EVALUATE THE EMPLOYEE'S PERFORMANCE AGAINST THE FOLLOWING PERFORMANCE FACTORS. Circle the numerical rating: 5. Outstanding 4. Good 3. Satisfactory 2. Fair 1. Unsatisfactory. Circle NO (not observed) if unable to evaluate the item. Each factor rating must be explained in the justification comment section.

PERFORMANCE CRITERIA AREA	Rating	COMMENTS
KNOWLEDGE OF THE WORK Understanding of the various phases, knowledge of the technical fundamentals of the position. Understands work output relationships and interdependencies within IBS.	5 4 3 2 1 NO	
QUALITY OF WORK Thoroughness, neatness, accuracy, completeness.	5 4 3 2 1 NO	
QUANTITY OF WORK Amount of work accomplished, ability to function effectively within time or work schedule, prompt completion of work.	5 4 3 2 1 NO	
INITIATIVE Ability to act on his/her own. Displays understanding of task or project and moves forward on own.	5 4 3 2 1 NO	
CARRY OUT INSTRUCTIONS Willingness and ability to take instructions and effectively follow through. Makes positive effort to suggest task/process improvement.	5 4 3 2 1 NO	
ATTITUDE Accepts suggestions, responsibility, improves work techniques. Displays cooperative, positive behavior patterns. Exerts positive influences on morale of co-workers. Exhibits effective interpersonal skills that contribute to department team goals and to IBS's mission.	5 4 3 2 1 NO	
ATTENDANCE/PUNCTUALITY Consistency in avoiding absenteeism and tardiness. Provides adequate notice of absence.	5 4 3 2 1 NO	
OVERALL EVALUATION	5 4 3 2 1 NO	

MAJOR STRENGTHS AND/OR WEAK AREAS NEEDING IMPROVEMENT—RECOMMENDATIONS
(ATTACH ADDITIONAL NARRATIVE SUMMARY SHEET, IF REQUIRED)

Signature _____ _____
　　　　　　SUPERVISOR　　　　　　　　　　　　　DATE

Signature _____ _____
　　　　　　EMPLOYEE　　　　　　　　　　　　　　DATE

Note: By signing this form, the employee acknowledges only that this evaluation was discussed and a copy has been received. It does not necessarily signify the employee concurs with the evaluation.

If a performance appraisal backfires, the manager should consider why it was unsuccessful. Could it be that:

- The manager lacks interviewing skills?
- Too many forms must be completed?
- Rater bias exists?
- There is no top-management support of the rating or consequences?
- The judgmental and helping roles of the manager conflict?

There are a number of personnel actions that can be taken as a result of a performance appraisal. On the positive side, the employee can be rewarded with a pay increase, a promotion, additional training, or a career move. On the negative side, the employee can be laid off or discharged.

EMPLOYEE TURNOVER AND RETENTION

Turnover costs a fortune. When workers leave their jobs in the business world it is referred to as **turnover**. You've got recruiting costs; interviewing, checking, and testing costs; orientation costs; and transitional time spent getting new employees on board. Customers lose their contacts when regular employees leave and generally morale sinks when other employees have to pick up the slack. Clients, competitors, and sometimes the media think there's something wrong at the company.[8] The U.S. Department of Labor conservatively estimates the cost of turnover to be 30 percent of each new hire's annual salary.[9] Though turnover is a natural occurrence in all organizations, it should be minimized as much as possible by retaining good employees for a good amount of time.

To obtain that end, companies no longer view employees as workers simply meant to carry out tasks according to their job descriptions. Companies now view workers as knowledge experts with specific, individual competencies that, when harnessed and further developed, drive corporate success.

To understand the need to reduce employee turnover, let's explore some reasons employees leave their jobs:

- Poor compensation
- Poor working conditions
- Inadequate training
- Relationship with their direct supervisors
- Feeling underappreciated or overworked
- Need for a more flexible working arrangement

When a company spends more money to replace workers than to retain them, it may be time to reassess hiring policies, career development tracks, and compensation scales. Companies need to work harder to find ways to retain good employees. Although most managers agree that the following employee retention techniques alone will not keep employees on board, these low-cost ideas are a necessary piece of a company's retention puzzle. Most employees won't use all of these techniques, but if even a few good workers are retained, it is well worth it.

- Provide flexible hours and other non-traditional work arrangements
- Encourage employees to train other employees
- Create and communicate clear career paths

- Update workers with cutting-edge technology and training opportunities
- Emphasize the value of benefits package
- Instill a supportive culture, and
- Offer small gifts and cash prizes for outstanding employee attitudes and performance.

While there are no guarantees, the following practices can help organizations hire and retain the best employees:

- Integrate recruiting and retention goals into the annual planning process.
- Develop a "joining up" program to track new hires. Make sure their entry into the organization goes well and that their

expectations are met. This is usually accomplished through a series of meetings over the first six months between employer and employee. Follow-up meetings throughout the first year will help employees connect to the company.

- Create a talent database that tracks specifics about your workers' talents and accomplishments, and identifies critical skill sets and gaps.
- Provide incentives that are based on years of service with the organization as a retention tool.
- Ask your best workers periodically about whether their expectations are being met—and how to recruit others like them.

MESSAGE FOR MANAGERS

Issues that affect workers on the job are as varied as they are many. An administrative manager is not expected to perform in an exemplary fashion 100 percent of the time. However, the AM is expected to understand organizational processes and know where to find answers to common workplace questions and on-the-job issues of concern to employees.

Read as many articles as you can from either online sources or from newspapers, magazines, and journals to stay updated on better approaches to improve your "people" skills. In addition, network with other managers in and out of your company by attending trade shows, conferences, and seminars. Chances are your colleagues will want to share ideas and

talk through problems with you as much as you do with them. One final suggestion: find a person you admire and regard highly. Study the techniques and attributes that draw you to that person. If it feels right to both of you, propose a mentoring relationship to help you become a better manager and stay focused on ways to improve yourself on the job.

Chapter Seven

S U M M A R Y

1. Employment recruitment is the process of generating a pool of qualified applicants for organizational job vacancies, both internally and externally.

2. Various external recruiting sources are available, which include computerized online job announcements, private and public employment agencies, temporary employment services, college placement offices, and job fairs.

3. The selection process includes the following seven steps: a) forward position requisition, b) complete application form, c) complete preliminary screening, d) administer employment tests, e) conduct job interview, f) check references and verify prior employment, and g) give physical exams.

4. The Affirmative Action Program provides guidelines to eliminate discrimination in the employment selection process. Unless the information you seek is directly related to job performance, questions regarding age, arrest record, citizenship, education, financial status, sexual orientation, health, childcare needs, military status, pregnancy, race or color, religion, or residence are not allowed and must be avoided.

5. A good orientation should provide information about the physical workplace, policies, procedures, and expected perform-

ance, as well as routine information such as payroll arrangement, breaks, benefits, and working hours.

6. The systems approach to training emphasizes formulating instructional objectives, developing learning activities to meet those objectives, establishing performance criteria to be met, and evaluating the results of training.

7. The most effective training is concise and interactive, interspersed with group projects, role-playing, and hands-on experiences.

8. Generally, problem employees are those with bad attitudes, those who are unskilled, or those who are simply misdirected. Organizations should strive to reduce the need for discipline, but if discipline becomes necessary, it should be administered immediately after the infraction in a fair, consistent, and impersonal manner.

9. Administrative managers need to understand what the objectives of an appraisal are, how to prepare for and conduct review activities, and what outcomes to expect at the conclusion of the appraisal process.

10. Recruiting costs, as a result of employee turnover, involve interviewing, checking, and testing costs; orientation costs; and transitional time spent getting new employees on board.

KEY TERMS

Affirmative Action Program
Behavioral interview questions
Buddy system
Employee recruitment
Employee selection
Employment application form
Orientation
Performance appraisals
Position approval form
Situational interview questions
Structured interview questions
Systems approach to training
Training
Train-the-trainer workshops
Turnover

REVIEW

1. Why is employee turnover so costly to organizations? Identify reasons why employees leave their jobs.

2. What are the advantages to recruiting internally?

3. What are some drawbacks for companies that recruit applicants through online job searches?

4. What are three types of interview questions commonly used in the job selection process?

5. During an employee orientation, what role does the human resources department play?

6. List several training methods used by organizations to upgrade employees' skills.

7. As a result of effective job counseling, what changes should you be able to observe in the worker?

8. Explain what is meant by the progressive discipline method in organizations.

9. What are several objectives of performance appraisals?

10. List some steps you can take as an AM to prepare for a performance appraisal.

CRITICAL THINKING

1. Why do employees leave their jobs and what can managers do to prevent excessive turnover in organizations?

2. Of the several sources that are successful for internal and external recruitment of employees, which three do you feel are the best to use, and why?

3. In your opinion, should any of the steps that companies follow when completing a typical employee selection process be deleted or changed? Are there any steps that should be taken during the selection process that aren't listed?

4. What is the most important part of a new employee orientation session as conducted by an administrative manager? Explain.

5. Why do companies use the systems approach to training?

6. In addition to those mentioned in the book, what are additional examples of the three categories of discipline problems found in organizations today?

7. Some people feel that the performance appraisal process is unnecessary as most everyone gets a good evaluation by their managers. Do you agree with this statement? Define your position with examples from your experience if possible.

CASE STUDY 7-1
CRITICIZING AN EMPLOYEE'S WORK

Bruce Gerhold, the administrative office manager at Home Appliance and Lighting Co., is not looking forward to the day. He has to conduct a performance appraisal with Molly at 10 a.m., and he has had it on his mind since arriving at work. He feels prepared—he's got his notes ready, the performance appraisal form is already typed, and he has a sense about how he wants to proceed in the interview.

Molly comes into his office at 10 a.m. sharp, and the conversation goes like this:

Mr. Gerhold:

I'm generally very pleased with your work, Molly—especially the way you're handling the arrangements for the sales conference next week. But there is one thing you need to work on. Maybe I haven't made it clear that you're also responsible for supervising all the promotional material, but lately I've found quite a few mistakes and some sloppy work.

Molly:

Mr. Gerhold, you know I have been working ridiculous hours to get everything done for the sales conference on time. I can't believe you're complaining about this, given all that I've done for you.

Mr. Gerhold:

Let me show you what I mean, Molly. Here are copies of the last three promotional pieces that you OK'd. I've marked the problem areas.

Molly:

I think you're being very unfair. On the whole, my work is excellent—you're just nit-picking. Mr. Gerhold, you've been overly critical of me since the first day I started working for you.

Discussion Questions

1. How is this performance appraisal going? How do you think it will end?
2. Could Mr. Gerhold have said or done anything differently?
3. Should Molly be issued a warning about her attitude? If so, how should Mr. Gerhold proceed?

Be prepared to discuss your reasoning in a group as directed by your instructor. Perhaps a role play of this situation would be useful. First role play an unsuccessful appraisal meeting, and then follow with a better scenario.

CASE STUDY 7-2
FALSIFYING AN EMPLOYMENT APPLICATION

In a desperate moment three years ago, you misrepresented your educational background when you completed the application form at your current place of employment. Ever since, that little lie has been like a time bomb ticking away in your personnel file. Tomorrow, you face an employee appraisal and a review of your qualifications for promotion. Today, you are in a quandary.

Discussion Questions

What should you do? Ask for your personnel file and delete the "padded" degree? Live with the lie and keep your mouth shut? Or what?

Be prepared to discuss this thoroughly in class. So what if you do get your personnel file? How could you make the changes? Should you make any changes in your information? You may want to discuss this with a person in HR to get an interpretation from an experienced human resources person. Bring your information and reasoning to class for a discussion as directed.

INTERNET RESEARCH ACTIVITY

Job interviews are always stressful for one reason or another. Preparation, however, is key to keeping those butterflies down to an acceptable level. Visit the suggested course web site at *http://odgers.swlearning.com*, as well as others on your own, and study the numerous tips and tricks you can use when interviewing for a position you really want.

Search words for you to consider may be job interviews; job skills; job search; or others that you think will help you locate job information. You can locate a company's web site by searching for the name of the company. The company's web site may contain valuable data that will help you in the interview.

Learning Activity:

1. From your research, what are the five most useful tips you discovered?
2. Which web sites did you find the most helpful and why?
3. What information did you find other than tips and tricks to interviewing success?

Your instructor may ask you to write an outline of the web sites you visited and your findings. Be prepared to discuss your findings in class.

Chapter 8

Employee Compensation, Recognition, and Company Policies

OBJECTIVES

After completing this chapter, you will be able to:

1. Discuss the two major pieces of legislation that govern employee compensation and benefits.

2. List the general categories of indirect compensation plans.

3. Discuss the purpose of promotions and employee recognition when furthering organizational goals.

4. Cite examples of a policy, a procedure, a rule, and a de facto rule or policy.

5. Identify the personal and legal aspects of terminations and lay-offs for employers and employees.

6. Contrast the power of the union-represented worker with the power of the employer.

In the previous chapter, recruiting, hiring, and training were discussed. In addition to employee recognition and compensation matters, Chapter 8 continues with workers' issues and deals with the administrative manager's role in administering, interpreting, and updating policies and procedures and the importance of employee handbooks as an organizational communication tool.

Typically, of course, wage rates and salary schedules are formulated by input from many sources such as top management, the human resources department, professional associations, the union contract, or government legislation or regulation. Nevertheless, within such limitations, AMs have some responsibility in establishing standards for promotion and compensation that will attract and retain a competent work force.

In business, compensation is a right;
recognition is a gift. —Rosabeth Moss Kanter

© Getty Images/PhotoDisc

TECHNOLOGY APPLICATIONS IN THE WORKPLACE

An Understanding of Spam and its Cost to Businesses

Spam, an unsolicited e-mail message sent to many recipients at once, is commonly known as Internet junk mail. The content of spam ranges from selling a product or service, to promoting a business opportunity, to advertising offensive material. It is strongly advised not to reply to spam messages for any reason if you want to keep your personal data private.

The cost of spam to companies is great. According to *Spam: The Silent ROI Killer,* a report conducted by Nucleus Research, the average cost of spam per year per business employee is $874. The major finding was that the average employee receives nearly 3,500 spam messages per year.[1]

EMPLOYEE COMPENSATION AND BENEFITS

For the employee, salary and benefits are tangible rewards for services rendered. For the employer, salary and benefits are the single greatest expense in the budget. Therefore, it is essential that the company have a sound compensation program to motivate employees, yet keep labor costs at an acceptable level.

Compensation Legislation

As with other human resources issues, an administrative manager should understand the legal basis for compensation activity in his or her company. The two principal laws governing compensation activities are the Fair Labor Standards Act of 1938 (and its amendments) and the Equal Pay Act of 1963.

Fair Labor Standards Act The Fair Labor Standards Act (FLSA), passed in 1938, is the major law affecting compensation administration. Over the years, the FLSA has been amended several times in order to raise the minimum wage rates and expand on the types of employees covered. Four issues stemming from the FLSA are important for any manager to know:

1. The three major components of the FLSA are to (a) establish a minimum wage, (b) encourage limits on the number of weekly hours employees work through overtime provisions, and (c) discourage oppressive use of child labor.

2. The Wage and Hour Division of the U.S. Department of Labor enforces compliance with the provisions of the FLSA. Companies must maintain accurate employee time records for three years. Penalties for violations can include awards of back pay for affected current and former employees for up to two years.

3. The FLSA classifies employees as exempt or nonexempt. **Exempt employees** are not paid overtime and usually are classified as being in professional or administrative positions. An administrative manager is an exempt employee. **Nonexempt employees** are paid overtime under the FLSA and are usually paid an hourly wage. There are, however, salaried-nonexempt positions like secretarial or clerical that fall under FLSA overtime provisions.

4. Compensatory time off ("comp time") is sometimes given in lieu of payment for time worked. In the private sector, comp time must be given at a rate of one-and-one-half times the hours worked during a 40-hour week.

©Getty Images/PhotoDisc

Workers who are nonexempt are usually paid on an hourly basis and can also earn overtime pay.

Equal Pay Act of 1963 A second important piece of compensation legislation, already mentioned in an earlier chapter, was passed as a major amendment to the FLSA. This amendment is called the Equal Pay Act of 1963 and is commonly referred to as the "equal pay for equal work" law. Except for differences that are justified on the basis of better performance, longer service, and quantity or quality of work, similar pay must be given for jobs requiring equal skills, equal effort, equal responsibilities, and similar working conditions.

Part of the task of an administrative manager is to determine what the average salaries or wages are for different types of positions. This topic of wage and salary administration is covered next.

Wage and Salary Administration

Appropriate compensation plays three vital roles in organizations. A good compensation plan (1) attracts capable employees, (2) motivates employees to perform effectively, and (3) helps retain capable employees.

Recognizing that jobs have different meanings to employers and employees, the goal of any compensation policy is to understand and reflect these differences equitably for both sides. Companies need to understand the politics and culture of an organization before a well-designed, useful compensation program can be implemented. A constant monitoring of the market to stay competitive is also necessary.

The first step in developing a salary compensation policy is to gather and analyze external and internal data. This process is sometimes referred to as conducting a **wage survey.** If it is not feasible for an organiza-

tion to conduct its own survey, an employer may use published wage surveys from sources such as trade associations and the U.S. Department of Labor.

Regardless of the source of the wage survey, the survey results must reflect several external and internal economic conditions. The external economic factors are

- The local supply and demand of qualified labor (Are there enough workers available?)
- The going wage rates for the area (Is the rate of pay competitive with other similar companies?)
- Cost of living factors (Will the wage offered be enough to pay rent, buy food, etc.?).

The internal factors that influence wage rates include

- The worth of the job to the company (How valuable are the responsibilities for the position to the success of the company?)
- The employee's worth (What are the education and years of experience an employee brings to the company?)
- The company's ability to pay (Is there enough budgeted to hire a person of this competence?).

Total Compensation Package

Although financial compensation is still important in fostering commitment and encouraging good performance, companies can further improve employee satisfaction and loyalty by making their employees feel they are needed, valued, and appreciated. Employers typically receive more loyalty from their employees if they offer benefits that go beyond the usual monetary rewards. The reason for that feeling makes sense because recognition goes beyond the need to receive money. Employees are demanding to know that their hard work means something. If it doesn't mean something within organizations, people will find another employer with whom their work does mean something beyond a paycheck.

An employee's **total compensation package** includes direct compensation and indirect compensation. **Direct compensation** is an employee's base pay as well as any incentive pay programs. **Indirect compensation** includes the whole array of benefits, some of which are required by law and others which are voluntary benefits offered by the company.

Direct Compensation Direct compensation to an employee is in the form of a wage (per hour amount) or salary (per month or yearly amount). Direct compensation can also include pay in the form of incentive plans. **Incentive plans** are optional but are usually based on set criteria established by the employer. The criteria for incentive plans for all employees should be spelled out in writing and made available to the employees.

As an example of an incentive plan, we will use merit pay. **Merit pay** is based on established criteria or performance at an exemplary level as usually reflected in an employee's performance appraisal. As with any incentive plan, merit pay has to be ad-ministered in a fair and equitable way for it to be motivating to the employee. Incentive plans, such as merit pay, can be a topic for discussion during orientation sessions.

Often the budget has a set amount of merit pay to be distributed. When administering merit pay, the administrative manager should:

1. Develop employee confidence and trust in the performance appraisal process;
2. Separate merit pay from regular pay, and, most importantly;
3. Establish job-related performance criteria against which merit pay will be determined.

Table 8.1 outlines the criteria on which incentive plans such as bonuses, commissions, gain sharing, merit raises, profit sharing, and stock options and ownership are based. Employees should have the criteria available in writing and understand it.

It is safe to say that corporate salary budgets are struggling, as evidenced by the *Salary Budget Survey* conducted by WorldatWork, the world's largest salary budget survey. In the latest survey, findings indicate that salary increases in 2003 will be about one-half of 1 percent lower than what was projected in 2002, which is the same decreasing trend the survey revealed between 2001 and 2002, the lowest level in the survey's 30-year history. The 2003 survey includes the responses of more than 3,100 diverse companies, representing a total of 15.8 million U.S. employees.

Although the work force can expect an average salary increase of 3.5 percent in 2003, increases fell short of the projected 4.1 percent, which continues the yearly decline to the present 30-year low. Company projections for 2004 look slightly better than the 2003 actual figures, with a projected increase of 3.7 percent.[2]

TABLE 8.1 Incentive Plans for Employees

Types	Based On
Bonuses	Established goals or criteria
Commissions	Amount of sales
Gain sharing	Improved productivity or cost savings shown
Merit raises	Established criteria and policies
Profit sharing	Organizational profits distributed proportionally to pay
Stock options	Achievement of specific goals
Stock ownership	Special purchase plans or bonus distributions. (Often based on rank in company or years of service)

Indirect Compensation Indirect compensation plans, or benefits, are financial rewards and services provided to employees in addition to their regular earnings. With salaries stagnating and health-care expenses booming, benefits are becoming an increasing portion of the total cost of employment. The U.S. Chamber of Commerce reported in January 2003 that employee benefits made up 39 percent of total payroll costs in 2001, up slightly from 37.5 percent the prior year.[3]

Employers have continued to make benefits a priority and recognize the importance of benefits in retaining employees in their companies. Often, job applicants weigh the total compensation, so a better benefit package can more than make up the difference in pay among competing employers.

Although there are different ways to categorize employee benefits, we shall refer to them according to these five categories:

(1) benefits required by law, (2) pay for time not worked, (3) insurance plans, (4) security and retirement plans, and (5) work/life benefits and services.

1. *Benefits Required by Law.* Federal and state governments require employers to provide benefits under these government programs:

- *Federal:* **Social Security,** also known as the Old Age and Survivors Insurance (OASI) Program, includes four categories of benefits to those who qualify. These benefits include old age benefits, survivor benefits, disability benefits, and medical benefits. To be eligible, a worker must have contributed taxes into the system for ten years or forty quarters (three-month periods of time).

- *State:* **Unemployment compensation,** also referred to as unemployment insurance, provides unemployed workers with benefits from a fund of payroll taxes imposed on employers. To receive benefits under the law, the unemployed worker is required to register for employment at a U.S. employment office and usually must have worked for a certain period of time at a company before becoming unemployed. Benefits are usually provided for a certain stated period of time.

Workers' compensation laws protect employees and their families from permanent loss of income and high medical payments as a consequence of accidental injury, illness, or death on the job. To collect workers' compensation, it does not matter who was at fault. Workers' compensation funds are provided primarily through employer contributions to a statewide fund. In some states, the amount to be paid for a given condition is stipulated in the law; in other states, guidelines are in place and judges and/or juries determine the fair and equitable payment, if any.

2. *Pay for Time Not Worked.* Most organizations today grant their employees pay for time not worked under certain conditions. These benefits normally include holidays, vacations, sick leave, jury duty, military service, and bereavement leaves. A **bereavement leave** is offered by

companies to provide eligible employees paid leave off in the event of a death in the employee's immediate family.

3. *Insurance Plans.* Among the popular company-sponsored insurance plans are group life insurance, health-care insurance (medical and hospital), vision-care insurance, and dental insurance. Of all the benefit plans, this category is currently the most volatile. In 2002, medical benefits, which accounted for 11 percent of total gross payout, made up the largest share of employee-benefits costs, surpassing pay for time not worked. According to several studies, premiums for employee health-care insurance went up by around 13 percent in 2002.[4]

Employers can expect more of the same in upcoming years: double-digit increases to the cost of their health plans. This forecast, according to Avon Consulting's Spring 2003 Health Care Trend Survey, represents figures from actuaries at more than 20 leading medical, dental, pharmacy, and vision insurers. Faced with rising expenses, companies are expected to increase co-pays and premiums for employees. The trend is toward plan designs that require more cost-sharing by the employee.

4. *Security and Retirement Plans.* For many retirees, the pension, 401(k) accounts, and health-care benefits provided by their former employers are the core of their retirement security—both financial and emotional. **Pension plans** are retirement benefits established and funded by employers and employees. These plans are always provided to the employee in writing.

ETHICS & CHOICES

Suppose you chose to take an extended unplanned weekend and not report to work on Monday. Would you call in sick just because you have unused sick leave available? Why or why not?

© Getty Images/PhotoDisc

Retirement opportunities are not as traditional as they once were—there are more variations. Rather than a full retirement, for example, more employers are embracing "phased retirement" approaches, such as shortening work hours and offering part-time or temporary work, to retain long-time employees, according to a survey of 586 large employers by Watson Wyatt Worldwide.[5]

The Senior Citizens' Freedom to Work Act of 2000, signed by President Clinton, made it easier for companies to hire Social Security recipients because they no longer had to worry about earning limits. While the legislation removes the earnings cap for people between the ages of 65 and 70, there is an earnings cap for those who take early retirement and collect Social Security before they reach their full retirement.[6] There can be many reasons why someone who took an early retirement may want to re-enter the work force. Some might not have liked retirement as much as they expected and now want to return to their jobs. Other workers might have retired to care for an ill spouse whose health situation has been resolved. It might also be that there are individuals who have irreplaceable skills that the employer wants back. Some may have lost their savings in the economic turndown. Or it could simply be they don't like "doing nothing" and want to feel they are serving a purpose with their lives again.

5. *Work/Life Benefits and Services.* With the reality of low wages, cutbacks in health insurance and the threat of being laid off are the very things that make families' lives so stressed. People must work longer

hours just to maintain their standards of living. Employers have found that even a handful of relatively inexpensive work-family benefits can play a role in eliciting greater employee participation, loyalty, and job commitment, even from those who don't use them.

Many older workers have found jobs that make use of their skills and that make them feel productive.

As a result, companies continue to explore nontraditional solutions that will help employees better integrate work and life as part of their commitment to be an employer of choice by employees. The basis of that belief lies in the concept that when people at work are distracted with personal issues, they are less effective in their jobs.

Therefore, in addition to standard benefits, such as life insurance and medical coverage, employers are providing unconventional perks, including tickets to cultural

© Getty Images/PhotoDisc

A health club provided free by the company provides employees with healthy exercise options.

events, free or reduced health club memberships, on-site day care, and payments for college tuition for children of employees who have been with the company for a specified number of years.[7] Moreover, companies are also helping employees cope with work and family demands by offering counseling, educational information, and referral assistance. As we discussed in an earlier chapter, companies offer alternative work schedules in the form of telecommuting, flexible work hours, and job sharing to ensure the high quality of employees' work and professional lives. These benefits result in a win-win situation for everyone who deals with hectic schedules and the day-to-day demands of life and work.

Employees enjoy the comfort offered by these nontraditional provisions while employers benefit from lowered costs, loyal employees, and improved relationships. With so many benefit options available and the dramatic rise in the cost of health care, the

dollars allocated to company benefits unfortunately are stretched to capacity. For that reason, many employers are providing employees with flexible benefit packages called a **cafeteria benefit plan.**

The cafeteria benefit plan is an outgrowth of Internal Revenue Code Section 125. Section 125 allows an employee to contribute a certain amount of pre-tax dollars to a plan to avoid income taxes on the amount allocated to these qualified benefit plans. The upshot is that it allows employees to actually receive the benefit of using pre-tax dollars to pay for qualified expenses such as medical expenses not covered by insurance plans or a dependent care reimbursement plan.

Under the cafeteria plan, all employees receive a statement of the total dollar amount of benefits they are entitled to, along with the amount earmarked for legally required benefits. Each employee then tells the employer how to allocate the balance among the programs available. The major advantage of this benefit allocation approach is that benefit packages are better tailored to individual employee's needs.

Table 8.2 outlines the relationships among the total compensation packages employers can offer.

One final suggestion: Because many companies put such substantial investments into benefits, employers should show their employees annually how much these benefits are worth. A total compensation statement given to employees annually can be a great retention tool that can benefit an organization.

Employees make commitments to companies for a number of reasons. Probably the

TABLE 8.2 Total Employee Compensation

Direct Compensation	Indirect Compensation
Base Pay:	Pay for Time Not Worked:
Wages and salaries	Vacations, breaks, holidays, sick pay, jury duty, and military duty
Incentives:	Insurance Plans:
Bonuses, commissions, gain sharing, merit raises, profit sharing, stock options, and stock ownership	Medical, hospital, dental, life, and surgical
	Security Plans:
	Pension, Social Security, disability insurance
	Employee Services:
	Educational assistance, recreational programs, food services

best reason is because they like the company and seek to be a part of its growth. Promoting those who achieve is one of the more important activities administrative managers perform.

PROMOTING EMPLOYEES

In the careers of most workers, there comes a time when recognition is received for a job well done. Recognizing or promoting an employee in some way is one of the most effective ways to reinforce an organization's culture, support its objectives, and retain top performers. Through genuine recognition, a work environment is created that allows people to be their best, to perform at higher levels, and to feel genuinely appreciated in the process. Communication, recognition, and rewards are often provided to the

employees through promotions and are critical to creating an energizing, enthusiastic, and enjoyable workplace.

Promotion from within helps companies retain and develop productive employees. It provides challenging assignments, prescribes new responsibilities, and helps employees grow by developing their abilities. One approach to promotion from within is **job posting**, which means that positions are announced on bulletin boards or in company publications as openings occur. Interested employees notify the manager or the human resources department which then helps make the fit between employees and positions. Two of the main advantages of job postings are that the job applicants already have been observed performing within the company and know the company's culture and goals.

The biggest disadvantage of job postings is that it doesn't bring in new ideas to the company from the outside.

Successful promotion plans are definite, systematic, fair, communicated to employees, and followed uniformly. A promotion plan, therefore, must have the confidence of the employees. In order to provide for promotions based upon objective data and not solely upon personal opinion and assessment, the human resources department should maintain a database of all personnel and make it available to managers on an as-needed basis. Commonly, promotions are granted as rewards for successful work done in a previous position. Sometimes when promotions are given, the recipient may be transferred to another department or division.

A few companies recognize the need to motivate all their employees and are grappling with ways to challenge their older managers. They encourage those they don't promote to make lateral moves that will broaden their experience. Companies also are receptive to veteran workers who raise their hands and volunteer for very different assignments than they have performed in the past.[8]

Whether an administrative manager is dealing with compensation and benefits or promotions, to be fair to all employees he or she must follow policies, outlined procedures, and rules to the letter.

POLICIES, PROCEDURES, RULES, AND HANDBOOKS

As companies learn more about what is required to remain viable in the 21st century's economic environment, it is important to examine policies to ensure that they are compatible with the organization's values and long-term objectives. Additionally, an employee handbook could be a valuable tool for an employer to communicate company policies and any procedural changes to workers. A good time to review these is during orientation sessions.

Policies, Procedures, and Rules

It is not possible for an organization to avoid having policies, procedures, and rules. Policies and rules determine or strongly influence how work is done and how people behave and are treated in the organization. Policies and rules must exist because in the absence of formal policies or rules, there will be *de facto* policies and rules (that govern *actual* practice), which spring up from having to make the same kinds of decisions repeatedly.

In the following remarks, we will focus on policies and rules which govern the decisions and behavior of people as they carry out the day-to-day work of the organization, or govern the reaction of an organization to employee actions. In order to have a common understanding of what a policy is and its relationship to written procedures, what a rule is, and finally what we mean by *de facto* policies and rules, it may be helpful to look at their definitions and a few examples that are shown in Table 8.3. Table 8.4 provides an example of a bereavement policy.

> **M A N A G E M E N T   T I P**
>
> Keep a stack of note cards on your desk, where you cannot ignore them. At the end of the day, take a few minutes to write personal thank-you notes to any employee who made a difference that day.

T A B L E 8 . 3 Definitions

	Definition	Examples
Policy	A plan or course of action adopted by a business organization is designed to influence and determine decisions, actions, and other matters.	Company absenteeism policy Purchasing policy Equal opportunity policy Posting all job openings policy
Procedure	A routine method of handling activities that is more specific than a policy; procedures outline the steps to be performed when taking a particular course of action.	Within a grievance policy is a procedure outlining the sequential steps to be taken by all affected parties to resolve the grievance Within an absenteeism policy is a procedure that spells out how to report an absence
Rule	An authoritative directive for conduct; an established standard or habit of behavior.	All outside doors will be kept locked between the hours of 5 p.m. and 7 a.m. Personal calls are not permitted on company phones. Food and beverages are not to be consumed in the computer server area. Anyone clocking in more than 10 minutes late will have his or her pay docked.
De facto	[Latin meaning "from the fact"]; reality or fact, actually. In other words, what *really* happens in practice.	We use substandard materials because we need them in order to keep production going. I know the rule says "no selling or solicitation in the plant or offices" but everybody does it. We don't report small cuts like that... they make the accident statistics look bad.

TABLE 8.4 Example of a Bereavement Policy

POLICY 410. BEREAVEMENT LEAVE

410.6.1 Purpose

To provide eligible employees paid leave off in the event of a death in the employee's immediate family.

410.6.2 Eligibility

Eligible employees are regular and probationary full-time employees working 30 or more hours per week, and full-time one-year temporary employees (as defined in 443.1.3.3, #1). Other temporary and part-time employees are not eligible. An employee must be on active pay status in order to receive paid bereavement leave.

410.6.3 Scope of Benefit

An eligible employee, upon giving as much notice as possible to his/her supervisor, shall be permitted up to three days in-state and five days out-of-state in the event of death in the immediate family. An additional three days leave of absence charged to the employee's accumulated sick leave may be granted.

410.6.4 Definition of Immediate Family

Immediate family is defined as a spouse, daughter, son, parent, parent-in-law, sister, brother, grandchild, grandparent, or any other relative who is a permanent member of the employee's established household. A parent is defined as a natural parent, step parent, adoptive parent, or surrogate parent (a person who raised the employee as his/her child). A child is defined as a natural child, adoptive child, foster child, or step child.

410.6.5 Request for Leave

A Leave Request Form must be submitted to the employee's supervisor substantiating the need for bereavement leave.

Although formal policies and rules are easily accessible to examination, **de facto policies** are embedded in the everyday work of the organization and are less visible. They may be completely contradictory to the formal values of the organization, but they may have developed as a result of a reward system that is strongly tied to short-term results.

A de facto policy becomes the accepted practice by default until a more formal and written policy is drawn up to replace it. With company intranets, many organizations are posting their entire group of policies on their computer servers for easy and confidential access to employees. Should questions arise, the policies should be clarified by the AM.

Table 8.5 describes how organizations should set policies in motion and monitor their appropriateness.

Policies and rules are usually good indicators of an organization's value system, its assumptions about people and human behavior, and its understanding of and beliefs about what makes organizations effective. What an organization says and does through its policies and rules has a major effect on how that organization is perceived by its employees and, in some cases, by its customers, suppliers, and community. This perception affects the employees' sense of identification with the organization and its objectives.

As a manager, one of your responsibilities will be to assist in administering, interpreting, and updating organizational policies, procedures, and rules. If policies and procedures were not in place, organizations would not function smoothly and administrative managers' jobs would be chaotic and more unpredictable. An effective way to ensure that all employees understand policies and procedures is to issue each worker an employee handbook the first day of work. Policies, procedures, and rules should be discussed during employee orientation, with an opportunity

for questions to be answered. Some companies provide games or give short quizzes with small prizes for participation in these orientation sessions.

Handbooks

Employee handbooks are commonly used manuals that communicate to workers numerous company policies, ranging from time off to insurance coverage to drug testing. Handbooks give employees a reference to research specific questions they may have. Typically, it is distributed as part of the employee orientation process. But despite their wide use, many companies are unaware of the legal issues, both the benefits and risks, associated with the handbooks.

Many states consider an employee handbook a contract if a clear promise is stated in a company's handbook and there's no disclaimer or stipulation that says the handbook is not a contract. For example, if a handbook specifies that a permanent employee will only be terminated after three written warnings, the employer may be considered in "breach of contract" by terminating the employee at will.[9] Legal counsel may be useful or necessary in these situations.

TABLE 8.5 Communicating Organizational Policies

POLICIES SHOULD

Cover only areas where employees and managers need guidance.

Be communicated by management to employees through training, orientation programs, and the employee handbook.

Be reviewed and updated on a continuous basis with any changes communicated to employees.

Be written as concisely and to the point as possible.

© Digital Vision

A policy manual or employee handbook clarifies questions employees may have.

Extra care should be taken not only in the drafting of a handbook, but also in the delivery and acknowledgment of its policies. Typically, employers should have items in their handbooks such as a disclaimer that is prominently placed in large bold letters on the first page, general company information, a welcome message, company history, a mission or value statement, philosophy of the organization, regular hours of work, equal opportunity and anti-harassment statements, work rules, benefits, and other items relating to the organization.

It's a good idea for employers to think about handbooks as an internal marketing tool. It's a way for them to remind their employees on a regular basis that

- This is a good place to work.
- These are the things we offer you.
- This is why it's a fair place to work.

All employers should consider providing employee handbooks because they are

extremely important as a guideline that offers information about the organization, identifies what expectations the organization has for its employees, and acts as high-quality orientation material.

One of the most important reasons to follow procedures and policies has to do with, unfortunately, when terminations and layoffs occur in the workplace.

TERMINATIONS AND LAYOFFS

The termination process is difficult and stressful. Simply put, **termination** is a request for an employee to leave a job. It is the last and unfortunate step in a relationship between an organization and an employee. It is to be avoided, if possible. Before taking this step, administrative managers need to be sure that everything has been done to prevent it. Has everything been done to help the employee be successful on the job? If so, it is time to make a clean break.

Consider this action deliberately, not at a time of anger or defensiveness. By controlling hard feelings, the employee is helped to acknowledge that all possible steps were taken to avoid this action. In today's world of complex labor laws, it is important and extremely necessary to assure the termination is carried out in a thorough and professional way.

Personal Aspects of Terminations

No manager likes the unpleasant task of terminating a worker, but the reality is that it happens every day in organizations. Regardless of the reasons or circumstances surrounding the dismissal, when an employee is released involuntarily from his or her job, the psychological bond is broken between employee and employer. What usually results is that the employee feels a loss of control, loss of security, and loss of loyalty. If left unchecked, these feelings can manifest into increased stress and distrust which we often hear about on television.

What is more, when an employee is terminated, the employer and remaining staff are affected as well. In organizations, terminations have a ripple effect on those who stay. For example, those who stay may feel that their psychological bond is no longer valid with the organization, their loyalty is shaken, and their security is eroded.

Typical reactions of those who stay may manifest as anger, distrust, guilt, relief, grief, and survivor shock. What should you as a manager do to allay these effects? Some suggestions are to increase communication with the remaining employees by being more visible and walking around the offices, providing consistent information, and soliciting employee concerns about future layoffs or terminations.

Legal Aspects of Termination

There are three legal terms associated with termination that AMs should understand when dealing with this topic. These terms are at-will employment, wrongful termination, and the Worker Adjustment and Retraining Notification Act (WARN) of 1989.

At-Will Employment In many states, employment is "at will." At-will employment means that the employer can fire the employee for no reason or any reason. If an employee is not under contract, he or she is an at-will employee in these states. An

employer can dismiss an at-will employee hired for an indefinite term at any time for any nondiscriminatory reason. Likewise, the at-will employee is free to terminate his or her employment at any time.

The two exceptions to this general rule are discrimination and contract considerations.

- *Discrimination.* Employers cannot discriminate against employees on the basis of age, race, sex, national origin, disability, and a variety of other reasons. Employers cannot discriminate against an employee because he or she has "whistle-blown," which is reporting illegal activity of the employer. They also cannot discriminate against an employee for engaging in other protected activities, such as filing workers' compensation claims. If an employer fires an employee because of one of these factors, that is against the law and the employee can sue.

- *Contract.* If any employee has a contract with the employer, the employee probably cannot be fired without just cause. Contracts can be written or implied. A common way for an employee to have a written contract is to be a member of a union.

Wrongful Termination Wrongful termination is a term that generally refers to a person being fired when they shouldn't have been. It can be a very misleading phrase. Many terminations that people think of as

© Getty Images/PhotoDisc

Handling layoffs might be one of the most regrettable administrative manager's tasks. It's sad, uncomfortable—and fraught with legal difficulties. In these tough economic times, the most positive thing AMs can do is to ensure that layoffs are handled correctly. The act of handing out pink slips to employees is bad enough. Don't compound the grief by opening the door for unfounded legal claims and lawsuits.[10]

Exit Interviews

Because organizations lose money when employees who have been trained leave, human resources departments often conduct an exit interview and complete an exit interview form on each employee's last day of work. The purpose of an **exit interview** is to obtain information from departing employees concerning their experiences with various aspects of their employment.

Management should see this as a means of evaluating its policies and procedures and not as a threat. Additionally, exit interviews are excellent ways to try to prevent important company business from disappearing along with the employee who is leaving. Given the importance of information management today, this is simply a prudent action on the part of organizations.

The mood should always be positive. All exit interview data are prepared in statistical and/or summary form so the respondents are not linked to the responses. An example of an employee exit interview questionnaire is shown in Figure 8.1.

If the termination was properly conducted, there should be no repercussions. If it wasn't and the company is unionized, the union will represent its member should the member say the termination was unfair.

Exit interview forms are completed by workers, usually during their last day on the job.

"wrongful" aren't. For example, if the employer fires an employee because of race or another illegal reason, that is "wrongful termination." However, if the employer fires the employee in violation of a contract, that is not, in legal terms, "wrongful termination." It is "breach of contract."

Worker Adjustment and Retraining Notification Act (WARN)

The Worker Adjustment and Retraining Notification Act was enacted in August 1988 and became effective in February 1989. WARN offers protection to workers, their families, and communities by requiring employers to provide notice 60 days in advance of plant closings and mass layoffs. This notice must be provided to either affected workers or their representatives (e.g., a labor union); to the state dislocated worker unit; and to the appropriate unit of local government. Employees entitled to notice under WARN include hourly and salaried workers, as well as managerial and supervisory employees.

FIGURE 8.1 Employee Exit Interview Questionnaire

INTERNATIONAL BUSINESS SERVICES

EMPLOYEE EXIT QUESTIONNAIRE

The following questionnaire was developed to obtain information from departing employees concerning their experiences with various aspects of employment. This questionnaire will assist IBS in evaluating its policies and procedures.

- This questionnaire will not become part of your personnel file and will not be seen by your former supervisor.
- The answers you give will be distributed only in statistical and/or summary form. Your answers will in no way affect your reemployment possibilities with International Business Services.

GENERAL INFORMATION

1. Your current position and department at IBS
   Position: _____
   Department: _____

2. Date hired into permanent position: _____

3. Separation Date: _____

4. Gender: ☐ Male ☐ Female

5. Ethnicity (please check):
   ☐ African American ☐ Asian/P. Islander ☐ Native American
   ☐ Hispanic ☐ White ☐ Alaskan Native ☐ Other

6. Job Classification (please check):
   ☐ Professional ☐ Administrative

7. Is your separation from International Business Services (please check):
   ☐ Voluntary
   ☐ Other (Layoff, etc.)

REASON FOR LEAVING

Please use the following scale when answering these questions:

Strongly Agree	Agree	Neutral	Disagree	Disagree Strongly	Not Applicable
1	2	3	4	5	NA

My leaving IBS is due to the following reasons: (circle your response)

1. I am leaving the Phoenix area for another job.   1 2 3 4 5 NA
2. Family circumstances/health reasons.   1 2 3 4 5 NA
3. I have another job in Phoenix.   1 2 3 4 5 NA
4. Spouse is relocating to different area.   1 2 3 4 5 NA
5. I am going to return to school.   1 2 3 4 5 NA
6. Maternity/paternity concerns.   1 2 3 4 5 NA
7. Retirement/leaving job market.   1 2 3 4 5 NA
8. I have been generally dissatisfied in my job.   1 2 3 4 5 NA
9. Salary is not adequate/acceptable.   1 2 3 4 5 NA
10. Unsupportive/hostile work environment.   1 2 3 4 5 NA
11. What was/were your major reason(s) for leaving IBS?

FIGURE 8.1 Employee Exit Interview Questionnaire (Concluded)

JOB SATISFACTION

Overall, I have been satisfied with . . . (circle your response)

1. the orientation/training.	1	2	3	4	5	NA
2. the physical condition of my work area.	1	2	3	4	5	NA
3. the work environment.	1	2	3	4	5	NA
4. the safety of my work surroundings.	1	2	3	4	5	NA
5. the support for a culturally diverse environment.	1	2	3	4	5	NA
6. my yearly salary.	1	2	3	4	5	NA
7. the benefit package.	1	2	3	4	5	NA
8. my career development at IBS.	1	2	3	4	5	NA
9. the additional training opportunities I received.	1	2	3	4	5	NA
10. co-worker relationships.	1	2	3	4	5	NA
11. the ease and effectiveness of IBS procedures.	1	2	3	4	5	NA
12. my ability to have input.	1	2	3	4	5	NA

WORK ENVIRONMENT

1. During your employment with IBS, do you believe that you have ever been sexually harassed?

   ☐ YES ☐ NO ☐ Not Sure

2. During your employment with IBS, do you believe that you have ever been discriminated against?

   ☐ YES ☐ NO ☐ Not Sure

3. If you answered "yes" to either question 1 or 2, did you report it? (If not, skip to the next part.)

   ☐ YES ☐ NO ☐ Not Sure

4. Do you feel satisfied with how your issues were resolved?

   ☐ YES ☐ NO ☐ Not Sure

If not sure, please explain: _____

PERFORMANCE APPRAISAL SYSTEM

1. Did you receive timely evaluations? ☐ Yes ☐ No
2. Did you believe your evaluations were fair? ☐ Yes ☐ No
3. Did you believe your evaluations were helpful? ☐ Yes ☐ No

*UPON COMPLETION, PLEASE RETURN THIS FORM
TO HUMAN RESOURCES AND
SCHEDULE AN APPOINTMENT TO MEET WITH THE DIRECTOR*

LABOR UNIONS

© Richard Lord/Photo Edit

Labor unions are associations of employees formed to represent work force concerns and interests during negotiations with management. In the past, workers have joined unions for the following reasons: higher pay, shorter hours of work, improved working conditions—both physical and psychological—and improved security. Although those reasons are still the central motivators for joining the union, over the years membership has shifted downward in traditional occupations.

As wages stagnate, as companies cut back on health insurance and pensions and as work hours grow longer, more and more workers want a voice on the job with a union. While there have been slight rises and dips in membership in recent years, the number of members in 2002, according to the AFL-CIO, is about the same level as it was in 1997, despite adverse trends in hard-hit sectors such as manufacturing and the effects of the current recession. The number of union members in the United States in 2002 was 16.1 million compared to 16.14 million members in 2001. The AFL-CIO represents 13 million working men and women. Two and a half million workers have formed new unions since 1996.[11]

The administrative manager needs to know how to function in unionized organizations because unions remain a force in many industries. Representation of workers by unions takes two forms. First, unions represent employees. They negotiate contracts with employers covering the workers they represent. The **union contract** usually specifies wages, benefits, work rules, and

other workplace procedures. Second, within the contractual framework negotiated with the organization, unions establish a formalized grievance procedure. This **grievance procedure** provides the mechanism whereby employee and union grievances can be aired and judged according to prescribed and agreed upon steps.

Unions are able to influence management decisions through their bargaining power. At the core of this power are these forms of influence:

1. *Picket.* Unions can enlist public support by barring customers, nonunion employees, and carriers from the premises.

2. *Strike.* Unions can impose significant costs on the enterprise by forcing the employer to cease operations.

3. *Boycott products.* Unions can discourage members and the public from patronizing the employer.

Labor unions are associations of employees formed to represent work force concerns.

An employer's power in a union organiza-tion comes from the following actions:

1. *Continue operations.* Hire replacements for strikers and encourage workers to return to work.

2. *Lock out workers.* Counteract union slowdown or vandalism.

3. *Subcontract work.* Force the union to give up the strike and continue to service customers with a substitute source of labor.

Thus, in a unionized company the ability to inflict costs operates in both directions. Although adversarial relations are still the rule, there is growing attention to labor-management strategies that emphasize mutuality of interests, cooperation, and "win-win" bargaining, whenever possible. Employees are less likely to want a third party's help if steps are taken to improve workplace policies and communication mechanisms.

Four elements of any proactive union-avoidance strategy that employers can follow are as follows:

1. *An open-door complaint procedure.* Most employees join unions to feel a sense of empowerment and to have a voice in the workplace. Providing a mechanism for voicing complaints and asking work-related questions satisfies this need. Without this channel, undiscovered prob-lems such as arbitrary treatment or unfair favoritism by a supervisor will fester, ruining morale and driving off good employees. A union representative will usually sit with a worker during any contract dispute or grievance discussion.

2. *Enhanced communication.* Whether through employee meetings (formal or informal), newsletters, memos from man-agement, or employee attitude surveys, employers must focus on improving two-way communications. Employees want to be heard, provide input, and receive timely information (both good and bad) about their workplace and issues of concern. Employee confidence can be strengthened by this input.

3. *Management training programs.* As legal agents of the employer, supervisors can bind the employer through their actions; further, they also can be the source of the problems leading to organizing efforts. Train managers on such matters as recog-nizing an employee's individual rights, improving employee performance, docu-menting misconduct, and imposing fair discipline. Training supervisors on the factors in a contract that if violated could create a grievance should build employee confidence in the supervisors' skill to manage.

4. *A personnel policies and procedures audit.* Unions frequently use various inconsistent employer policies as rallying cries to turn employee interest toward unions. Thwart such efforts with an internal audit of those policies and procedures. As mentioned, if supervisors understand the contract and work for consistent application of work policies, rules, and procedures, the company should maintain a happier and more productive work force. This is something that is likely to be appreciated by the union, the workers, and management.

MESSAGE FOR MANAGERS

Recognition, compensation, and rewards have to do with understanding how the organization values the contributions of employees. The employees with their specialized skills help the organization achieve its mission and purpose in the marketplace. Administrative managers are positioned well in the organization to show workers that rewards and recognition go beyond compensation. They, in fact, regularly have opportunities to communicate to employees the special value the organization places on specific behaviors. Administrative managers should take the time to tell employees that their work means something to the organization. Incentive plans with monetary rewards are just one way to do this.

Any time people are a part of any workplace, conflicts can arise. Unions were eventually established to give the workers a voice in the workplace. For many years now, labor unions have been a permanent part of our free-enterprise economy. A union, just like any other institution, has the potential for either advancing or interfering with the common efforts of an organization. Thus, it is in management's self-interest as well as in the interest of the work force, to develop a union-management climate that is conducive to constructive relationships.

When relationships run counter to the interests of the workers and management, strikes and other organized reprisals can take place. Unfortunately, they can become violent as we sometimes see on TV or read about in the papers. Administrative managers and others can do much to maintain positive working relationships before relationships break down.

S U M M A R Y

1. The two principle laws that form the basis and govern compensation activities in organizations are the Fair Labor Standards Act and the Equal Pay Act.

2. A good compensation plan attracts capable employees, motivates employees to perform effectively, and helps retain capable employees.

3. An employee's total compensation package includes direct compensation (an employee's base pay as well as any incentive pay programs) and indirect compensation (an array of benefits offered by the company).

4. Five categories of employee benefits are benefits required by law, pay for time not worked, insurance plans, security and retirement plans, and work/life benefits and services.

5. Recognizing or promoting an employee in some way is the most effective way to reinforce an organization's culture, support its objectives, and retain top performers.

6. Organizational policies, procedures, and rules determine or strongly influence how

work is done and how people behave and are treated in a company.

7. Employee handbooks are commonly used manuals that communicate to workers numerous company policies and can serve as a high-quality method to assist in orienting new employees.

8. Regardless of the reasons or circumstances surrounding the dismissal, when an employee is released involuntarily from his or her job, the psychological bond is broken between employee and employer.

9. An exit interview obtains information from department employees concerning their experiences with various aspects of their employment.

10. Labor unions are associations of employees formed to represent work force concerns and interests during negotiations with management.

11. A written grievance procedure provides the mechanism whereby employee and union grievances can be aired and judged according to prescribed and agreed upon steps, usually as part of the union contract.

KEY TERMS

At-will employment
Bereavement leave
Cafeteria benefit plan
De facto policies
Direct compensation
Employee handbook
Exempt employees
Exit interview
Fair Labor Standards Act
Grievance procedure
Incentive plans
Indirect compensation
Job posting
Labor unions
Merit pay
Nonexempt employees
Pension plans
Policy
Procedure
Rule
Social Security
Spam
Termination
The Worker Adjustment and Retraining
    Notification Act (WARN)
Total compensation package
Unemployment compensation
Union contract
Wage survey
Workers' compensation
Wrongful termination

REVIEW

1. Define promotions and how recognition can be achieved without promotion.
2. Discuss the procedures for termination. Do you agree with these steps?

3. How are wage rates and salary schedules formulated?
4. What does at-will employment and wrongful termination mean?
5. Explain what a wage survey is and how it is typically conducted.
6. In addition to salary and wages, what are some examples of incentive plans for employees?
7. What are benefits required by law that organizations must provide for employees?
8. Out of all the benefits offered to employees, why is the health benefits package of most concern to companies?
9. Describe what is meant by a cafeteria benefit plan.
10. Why do employees join labor unions?
11. List several ways that organizational policies, procedures, and rules are communicated to employees.

CRITICAL THINKING

1. What are the advantages to a company to promote and formally recognize employees?
2. If you were to advise someone on the legal aspects of terminations and layoffs, what would you say?
3. What reasons can you give that the two major pieces of legislation that govern employee compensation and benefits are still in force since being enacted in 1938 and 1963, respectively?
4. Of the five general categories of indirect compensation plans, which ones do you think employers should always provide for employees?

5. Do you think the power of unions does a good job in representing workers today or facing the usual dollar crunch, Danny plans to offer him a starting salary of $50 per week more than the midpoint of the salary range established for the position. Danny plans to offer Slezak a starting salary of $10 per week less than the midpoint since her financial obligations are fewer and she has no dependents to support.

Why or why not?

6. Cite one example each of a policy, a procedure, a rule, and a de facto rule or policy.

7. As a cost-cutting method, companies are now putting their total employee handbook on their intranet web site. Do you think an electronic form is better than a written form? Which do you think is better? Why?

Realizing that Hagman is a "family man"

Discussion Questions

1. As Danny's superior, what are your reactions to the starting salaries he has recommended?

2. What, if any, additional information about the two applicants do you need before you decide to approve or disapprove Danny's salary offers?

   Reflect on the facts, research any employment laws that apply, then write brief answers to the questions. Be prepared to discuss your opinions in class.

CASE STUDY 8-1: DETERMINING A STARTING SALARY

Danny Costner, purchasing manager for Trout Manufacturing, has been interviewing applicants for the position of purchasing clerk. Danny has narrowed down all applicants to two people, one of whom, if the starting salary is acceptable, will commence work next Monday morning.

From their interviews and applications, Danny has summarized the following information about the two applicants:

Marila Slezak: 18 years old, single, no dependents. Graduated last year from North High School; cumulative GPA 3.7 out of 4.0; area of concentration: computer technology specialist. Presently unemployed. No prior work experience in the field of business.

Anthony Hagman: 20 years old, married, one child. Graduated two years ago from North High School; cumulative GPA 3.8 out of 4.0; area of concentration: electronic accounting. Part-time employed as short-order cook. No prior work experience in field of business.

CASE STUDY 8-2: CHALLENGING THE VACATION POLICY

Looking forward to early retirement within one week, Sean Arless has decided to give his employer a claim for unused vacation time. Sean calculates that he has accumulated 20 weeks of unused vacation time, which is the cash equivalent of $18,000.

When he met with Tim Geren, director of human resources, Sean was told, "Look at your employee handbook, Sean. It states very clearly that vacation days must be taken by the end of the year or be forfeited."

Sean argued, "Yeah, Tim, but the company policy also says I am entitled to 15 paid vacation days for every year on the job. As I see it, that's part of my salary. You can't take my vacation days away once I have earned those days even if I don't use them."

Discussion Questions

1. Assuming Sean decides to press for payment in the court, how would you expect the judge to rule?

2. To protect itself from any future legal actions, how should Geren restate the company's vacation policy?

Review the case and research employment laws and regulations that apply. Decide whether the company handbook is at fault and how it should be remedied. If so, write a brief analysis of the case, reflecting on your research and the answers to the questions. Be prepared to discuss the case in class.

INTERNET RESEARCH ACTIVITY

Wage and benefits information is available on the Internet at several web sites. The U.S. Department of Labor should provide several bits of comprehensive information on current occupational earnings, compensation cost trends, and benefit plan provisions. Detailed occupational earnings may be available for metropolitan and non-metropolitan areas, broad geographic regions, and on a national basis. Access the web site for your city or town to find out if there are any salary trends for your area. Also check your state's web site and review any links to employment, salary, and other information that may be listed.

Access the course web site *http://odgers.swlearning.com* for additional links.

Learning Activity:

Your instructor may ask you to compare your city or state's salary trends nationally or with other specific states.

1. What national or state salary trends did you locate? How does your city compare with national or state salary information?

2. If you were an employer, how would you use salary statistics to set wages or salaries for your company or department?

Do the research for this activity and draft your analysis. Be prepared to submit your findings if directed by your instructor or to participate in a class discussion.

Chapter 9

Health-Related and Other Workplace Issues

The personal issues and problems of workers often spill over into the workplace and, as a result, affect job performance and productivity. When a personal problem is brought into the workplace, it becomes a personnel problem for AMs, who must assume responsibility for assisting in solving personnel problems.

In this chapter, we shall examine those work force issues and problems commonly found in offices of all sizes. First, we shall direct our attention to those issues that affect the physical health and mental well-being of employees, such as substance abuse, depression, workaholic behavior, AIDS, and smoking. Then, we will examine other noteworthy workplace issues dealing with nepotism, office parties, and office romances that raise concerns for many managers.

Being tolerant means that I acknowledge another one's right to obey his own conscience. —Victor Frankl, "The Will to Meaning"

© Digital Vision

TECHNOLOGY APPLICATIONS IN THE WORKPLACE

Computers – Striking a Balance

Computers do a lot for us in our lives. For example, they make education more compelling than words and pictures on paper. In addition, they make our jobs easier to do. It's no wonder people love these machines.

But some people love them too much, and experience "computer addiction." Computers or computer use can be harmful if they isolate you from other areas of life and from other people. If you forgo important social, occupational, educational, or recreational activities in favor of time in front of your computer screen, you've probably taken things too far.

But while computers or computer use can isolate, it can also connect. Many people have developed online friendships and romances or have used the Internet to find and reconnect to old friends and classmates. E-mail can be an easy, low-cost way for family and friends to stay in touch with one another, even over great distances. As with almost everything, striking a healthy balance is necessary while using computers.

ISSUES TO THINK ABOUT:

1. To what extent do you think computer addiction is a concern in our society?
2. Does computer addiction negatively affect the amount or quality of work that gets accomplished in the workplace?

HEALTH-RELATED WORK ISSUES

Health-related work issues affect an administrative manager's performance. These issues may involve dealing with employee substance abuse and depression in the workplace, managing a workaholic, supervising an employee who has AIDS, or monitoring smoking concerns in the workplace, to name a few.

Problems of Substance Abuse

Significant and costly challenges to society have emerged in recent decades. In particular, some that are taking an inordinate amount of managerial time are the problems of alcoholism and drug abuse. The Department of Labor estimates that 73 percent of drug users hold jobs and the combined cost of drug and alcohol abuse is $276 billion annually. Studies also indicate that those who suffer from addiction have more on-the-job accidents, higher absenteeism rates, and increased health-care and workers' compensation claims.[1]

These problems are costly to industry and society in terms of lost work time, health and medical care expenses, property damage, and wage losses. According to the Institute for a Drug-Free Workplace, 1 out of every 12 employees (and 1 out of 5 employees between 18 and 25) use some illicit drug at least once a month. The drugs most commonly abused are marijuana, cocaine, barbiturates, amphetamines, and heroin.[2]

These statistics are profound, and businesses are responding because substance abuse affects its most important asset and expense—members of the work force.

According to a Benefits Survey by the Society for Human Resources Management, more and more companies are adopting proactive policies and procedures related to drug abuse in the workplace—and the pluses are obvious. In addition to developing policies and procedures, the survey found that 52 percent of human resources professionals revealed their organizations currently offer wellness programs, resources, and substance abuse information to employees.[3]

A drug-free workplace program may contain several components and, depending on the level of concern about the problem and the potential for abuse at the work site, companies can implement all or a few of the following prevention and testing activities.

- *Policy development.* Employees must have in writing how the company feels about and will deal with substance abuse in the workplace. An example of a drug-free policy used in an educational environment is shown in Figure 9.1.

- *Employee education.* Once a policy is written and goes into effect, employees must be clear as to its content and the consequences that result from violating that policy.

- *Supervisor training.* Should employees violate the policy, supervisors must be trained to know how to proceed when confronting employees, as there are legal ramifications for not proceeding appropriately.

- *Employee assistance.* Providing help with ways workers can overcome their use of substances is what most companies view as the right thing to do.

FIGURE 9.1 Drug- and Alcohol-Free Workplace Policy

Policy:

The college president or designee shall develop procedures to ensure compliance with state and federal regulations regarding a drug- and alcohol-free workplace/school environment. Such procedures shall include development and implementation of a substance abuse awareness and prevention program in compliance with the U.S. Department of Education Drug Prevention Program Certification requirements.

Procedure:

Purpose

To ensure that employees and students comply with state and federal regulations regarding a drug- and alcohol-free workplace/educational environment.

Employees and students will be notified that the college provides a drug- and alcohol-free workplace/educational environment through regular publications such as class schedules, catalog, and yearly reminders. These publications will also include information regarding the dangers and health risks of substance abuse as well as a description of the applicable legal sanctions under local, state, and federal law for unlawful possession, use, or distribution of illicit drugs and alcohol.

No employee or student will manufacture, distribute, possess, or use a controlled substance or alcohol in the workplace/facilities owned or leased by the college. No employee or student will be allowed to work or attend classes and/or functions that is under the influence of, or has recently used, alcohol and/or a controlled substance to the extent of causing disruptive behavior or impairment of job or academic performance.

Definitions

As used in this policy, "substances" means any/all of the following:

- Illegal drugs/controlled substances.
- Legal drugs (either by prescription or over-the-counter) if these legal drugs are illegally possessed, misused, or overused to such an extent as to cause impairment of job performance.
- Intoxicating beverages.
- Other mind-altering chemicals, materials, and/or substances.

- *Drug testing.* Although drug testing can be a source of controversy, *anxiety*, and concern among employers and employees, it's also helpful. But a successful drug-testing program requires careful planning, consistently applied procedures, strict confidentiality, and provisions for appeal.

How can an employer or manager set up a prevention and testing program that works? First, it's imperative to have the proper policies and programs in place. Then, the employer should spell out the drug-free workplace program to employees. Give each employee a copy of the policy for his or her employee handbook; ask each to acknowledge that he or she has received it by signing and dating a form. Keep the signed and dated form in the files. As a result of workers having this information emphasized and a form acknowledging this has been signed and dated, there are no misunderstandings about what the company expects from its employees. Finally, discuss the handbook contents with workers during the orientation period and ask for questions to clarify the information therein.

Companies should be aware of any outward signs of problems such as increased absenteeism, irritability, and erratic behavior by workers. They should also reassure employees that they can seek help without fear of losing their jobs. If a violation occurs, an employee is typically given a choice: rehabilitation, investigation, or resignation. In other words, the employee *could* enter a rehabilitation program; he or she *could* raise a defense, which then would be investigated; or the employee *could* choose to resign. Workers can ask for help in making their decision in order to select one that benefits them the most. Some companies will offer counseling services in these situations.

In 1988, the **Drug-Free Workplace Act** was passed to ensure that employers who have contracts with the U.S. government maintain a drug-free environment for their workers. Failure to do so can lead to contract termination. A company is not covered by the Act unless it has a single contract with the federal government of $25,000 or more, or it receives a grant from the federal government. To be compliant with this legislation, employers must do the following:

1. Inform employees of drug-free requirements.

2. Clearly outline actions to be taken for violations.

3. Establish awareness programs and supervisory training.

There are do's and don'ts for a manager to consider when approaching an employee about suspected abuse. This checklist is shown in Table 9.1. You should expect workers to display a variety of emotions. Sometimes substance abuse leads to depression or vice versa. Workers may feel depressed over the fear of losing their jobs or any number of problems as described next.

ETHICS & CHOICES

Lately, your top sales manager Tony has been very drowsy after lunch each day and is noticeably less productive than normal. Mary Ellen, a coworker, spots Tony in a sports bar restaurant during lunchtime having at least two beers. She comes back to the office and tells you. As an AM, what would you do?

TABLE 9.1 Suspected Substance Abuse Checklist for Managers

Remember to . . .	But . . .
Prepare what you're going to say ahead of time. Have a plan and stick to it.	Don't try to diagnose the cause of the employee's job performance or conduct problem.
Find a place to meet that's private. Keep what is said in the meeting confidential.	Don't be distracted by tears, anger, or other outbursts. Stay focused.
Focus on job performance and conduct.	
Present written documents of the job performance and/or conduct problems.	Don't threaten discipline unless you're willing to carry it out.
Treat all employees the same.	Don't argue with an employee. If the employee becomes resistant, reschedule the meeting.
State your expectations for improved performance and/or conduct and what will happen if the expectations aren't met within a specific period of time.	
Offer available resources.	
Arrange for another meeting to evaluate progress.	

Depression in the Workplace

The effect of depression on the work force is both broad and deep. According to *Webster's Dictionary*, **depression** is defined as 1) a state of being sad, or 2) a psychoneurotic or psychotic disorder marked especially by sadness, inactivity, difficulty in thinking and concentration, a significant increase or decrease in appetite and time spent sleeping, feelings of dejection and hopelessness, and sometimes suicidal tendencies.[4]

Depression is a common, debilitating, and costly condition—especially to the employer in terms of lost productivity. Depressed employees are more likely to be absent from work, less creative, more argumentative, and more likely to lose their jobs. Depression is increasingly the reason stated by employees who request leaves of absence, disability benefits, job changes, and reasonable accommodations. Statistics show that diagnosis of depression is increasing.

Experts aren't sure what has caused the increase in cases of depression in the workplace, but they offer a variety of potential factors. Some of these factors include

- Rising divorce rates
- The loss of community
- A greater awareness of depression, and
- A decrease in the stigma attached to seeking help.[5]

Effects of depression in the workplace are broad and deep.

© Getty Images/PhotoDisc

Depression affects nearly 10 percent of the U.S. population at any given time. Among the 19 million people who will experience the disease, nearly three out of four are in the work force, according to the Washington Business Group on Health. Estimates of the total U.S. cost of depression run as high as $44 billion, with lost work-days accounting for $12 billion.[6]

Depression is probably the most expensive illness for employers because it is often associated with other ailments, such as back pain, headaches, and stomach problems; and it undermines people's ability to work. Depressed workers lose about 5.6 hours a week because of health problems, compared with the average of 1.5 hours, according to Dr. Walter Steward, leading author of the workplace study on depression.[7]

In order to address these statistics, employers are spending more money on health care because proper treatment is effective in more than 80 percent of the cases. The result is that treatment reduces lost work time and expenditures for other types of health care. A 2002 study conducted by the group, Disease Management Health Outcomes, found employers saved $93 per patient-employee in direct disability payments within the first 30 days following initial treatment for major depression.[8]

Most mental health experts agree that depression is best treated by a combination of medication and therapy. Typical anti-depressant medications are intended to help improve mood, increase the sense of pleasure, help with energy, and make people feel more hopeful. Overall, therapy helps patients work out their problems, provides emotional support, and offers techniques for improving one's life.

Treating depression is an expensive undertaking with escalating costs of anti-depressant drug prescriptions and patient therapy sessions. The costs of untreated depression, however, can be much higher than the treatment costs. When depression is not managed, it can manifest itself in other physical ailments for which the employee might seek treatment. According to the National Mental Health Association, up to one-half of all visits to primary care physicians are due to conditions that are caused by mental problems. Moreover, people with depression are four times more likely to have a heart attack than those with no history of depression.[9]

What is the role of the administrative manager when depression in a worker is suspected? Primarily keep in mind that the AM shouldn't get involved in dictating or advising employees on how to treat depression—or any other serious condition, for that matter. So for a legally responsible way, experts offer the following suggestions:

- *Refer employees to the Employee Assistance Program (EAP).* When an employee tells you that he or she is depressed, you must be careful not to offer medical advice; instead, your emphasis should be on helping that employee identify the best provider, either within your managed care network or EAP, or elsewhere to properly diagnose and treat the employee. The manager's role is to help direct the employee to the best treatment resource—never to treat.

- *Be careful how you bring up the subject of depression with the employee.* Making statements like "It seems to me you're depressed" and asking related questions may violate provisions in the Americans with Disabilities Act. Instead, open with a job performance-based discussion. The discussion may appropriately lead you to suggest that the worker make use of the Employee Assistance Program.

- *Follow up with employees after suggesting they contact the EAP.* By setting the expectation that you'll follow up, the employee is more likely to make the appointment.

- *Through the human resources department, schedule depression screening events at the work site or link mental health web sites to the company's intranet.* Depression screenings help identify symptoms of depression and can be conducted on-site, online, or via telephone using a recorded questionnaire.

- *Don't think of depression as a character flaw or assume the person is lazy and doesn't want to work.* Many times, the depressed person may be making great efforts just to get to work.[10]

In addition to employee depression in the workplace, administrative managers must also recognize that their subordinates may include those who tend to be workaholics.

Workaholics vs. Hard Workers

Not everyone who puts in long hours is addicted to work. Some people are inspired and energized by what they do for a living, and their sense of well-being and fulfillment is proof that they are not engaging in obsessive activity. But for others, the diagnosis may be quite different.

A **workaholic** is a compulsive worker. The person for whom work has become an unhealthy obsession may show the following signs: enjoys little, if any, relaxation or play time; consistently tries too hard and is rarely satisfied with work results; complains of physical symptoms such as headaches, back pains, fitful sleeping, and even ulcers; doesn't enjoy much of a social life; and is single-mindedly dedicated to work to the exclusion of other life activities.

When compared with other workers, compulsive workers are less likely to feel

---

MANAGEMENT TIP

When counseling employees, address employee behaviors, not attitudes. Inappropriate behavior is easy to point out—and easy to explain why it is inappropriate—while a challenge to a person's attitude often will be taken as a personal attack.

happy or satisfied with their lives—even though they are just as likely to enjoy their jobs. Additionally, workaholics generally express the following attributes to a greater degree than non-workaholics:

- Overly stressed or worried
- Feel guilty about not devoting enough time to family and friends
- Unsatisfied with the way they spend their remaining off-work time
- Feel trapped in a daily routine
- Believe they have no time for fun
- Stress at trying to accomplish more than they can comfortably handle.

When an AM senses a worker is displaying workaholic tendencies that appear to be affecting his or her productivity on the job, one of the best approaches is to refer the worker to an Employee Assistance Program.

AIDS Concerns

AIDS (Acquired Immune Deficiency Syndrome) and HIV (Human Immuno-deficiency Virus) are related issues that are problematic for managers and organizations. The concerns are twofold. First, managers are concerned with the eventual decline in productivity and attendance brought on by the inevitable diseases that can afflict an employee with AIDS or HIV. Second, the fear and panic in the workplace brought on by misunderstanding and misinformation can cause colleagues' productivity to change.[11]

Yet, with more and more people living with HIV/AIDS for longer periods of time—and remaining vital contributors to the work force—the stakes have never been higher to stop the discrimination that surrounds the

disease. HIV is defined as a disability under the federal Americans with Disabilities Act with protections akin to those accorded race, religion, sex, or sexual orientation. In the fight against all forms of discrimination, as in the fight against HIV/AIDS, education is the most effective vaccine.

The American College of Occupational and Environmental Medicine has issued recommendations for dealing with HIV/AIDS in the workplace. The recommendations address the role that physicians have within the context of the Americans with Disabilities Act of 1990 (ADA) and the Family Medical Leave Act of 1993.

One of the recommendations is that a physician who performs preplacement medical examinations should ask newly hired employees if they are able to perform the essential functions of the job. Then determine whether any accommodations are necessary. If an employee reports that he or she has AIDS or HIV, reasonable accommodations required by the ADA might include the company modifying facilities, restructuring jobs, changing schedules, or transferring some job functions to another employee. The physician should work with administrative personnel to make sure that the accommodations are appropriately implemented without revealing the employee's health condition.[12]

Workplace Smoking Concerns

In many states, smoking is not allowed in enclosed spaces at all. In other states there are no fixed rules on smoking, or smoking is allowed only in designated areas in the workplace. Management's prerogative to maintain an orderly workplace and address safety and health concerns generally over-rides concerns from employees that their privacy has been restricted and their indi-vidual freedoms have been impinged upon.

The first surgeon general's report in 1986 dealing with the health consequences of smoking and subsequent reports demon-strated the risks of exposure to other people from tobacco smoke. The effects of these reports in the workplace were significant.

1. The focus on involuntary exposure was followed by the 1992 Environmental Protection Agency risk assessment that established environmental tobacco smoke as a Class A carcinogen associated with lung cancer in adults and respiratory disorders in children.

2. The report and risk assessment fueled efforts to restrict smoking in public places.

3. While people have a choice with respect to the frequency and duration of visits to most public places, workers frequent their workplaces consistently and remain at work for considerable amounts of time. Therefore, in workplaces, the degree of "voluntariness" with respect to exposure is questionable; hence, the government protects workers through regulation and legislation.[13]

Smoking in the workplace is beginning to disappear in many organizations. Few organ-izations allow their employees to smoke at will—a reversal of employment policies in place a few decades ago. In other words, previously the right to smoke on the job was generally recognized, and non-smokers had to accommodate themselves as best they could.

Today smoking in the workplace raises two issues for companies: public health con-cerns and organizational costs of smoking.

- Public health concerns center on the issues that smoking has an addictive nature in the form of nicotine and that environ-mental or passive smoke risks must be considered as harmful to others.

- Organizational costs associated with allowing a workplace smoking environ-ment are considerable. These costs can be incurred by organizations through safety risks, fire insurance, effects of smoking on equipment, and the loss of customers who find smoking distasteful.

These problems have formed the basis for this shift in orien-tation. Collectively, smokers incur higher health-care costs (typically supported financially by the employer with insur-ance programs) and higher rates of absenteeism than nonsmokers, which are attributed to their status as smokers. Moreover, employers and nonsmoking employees perceive smokers as less produc-tive because of the time they spend on smoking-related activities, such as breaks.[14]

Smoking should be managed in the context of employment. To that end, compa-nies are developing a smoking policy similar to the one in Figure 9.2 on the next page. Smoking in organizations is a topic that has engendered strong feelings on the part of smokers and non-smokers alike.

FIGURE 9.2 Smoking Policy

Policy

XYZ Corp. is committed to promoting a safe and healthy environment for all individuals within the facility in compliance with state laws and city ordinance. Therefore, smoking is prohibited in all company buildings except in areas specifically designated and identified as "smoking" areas.

Visitors who smoke are expected to abide by this smoking policy. Visitors who, after notice of the policy and its requirements, fail or refuse to abide by this smoking policy may be asked to leave the facilities.

Violators of this policy may be subject to disciplinary action, or may be subject to other rights and remedies provided to the company by law.

Can a company simply refuse to hire smokers? The restrictions on discrimination in hiring are flexible, but there are some pretty fixed boundaries. To single out a group and treat them different from another group—not for job skill or business-based criteria but rather for a lifestyle choice—is something most courts and EEO agencies would question.[15]

In addition to health-related issues, there are other workplace issues that affect the way administrative managers do their jobs. These topics will be covered in the next section. While these issues are not problems that you will readily see in most companies, they can be problematic.

OTHER WORKPLACE ISSUES

Other issues in the workplace that require a manager's ability to determine the proper actions to take with subordinates involve relatives working in the same company

(nepotism), and organizational concerns about office parties and office romances.

Nepotism

Webster's *New Collegiate Dictionary* defines **nepotism** as favoritism shown to a relative (such as giving an appointive job) on the basis of relationship.[16] Most employers have policies that restrict or prohibit this practice. At issue is the potential collusion or conflicts that could occur if spouses, brothers, sisters, mothers, fathers, sons, and daughters work directly for a relative. Continuity of a family company is normally the justification for nepotism. Both of these situations are valid and can occur in any business today.

Therefore, nepotism must be covered in a policy so that job expectancies are clear to employees who are related.

In general, nepotism is thought to have more negatives than positives. Business owners and their advisers have often feared

© CORBIS

Do parties improve morale or create problems in companies?

that non-family employees would resent and possibly treat unkindly family members brought into the business or would see the family members as roadblocks to their own career success. They also feared that some family members might be incompetent or lazy, yet have an attitude of entitlement.

To clarify the extent of coverage in a policy on nepotism or employment of relatives, refer to Figure 9.3 on the next page. The purpose of the procedure, standard of employment, and definition of relatives are clearly spelled out in a policy of this nature.

Another issue that involves the AM and employees' behavior on or off the job is that of office parties.

Office Parties

There is an art to holding a successful office holiday party. And there's literature, too—hundreds of court cases that explore the various pathways to employer liability. Under the heading of sexual harassment claims alone (skipping past assaults, illnesses, and accidents), there are volumes of litigation devoted to inappropriate entertainment, provocative gifts, and lewd table decorations. The institution of the holiday or promotion party has undergone profound changes lately. A survey by career research firm Vault in 2002 found that only 56 percent of companies planned to hold parties, and only 51 percent of employees planned to attend, down dramatically from the last study conducted two years earlier. Budget crunches also have caused changes.

There are two sides to this issue. Some people find it difficult to make merry with the same people they have been working with all year. But other people feel office parties improve morale and, indeed, there

are businesses where the workers genuinely look forward to socializing after hours. Instead of having a big party, however, some companies are doing alternative activities to improve morale and promote team spirit. The activities may include helping to serve food at a shelter, renovating a home or institution for the disabled, or being involved in a general day of caring for less fortunate members of the community.

Other companies are turning their parties into family occasions that take place around lunchtime, or they have moved the parties off the premises to a commercial eating site where beverages are dispensed by professional bartenders. Increasingly, company parties ban alcoholic drinks due in part to management's concern about drunk driving and being held liable. There is also a self-serving fear that a few glasses of wine could dissolve the sense of restraint that keeps employees from expressing their true feelings about their jobs or their coworkers.

FIGURE 9.3 Employment of Relatives (Nepotism) Policy

Purpose

The purpose of this procedure is to avoid real or perceived conflicts of interest and other problems that can be caused by nepotism.

Standard of Employment

XYZ Corp. permits the employment of qualified relatives of employees as long as such employment, whether full time, part time, regular or temporary, does not create actual or perceived conflicts of interest.

An employee may not initiate or participate in any institutional decision involving a direct benefit to a member of his/her immediate family, including serving as the immediate supervisor.

Such involvements include, but are not restricted to, participation in recommendations regarding initial employment, retention, promotion, salary determination, leave of absence, sitting as a member of a grievance or conflict resolution committee, evaluation, discipline, and dismissal. Also, no employee will be permitted to work within the "chain of command" of a relative such that one relative's work responsibilities, salary, or career progress could be influenced by the other relative.

If a conflict or an apparent conflict arises involving employment of relatives, one of the employees must resign or transfer to another position within a reasonable period of time, or an agreeable alternative reporting arrangement must be implemented. The determination of what constitutes a reasonable period of time will be made by the president of XYZ Corp., or designee, based on all the facts and circumstances of the particular case.

Definition of Relatives

A relative is defined as a spouse, child, parent, sibling, grandparent, grandchild, aunt, uncle, niece, nephew, first cousin, or corresponding in-law or "step" relation.

While this procedure explicitly applies to legally recognized family relationships, employees are advised that it may be applied in situations where a conflict of interest could occur in relationships which are not legally recognized; for example, employees who maintain a relationship similar to the relationships prescribed above.

Employees who become relatives by marriage while employed will be treated in accordance with these guidelines.

Sometimes workers may find themselves romantically involved with a colleague at work. The AM may be enlisted to make or enforce policies regarding office romances.

Office Romances

Business colleagues share interests and values, goals and fears, triumphs and setbacks, and, of course, time—lots of time. Given all this, it is not surprising that many women and men find the prospect of an office romance too exciting to resist. Romantic relationships in the workplace have both good and bad consequences.

On the positive side, they can boost employee morale, improve attitudes, minimize personality conflicts, and improve teamwork. On the negative side, workplace romance can give rise to sexual harassment complaints, particularly when a romantic relationship between a supervisor and a subordinate goes awry. Companies can avoid the adverse effects of office romance by implementing a written policy.

A well-written office romance policy should

- Recognize that office relationships exist
- Establish a mechanism whereby relationships and problems are to be reported to the parties' managers confidentially
- Employ mediation (with an unbiased third party) to solve relationship problems but still reserve the use of warnings and extreme discipline measures
- Separate romance from sexual harassment but retain the discipline measures for unreasonable or serious noncompliance; and
- Create a general environment of trust and support for employees.

Despite the rising prevalence of office relationships, coworkers generally continue to find such pairings problematic and risky as well as embarrassing at times.

Risks and Legalities What makes office romance so difficult is the fact that it may affect the work of both parties involved. For example, if a couple has an argument during a coffee break in the morning, will this argument affect their work performance throughout the entire day?

Let's look at the legalities of this dilemma and examine the reasons that companies establish policies against office romances.

Discrimination based on marital status is unlawful today in most states. However, even though employers are not allowed to prevent married couples or significant others from working for the same company or even within the same department, employers are allowed to prevent such couples from working for each other (i.e., in a "reporting to" supervisory situation).

Preventing couples from working for each other protects the employees as well as the company from financial and legal risks. The following three examples help to illustrate the potential risks involved for an administrative manager, an administrative assistant and the company if the manager and the assistant are involved on a romantic level:

1. *Personal risk to the administrative manager.* If the relationship fails, the administrative assistant could claim, under federal guidelines of sexual harassment, that the boss coerced the administrative assistant into the relationship (e.g., with promises of a salary increase).

2. *Risk to the administrative assistant.* When in control of performance reviews, salary increases, and promotions, the AM may not disclose information about promotional opportunities for fear of losing the relationship.

3. *Risk to the company.* Another employee could have a basis for a claim against the company, stating that the administrative assistant involved was receiving preferential treatment in the form of better bonuses or additional benefits. Even if it were untrue, because of the administrative manager and administrative assistant's relationship, the situation could provoke an unpleasant atmosphere wherein other workers feel betrayed. Some may make comments that if they were involved with a manager, promotions or other favors would be easier to get.

Crisis Control If an office romance should happen to you, it may work out with no problems. However, it could go the other direction and you may, at some point, need to manage a breakup situation. If the romance turns sour—or just begins to curdle—think seriously about cutting your losses early. Break up while you can still be friends or, at the least, colleagues. You may consider seeking professional help either to mend the relationship or to end it with both egos intact.

Although dozens of ultimately happy unions begin in business settings, the bottom line is that mixing love and work can be risky business. However, note the reactions in the following study of over 31,000 responses.

The groundbreaking Office Sex and Romance Survey conducted by *Elle*, the world's largest fashion magazine and MSNBC.com in early 2002, was the first to measure the real personal consequences of men and women working side by side. The 44-question survey, polling both female and male respondents 18 and older, collected 31,207 responses. The topics ranged from the sexual climate in the office to the fallout of coworkers' romantic affairs.

Previous surveys showed that most Americans endorsed the statement that having an office romance is like "playing with fire," but this 2002 survey data clearly indicated it's more like playing with matches – "there's the chance of danger, but its slim." Given the potential rewards (at least for any single people), the risks may be worth it. Some of the statistical findings obtained from the survey include:

- 92 percent said a coworker they found "attractive" had flirted with them
- 62 percent of respondents have had at least one office affair; whereas, only 14 percent said they would never date someone from work
- 42 percent of respondents were married or in a concurrent relationship at the time of the office affair
- 12 percent left the company or got transferred as a result of the affair, 4 percent felt stalked at work, 3 percent lost their job, 49 percent reported no problems

after a breakup, but 9 percent said their affair led to divorce or separation

- 25 percent of women say they have benefited because a supervisor found them attractive
- 4 percent of women said they had paid a price for rebuffing a supervisor's advances
- 24 percent of men say they are reluctant to flirt because of the sexual harassment policy

- 60 percent believe an employer should not have any say regarding who they date.[17]

According to the survey, it sheds a new light on an old taboo—office affairs are becoming the norm rather than the exception. However, you should probably weigh the advantages and disadvantages of such an alliance. This, of course, may be easier said than done once a relationship has started.

MESSAGE FOR MANAGERS

Companies can avoid the adverse effects of several health-related and other workplace issues by writing policies and sending the message that management is here to help, rather than to "getcha." Successful managers proceed with employees carefully by first showing they care and then picking the right moment to offer assistance. Avoid giving the impression that you are more concerned with seeing your recommendations put into practice than in helping the other person. In addition, show how the person will benefit from taking the actions you suggest. None of the issues discussed in this chapter are easy ones for administrative managers, but all will inevitably surface in any AM's career and are a critical part of the position.

Chapter Nine

SUMMARY

1. Substance abuse problems are costly to industry in terms of lost work time, health and medical care expenses, property damage, wage losses, and costs associated with traffic accidents. Companies should be aware of any outward signs of problems such as increased absenteeism, irritability, and erratic behavior by workers. They should also reassure workers that they can seek help without fear of losing their jobs.

2. A strong drug-free workplace program contains the following components: policy development, employee education, supervisor training, employee assistance, and drug testing.

3. Depression is a common, debilitating, and costly condition and employees who suffer from depression are more likely to be absent from work, less creative, more argumentative, and more likely to lose their jobs.

4. Administrative managers shouldn't get involved in dictating or advising employees on how to treat depression—or any other serious condition, for that matter. Instead, one approach is to refer employees to the Employee Assistance Program available through the company.

5. A workaholic is a compulsive worker who has an unhealthy obsession with work. Signs to look for that may indicate that work has become an unhealthy obsession are: the person who enjoys little relaxation or play time, consistently tries too hard, and is rarely satisfied with work results. When an AM senses a worker is displaying workaholic tendencies that appear to be affecting his or her productivity on the job, he or she should take some action. One of the best approaches is to refer the worker to an Employee Assistance Program.

6. When managing an employee with HIV/AIDS, managers are concerned with the eventual decline in productivity and attendance brought on by the disease and the fear and panic in the workplace brought on by misunderstanding and misinformation.

7. In general, companies recognize that smokers incur higher health-care costs, higher rates of absenteeism than non-smokers, and can be less productive because of the time they spend on breaks. In many workplaces, smoking is not allowed in enclosed areas or it may be allowed in designated areas only.

8. Nepotism is the practice of allowing relatives to work for the same employer, and most employers have policies that restrict or prohibit this practice.

9. The institution of the holiday or promotion party has undergone profound changes lately and, according to some studies, appears to be on the decline. However, some organizations still see them as a benefit.

10. Romantic relationships in the workplace have both good and bad consequences and one should be aware of these before beginning an office liaison. It's always advisable for companies to avoid the adverse effects of office romances by implementing a written policy dealing with consensual amorous relationships.

KEY TERMS

Depression

Drug-Free Workplace Act of 1988

Nepotism

Workaholic

REVIEW

1. Why do problems of substance abuse cost companies so much money?

2. Briefly state what content a drug- and alcohol-free workplace policy should contain to be effectively written?

3. What is the purpose of the Drug-Free Workplace Act of 1988?

4. According to health professionals, how is depression best treated? What is the appropriate role of AMs in treating depression or any other serious condition?

5. What is the difference between a hard worker and a workaholic?

6. According to the Americans with Disabilities Act, what reasonable accommodations can companies make for workers with HIV or AIDS?

7. What are the costs to companies of employees who smoke compared to employees who are non-smokers?

8. Define nepotism and the reason that companies are concerned with this relationship among workers.

9. Cite three examples of new approaches or alternatives to *safer* office parties and other events.

10. What are some risks associated with office romances, for example, for an *involved* administrative manager? What should the manager do?

CRITICAL THINKING

1. How is the increase in substance abuse affecting the workplace and the job an administrative manager performs?

2. In what ways does depression affect employees' productivity in the workplace?

3. Describe the behaviors of two people you know who you consider one, a workaholic and the other, a hard worker. Summarize the differences.

4. In the role of an administrative manager, how does HIV/AIDS affect productivity in the workplace?

5. To what extent do you think smoking policies are a problem for smokers in the workplace? In your opinion, are smoking policies, like the one shown in Figure 9-2, fair to all workers?

6. Do you think office parties and office romances in the workplace are legitimate concerns for companies and administrative managers? Why or why not?

CASE STUDY 9-1:
HIRING A VICE PRESIDENT'S DAUGHTER

The Dalton Co. is considering hiring the daughter of one of the vice presidents for the position of administrative manager. The daughter, Joyce McGregor, is as well-qualified for the position as any other person who has been interviewed. The position involves responsibility for planning and controlling areas where services and technology are undergoing great change.

The company wants a manager who can "grow with the job," for the position is expected to grow rapidly in scope and status. Although the company has employed relatives of executives for other managerial posts in the company, there is no consensus that employing a relative for the administrative management job will work equally well.

The four executives who have the responsibility for making the final decision have evaluated the situation as follows:

1. Alex McGregor, Joyce's father, feels that since his daughter is well-qualified for the position, she should be hired.

2. Joan Flores, vice president of human resources, also feels that Joyce should be hired. But Flores is aware that the position is subject to much stress and change. Therefore, she feels that special measures must be taken to see that Joyce's performance is evaluated objectively and impartially. Flores firmly believes that if Joyce should fail to measure up to the job, she should be replaced immediately.

3. Donna Renz, vice president of finance, feels that nepotism in a situation such as this is too much of a gamble. She sees that McGregor's daughter may not measure up, and as a result, the company will be faced with a messy and extremely unpleasant decision. (Why does she feel that the daughter may not measure up, in your opinion? On what basis do you think she is making this assessment?)

4. You, as president of Dalton Co., are trying to reconcile the different points of view and reach a decision.

You hold a great deal of admiration and respect for the ability of Alex McGregor, but you know that this is no guarantee that his daughter will perform equally well. Still, as you realize, there is a family tie here. And if you vote against Joyce, what will be the effect upon the father?

You appreciate Flores' point of view and agree wholeheartedly that if Joyce is employed, her performance must be evaluated objectively, and her rating must not be influenced by the position of her father. But, you ask yourself, how can a relative's performance be evaluated objectively? Who will be responsible for conducting the performance appraisal for Joyce? Should she be required to complete a goals assessment similar to others?

Renz has made a good point, too, for you recall that 10 years ago the former president's son-in-law was hired and turned out to be a misfit. It was a sticky situation, and the company had no alternative but to let the son-in-law "gracefully resign." After that, things were never the same with the former president up to the day he retired. After listening to Alex McGregor, Flores, and Renz evaluate Joyce's capabilities and express their viewpoints on nepotism, you realize the next step is up to you.

Directions

Cast your vote and defend your stand by answering each of the following questions.

1. What is your vote?
2. How would you justify your position to each of the three vice presidents if you were asked to do so?
3. How would you proceed to evaluate objectively the performance of an executive's relative such as Joyce McGregor?

Review the facts of the case. Research information on nepotism in the library or on the Internet to see if any factors are involved that you didn't realize at first. Then, take a stand that you can objectively defend from your research in a two-page paper. You may also want to take the approach from the daughter's viewpoint. Do you think she would want to work in this setting with her father as one of the vice presidents? Give your reasons for your stand if you take this approach. Your instructor may ask you to submit the paper after a class discussion.

CASE STUDY 9-2: HOLIDAY PARTY THIS YEAR?

Ms. Saikley, AM at International Business Services, is wondering whether to vote to have a holiday office party this December. She has just spoken with the sales manager, who told her about an incident that happened at another company last holiday season. It seems that the other organization decided to have an "employees only" office party on Friday night from 5 to 8 p.m. at a local downtown restaurant.

Two weeks later, the wife of one of the workers burst into the office area and began shouting accusations at an office worker who she thought was having an affair with her husband. It was embarrassing to everyone in the organization, and most agreed it was unnecessary. The tantrum became loud and abusive on both parties' parts—the wife making accusations and the office worker denying them. The situation became pretty tense at this point.

Discussion Questions

1. If you were the AM of that organization, how would you have reacted to the situation just described? The office worker would have reported to you, and you were the first manager on the scene.
2. Should a policy be written covering office parties? If so, what would be your input

on this policy? Should a policy be written concerning visitors who enter the workplace (even family members) and create a disturbance?

Reflect on the scenario involved in this case. Incorporate your conclusions about what should have been done and how you would write a policy to prevent this type of incident from happening in the future. Can you justify having a guard, or other security policies such as a visitor must be escorted to a particular area? Draft your policy and other actions in a one- to two-page report. Prepare to participate in a group discussion directed by your instructor. Your instructor may ask you to submit your paper in a particular format after the discussion has ended.

INTERNET RESEARCH ACTIVITY

The importance of understanding and treating substance abuse in society is an area the workplace must come to grips with because the issue affects the bottom line and profitability of corporations. Visit the web site *http://odgers.swlearning.com* and others of your choosing and get an update on substance abuse since the publishing of this textbook. You may find search words/phrases such as substance abuse in the workplace, drugs in the workplace, smoking on the job, and others you determine to be useful as you search the web for information on this topic.

Your instructor may ask you to write an outline of your findings with any new web sites that you locate and be prepared to discuss them in class. Be prepared to defend your research efforts.

Chapter 10

Work Ethics and Business Etiquette Issues

After completing this chapter, you will be able to:

1. Discuss the importance of corporate values and business ethics.

2. Describe the types of employee loyalty corporations can expect in today's workplace.

3. Cite examples of desirable business etiquette and behavior relative to work settings, meeting people, using telephonic devices, and dining out.

4. Describe the reasons for appropriate standards of business attire and grooming for men and women.

6. Describe etiquette tips that should be followed when conducting international business.

Employers value well-mannered employees because they are a reflection of the company. Although work ethics and business etiquette reflect social and cultural factors, they are also highly personal and are shaped by an individual worker's own values and experiences.

Chapter 10 looks at ethics and etiquette issues from a number of viewpoints. Organizations pay attention to ethics and etiquette because the public expects a business to exhibit high levels of ethical performance and social responsibility. The public also expects managers and workers alike to be appropriately attired and to project a professional image at all times. These expectancies extend to doing business in the international arena.

Chapter Ten

An infectious greed seemed to grip much of our business community. —*Alan Greenspan*

TECHNOLOGY APPLICATIONS IN THE WORKPLACE

© Getty Images/PhotoDisc

Protecting Company and Customer Information

Identity theft is a booming and growing business with plenty of customers willing to pay to become someone else. Stories about hackers breaking into systems and taking personal information are abundant in the news. This information can be used to obtain credit cards and loans. It can also be used to assume someone else's identity. For example, a person with a criminal record or an illegal immigrant may want a new identity so that he or she can get a decent job. An estranged parent may want a new identity to avoid paying alimony or support, similar to debtors who may want to avoid paying their obligations.

Whatever the reason for the new identity, there is a large market waiting to be filled. With this type of demand, it is no wonder that hackers are constantly probing company networks looking for weaknesses. When they find poorly secured systems, they exploit them in the hope that they can penetrate the defenses and reach their goal, the personal information of customers, clients, and business partners. These people have no interest in ethics.

ISSUES TO THINK ABOUT:

1. How vulnerable do you think businesses are to hacking and identity theft?
2. Who is responsible for taking the steps to prevent this from occurring—the government or the company? Why?

CORPORATE VALUES AND BUSINESS ETHICS

Every organization has a soul. When done right, the soul is a set of basic beliefs, ethics, and values that stand above and beyond their effect on any particular product, market, capability, or result. Beliefs, values, and ethics sustain growth and success over time and add real value to employees, customers, and investors.[1]

Value-driven management is a concept that defines successful companies. A **value-driven company** is one that consistently produces a high-quality product or service, treats employees with respect, and has demonstrated ways in which it incorporates the values it holds into the fabric and culture of its business. Moreover, value-driven companies find ways to link their daily operations to social and environmental concerns and integrate employee and community well-being into their decision-making. Companies like these define their cultures in terms of common sense and what they think it means to do the right thing.

When an organization's values statement is crafted, it should show the best side of a company's personality. The statement usually offers ambitious commitments to quality and service. Unfortunately for many organizations, the values statement is window dressing—an image thing. When companies put statements on paper and then ignore them, it is an easy and almost certain way to lose credibility with the work force and esteemed customers.

Every company faces ethical dilemmas. The question is — how does a company treat employees when they bring manage-ment bad news or unpopular opinions? If managers expect employees to bring bad news to their attention, then employees need to feel that they're going to be treated fairly. They want to know that management is going to actually follow through, that they care that something might be going on that is wrong, and will take the steps to do something about it.[2]

How do you make sure sound beliefs and ethics are at work in an organization? Discussion of the following three questions will help in finding answers.

1. What are basic beliefs, values, and ethics?
2. How are ethical behaviors communicated?
3. How can they be made to work?

Basic Beliefs, Values, and Ethics

Basic beliefs are deeply felt moral and ethical principles that guide decision-making and behavior. They begin with the feelings, character, and experience of the original founders and owners of the company. Succeeding managements further shape the original basic beliefs as they face economic, environmental, political, technological, and competitive change and their effect on the company.

Values and ethics aren't the same; there's a crucial distinction that should be noted. Values are our fundamental beliefs or principles. They define what we think is right, good, fair, and just. Examples of specific ones are to tell the truth, operate within the law, and assure employee equality in gender and ethnicity.

Ethics, on the other hand, are behaviors and tell people how to act in ways that meet the standard our values set for us. The crux of that distinction for organizations is this:

© Getty Images/PhotoDisc

It's not the company's place to tell workers what their values ought to be. Values come with workers when they enter the workplace. But it is the company's responsibility to set behavioral standards, and it has an obligation to train employees in what those standards are—relative to ethical issues.

In business, examples of ethical issues include, but are not limited to, sexual harassment, employee privacy, nepotism, environmental concerns, security of company records, usage of computer and network systems, workplace safety, product safety standards, fair treatment of customers, and financial and cash management procedures. Acceptable behaviors regarding the foregoing ethical issues are normally spelled out in various company policies. Policies must also spell out acceptable practices relating to acceptance of gifts from vendors and others.

Can you train an employee to be ethical? Not if his or her values run counter to the organization. Ethics violations don't occur for the most part because employees are bad people. On the contrary, most violations are committed by people who think they are doing the right thing within the boundaries set by supervisors and upper management.

Values statements and codes of conduct are the infrastructure of an effective ethics program. Codes of conduct don't need to re-articulate every possible situation that could arise, nor do they need to cover every rule and regulation. But they should address the areas of uncertainty, confusion, and risk that the organization faces today and in the near future.

Employees will be motivated in an organization with values compatible with their own.

Ethical Behaviors and Ethics Training in the Workplace

The business world is not a separate universe of economic values and goals distinct from society but an aspect of the behavior of society as a whole. To be effective, ethics cannot be a mere restraint on the unsocial or criminal behavior of managers or a response to consumer pressure. Because values precede behavior as we've just stated, it's safe to predict that companies need to take employees' values seriously. Workers at all levels want to know what the organization stands for and whether it is something they can feel a part of and identify with as well. Knowing that their company stands for values they themselves hold can help employees decide to be loyal and give their best effort when on the job.

Many companies develop detailed codes of conduct and policies; yet many of these firms actually pay only lip service to the ethics they supposedly espouse when it comes to their daily activities. The gap between what the company actually practices and what it supposedly upholds promotes cynicism, which in turn nurtures and reinforces mistrust. Cynicism and mistrust encourage unethical behavior.

Companies can create an ethical environment by ensuring the presence of four conditions: ethical awareness, reasoning, action, and leadership. An organization may possess:

- *Ethical awareness* if employees are able to recognize ethical problems when they occur.

- *Ethical reasoning* if employees are provided with the right tools for understanding and dealing with ethical dilemmas. These tools include a common language and method of evaluating the courses of action they can take in the face of moral dilemmas.

- *Ethical action* when structures and approaches enabling employees to freely discuss and resolve ethical issues are established.

- *Ethical leadership* when leadership is applicable to all levels of the organization and can be achieved by allowing *everyone* to be a moral leader.

The Ethics Resource Center, a nonprofit educational organization in Washington, D.C., issued its findings from the 2001 National Business Ethics Survey: How Employees Perceive Ethics at Work. The report's authors identify these potential benefits when companies are linked to an effective ethics program:

- Recruiting and retaining top-quality people;

- Fostering a more satisfying and productive work environment for employees;

- Building and sustaining a company's reputation within the communities in which it operates;

- Maintaining the trust of employees to ensure continued self-regulation;

- Legitimizing an open dialogue concerning ethical issues;

- Providing ethical guidance and resources for employees before making difficult decisions; and

- Aligning the work efforts of staff with their company's broader mission and vision.[3]

An ethics program requires commitment and training. Three noteworthy objectives of any workplace ethics training program are to:

1. Raise awareness that corporate values are important to the organization;

2. Give people the tools to make ethical decisions; and

3. Teach people to consider the consequences of their actions.

At the heart of communicating and teaching ethics, every employee needs to know how to apply beliefs to his or her decisions and actions, what to do when trouble occurs from failure to apply a belief, what rewards exist for application of sound ethics, and what penalties may occur for failure to apply fitting ethical standards. It is better to discuss typical situations in advance during a training setting, rather than let trouble occur and then consider what might have been done to prevent or control it. Role playing in training sessions may be helpful.

Ethical Leadership and Decisions

By virtue of their positions, administrative managers have always had to deal with ethical issues. These issues ranged from the "little white lie" told over the telephone and face-to-face, to being asked by a supervisor to perform illegal, immoral, and unethical tasks on the job. A person with strong work ethics has the ability to recognize ethical problems, exercise ethical reasoning skills, resolve ethical conflicts, and implement ethical decisions in the face of these situations.

The bar is set high for company leadership with regard to ethics: It's not enough to be an ethical person. Leadership must be visibly ethical. How do managers do that? They create an expectation in others that they (the managers) will act ethically and expect the same actions from everyone else in the organization.

Let's take the infamous Enron Corp. as an example of "values in words only." Unfortunately, Enron is out of business, taking with it billions of investor dollars and the jobs of more than 4,000 employees, as well as their retirement funds. The company's core values—respect, integrity,

communication, and excellence—were once proudly etched on paperweights. Now they're an ironic joke. As events in the business world have shown, values statements that are contrary to actual practices by a business can result in a sense of insincerity. Companies need to concentrate on their basic values if only to avoid being considered hypocritical.[4]

When leaders make ethical decisions, those decisions are usually based on the following six behavioral and moral standards: honest communication, fair treatment, social responsibility, fair competition, responsibility to the organization, and respect for the law. Table 10.1 offers some business-related examples for each of the six standards.

Having seen some leaders go to jail for unethical practices, the threat of legal punishment has prompted many organizations to put compliance-based ethics programs into effect. Management can take these five steps to establish ethics in the workplace.

1. *State corporate values in three sentences or less.* Make sure all employees understand what these values are and how they apply to daily activities. Publish the values so that associates and customers also understand them. Some examples of value statements from various organizations include the following:

- Our customers are the only reason we are in business.
- Quality in delivering our products and service is No. 1 with us.
- Every college employee helps students to learn.

TABLE 10.1 Six Ethical Standards for a Value-Driven Company

Ethical Standards	Examples
Honest communication	Evaluate subordinates candidly. Don't slant proposals to senior management.
Fair treatment	Pay equitably. Don't use lower-level people as scapegoats.
Social responsibility	Show concern for employee health and safety.
Fair competition	Avoid bribes and kickbacks to obtain business. Don't fix prices with competitors.
Responsibility to the organization	Avoid waste and inefficiency. Act for the good of the company as a whole, not out of self-interest.
Respect for the law	Avoid taxes, don't evade them. Follow the letter and spirit of laws.

2. *Act according to these published values.* One interpretation of this simply states: "We are what we do, not what we say."

3. *Outline specific responsibilities for decision-making to ensure accountability.* Policies and lines of responsibility must be clearly stated. Be willing to take action if the code of ethics is violated.

4. *Encourage open discussion.* Discussions among company employees about controversial issues, ethical questions, and anything that might fall into gray areas should occur frequently. Keep in mind that people must feel safe before they will speak openly.

5. *Conduct ethical-awareness training for employees.* Allow workers to see how the company's ethical system applies to everyday problems and blurred areas throughout organizations.

LOYALTY IN THE WORKPLACE

The days of one employee working for one company for an entire career and ultimately retiring from that company with pride and pension are, to a great degree, going away. With today's mergers and acquisitions, company closings, downsizing, accounting irregularities, tarnished images, and intense economic pressure on company portfolios and pension plans, an employee is likely to leave with neither pride nor a healthy pension, and maybe depart even sooner than an anticipated retirement. Loyalty in the workplace has become a radically misunderstood concept. The questions of how to build workplace loyalty among those employees who stay and what their loyalty means for profits have never been so relevant.

Manpower Inc. announced the results of an international survey, which found that employee loyalty is alive and growing; but there are many variations in loyalty levels across the world as well as among the demographic groups that comprise each organization's work force. Across the eight countries included in the survey, managers reported that loyalty has increased in the past three years, and they are very optimistic about loyalty increasing over the next three years.

The groundbreaking study consisted of more than 2,600 telephone surveys of human resource managers in eight countries—France, Germany, Italy, Japan, Mexico, the Netherlands, the United Kingdom, and the United States—as well as more than 1,400 interviews of employees in the United States and the United Kingdom. The highest levels of loyalty to employers were reported in Mexico, the Netherlands, and the United States; the lowest, in Japan and Italy. The findings of the loyalty survey resulted in describing employees in four ways—mutual loyalists, blind loyalists, mercenaries, and saboteurs.

- *Mutual loyalists* (53 percent of employees surveyed) are loyal to their employer and believe this loyalty is deserved. These employees are likely to see their psychological contract as a two-way street, where their own efforts and performance are rewarded with investment from the company. To some degree, this is the ideal scenario: true, mutual loyalty. This group is composed of a higher proportion of U.S. employees, women, and senior managers.

- *Blind loyalists* (19 percent of employees surveyed) express loyalty toward their company despite not feeling that the company deserves it. To some extent, this segment is expressing blind or misplaced loyalty toward the company. The challenge for companies with large numbers in this employee segment is how to generate more positive perceptions of deserved loyalty through improved practices. This segment is composed of a higher proportion of women and U.K. employees.

- *Mercenaries* (6 percent of employees surveyed) feel that the company deserves their loyalty, but they sense no loyalty toward it. Only about half intend to be with the same company in three years. Mercenaries are represented by a higher proportion of non-managerial employees and employees with lower scores on awareness and understanding of the company's values.

- *Saboteurs* (21 percent of employees surveyed) feel that the company does not deserve their loyalty, nor do they feel any loyalty toward it. Only one in four of this group would speak highly of their company as an employer, and a similar proportion would actively criticize the business as an employer. Only about half feel any sense of motivation in their jobs, and more than half feel their company does not reward loyalty. Saboteurs are composed of a higher proportion of men, U.K. employees, and those with three to five years of service with their current employer.[5]

The larger the company, the more likely there is to be decreasing employee loyalty, according to research conducted at NFI Research.[6] The conclusions reported that at large companies (those with 10,000 employees or more), employee loyalty is dramatically decreasing; while at small companies (those with fewer than 100 employees), loyalty is actually increasing. For the most part, the larger the company, the less loyal the employees are; and the smaller the company, the more loyal the employees are.

The good news is that businesses have an opportunity to increase employee loyalty by taking action. Here are some suggestions for organizations to maintain or improve employee loyalty.

1. *Increase confidence in leadership.* Employees want to feel their leaders know where they're going, since the employees have to follow that path.

2. *Improve company culture.* What it's like to work at a company is more important

> **MANAGEMENT TIP**
>
> The Pygmalion in Management Theory argues that managers' expectations of their subordinates serve as self-fulfilling prophecies. In other words, managers who expect creativity, productivity, and ethical behavior from their employees usually get it—and vice versa.

than salary when it comes to increasing loyalty. This means people need to be treated fairly.

3. *Increase trust.* It isn't the monetary rewards that build loyalty — it is the feeling of adding value, making a contribution, and being trusted that matters most in building an organization of loyal employees.

4. *Create advancement opportunity.* Employees want to progress but want businesses to provide a growth path they can follow.

5. *Promote stability of company.* In this economy, employees in general do not expect substantial financial increases. Job and company stability and staying power are more important in most employees' (and managers') minds.

6. *Provide autonomy and challenge.* Provide some tough challenges for employees and then get out of the way! When given the chance, many conscientious employees will rise to a challenge because they desire to make a meaningful contribution.

7. *Provide stability of job.* It's tough to make or get guarantees these days, but job stability stands for a lot when everything else around the employee seems to be changing.

8. *Provide flexibility.* Many are looking for a more balanced work and personal life, especially in these trying times.

9. *Monitor benefits.* It's not just the salary that matters for loyalty from workers; it's the other company programs, such as health-care coverage, matching company contributions, and employee stock ownership plans that can more closely link an employee to a company.

While a company may not use all of these, these actions will provide approaches that organizations can use to obtain a greater sense of loyalty from their employees.

BUSINESS ETIQUETTE AND BEHAVIOR

In light of our shrinking world and expanded media coverage throughout the world, good business etiquette is crucial as behaviors are more closely scrutinized than ever in the past. Business etiquette is much more than knowing how to use the correct utensil or how to dress for certain occasions. Today's businesspeople must know how to be at ease with strangers, people from other cultures, or in groups; they must know how and when to congratulate someone; they must know how to make introductions; and they must know how to conduct themselves on cell phones and at company social functions, receptions, and meals. Table 10.2 lists some basic etiquette rules for the workplace relative to general office etiquette, general courtesy, introductions, and travel. Review these general rules of etiquette and think about how you are perceived at school and in the workplace (if you currently work).

Etiquette is about presenting yourself with the kind of polish that shows you can be taken seriously. Etiquette is also about being comfortable around people and making them comfortable around you. Many potentially worthwhile and profitable alliances have been lost because of an unintentional breach of manners. Most behavior that is perceived as disrespectful, discourteous, or abrasive is unintentional and could have been avoided by practicing good manners or etiquette. Basic knowledge and practice of etiquette is a valuable advantage, because in a lot of situations,

a second chance may not be possible or practical. One such second chance that never repeats itself is when you meet someone, introduce yourself or others, and/or exchange business cards. Definite rules are in place for these actions. Business introductions are important, and business cards must be looked at and handled with respect, as you will learn in the following sections.

Elements of business etiquette not only focus on work behavior, but on meeting people, telephone etiquette, and dining etiquette as well.

At Work

As businesses continue to reduce staff and compress layers of management, companies are catapulting administrative managers into positions of increased responsibility and exposure to people both inside and outside the organization. Today, you must look and act the part—exude style, competence, and authority—to ensure that your ascent up the ladder does not end in a crash landing.

Rudeness and bad manners have become alarmingly common in the workplace in the United States, according to research by psychologist Lilia M. Cortina at the University of Michigan. Her research found that 71 percent of workers surveyed have been insulted, demeaned, ignored, or otherwise treated discourteously by their coworkers and superiors. Employees who experience uncivil treatment report lower job satisfaction and are more likely to withdraw from their jobs by being tardy repeatedly, taking unnecessary sick days, or by simply not working very hard.

MANAGEMENT TIP

The important thing to remember about business etiquette is this: If you strive to make the people around you feel comfortable and valued, to a large extent, you have succeeded.

TABLE 10.2 General Business Etiquette Rules

General Office Etiquette	Offensive language, be it gender-, culture-, race-, or religion-based, does not belong in the workplace.
	Sexual innuendoes and off-color jokes should be avoided.
General Courtesy	Business etiquette is genderless and generationless—everyone should be treated equally.
	Men or women should never loosen their ties or remove their jackets unless the host or hostess does.
	A person should never be kept waiting longer than 10 minutes.
	Thank-you letters should still be sent after meals and interviews.
Introductions	Men and women should always extend the right hand when being introduced.
	Men and women should both stand when a guest from outside the company enters a room.
Travel	Men no longer need to feel obligated to assist women with their luggage.
	A male or female driver should unlock all doors for passengers before getting into a car.

Source: Jim Rucker and Jean Anna Sellers, "Changes in Business Etiquette," *Business Education Forum*, February 1998, pp. 43–45.

When employees speak up about rudeness from their superiors, Cortina's research indicated they experienced both social and professional retaliation. When employees are silent, they experienced a higher level of psychological problems, including depression and anxiety. So there's a real dilemma about how to respond to rudeness.[7]

Practicing a positive attitude and saying "please" and "thank you" frequently are suggestions that are always advisable. In addition, remember to also address work

conflicts as situation-related, rather than person-related. Apologize when you unintentionally hurt someone by your remarks, as you show respect and courtesy to everyone, regardless of their position.[8]

In an increasingly competitive business environment, good manners can make the difference in completing a sale and getting or losing a new or repeat customer. Using good etiquette at work includes all aspects of the work environment—completing work on time, getting to work on time, being courteous to others, being an active member of the work team, practicing good human relations, listening, following through on commitments made, and solving problems in a manner that involves good etiquette.

Meeting People

Workplace courtesy should be a matter of policy. Etiquette when meeting people involves receiving guests, making their visit pleasant and worthwhile, introducing people, presenting gifts, shaking hands, giving and receiving business cards, and remembering names. The ability to make introductions graciously and with sensitivity to the status of the person or people involved is a simple enough skill to acquire, with a small amount of time devoted to practice. Displaying this ability will show that you are a professional and take your job seriously.

Introducing people correctly is actually quite uncomplicated. Always use the name of the older or higher-ranked person (if this is a business-related introduction) first. For example, you should introduce

- A junior executive to a senior executive. Mr. Senior, this is Miss Junior.
- A younger person to an older person. Mrs. Holloway, I'd like you to meet my daughter, Melissa.
- Someone from the company to a customer or client. Mr. Haggerty, this is Ms. Warren, the head of our advertising department. Ms. Warren, this is Jim Haggerty from the Wilson Co.
- A non-official person to an official person. Mr. Sudek, I'd like you to meet Janice Haynes, our director of human resources.

It's usually helpful if you provide a little bit of information about the people you're introducing, although this might not always be necessary or possible. [9]

Whether you're a man or a woman, jobs can still be won or lost on the basis of a firm handshake. Men and women should shake hands with each other the same way a woman would shake another woman's hand or a man would shake another man's hand. Offer your hand turned at a 90-degree angle to the floor and don't hold just the fingers or try to crush the other person's hand with an iron grip.

Another hallmark of good manners and professionalism is the ability to recall names at will. Many people admit that they're able to recognize a familiar face but can't always recall the person's name. The key to developing a good memory for names is concentration, especially when you first hear a person's name. Here are some techniques to practice:

- *Make sure you hear the name clearly.* If you're not sure you've heard the name correctly, don't hesitate to say, "I'm sorry, but I didn't catch your name. Could you tell me again?" If the name sounds foreign or is difficult to pronounce, ask the person to spell it. A friendly smile can help you do this pleasantly so that you don't act embarrassed.
- *Use the person's name immediately.* This helps to impress the name upon your memory. You might say, "It's nice to meet you, Mrs. Flanagan." Then, if you make a mistake, the person can correct you. Repeat the name again if you are corrected—with a smile.

- *Repeat the name often (but don't overdo it) as you converse.* Repetition fixes the name more firmly in your mind.

- *Connect characteristics with names.* Take note of such things as the person's occupation, eye color, unique handshake, style of dress, or manner of walking. For example, you might associate "Mr. Burns" (as in red fire) with red hair. Or "Miss Parker" with the ski jacket or parka she's wearing. No matter how far-out the association might be, it's legitimate as long as it helps you remember the name without confusing it with your memory aid. A case in point of what not to do—an assistant was introduced to a client whose name was Mr. Fox. She thought she could remember that easily by associating it with the fox and the crow fairy tale. When Mr. Fox came in for his next appointment, the assistant greeted him very enthusiastically as, "Hello, Mr. Crow." Was she embarrassed!

- *Look away and try to visualize the person.* You can do this while you're still in the same room with the person and again after he or she has left. It will help you associate the face with the name.

- *Record names.* When you return from a business meeting or social gathering, write down the names you want to remember. You might want to carry a small notebook for this purpose. Exchanging business cards with others can be an excellent way to help remember names. Business card etiquette is an important tool for you to use.

- *Accept it when memory fails.* If you do forget a name, don't be shy about admitting it. It's better to admit having a memory lapse than to embarrass yourself or the person by using the wrong name.

- *Be sympathetic to people who forget your name as well.* Offer your hand, and say, "I'm Georgie Steele, Dr. Janey's assistant. I met you at the conference in Phoenix."[10]

After introductions are out of the way, some small talk may be suitable. The purpose of small talk is to find something in common and create a bond. The best way to do this is to ask people questions. Being observant and asking good questions is more important than trying to be witty. Politics and religion are best avoided as topics of conversation unless you know the person you're talking with has similar interests. Never bring up sex in any context and never swear. People often get into a social situation, and they let their guard down. Don't let this happen to you.

Telephonic Devices

The telephone naturally de-emphasizes status, gender, and age distinctions. One way to look at the telephone is that it allows us to respond to content, not context, thereby facilitating equality. On the other hand, telephone rudeness can inadvertently occur and may have a devastating and long-term effect on an organization. All too often companies lose clients because of indifference or negative treatment they received on the phone.

Using office and cell phones presents special etiquette concerns. Telephone services will be covered in more depth in Chapter 15; however, they affect the study of etiquette now. Remember these etiquette rules with office phones:

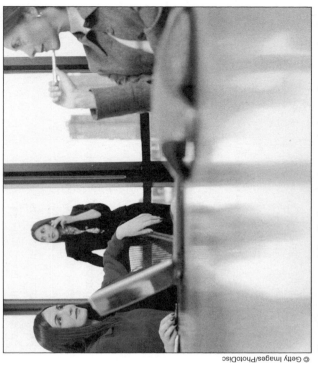

© Getty Images/PhotoDisc

- Answer the phone by the third ring.
- Say "Good morning" or "Good afternoon."
- Identify your company, your department, and yourself at the start of the phone call.
- Listen attentively to the caller to determine the nature of the call so you can serve the needs of the customer or client quickly and efficiently.
- Try to direct the caller to a person who can help him/her.
- If you must put a caller on hold, do not keep the caller waiting without checking back to find out if the person wants to continue holding or call back later.
- Remember to ask first before transferring a call. If you must transfer a call, keep it simple and positive, and do not transfer the person if that is not his or her preference. Ask for permission to put the person on hold while you check with the person or department to which you are making the transfer. Give the caller the extension or the complete number of the transfer location.
- Always end the call on a pleasant note and say "Goodbye."[11]

When using your cell phone in a business setting, remember to keep it in your purse or briefcase—with the ringer turned off. If you are expecting an absolutely urgent call, be sure to make your guests aware of it at the beginning of the meeting or a meal. Then, when your phone rings, excuse yourself from the table and keep your conversation brief.[12] Especially during business lunches or any other meeting, avoid taking cell phone calls. It sends the message that the client you are

Practicing respectful cell phone etiquette is becoming a serious concern during business meetings.

with is not as important as the person calling. In addition, it interrupts the flow of the conversation and is annoying to the other attendees.

Dining Out

Etiquette for breakfast, lunch, or dinner meetings involves planning the meeting, arranging for seating, paying the bill, and tipping. For starters, the following information can ensure a smooth dining experience:

- *Choose the right location.* Bypass the trendy new hot spot for a more-quiet and easy-to-find restaurant that you know provides excellent food and service. Make sure a variety of menu options are offered so people with dietary restrictions will be accommodated.

• *Arrive early.* Get to the restaurant before the people you are meeting. That way you can select a comfortable and quiet table and be there to greet them. Arrange seating in advance. Discuss with the maître d' or wait staff the requirements for seating and explain that you will be receiving the check. You may also want to discuss how you will pay for the meal and/or the room if one is also provided for a charge. If appropriate, you may want to remind the wait person not to interrupt a person's speech to discuss something about the meal, but to stand by until a convenient time to ask or give information.

• *Keep it short.* While you want to postpone talking business until after you have ordered, don't let the lunch go on too long, since your clients may have limited time to meet. The guest should order first (unless the guest asks you, as the host, to do so). The guest should be served first. You can let the server know who your guests are ahead of time or when the order is being taken.

• *Give your undivided attention.* As the host, it's your job to make sure the meeting is productive and on topic. Do not comment on whether someone did or did not eat all of the food on the plate. It is considered rude to notice and mention it one way or the other.

• *Pay and tip appropriately.* Establish with the waiter that you will be paying the check. Tip the waiter approximately 15 percent; more if service is especially good, less if service is bad. Never make a scene about bad service.[13] A letter to the manager after the meeting should be sufficient to let the restaurant know you were dissatisfied.

BUSINESS ATTIRE AND IMAGE SKILLS

You must have technical skills, communication skills, and interpersonal skills; but, to succeed, you also need image skills. Most people just dress for their job with very little thought to their choice of attire or accessories. The importance of image and attire in the business world is very real. Your image is like the weather—people notice when it is extremely good or extremely bad. Put another way, your image is your reputation and a reflection of how others perceive you, either through your conversation, appearance, or written words. More and more, corporations are taking on the role of professional etiquette and image training for up-and-coming executives by providing classes in etiquette and image building.

Unless you work for one of the handful of surviving Internet start-ups, wearing vintage Pumas and a Def Leppard T-shirt to work may no longer be the thing to do. Be aware that the manner in which you present yourself can negatively affect your career. That is what has happened with people dressing too casual.[14] It is, therefore, important to take the necessary steps to develop the awareness, judgment, and a system that leads you to consistently present yourself to achieve the success you desire.

According to the American Industry Dress Code Survey completed in December 2001, a national poll of 201 senior executives at companies with more than $500 million in annual revenue, reported that more than half of large businesses (56 percent) maintain a business attire policy—that means a suit and tie for men and a suit or dress for women.

What's more, the study reveals that of those companies with a business dress code, 19 percent have reinstituted their policy since 2000.

Companies have their individual reasons for promoting a dress code in their organizations. Some respondents in the survey, for instance, predicted that the switch from a casual to a professional business dress code could result in an average 3.6 percent productivity gain for their company. Other executives surveyed believe a professional image can translate into improved work ethics and spur growth in overall productivity.[15]

The bottom line, however, is that people want to be taken seriously, and attire can help or hurt in that regard. When people look at you and see the way you act, as well as the way you dress, they draw impressions concerning your ability, your credibility, and, most importantly, whether you are serious and should be taken seriously.

When you go to work, be appropriately dressed and prepared for anything, because you could be in contact with people at all levels and in all walks of life. Work attire should reflect the position you hold, the organization you represent and, of course, a little about you personally. Being well groomed from head to toe is part of that preparedness.

A positive public image is a way of life in which your wardrobe style, voice tone, grooming habits, etiquette, office decor, body language, and business presentations (oral and written) denote a style of performance commensurate with success. Given the standard five seconds it takes a person to make a visual first assessment, most people agree that your appearance sends a powerful

message. For some women and men, what one wears to work is almost as important as job performance.[16]

Dress and Grooming Policies

When it comes to employees' clothing, how much can a company dictate? It depends on the situation. An employer is certainly entitled to address the subject and tie it to the workplace and the business needs of the company. It's definitely a good idea to discuss dress and grooming standards in company policies. That way, the company's procedures will be clearly stated in writing, which is always a good idea when you're addressing personal preferences of workers.

Written dress and image policies vary from company to company. For example, policies can instruct employees to dress in accordance with their position and to always be "neatly attired." (That's the language that's often used.) If you're in a very formal work environment where all customers and

© CORBIS

To succeed in business, you need to look and act professionally.

clients are more formally dressed, then using a rule of thumb that would require employees to be appropriately dressed in meetings with clients and customers is reasonable. In contrast, companies can allow for casual dress where there's no direct contact on a regular basis with clients and customers.

How should policies be written that address hairstyle and grooming issues? Businesses need to be appropriate with respect to grooming standards, and those standards must always be business-based rather than personally-based.

There has been, for example, litigation over requiring men to have short hair, where there was no business basis for that requirement.

Can you center these guidelines on your customers' expectations? For instance: Our clients expect men to have short hair or our clientele expect women to wear skirts. That would be a gray area. To be reasonable, most grooming policies must focus on presenting a neat and professional appearance and should reflect the needs of the working environment. For example, there may be safety reasons, particularly in a manufacturing situation, where long hair (if it's not restrained) or wearing certain pieces of jewelry on the job, may pose a safety hazard. Obviously that's a legitimate restriction on one's grooming and dress.

What happens when dress codes intrude on an employee's religion or ethnicity? Managers must have a valid business reason for the dress code to restrict an employee

> **MANAGEMENT TIP**
>
> *Pointer for success—*You never get a second chance to make a first impression.

from dressing in accordance with his or her religious beliefs. It's fair to say that if an employee's religious beliefs require wearing a hair covering or a particular style of clothing, employers are required to reasonably accommodate this request when it doesn't impose an undue burden on getting the job done in the workplace.[17]

Dress Code Terms

Business dress used to mean just that, but today even the most fashion-conscious among us are puzzled on occasion. Dress-code terms found on invitations and in business conference and registration material can be perplexing. Here are some interpretations that might help.

- *Smart casual:* Also called dressy casual, or Friday casual, appropriate wear includes sweaters, turtlenecks, blazers, collarless or open-collar tops, and pants such as khakis or corduroys. For women, slacks and skirts also should be suitable.

- *Resort casual:* Often called for in warm destinations, attire includes mid- to knee-length shorts; collarless or golf shirts; khakis and sandals. Women can wear linen sheaths, casual skirts, or sundresses.

- *Business:* For men, a collared shirt, tie, and jacket or suit are always correct. For women, pants, skirt suits, or business dresses.

- *Cocktail:* Men should wear nothing less formal than a blazer and slacks; for women, dressy pantsuits or short, dressier dresses would be acceptable.

- *Black-tie optional:* Men can wear a tuxedo or dark business suit; for women a long, formal gown or a shorter, elegant dress or nice suit would be appropriate.

INTERNATIONAL POLITENESS

The thing about different cultures is just that—they're different. And no one can expect to know every nuance. So mistakes will be made and unintentional blunders committed. But some of these errors can be avoided by suppressing one's own cultural biases. Most mistakes come in the form of spoken and body language or omitting something that should have been taken care of. People from other countries spend a great deal of time studying the culture of those who live in the United States. A good host should be willing to spend time and effort studying the guest's culture. Attention to detail is not only a polite practice; but in today's economy, it is a very smart business practice. Remember that communication is between two people, not two cultures. Few people are a perfect example of their culture—we all have some differences or preferences that aren't what a person of that culture would normally say, think, or do.

As the United States gains greater access to other countries and as businesspeople from abroad come to the States, our knowledge of etiquette needs to become more universal. We have to learn about and remain respectful of each other's particular ways of greeting people, eating, dressing, and making conversation. With international business competition heating up, manners could mean the difference between corporations making money or losing the opportunity of being invited to do business in a foreign country. Why then should we so keenly study foreign cultures? One explanation is that we don't want to omit someone who prefers not to

Regardless of how informal the outfit or the stated dress code, clothes should always be clean and pressed, stain- and odor-free, and not ripped, torn, or frayed. In a business setting, it is not advisable to wear Spandex, muscle T-shirts, sweat pants (although company-logo sweats and jackets may be fine in a casual setting), running shoes, ultra-tight or sexually provocative clothes.[18]

If in doubt about the appropriate attire, always err on the side of conservative. If you think jeans may be OK for a social event but aren't sure, wear ironed khakis and a nice golf shirt. If you have any inkling that a suit may be called for, dress in a suit. It's always advisable to be overdressed for an occasion, rather than underdressed. Decisions regarding appropriate women's clothing are a bit more complicated, but again, err on the side of conservative and dressy. One more thing—remember to practice impeccable grooming, however, even in a jeans' environment!

As the administrative manager, you may be responsible for meetings, conferences, or social occasions. If so, be sure to indicate what dress is expected so that employees know what is the appropriate attire for the occasion. Be sure to use terminology that the employees will understand. For example, one manager of an organization sent out invitations to the employees for a formal dinner and listed the attire as Business Casual: Cocktail. You can imagine that some employees were confused since the dinner was at a resort club that normally had a casual attire policy. At times the administrative manager may be asked to clarify the attire expected at office functions, such as holiday parties.

adapt to the ways of those from the United States. The economy won't let us forget about consumers if we intend to do business globally. Another explanation is that those in foreign markets are not likely to have the same needs, wants, habits, or tastes as the U.S. market. We don't want to abandon them, and most of all we don't want to offend them with our branding of products, our advertising, or our marketing strategies. Keep in mind that even though someone may look and act like he or she is part of the U.S. culture, he or she may still be thinking in the native language.

We all carry our own culture with us, so everything we see, hear, or feel is filtered through our cultural biases. We, who live in the United States, are often so noticeable because we tend to be so unreserved in our behavior and so informal and casual right from the start in both business and social relations. For example, many of us are more apt to use an acquaintance's first name after meeting him or her. But it is a tradition unheard of in some cultures. It's somewhat offensive to some, especially in countries where it's very important to build relationships *before* business takes place. Most of the resources available on the subject usually compare different countries and the ways in which they perceive and react in several major cultural areas such as time, greetings and names, gift giving, gestures, and personal space and touch.

- *Time.* Differing attitudes toward time are a major source of annoyance in international interactions, yet few people give it much thought. How far in advance appointments and bookings must be scheduled, and to what extent punctuality is stressed or ignored are all important considerations to remaining in control during international meetings and negotiations. It can be totally unnerving when a task-oriented American, who considers time a commodity to be managed, is confronted with a relationship-oriented Arab, European, Asian, or Latin American, who considers time as flowing and flexible, beyond human control, and to be accepted whatever happens—regardless of who may interrupt and how frequently the interruptions may occur. It pays to develop some flexibility relative to time to avoid angry outbursts.

- *Greetings and Names.* When executed properly, greetings and introductions are a clear indicator of status, even in our culture. Who acknowledges whom, how deeply one bows in certain cultures and for how long speaks volumes. If you haven't mastered the intricacies, stick to the handshake, but don't expect to get a like handshake in return. It's gauche in France, for instance, to pump more than once from the elbow.

One of the most confusing aspects of meeting people with foreign names is not knowing whether to use the first name or the last name upon meeting the other person.

ETHICS & CHOICES

Huy Nguyen has moved from the Far East branch office to San Francisco. As a manager, he interacts with employees throughout the day. Because of his broken speech patterns and the effort it takes to understand him, he is often avoided by coworkers. What should the company do?

For that reason, learn which cultures place the surname first so you won't be addressing someone with the Chinese equivalent of "Mr. Bob." Never call someone by the first name unless you are specifically asked to do so by the person. Virtually nowhere else are people as informal in the manner of address as in the United States. Don't forget the honorifics or titles that go with the name. They are usually a point of pride in many countries. As in Germany, you might use a whole string of titles to address someone, while in Italy it's an honor to be addressed by your profession.

Another cultural reminder is if you are doing business internationally, the first indispensable tool you must have is a nice personal business card. Your international clients will be pleasantly surprised if you present them your business card in their language. This practice projects two very positive images: You are prepared to go the extra mile, and you respect their culture. It is also the best way to create instant good-will and to make an excellent first impression.

- *Gift Giving.* When going abroad, especially on business, people from the United States worry about gift giving. Except in Japan, it is seldom as important as we think it might be. That does not mean you can overlook your homework. Giving too much and too often can be just as offensive as not giving at all. Always consider the basic questions: To *whom* must you give gifts, *what* should you give or avoid giving, *when* should you give it, and *how* should it be presented? The answers vary from culture to culture, so be prepared. Gift giving can hold great significance in some countries. For example, you would

want to avoid giving handkerchiefs to Chinese or Brazilian counterparts because handkerchiefs are associated with mourning. Knives, to some Latin Americans, can symbolize severing a friendship. And unwrapping a gift in front of some Asian colleagues could be deemed rude.

- *Gestures.* Relative to proper gestures to use, if you are in a country where bowing is the custom, you are not expected to bow as well. If you plan to, practice first to avoid "head bonking." And there's a trick to knowing how long to bow, how deep to bow (it depends on rank and status). So if you normally extend your hand for a handshake, do it naturally. But don't judge anyone by the strength of his or her grip. That's one of our cultural nuances.[19]

- *Personal Space and Touch.* The differences in space and touch among cultures reflect each society's attitudes and values. Understanding and appreciating these differences is vital to successful intercultural communication. **Personal space** is defined as the flow and shift of distance between people as they interact and communicate. Americans today have gradually grown more attached to the bubble of invisible space that surrounds them. Woe unto him, or her, who crosses that imaginary line and steps into the highly valued and highly protected area deemed "personal space." In similar individualistic cultures, such as Germany, England, and Australia, personal space is viewed as sacred. Members of these cultures may take on an aggressive manner when their space is violated. When you are communicating with people from cultures with highly valued personal space, it is important to note personal boundaries and take care not to cross them. The failure to do so in a profit-oriented economy may have disastrous business results that would not be good.

In other cultures, however, the perception of personal space is very different. Members of Arab cultures hold conversations in very close proximity and often touch each other while they talk. Africans will come extremely close to people, even strangers, when speaking.

Another aspect of intercultural communication is touch. A single touch can communicate as much as an entire paragraph of words. Different cultures have different ideas about what touch is appropriate and what touch is not. People in Europe, Portugal, and Arab countries often greet each other with a kiss. Americans, on the other hand, prefer a nice firm handshake. In Asia, people avoid touch as much as possible. Some members of the Hindu religion will show disrespect by touching the feet.

S U M M A R Y

1. Value-driven companies find ways to link their daily operations to social and environmental concerns and integrate employee and community well-being into their decision-making. A value-driven company is one that consistently produces a high-quality product or service, treats employees with respect, and has demonstrated that it incorporates the values it holds into the fabric and culture of its business.

2. Basic beliefs are deeply felt moral and ethical principles that guide decision-making and behavior.

3. Values are our fundamental beliefs or principles that define what we think is right, good, fair, and just; whereas ethics are behaviors and tell people how to act in ways that meet the standard our values set for us.

4. Ethics are behaviors that tell people how to act in ways that meet the standard our values set for us. A leader with strong ethics has the ability to recognize ethical problems, resolve ethical reasoning skills, resolve ethical conflicts, and implement ethical decisions in the face of critical situations.

5. When leaders make ethical decisions, those decisions are usually based on the following six behavioral and moral standards: honest communication, fair treatment, social responsibility, fair competition, responsibility to the organization, and respect for the law.

6. According to loyalty surveys, loyalty is growing in the workplace. Studies indicate that the larger the company, the more likely there is to be decreasing employee loyalty; and the smaller the company is, the more loyal the employees are.

7. Etiquette is about presenting yourself with the kind of polish that shows you are a professional. Elements of business etiquette focus on behavior at work, when meeting people, telephone usage, and dining manners.

8. Business attire and image skills become important when people draw impressions concerning a worker's ability, credibility, and whether he or she is serious and should be taken seriously.

9. A positive public image is a way of life in which your wardrobe style, voice tone, grooming habits, etiquette, office décor, body language, and business presentations (oral and written) denote a style of performance commensurate with success.

10. A dress and grooming policy is advised because companies are addressing employees' personal preferences.

11. Individuals in business carry their own culture with them, so everything that is seen, heard, or felt is filtered through those cultural biases. Knowing the cultural attitudes about time, greetings and names, gift giving, gestures, and personal space and touch will make you more comfortable in your international transactions.

12. Relative to conducting international business, countries differ from each other with respect to several major cultural areas such as time, greetings and names, gift giving, gestures, and personal space and touch.

KEY TERMS

Basic beliefs

Ethics

Personal space

Value-driven company

Values

REVIEW

1. When it is said that an organization has a soul, what does this mean?

2. List several ethical issues in the business world.

3. What is one way unethical behavior is fostered in organizations?

4. Identify three objectives of a workplace ethics training program.

5. What are six behavioral and moral standards that leaders base decisions upon?

6. When making proper introductions, what are some rules to keep in mind?

7. To ensure a smooth business dining experience, what are some actions you might take? What should you do if the service is unsatisfactory?

8. What is the difference between smart casual and business dress codes?

9. Why is international politeness and manners important to the future of a business?

CRITICAL THINKING

1. Why should corporate values and business ethics be incorporated into the day-to-day activities of successful companies?

2. According to current research, to what extent is employee loyalty visible in today's workplace?

3. From the major areas of business etiquette and behavior relative to work settings, meeting people, using telephonic devices and when dining out, which ones do you think are the most important for every employee to exercise. Why?

4. In your opinion, what negative effects do casual manners in the United States have on international business? How can you prevent these negative effects?

CASE STUDY 10-1: WOMEN IN INTERNATIONAL BUSINESS

When recently given an assignment in the Far East, Debra was sent some literature by her manager, Tim Mohr, to read. In part it said, "Women can represent their companies almost anywhere in the world, but how they conduct themselves while doing business is important. In Asian countries, men are often uncomfortable doing business with women, but are more accepting of women if they are not too aggressive, immediately establish their credentials, and dress conservatively. On the plus side, women doing business in Japan can have a distinct advantage, since they are not expected to stay out most of the night drinking with their hosts."

Although Debra has never been a staunch "feminist," she takes offense to this attitude and feels she should be treated as her male counterpart. She has made an appointment with Tim Mohr to discuss her concerns.

Discussion Questions

1. Do you feel Debra is correct?

2. If you were Tim Mohr, how would you approach your discussion with Debra? In other words, do you think it fitting that Debra be sent to the Far East on a business trip with this attitude?

Study the facts in this case. What do you see as the basis for Debra's thinking? Outline your analysis of this case and include the questions to be prepared so you can discuss it in class.

CASE STUDY 10-2:
FORMER MODEL TURNS RECEPTIONIST

Roxanne Frederick recently went to work for an interstate transportation company in Detroit as its receptionist. The first week or so, several of the employees went out of their way to go by the lobby to take a second look at her. She is very attractive and most soon learned she was a former model at car shows at General Motors Corp.

Her image, however, started to create problems in the company. Though Roxanne was a nice person and didn't appear conceited, she was unique to the organization. As the AM is finding out, work has slowed down since she was hired. For instance, truck drivers were stopping by and spending time chatting with her; other female workers were saying "catty" things behind her back and seemed to be spending more time in negative conversations. Three comments overheard were "She's too perfect," "She wears heavy makeup," and "She dresses too nice for this place."

Roxanne's fault, in your opinion?

3. In your personal opinion, is it wrong for someone to be regarded as "not fitting the image" of the organization? Where, do you think, did the worker get that idea?

Read through the case and make notes regarding what is happening here. Include the receptionist, the visitors to the front lobby, the other employees, and the administrative manager's roles in this situation. Each person or group is playing a role. Be prepared to discuss how this situation should be resolved. Would you include this situation in the revision of the handbook? Be prepared to discuss your reasoning with the class as directed by your instructor.

INTERNET RESEARCH ACTIVITY

Several web sites offer travel tips for business travel. A few popular and complete tourism web sites are noted in the course web site *http://odgers.swlearning.com*. When using the web site, first select a country from each of the following areas: Europe, Asia, Latin America, and Africa. Second, within each country, click on the Etiquette link. You can then research each country's travel and business etiquette tips regarding business meetings, business lunches, dress, time and space orientation, and gift giving.

Learning Activity:

Upon the direction of your instructor, prepare a research paper or oral report of your findings. Be prepared to share your report with the class in a presentation using PowerPoint, if available. You may want to develop handouts of the information.

Discussion Questions

1. Do you think the administrative manager should view this problem as one that will work itself out with time?

2. If it doesn't, what steps might you take as the administrative manager to get work back on track? What should you say to the other workers? Is any of this

Part 3

Practicing Leadership and Communication Skills

Workplace

GEORGE S. PEARL

President
Atlanta Legal Photo Services Inc.
Atlanta, Ga., USA

After acquiring a Bachelor of Science degree in Radio Television & Film from the University of Southern Mississippi, I served four years in the U.S. Navy. This experience led me to what I really liked the most: *photography!*

Upon deciding I wanted to have my own photo business, I chose *civil evidence photography* in an attempt to be different enough in a technical area that most other photographers would not want or know how to follow. I read every book, attended seminars, and took courses to gain the specialized knowledge required. Today I own a 5,000-square-foot building and have seven employees producing not only evidence photography but *demonstrative evidence* on 1,500 cases a year.

Question

In your opinion, has the nature of leadership and communication skills changed over the past few years? To what extent are effective communication skills important to worker success?

Response

As we receive jobs, a special form is filled out by one of us dealing with that client. The form is made in such a way that if a person will just go right down the form filling in the blanks in his or her own handwriting, then he or she will also be getting all of the important information required for the work to be done.

An employee must be able to write down a message so it can be read easily by anyone else! *I do not hire anyone who has bad handwriting skills.* If I can't read the work application, then it makes no difference how great an education he or she might have—the person will not be

working for us. Bad handwriting is not a little thing. It can mean the loss of thousands of dollars or incorrect work being done simply because someone's handwriting cannot be read.

In my business the telephone is still the lifeblood of the company. I have instructed all of my employees to answer the phone in *two rings*. When a client calls us, the phone will be answered by a real person within two or three rings. That person will be friendly, communicative, and helpful. Without fast exchanges over the telephone, a company will not survive.

Communicative skills are what we are hired to provide attorneys for their legal cases. After studying the case, we decide how best to communicate critical facts to a jury. Ours is a unique business of special communicative skills that when done correctly can be worth millions of dollars in a civil lawsuit or result in a person spending his or her life in jail.

Chapter 11

Leadership, Motivation, and Problem-Solving in Organizations

OBJECTIVES

After completing this chapter, you will be able to:

1. Describe an effective leader relative to leadership characteristics, habits, attitudes, and styles.

2. Identify techniques that work when motivating different types of workers and motivational problems and behaviors that may be encountered in the workplace.

3. Distinguish between position power and personal power in organizations.

4. List the seven steps in the problem-solving process.

Every researcher has his or her own perspective on what constitutes an effective leader. Some people study leadership traits, others identify leadership behaviors, and still others match leadership actions with leadership situations. Add to this the fact that people still can't agree on whether leaders are born or made, and whether leadership is an art or a science, and you begin to see why it's so difficult to determine what is lacking—and what is necessary—in today's leaders. This understanding of leadership is vital because leaders motivate employees and solve problems in organizations.

Merely placing people together does not guarantee success in organizations composed of individuals with diverse backgrounds and perceptions. The real challenge for administrative managers comes in effectively leading, motivating, and solving problems.

Chapter Eleven

Management is doing things right;
leadership is doing the right things.

—*Peter Drucker, management guru*

TECHNOLOGY APPLICATIONS IN THE WORKPLACE

The Digital Divide and Leading the Work Force

A major concern of the U.S. government and many citizens around the world is the digital divide. The phrase **digital divide** is used to describe the idea that people of the world can be divided into two distinct groups: (1) those who have access to technology with the ability to use it and (2) those who do not have access to technology or are without the ability to use it.

Society's goal is to narrow the gap, or bridge the divide, between those who have access to technology and those who do not. The National Policy Association's Digital Economic Opportunity Committee recently released its final report, "Building a Digital Workforce—Confronting the Crisis," at a Washington news briefing. The report says that action by Americans to close the information-technology skills gap in the current and future work force is a critical challenge for business, labor, education, government, and the nonprofit sector.[1]

ISSUES TO THINK ABOUT:

1. Do you think the U.S. work force experiences the digital divide phenomenon or is it limited to workers in other countries? Explain.
2. Project ten years from now and forecast the extent to which the digital divide will affect global business, and as a result, the way workers are managed.

EFFECTIVE LEADERSHIP

Effective leadership involves exerting influence in a way that achieves the organization's goals through enhancing the productivity and job satisfaction of the work force. Successful leaders can increase their effectiveness by expecting the best from people, maintaining a positive self-regard, developing a desire for the entire team to achieve, and by simply saying "thank you" to workers and customers.

The increasing rate of change in the business environment is a major factor in this new emphasis on leadership. Whereas in the past, managers were expected to maintain the status quo in order to move ahead, new forces in the marketplace—such as the Internet, telecommunications, and technology, in general—have made it necessary to expand this narrow focus. The leaders of tomorrow are both learners and teachers. Not only do they foresee changes in society, but they also have a strong sense of ethics and work to build integrity in their organizations.

Managers versus Leaders

The age-old question of whether a boss is a manager or a leader still remains. Although you may hear these two terms used interchangeably, they are in fact very different from each other in terms of personalities and world views. By learning whether you are more of a leader or more of a manager, you will gain the insight and self-confidence that comes with knowing more about yourself. The result is greater impact and effectiveness when dealing with others and those whose work you oversee.

Table 11.1 compares the characteristics of managers versus leaders. It illustrates the different personality styles of managers versus leaders, the attitudes each category has toward goals, their basic conceptions of what work entails, and their relationships with others.

As you can see, managers and leaders are very different. It is important to remember that there are definite strengths and weaknesses in both types of individuals. This is to say that managers are very good at maintaining the status quo and adding stability and order to the culture. On the other hand, leaders are very good at stirring people's emotions, raising their expectations, and taking them to new levels and in new directions (both good and bad).

Organizations need both leaders and managers to be able to function effectively. Without both, an organization and its leadership may stagnate.

The Nature of Leadership

According to David Brewer of the Leadership Consulting Group in San Francisco, **leadership** is the art of enlisting people to embrace a vision or a goal as their own, and then inspiring and encouraging them to sustain their commitment so that by their own action and initiative they turn that vision into a reality. Leadership can be exerted at all levels in the workplace, not only by managers and supervisors but also by peers and individuals, sometimes in ways that influence those with much greater formal power. That is because leadership is persuasion, not domination. Persons who can require others to do their bidding because of their power are not leaders.[2]

TABLE 11.1   Characteristics of Managers Versus Leaders

Characteristics	Managers	Leaders
Styles of personality	• Are problem-solvers who focus on goals, resources, organization structures, or people • Are persistent, tough-minded, hard-working, intelligent, analytical, tolerant, and have good-will toward others	• Can visualize a purpose and generate value in work • Achieve control of themselves before they try to control others • Are imaginative, passionate, non-conforming risk-takers
Attitudes toward goals	• Decide upon goals based on necessity instead of desire and are, therefore, deeply tied to their organization's culture • Tend to be reactive since they focus on current information	• Shape ideas instead of responding to them • Provide a vision that alters the way people think about what is desirable, possible, and necessary
Conceptions of work	• Establish strategies and make decisions by combining people and ideas • Are good at reaching compromises and mediating conflicts between opposing values and perspectives	• Develop new approaches to long-standing problems and open issues to new options • Focus people on shared ideals and raise their expectations • Possess strong dislike of mundane work
Relations with others	• Prefer working with others • Are collaborative and attempt to reconcile differences, seek compromises, and establish a balance of power • Maintain controlled, rational, and equitable structures	• Relate to people in intuitive, empathetic way • Focus on what events and decisions mean to participants • Create systems where human relations may be turbulent, intense, and at times even disorganized

In summary, management entails completing the operational and routine aspects of everyday tasks, while conforming closely to department policy, procedures, rules, and regulations. Leadership, in contrast, as shown in Figure 11.1, encompasses the spirit, vision, and ethical considerations that accompany the strategic planning and decision-making processes companies must perform in order to achieve success. These topics will be covered later in the chapter.

Morale can easily decline if companies have more managers than leaders. You really need a balance. While a leader must possess certain inherent leadership qualities, raw charisma alone does not ensure success. Leaders must determine their own strengths and weaknesses so that, in times of crisis, they can react with authority and calm. Leaders must first demand of themselves what they expect from others. When leaders

show consistency, their subordinates trust them. True leaders do not make impulsive decisions, waver, or agonize over political outcomes, nor do they depart from convention merely for the sake of personal convenience. Instead, they possess character and a spirit of fairness that dictate each decision. Instilling ideas that inspire a sense of ownership, pride, and commitment that make all subordinates eager to fulfill their duties is the job of a leader, not merely a manager.

Does that mean being "just a manager" is not good? According to Craig R. Hickman, author of *Mind of a Manager, Soul of a Leader*, organizations need both leader qualities (visionary, empathetic, and flexible) and manager qualities (practical, reasonable, and decisive). He states that the ability to provide balanced managerial leadership is the essential skill. Further, the question is not "What approach works

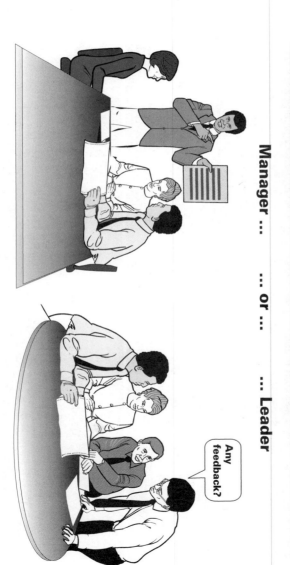

FIGURE 11.1 Management or Leadership?

Manager ...   **... or ...**   **... Leader**

better?" but, rather, "What combination works best?"[3]

What this means is that at the least leadership has to become a shared responsibility. While the person at the top (i.e., president or CEO) can set and communicate the corporate vision, executing it takes a lot more people working together now. Therefore, leaders have to be cultivated at all organizational levels (i.e., middle management, supervisory, etc.) because they:

1. Make the company's mission clear and compelling to everyone involved, including the executive team, customers, suppliers, stockholders, and the board.

2. Are team-oriented. Successful leaders cultivate talent in others and give credit where credit is due.

3. Are consistent in their execution. Research shows that good leaders know they have to build an infrastructure in which everyone's efforts are coordinated and integrated so that work is performed consistently over time. [4]

Qualities of Leaders

Though effective leaders are individuals and unique unto themselves, they tend to possess many of the following traits:

- *Emotional stability.* Good leaders are able to tolerate frustration and stress more easily than others because they confront new situations regularly.

- *Dominance.* Leaders are oftentimes competitive and decisive and usually enjoy overcoming obstacles.

- *Enthusiasm.* Leaders are usually seen as active, expressive, and energetic, optimistic, and open to change.

- *Conscientiousness.* Leaders usually have set a very high standard of excellence and have an inward desire to do one's best. They have a need for order and tend to be very self-disciplined.

- *Tough-mindedness.* Good leaders are practical, logical, to-the-point, and comfortable with criticism. They don't take criticism personally.

- *Self-assurance.* Leaders have little or no need for approval and are usually unaffected by prior mistakes or failures. Effective leaders use mistakes as learning opportunities for bettering their leadership skills.

- *Maturity.* Leaders recognize that more can be accomplished by empowering others than by ruling them.

- *Charisma.* Leaders who have charisma are able to arouse strong emotions in their employees by defining a vision in such a way that it unites and captivates them.

- *Adaptability:* Leaders must be adaptable to change. The last thing a leader wants is to be the keeper of the tradition that creates the roadblock to progress.

- *Consideration:* Leaders recognize, reward, and praise their followers frequently. Further, leaders don't just tell employees they're doing a good job. Instead, effective leaders use phrases such as these seven to show that they really care about employees:

1. "You've made my day because...."
2. "One of the things I enjoy most about you is...."
3. "I'm impressed with...."
4. "You can be proud of yourself...."
5. "You are doing an excellent job...."

Leadership Habits, Attitudes, and Styles

Leaders have many unique facets about them that promote their overall effectiveness with people. A person's habits, attitudes, and leadership styles make him or her truly one of a kind.

Leadership Habits Stephen R. Covey wrote the popular book, *Seven Habits of Highly Effective People* as a guide for business-people to recognize that character is a component of a person's habits. Covey presents seven habits that, by becoming the basis of a person's character, will create an empowering center of correct maps from which an individual can effectively solve problems, maximize opportunities, and continually learn and integrate other principles in an upward spiral of growth. The seven habits he identifies and explains are:

1. Be Proactive.® You are responsible for your life. Decide what you should do and get on with it. Don't blame others or the circumstances.

2. Begin With the End in Mind.® Think of how you want to be remembered at your funeral. Use this as a basis for your everyday behavior.

3. Put First Things First.® Devote more time to what is important but not necessarily urgent.

4. Think Win-Win.® Have an Abundance Mentality; Seek solutions that benefit all parties.

5. Seek First to Understand, Then to be Understood.® Don't dive into a conversation. Listen until you truly understand the other person.

6. Synergize.® Find ways to cooperate with everyone. Value the differences between people.

7. Sharpen the Saw.® Continually exercise and renew four elements of your self: physical, mental, emotional/social, and spiritual.6

Leadership Attitudes Leadership attitudes often form out of a belief concerning why people work. Most notable of these notions are the ideas of Theory X and Theory Y as proffered by Douglas McGregor, author of the classic management book, *The Human Side of Enterprise.*7

The idea that people work because they have to work is illustrated by the Theory X view of people. **Theory X** includes assumptions that people generally dislike work, lack ambition, and work primarily because they need to have money to live. According to Theory X, these workers prefer to be followers rather than leaders. Managers and supervisors who evaluate worker behavior from this point of view conclude that restrictive controls are necessary. An example of such restriction is the supervisor who exercises "tight" control over all aspects of employee performance. Punishment, threat, and close supervision might be necessary to motivate those individuals.

Theory Y, on the other hand, assumes that work is as natural as rest or play and that workers will accept responsibility when self-direction and self-control can be used to pursue valued objectives. Further, it can be argued with Theory Y that work can be inherently motivating in and of itself. Capable of self-direction and self-control, the workers are able to use their imagination and originality. Supervisors try to create conditions under which all workers have the opportunity to achieve their full potential.

William Ouchi, who wrote the book *Theory Z*, in which he contrasted American and Japanese industry, concluded that Japanese industrial success and world-class productivity were results of better management, an approach he called Theory Z.[8] **Theory Z** emphasizes long-range planning, consensus decision-making, and strong mutual worker-employer loyalty. Ouchi stresses that the special abilities of the individual worker are more important than the contents of the job description. According to Theory Z, workers should be hired for their talents. Further, jobs should be designed around the workers' talents rather than trying to fit workers into a preset job description. The key to increased productivity, therefore, is

to get employees involved by developing interpersonal skills, and broadening career path opportunities and development.

Leadership Styles Leaders can be categorized also by the styles they use to get a job done. Leadership experience reveals that, in some situations, an autocratic approach might be best; in others, a participative approach; and in still others, a free-rein approach. This conclusion emphasizes that leadership is complex and that the most appropriate style depends on several interrelated variables, such as a leader or follower's level of experience, task and environmental safety concerns, and the routine or unique nature of the task to be done.

- *Autocratic.* An **autocratic (authoritarian) leader** is one who makes most of the decisions alone instead of allowing followers to participate in the decision-making process. He or she feels that efficient operations result from arranging the work conditions in such a way that human elements minimally influence the task. The authoritarian leader sets the agenda, determines the group's policies, assigns tasks to the members, and makes decisions for the group without consulting them. In the end, the leader takes responsibility for the group's progress. Rarely do the group members communicate with one another, but they communicate with the leader.

- *Participative.* In sharp contrast, a **participative (democratic) leader** involves followers heavily in the decision-making process by using group involvement to set basic objectives, establish strategies, and determine job assignments. With this leadership style, a cycle is established. The cycle begins with the employee participating in decision-making. As decision-making improves, worker satisfaction and morale improve, which then recycles back to the employee wanting to participate more often in the success of the organization. The participative leader provides directions, but allows the group to make its own decisions. This leader offers suggestions and reinforces members' ideas. After offering these suggestions, providing information, and clarifying ideas, however, the leader allows the group to make the decision. Using employee participation, the leader shares responsibility of the decision. In terms of leadership styles, the participative leader is in the middle of the styles.

• *Free-Rein.* A **free-rein (laissez-faire) leader** focuses on the welfare and feeling of followers and has self-confidence and a strong need to develop and fully empower team members. Laissez faire comes from the French and means *allow to do.* The laissez-faire leader takes no initiative in directing or managing the group. In other words, the leader allows the group to develop on its own, as it has no real authority figure. Specifically, the leader answers questions and provides information but evaluates and criticizes little, and is thereby non-threatening to team members. Ultimately, the free-rein leader allows the members to make their own decisions. [9]

Steps to Effective Leadership

Volumes have been written about how to become an effective leader. But for many questions, there are no definitive answers. For example, you might ask: How should leadership be defined? How does one acquire the ability to exercise it? In response to these queries, what have evolved are six principles or guidelines that are important for effective leadership in any arena or organization. Review these guidelines and assess your leadership attributes. Are you skilled in each of these principles? If you identify a weakness, determine how you can work to improve yourself in that area.

1. *Surround yourself with colleagues who are as good as or better at their job than you are at yours.* Of course, they should be loyal to their leader; but loyalty must never be a substitute for competence. One sign of a good leader is the ability to hear and learn from colleagues.

2. *Delegate authority and require results.* How can workers learn how to get things done if they are never given the opportunity? In delegating authority to one's staff, a leader must also be clear about the results that are expected, the rewards for well-executed work, and the consequences that follow when work is poorly done.

3. *Model the behavior you expect of others.* From punctuality to ethical behavior, what is required of staff should be no more and no less than what leaders require of themselves. Employees usually look to their management as examples and learn by following the examples set by effective leaders.

MANAGEMENT TIP

As a leader, do not get stressed over issues that you cannot control.

STAFF MOTIVATION

As administrative managers focus on how to motivate staff, an understanding of several issues is important. For example, how should staff be recognized for outstanding work? How do employees' needs influence the motivational techniques used by managers? How do you motivate different types of employees? What kind of motivational problems and behaviors can AMs expect to encounter and resolve? These issues are discussed now.

ETHICS & CHOICES

Ruth is an overachiever and wants to please so much that you as her friend know she is getting physically sick with the pace she has set for herself. Since you both work for the same manager, would you say anything to Sally or to your manager?

Motivating Factors and Recognition

Promoting genuine and lasting employee motivation is not something management does; rather, it is a process that management fosters and allows to happen. Most employees are already motivated. Managers simply need to provide an environment that supports their motivation. Most employees want to do a good job. They want to excel and are naturally motivated to do so. The challenge is to release that motivation. This is easier said than done because the motivation to work is a complex drive influenced by both external and internal factors.

- *External Motivating Factors.* External factors can be either positive or negative. Punishment, a negative factor, may

4. *Believe in and inspire positive change.* It is not easy to counter resistance to innovation, but effective leaders are often able to do so by demonstrating their own respect for traditions while presenting the advantages of doing things differently. Inspiring an effective combination of continuity and change is surely a hallmark of strong leadership.

5. *Never take yourself too seriously.* Successful leaders do not behave as if they are personally more important than the work. Healthy doses of humility and good humor help a leader avoid fatal mistakes, such as adopting the attitude that it is the leader's way or no way, or that without the leader, the organization would cease to exist. A good attitude and a sense of humor often help one through rough spots, too.

6. *Serve others, not one's self.* Every leader of an educational institution, corporation, faith-based institution, political constituency, or social service agency must clearly and consistently articulate how the mission of their organization will be carried out.[10]

The major difference between most people and extremely successful people is the gap between what they *know* and what they *do*. Both groups have about the same knowledge base. Extremely successful people, however, are just better at doing what they "should" be doing. Helping workers bridge the gap between what they know and what they do is an important aspect of an administrative manager's job. Some would call this part of the job staff or task motivation.

include the threat of dismissal, a refusal to increase salary, or a reprimand. Rewards, a positive factor, may include a salary increase, job promotion, or recognition at a meeting. The problem most managers soon face when motivating exclusively with rewards is that they often run out of rewards. The problem with motivating by threat of punishment is that it breeds fear and resentment, which are likely to be expressed in behavior that interferes with achieving company goals. Common examples of this negative behavior are complaints, criticisms, absenteeism, wasted time, forgotten important details, communication of false information, rudeness to customers, and decisions that take the path of least resistance.

- *Internal Motivating Factors.* Internal motivation most often occurs when an employee's qualities match the requirements of the job. Motivating supervisors compare employees to checking accounts: You can only make withdrawals after you build up a balance. Managers need to steer clear of sweeping statements such as "You're terrific," and focus instead on targeted praise, such as "Getting the report out on time last week was crucial; you really came through. Thanks." People remember this kind of constructive feedback and recognition.

It helps to hire people who already feel motivated to work with your office team—those who love your business and who enjoy doing the tasks required. You can usually train your staff in the basic skills needed to do their jobs, but you can't teach energy, a positive attitude, and attention to detail.

As a result, high-performance companies understand the importance of offering awards and incentives that recognize, validate, and value outstanding work. Awards and incentives help keep employees motivated and productive and are effective methods of reinforcing company expectations and goals.

Non-cash awards and incentives—ranging from a Post-it note that says, "Good Job," to a set of golf clubs or a vacation package—can be not only cost-effective but also valuable tools that help raise morale, increase productivity, and improve quality, safety standards, and customer service.

However, at a time of budget deficits, frozen wages, and wrenching layoffs, lavishing employees with cash awards and stock options for excellence is a luxury that few companies can afford. Given this reality, one of the most urgent dilemmas facing managers is how to maintain and improve worker morale while holding down costs.

These guidelines for successfully recognizing employees are offered.

- Emphasize success. Don't dwell on the things that go wrong.
- Deliver recognition and reward openly and publicly.
- Give recognition in an honest manner. Avoid being too slick or "overproduced."
- Tailor the recognition and reward to the unique needs of the people involved.
- Timing is crucial. Reward the employee's contribution close to the time when an achievement is realized.
- Make sure people understand why they received an award and what criteria were used to determine it.[11]

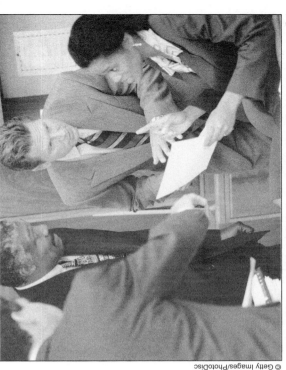

© Getty Images/PhotoDisc

Effective leadership requires good communication skills.

Employee motivation is highly individualized. Recognition should be, too. Instead of highly structured motivation programs such as employee of the month designation, informal recognition programs are preferred because they focus on spontaneous, sincere, and personal appreciation of employee efforts. Some examples of simple, informal recognition techniques that companies use to improve employee morale and productivity include the following:

- Buy "Welcome to the Team" flowers for an employee on his or her first day of work.
- Give *time off* certificates to employees.
- Hand out thank-you cards with candy or flowers.
- Provide movie tickets for a job well done.
- Take an employee out to lunch.
- Wash an employee's car for him or her during lunch.

People are inspired to do their best when you go one step further by doing the following:

- *Pay them more than money.* While employees have the need to earn a living, salary and benefits alone don't serve as motivators. They're an entitlement, not an incentive. Even a fair wage plays little role in determining whether someone is a motivated, satisfied employee.
- *Provide more than just a job.* Create an environment where employees want to work. Keep your office clean and pleasant. Make sure you, as the manager, enjoy what you do. When you're happy, it rubs off on those you supervise.

- *Offer variety.* Employees are motivated by a mix of responsibilities. Cross-train your staff so they can perform a variety of duties and cover for others on their days off. At the same time, they'll enjoy the challenge of learning new tasks.
- *Expand the boundaries.* Explain to employees how their jobs relate to other positions in your office and to the business as a whole.
- *Recognize employees' long-term goals.* Ask employees where they want their careers to be in five years, then do what you can to help them achieve that, whether it's training them to improve their telephone communication skills or teaching them a new computer program. Because you're giving them opportunities that contribute to meeting their goals, they'll feel motivated to work and more committed to you as a loyal employee.

- *Be more than an employer.* Serve as a coach and mentor, too. Take the time to talk—and listen—to your employees. Get to know them. Everyone is different, so forget the cookie-cutter approach. Go to lunch with your staff and spend time with them on their breaks. Make sure you and your managers make yourselves visible and accessible by walking around and interacting with staff in the office, instead of sitting behind some desk.[12]

- *Recognize that motivators differ from person to person and for the same person over time.* Spend a few moments each month asking about your employees' career goals, personal hobbies, and families, without getting too personal. Their answers will give you clues as to how you can help them continue to feel motivated at your office.

- *Have a little faith.* It's not enough just to feel appreciation toward your employees; you've got to prove it with your active trust in them. Delegate. For certain tasks, give them the authority to make decisions and act without your supervision. When you have high expectations of people, they usually rise to meet them. When you focus on the things a person is doing right, he or she does more of it. Most people want to please.[13]

Motivation and Maslow's Need Theory

The relationship among motivation, ability, and performance would be simple if productivity were a function of ability alone. If it was, output would vary directly with increases in a worker's ability. However, because employees have their freedom of choice to perform either effectively, ineffectively, or not at all, motivation is necessary to increase output. On-the-job performance and success are related to the type and extent of motivation involved.

Although managers can certainly create a climate of positive motivation, in the final analysis, motivation comes from *within* each person. Theories of motivation, such as Maslow's need theory, focus on the question of what causes behavior to occur and to stop. The answers usually center on the needs, incentives, and perceptions that drive, pressure, spur, and force people to perform. The needs and perceptions are internal to the individual; the incentives are external factors that give value to the outcome of people's behavior.

For example, Maslow based his concept of a hierarchy of needs on two principles. First, human needs may be arranged in a hierarchy of importance, progressing from a lower to a higher order of needs. Second, a satisfied need no longer serves as a primary motivator of behavior.

The five needs are briefly described next:

1. *Physiological or biological needs.* At the lowest level of the hierarchy of needs, but of primary importance when they are not met, are our physiological or biological needs, such as food, clothing, and shelter. Satisfaction of these needs is derived in part from money.

2. *Safety or security needs.* When the physiological needs are reasonably well satisfied, safety and security needs become important. For many people, this need involves the freedom from fear and anxiety that results in being able to plan ahead with confidence. Feeling safe at work or having

medical and life insurance plans provided are examples of workplace benefits that satisfy this need.

3. *Social or belonging needs.* Social needs include the need for belonging, association, and acceptance by colleagues, and giving and receiving friendship and love. When people's social needs—as well as their safety needs—are not satisfied, they may behave in ways that tend to hinder motivation and, worse, defeat organizational objectives.

4. *Esteem or ego needs.* Above the social needs, esteem needs are of two kinds: those that relate to one's self-esteem (needs for self-confidence, independence, achievement, competence, and knowledge); and those that relate to one's reputation (need for status, recognition, appreciation, and the deserved respect of one's colleagues).

Examples of Maslow's needs' hierarchy and how these needs relate to worker motivation are shown in Table 11.2.

TABLE 11.2 Maslow's Need Theory

Needs	On-The-Job Examples	If Need Not Met, Worker May Feel:
Physiological	Pay	Anxious
	Breaks	Physical pain
Safety	Benefits plan	Frightened
	Fair treatment	Suspicious
	Safe and clean working environment	Distrustful
Social	Work groups	Hurt
	Company-sponsored events and activities	Withdrawn
Esteem	Praise and recognition	Discouraged
	Promotion	Inferior
	Being asked for help or advice	Resentful
Self-Actualization	Learning new skills	Dampened enthusiasm
	Growing and developing	Nervous

5. *Self-actualization or self-fulfillment needs.* These needs include feeling self-fulfilled, realizing one's own potential, continued self-development, and being creative in the broadest sense of that term.

Motivating Different Types of Workers

Those of us in the work force today can be categorized in four groups. The four groups include:

- *Radio Agers* (born before 1946);
- *Baby Boomers* (born between 1947 and 1964);
- *Generation X* (born between 1965 and 1976);
- *Generation Y or "Millennials"* (born 1977 and after).

Many Radio Agers and Baby Boomers are either already retired or are trying to retire from first, second, or third careers! Today's workplace, then, is populated mostly by Gen-Xers and a growing number of Gen-Yers. Let's look at what makes each category of worker a special challenge for managers in the workplace.

The Older Worker

For many, work doesn't need to end with retirement. As life spans lengthen and living costs increase, researchers say more older people will want and need jobs. For most retirees, retirement doesn't signal the end of work life, but a chance to pursue interests, change careers, or start new businesses.[14]

When businesses do hire older workers, the results can be beneficial for everyone. Older workers are dependable, they have a

strong work ethic, and they are willing to accept flexible schedules. In addition, employers appreciate the value of seasoned judgment and a lifetime of experience. However, keeping older workers in the work force longer will likely require organizations to fund new education and training programs to keep their skills up to date. Attitudes will also have to change to reduce discriminatory practices that undervalue the intangible assets that older workers bring to their jobs, including experience, corporate memory, and relationships.[15]

By 2010, as 76 million Baby Boomers begin to hit retirement age, the United States will have 10 million more jobs than it will have workers to fill them, according to the U.S. Bureau of Labor Statistics.[16] It's feared there won't be enough Generation X or Y workers to fill the gap.

Generation X

Generation Xers were born between 1965 and 1976. We have already begun to see the development of new business structures, ideas, and products that take into account Generation Xers' preferences and unique characteristics. The Generation X discussions have focused mainly on their supposedly short attention spans and that this generation thinks and sees the world in ways entirely different from their parents. Their developing minds learned to adapt to speed and thrive on it—they grew up on video games, MTV, and nonstop-action films.

With those in mind, what are some work-related characteristics of this generation of workers that administrative managers need to recognize?

- *Multitask processing ability.* Working on multiple projects with little supervision comes naturally to this generation. They feel more comfortable than their predecessors in doing more than one thing at once (for example, doing homework while watching TV). This parallel-processing ability will allow workers to be better able to wear multiple hats and perform multitasking on the job.

- *Random-access thinking.* The Gen-Xers were the first to experience hypertext and "clicking around." Therefore, they can more easily make connections and are free from the constraint of a single path of thought.

- *Connected.* The previous generation was linked by telephone, a system that is synchronous (i.e., both people have to be there). In contrast, the Gen-Xers have been reared with the one-way worldwide instantaneous communication of e-mail, broadcast messages, user groups, and Internet searches. As a result of this "connected" experience, Gen-Xers tend to think differently about how to get information and solve problems.

- *Technology as friend, not foe.* To the older generation, technology is generally something to be feared, tolerated, or at best harnessed to one's purposes. To this generation, however, the computer is a friend. Being connected is a necessity. "What technology will I have?" is often the key factor in a Generation X worker's decision about what job to accept.

As a recap, to manage and motivate a Gen-Xer, first understand that most of them

were using computers by the fourth grade. They have a different way of processing information than did the previous generations. Gen-Xers understand and embrace the need to multitask, to make contributions, to be proactive, and to foster process changes when necessary. Consequently, feedback is one of the most important tools to use in communicating with Gen-Xers. Consistent, specific feedback from managers and peers is vital in the development of Gen-Xers because they need continued learning and increased opportunities.

Here are some practical guidelines anyone can use to better communicate with, manage, and cultivate Gen-Xers:

- Let workers know that they have direct access to you if they need it.
- Encourage workers to take courses or attend seminars to improve skills or learn new ones.
- Award or reward workers who have done a good job by giving them something unexpected, like a lunch or a day off. Promote workers based on their performance. Take the time to say thanks for a job well done.
- Help each worker to see how he or she fits into the plan for meeting goals.[17]

Generation Y Generation Yers were born after the year 1977. In 1998, they began graduating from college and entering the work force in earnest. Keeping them happy is especially important because of their workplace potential and their large numbers. Members of this burgeoning group tend to have a lot of raw energy, unbridled enthusiasm, and the skills and experience of those much older.

They are up for any challenge ("bring it on" may well be their motto) and have an astonishing amount of expertise in technology. Multitasking is second nature to them. They work well in team environments.

While there are about 77 million Baby Boomers and 44 million Generation Xers in the work force, Generation Y will number 80 million. Their considerable volume makes retaining them a top management priority. The oldest members of Generation Y are entering the work force just as the oldest members of the Baby-Boomer generation are poised to retire.[18]

Developing experienced and skilled young managers will become vital to any organization hoping to compete in the future. Given their expertise and enthusiasm, members of Generation Y will be able to meet the need, but retaining them is expected to be a real challenge for management because if they aren't happy at work, they won't stay.

The best approach to keeping Generation Y workers is to adopt a coaching style of management. The traditional "I tell/you do" school of management will not work with Gen-Yers. An effective coaching strategy includes the following actions:

- Developing and training people. Generation Y employees live to be trained.
- Involving them in decisions. Actively solicit their ideas and contributions.
- Giving them opportunities to move up in the organization.
- Providing challenging and meaningful work. These young workers do not want to be bored. Plus they want to know how their work fits into a company's big picture.

- Balancing corrective feedback with praise. Catch them doing something right and reward them when you do. Members of Generation Y thrive on recognition.

Whether an employee is from any of the four generations just mentioned, motivational problems and difficult employee behaviors develop and administrative managers must deal with them.

Motivational Problems and Behaviors

Managers must regularly deal with other motivational problems, specifically on-the-job personality disorders. **Personality disorders,** such as excessive absenteeism, tardiness, withdrawal, and personality conflicts are behaviors motivated by the need to survive. Self-preservation is an inherent inborn instinct, and survival is the primary motivator for all of us. Because people with personality disorders know of no other way to survive, they often exhibit defensive behavior. These behaviors can negatively affect morale and restrict the performance of other motivated workers in the organization.

Nearly everyone has felt defensive at one time or another. For example, when someone is coming toward you with a raised fist or when you are being unfairly criticized, you are going to do whatever is necessary to protect yourself. You naturally put up a defense with actions or words. A **defensive reaction** is a way of thinking that cushions the blow resulting from an immediate inability to overcome an obstacle or barrier that has been placed in your path.

Defensive reactions allow you to maintain a positive self-image. In motivating workers, managers can expect workers to exhibit these common defensive reactions:

- *Rationalization:* making an excuse;
- *Projection:* blaming others for his or her shortcomings;
- *Aggression:* treating others in a conde-

scending, overbearing, threatening, and demeaning manner;
- *Scapegoat:* using aggressive behavior against those who cannot fight back; and
- *Withdrawal:* avoiding conflicts by leaving a situation physically or mentally.

Table 11.3 gives examples of defensive reactions specific to work environments.

T A B L E 1 1 . 3 Examples of Defensive Reactions by Workers

Defensive Reaction	Examples
Rationalization	"The report is late because no one told me it was due today."
Making an excuse	"I'm late to work because my car ran out of gas."
Projection	"I didn't get the work from Harriet soon enough to finish on time."
Blaming others for your shortcomings	"There are errors in this report because my secretary has been preoccupied with family matters."
Aggression	"Let me explain it to you again!"
Treating others in a condescending, overbearing, or threatening manner	"There's no excuse for your not being prepared."
Scapegoating	"The new woman in the marketing department is the one who made the mistake, not me. But she will learn."
Using aggressive behavior against those who cannot fight back	"Jack must have forgotten to order copier paper before he left on vacation."
Withdrawal	"I can't take her constant chatter anymore. I'm going to lunch early."
Avoiding conflicts by leaving a situation physically or mentally	"I've got another meeting to attend. Will you tell me who decided what?"

© Digital Vision

Defensive reactions allow you to maintain a positive self-image.

POWER, OFFICE POLITICS, AND MOTIVATION

The way managers and others use power in an organization can affect motivation. Power dynamics requires that individuals develop a personal power base in order to successfully accomplish their goals and tasks. **Power** is not an attempt to influence but the *ability* to influence others. Effective leaders know how and when to use their power, whether that power is position or personal power.

- **Position power** is formal authority to tell others what to do that is granted by the organization. Generally, the more position

Often motivational problems manifest in creating a workplace that promotes unwise use of power and office politics. Administrative managers need to understand power, office politics, and how these dynamics positively or negatively influence a worker's motivation on the job.

power held by the leader, the more favorable the leadership situation. For example, managers, supervisors, and military officers have strong position power. The major benefit from position power is that leaders who have it can access needed resources in order to meet objectives. Position power also allows leaders to carry out their responsibilities with relative autonomy.

- **Personal power**, on the other hand, is informal power that is manifested by the extent to which followers are *willing* to follow a leader. Personal power, unlike position power, comes from below. Personal power is a day-to-day phenomenon. One day you might have it, and the next day you might not.

To be an effective motivator, leaders need to have both types of power, as shown in Figure 11.2. Additionally leaders need to recognize the effect that office politics has on the way organizations function, leaders lead, and workers work.

We would all like to claim that politics do not exist in organizations. However, human nature, being what it is, will always breed a certain amount of politics, intrigue, and alliances. Although it is not something you want to foster, organizational politics is something that leaders should acknowledge as part of organizational culture, learn to live with, and, if possible, learn to use constructively.

Some managers think of **office politics** as leveraging, positioning, and building alliances. In these cases, smart office politics refers to communicating well with superiors, drawing out the best in subordinates, and

FIGURE 11.2 Is it better to have position power or personal power or both?

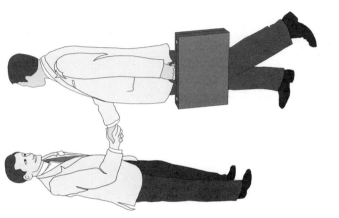

Position   **or**   **Personal**

POWER

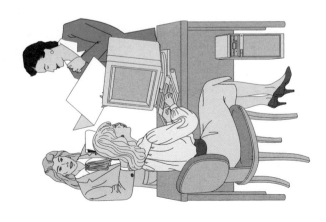

working easily with colleagues. Still, others think of office politics in less-glowing terms. For example, in military lingo, it could be said that office politics is keeping your eye on the target, but remembering to watch your flank. Office politics is a complex issue.

In dealing with power, office politics, and game players, managers may want to consider the two strategies that follow:

1. *Avoid taking sides in power struggles.* Your goal is to be recognized as your own person and to gain a reputation for objectivity and fairness. You can be supportive of others, where appropriate, and still draw the line at fighting their battles for them.

2. *Keep social contacts constructive.* No matter at what level of the organization you might socialize, if you are part of a group that meets regularly for any reason, be aware of the presence of the "three P's:"

- *Politics:* Is anyone using this group to build themselves up or tear others down?

- *Pretense:* Are you free to be yourself and say whatever is on your mind, or must you be on guard and aware of what others will think?

- *Pettiness:* Are these get-togethers vicious, and are you afraid people will talk about you if you are not there?

The following tips will help to reduce conflict and power games in the office:

- *Create an open environment.* Office politics are often fueled by insecurity, so try to keep employees well-informed of internal company news. Avoid closed-door meetings when possible, as they can give rise to speculation that can manifest into suspicion.

- *Seek employees with integrity.* Just one unethical or dishonest worker can generate significant tension in a group. During the hiring process, ask prospective employees' references about the applicants' ethics and honesty, and at every opportunity emphasize to your staff the strong value you place on these traits.

- *Eliminate office rivalry.* While a certain amount of competition can be healthy, too much is disruptive. If workers feel they are judged not by their individual merits, but by how they compare with others, the competition level could be counterproductive.

- *Watch out for burnout.* An office filled with overburdened workers is primed for conflict. Bring in outside help, when needed, to ensure that assignments are evenly distributed. Typically, staff members who have taken on more than their fair share of work are the first to experience burnout.

Decision-making and problem-solving are what managers are hired to do. Whether it is dealing with motivational issues or office politics, many managers find decision-making difficult. One thing is clear, however, and that is unless administrative managers can overcome their fear of making decisions and solving workplace problems, their careers will stall.

DECISION-MAKING AND PROBLEM-SOLVING

Poor decision-makers may be smart and diligent; however, when it comes to settling on a course of action, they may resort to delay tactics or blaming others in order to duck responsibility. At work, you aren't penalized nearly as harshly for making a poor decision as for not making a decision at all. Avoiding this responsibility and failing to make a deadline are actions that few organizations will tolerate.

The Decision-Making Process

Decisions are based on facts, intuition, and past experience. On paper, decision-making is a relatively simple process. The process starts with a need to make a decision. Then, at least two alternative courses of action are determined, followed by a selection of the better choice from the alternatives. In practice, however, decision-making is a very conscious process that involves the future. Keep these factors in mind when making decisions:

- The right person should make the decision.
- Decisions should contribute to objectives and reflect the organization's vision.
- Effective decision-making takes time and effort but cannot be put off until later.
- Though there is seldom only one acceptable choice, one usually surfaces as the best direction to take at the time, given the particular circumstances.

- Deal sensibly with uncertainties while taking into account your risk-taking attitude.
- Decision-making improves with practice. The more you do it, the easier it becomes.
- A decision may not please everyone. That is not its intent.
- A decision begins the process for other activities to go forward.

How can you ease the task and guide effective business decision-making? When making decisions, managers should ask themselves five questions:

1. What is the basic issue that must be addressed and resolved?
2. Has all the needed information been gathered and made available to the right people to make a timely and informed decision?
3. How have similar issues been handled in the past? Should anything be done differently this time?
4. If the stakes appear too high, is there a compromise that can be settled on as a safety net?
5. Should decisions be made by an individual or by a group? Think about how you would make this decision in a problem situation.

Clearly, the trend is toward empowerment and group decision-making; however, to keep some perspective, Table 11.4 lists both the advantages and disadvantages of group decision-making.

TABLE 11.4 Group Decision-Making

Advantages	Disadvantages
Provides the manager with a broad range of information.	Holds the manager accountable for the group's decision.
Lends a more "creative" approach to problem-solving.	Takes the work group's time away from other aspects of their jobs.
Improves communication in the department.	May result in "choosing sides" and cause morale problems.
Creates high morale in the work group.	Allows for strong personalities to dominate the work group.
Stresses a stronger commitment to decisions made.	Requires more supervisory skill.
	Is difficult to use if the decision must be made quickly.

Each week, you probably make hundreds of decisions. Most of them are manageable. But the larger ones—in which more is at stake—can be distressing. Use these tips to make decisions easier:

1. *Don't agonize over minor decisions.* You'll only waste time you could spend on important issues. Plus, delaying minor decisions could turn them into major problems.

2. *Gather enough information to make a sound decision.* But recognize that you don't have to collect every possible fact. Spending extra days or weeks searching for all available data could cause you to miss an opportunity.

3. *Narrow your options.* It's easy to be overwhelmed when you don't know where to start looking for a solution. So quickly review all your options, eliminate those that are questionable, and consider only two or three of the best options when making the final decision.

4. *Don't rush to judgment, instead try the "rule of three."* When all else fails, wait three days before deciding on any nonurgent, but significant decisions. In that time, the problem often either resolves itself or intensifies to the point of needing one's full attention.[19]

Decision-making is a forward-looking process so you have to be comfortable enough with the decisions that you've made so you can move on.[20] Don't play the *what-if game.* And to the extent you make a mistake or create a problem, you need to simply do your best to fix it as soon as you are reasonably able.

This leads us to the correct process to take when solving problems, because they surely will occur in the life of every manager who is responsible and is in the position of taking risks and making decisions.

Problem-Solving Steps

Problem-solving is not a skill that people are born with; it is an art that is learned and fine-tuned over the years. Typically in a work setting, the problem-solving process is learned by observing and emulating others.

The seven steps in the problem-solving process are to 1) define the idea or problem that needs attention; 2) collect, interpret, and analyze information; 3) develop possible alternative solutions; 4) analyze the implications of selected alternatives; 5) select the preferred alternative; 6) implement the decision; and 7) follow up, evaluate, and modify the decision, if necessary.

1. *Defining the Problem.* The idea or problem that needs attention must be very definite and specific. Answering these questions may help define the problem more succinctly:

• Precisely, what is the problem?
• Can the problem be stated in 25 words or less?
• Does the problem have a history? If so, can it be stated?

2. *Collecting Information and Analyzing the Problem.* Information surrounding the problem must be collected and analyzed to understand all aspects of the problem.

3. *Suggesting Possible Solutions.* Suggestions to solve the problem should be given and a list of the solutions should be made.

Brainstorming, piggybacking, and posting will help in this process. **Brainstorming** is the process of providing as many solutions as possible; **piggybacking** is the process of revising and expanding on suggested solutions, thus the idea of riding one idea on another; and, **posting** is the process of prioritizing the ideas from most important to least or vice versa.

4. *Analyzing and Comparing Possible Solutions.* Research and review are important at this step. Here techniques used to solve similar problems should be analyzed and criteria for solving the problem should be determined. At this step, one solution is compared to another until the better of the solutions has been developed or selected. Generally, the solutions should be compared on cost, efficiency, timeliness, and overall benefits to the

company. Consequences of the solutions must always be considered before moving to the next step.

5. *Selecting the Solution.* Make sure the solution that is selected is viewed with the results you expect to happen. If this process of selecting a solution is not handled well, the chosen solution could be worse than not having a solution at all.

6. *Implementing the Solution.* At this step, consider the steps needed to implement the solutions. Be as thorough as you can at this step.

7. *Monitoring progress.* Evaluate whether or not the solution is working to solve the problem. If it is not, then modify and adjust. It may be necessary to return to a previous step in order to correct the problem.

MESSAGE FOR MANAGERS

The ability to keep calm in a crisis is one of the qualities that distinguishs the good manager from a run-of-the-mill one. Not everyone is cut out to be an organizational leader. It is a tough job that includes making thoughtful decisions and understanding how to best interact with and motivate each of those people who report to you and for

whom you are responsible for their progression. When you become an administrative manager, remember to give sincere praise on a regular basis to those you supervise. The rewards from recognizing praiseworthy employees motivate them and result in making your job easier. When you acknowledge good performance in others,

be sure to specify the behavior, its results, and your feelings. Another idea is to let people tell you the story of their own success and how they did it, and then listen intently. After all, nothing encourages successful performance like a receptive audience.

Chapter Eleven

S U M M A R Y

1. Managers and leaders are very different. Managers are very good at maintaining the status quo and adding stability and order to the culture. On the other hand, leaders are very good at stirring people's emotions, raising their expectations, and taking them to new levels and in new directions. Organizations need both leader qualities (visionary, empathetic, and flexible) and manager qualities (practical, reasonable, and decisive).

2. Leadership is the art of enlisting people to embrace a vision or a goal as their own, and then inspiring and encouraging them to sustain their commitment so that by their own action and initiative they turn that vision into a reality.

3. Effective leaders possess many of the following traits: emotional stability, dominance, enthusiasm, conscientiousness, tough-mindedness, self-assurance, maturity, charisma, adaptability, and consideration.

4. McGregor's Theory X and Theory Y describe leadership attitudes often formed out of a belief concerning why people work. In brief, Theory X assumes that people generally dislike work; whereas Theory Y assumes that people view work as natural as rest and play.

5. Leaders can be categorized by the styles they use to get a job done. For example, the autocratic leader is one who makes most of the decisions alone instead of allowing followers to participate; a participative leader promotes group involvement to set basic objectives, establish strategies, and

determine job assignments; and a free-rein leader focuses on the welfare and feeling of followers and has self-confidence and a strong need to develop and empower team members. Experience reveals that in some situations an autocratic approach might be best; in others, a participative approach; and in still others, a free-rein approach.

6. Motivation is a complex drive influenced by both external factors such as punishment or a salary increase and internal factors that include non-cash awards and incentives.

7. Today's workplace is populated mostly by Generation X (born between 1965 and 1976) and Generation Y (born after 1977) workers, and each category of worker presents a special challenge for managers in the workplace.

8. Managers must regularly deal with other motivational problems, such as personality disorders that include excessive absenteeism and personality conflicts.

9. Position power is formal authority to tell others what to do that is granted by the organization. Personal power is informal power which comes from people below or followers.

10. The steps in the problem-solving process are to 1) define the idea or problem that needs attention; 2) collect, interpret, and analyze information; 3) develop possible alternative solutions; 4) analyze the implications of selected alternatives; 5) select the preferred alternative; 6) implement the decision; and 7) follow up, evaluate, and modify the decision, if necessary.

KEY TERMS

Autocratic (authoritarian) leader

Brainstorming

Defensive reaction

Digital divide

Free-rein (laissez-faire) leader

Generation Xers

Generation Yers

Leadership

Office politics

Participative (democratic) leader

Personal power

Personality disorders

Piggybacking

Position power

Posting

Power

Theory X

Theory Y

Theory Z

REVIEW

1. Compare the characteristics of managers versus leaders.

2. List the qualities that characterize successful leaders.

3. Describe the three leadership styles described in the chapter.

4. Contrast the underlying assumptions of McGregor's Theories X and Y of worker behavior.

5. Cite some examples of simple, informal recognition techniques that companies use to improve employee morale and productivity.

6. Describe the different kinds of needs found in Maslow's hierarchy of needs.

7. What are some motivational problems and behaviors that administrative

managers have to deal with in the workplace?

8. List some defensive reactions demonstrated by workers.

9. What are two strategies managers can use in dealing with power and politics on the job?

10. When making a decision, what factors should you keep in mind?

11. How do brainstorming, piggybacking, and posting help in the problem-solving process?

CRITICAL THINKING

1. Describe a person you know who has a leadership position relative to his or her specific leadership characteristics, habits, attitudes, and style. Would you like to work for this person? Why or why not?

2. If you had a choice of leading workers who were predominately either from Generation X or from Generation Y, which would you choose? What specific techniques would you use to motivate that type of worker?

3. Is it possible for a leader in an organization to have both position power and personal power? Explain your response.

4. Assume you are 25 years old, married, and the parent of a toddler and need to make a decision whether to accept a job in a nearby state. Your spouse does not want to move and you do because the new position appears to be everything you are looking for. How would you apply each of the seven steps in the problem-solving process to reach a decision that ultimately will affect you and your family's future?

CASE STUDY 11-1:
THE BEHAVIOR STYLES OF TWO MANAGERS

Assume you are on an interview team to select a new president and CEO for your organization.

During the course of the interviews, two of the candidates expressed the following behavior styles of leadership.

Candidate A said:

In turning troubled companies around, I would use this technique. I would first observe how people work and then reorganize. I would promote the top 10 percent and fire the bottom 10 percent. It's amazing how much energy it gives to the remaining 80 percent. Persuasion alone won't do the job. I would further pick role models on either end of the spectrum and do something with them. I believe this would promote a tighter team with a lot of deadwood and office politics gone. Actions speak louder than words!

Candidate B said:

I would push decision-making down into the middle ranks and create a corporate culture that questions the status quo, welcomes change, and encourages teamwork. Both men and women thrive in a boundaryless environment. To that end, I would want to have my employees determine how to spend the day or week. If they believe they need to take a supplementary course or spend a week at a customer site to improve their knowledge of a key subject, then I say let them do it. It's understood that everyone is working toward our team's common goal, and we all want to be successful.

As each candidate spoke frankly about his or her style of leadership, several thoughts come to your mind. You wonder whether as a worker or manager here, under which type of management would you prefer to work? Why, you ask yourself, would you like that style over the other?

Discussion Questions

1. Discuss the advantages of each style of leadership, as well as some possible disadvantages that could surface with each style.

2. Given only these two candidates, which one would you choose to be president and CEO? Why?

Reflect on the facts presented in the case. What other information would you need to evaluate their statements and their candidacy for the position? Be prepared to present your decision-making process in a class discussion or in writing as determined by your instructor.

CASE STUDY 11-2:
OFFICE POLITICS GONE TOO FAR

Maxie Coppinger, an office worker at Toledo Technical School, is waiting for the administrative manager to return from lunch. Maxie has borne the brunt of several offensive office political games within the past six weeks. In her wait for Mr. Darrell Williams, the administrative manager, to return she contemplates what she should do about this latest trick. Should she make a scene and confront the two women she suspects are behind these acts, should she quit her job, or should she seek legal counsel? This latest tactic has crossed the line, and Maxie has had it.

When Mr. Williams returns, Maxie follows him into his office, places a letter addressed to her husband on Mr. Williams' desk, and asks him to read it. Mr. Williams is perplexed but begins to read. He can see real anger in Maxie's face and overall demeanor. In a very few sentences, he ascertains that the letter strongly suggests to her husband that Maxie is having an affair at work. Maxie wants to know what Mr. Williams plans to do about this accusation and outright lie. She denies any affair is going on and is willing to confront her accuser(s)—whoever they may be. Her husband feels Toledo Technical School should put an end to these games.

think there is any merit to Maxie's claim of being harassed? Analyze the case; then prepare a statement including the answers to the questions. Be prepared to discuss the case in class as directed by your instructor.

INTERNET RESEARCH ACTIVITY

There are several web sites that allow you to take a leadership-style quizzes and then will score it for you. Following instructions given to you by your instructor, use the course web site below, or another one that you locate to determine how effective a leader you would be. Identify for yourself the specific characteristics you exhibit and possess that predict the kind of leader you might become. The course site is:

http://odgers.swlearning.com

Learning Activity:
Take one or more leadership-style quizzes. Summarize a description of your specific leadership style in a one-page report that you either present in class or hand in as a written assignment.

Discussion Questions

1. If you were Mr. Williams, what would be your initial reaction?

2. In your opinion, does the company become responsible for serious allegations made by a coworker to another coworker?

3. If you were Mr. Williams, how would you advise Maxie?

Reflect on the facts presented here. What are the problems as you see them? Do you

Chapter 12

Group Dynamics, Teamwork, and Conflict Issues

OBJECTIVES

After completing this chapter, you will be able to:

1. Discuss the effect that groups and teams have on an organization and how work is completed.

2. Identify conflict styles and negotiation strategies managers can use to manage and resolve conflicts in the workplace.

3. Describe approaches and strategies managers can use to manage multiple projects, cope with job stress, and maximize use of time for themselves and employees.

4. Explain the value of office manuals to organizations.

Since much of the work in organizations is accomplished through group and team effort, an understanding of how they function and their effect on both organizational and individual behavior is essential for an effective administrative manager.

Chapter 12 covers a range of issues dealing with managing groups and teams, as well as issues producing conflict in organizations. Some examples of these conflict-producing issues include managing multiple projects, coping with job stress, and using time management techniques effectively. Finally, office manuals are introduced as a means of establishing sound administrative work systems.

We must be the change we wish to see in the world. —*Gandhi*

TECHNOLOGY APPLICATIONS IN THE WORKPLACE

© Getty Images/PhotoDisc

Organization Affects Technology Expenditures

Businesses with well-organized people managing technology have systems that run better and cost less than businesses employing managers with only technical skills.[1] In general, organization wins over sloppiness, but with the complicated nature of technology, organizational skills pay big dividends. For example, an organized information technology person will standardize logins and passwords for server logins, e-mail, specialty applications, computers, databases, and any system requiring security.

Relative to the company networking databases and files, companies that value organization create an **acceptable-use policy** that prohibits employees from installing software, downloading programs from the Internet, passing pornography around the office, and the like.

Organization doesn't eliminate all computer hassles. It just makes all computer hassles easier to deal with, and that's good for any administrative manager!

ISSUES TO THINK ABOUT:

1. Why is hiring a person who is organized an important technology issue in the world of business?
2. Do you agree that a technology worker should be organized as well as technically savvy? Why?

THE NATURE OF GROUPS AND TEAM-BUILDING CONSIDERATIONS

To begin our study of groups and teams, it is necessary to distinguish between them because they are not the same in meaning. Putting a variety of people with varying skills together in a room does not make a team—it makes a group. Many times companies think putting people together for a meeting creates collaboration and coopera-

tion, and that's not the case.

Teams come together for a specific purpose. The key issue to be considered is knowing the distinction between working as a team

and working as a collection of individuals. This is perhaps the biggest hurdle to overcome in being on a successful team, since our natural tendency is to do what is best for us as individuals. Good team players participate in the team based upon their own belief system, yet with their focus on the team's mission or agenda. Teams are most successful when the people involved are willing to share their efforts and accomplishments.

Besides the team having clearly defined goals, the individuals who comprise a team must know what's in it for them. The major benefits of being on a team are that team members broaden their experience base and increase their visibility in the company. The foregoing enhances career opportunities inside the company. In terms of management, the concept of organizational teams is

built upon the idea that input from several people is usually better than the opinion of one. The points that need to be made are simply more strongly presented.

Types and Characteristics of Groups

When individuals associate on a fairly continuous basis, groups will form, with or without the approval of management. Individual members receive a great deal of satisfaction from being part of the group. A group can be either informal or formal.

Types of Groups Informal groups arise spontaneously throughout all levels of the company. They evolve out of employees' needs for social interaction, friendship, communication, and status. In contrast, **formal groups** are deliberately formed and created by management to attain organizational goals and objectives. Two examples of formal groups are **problem-solving committees** that meet on an as-needed basis and are relatively permanent, and **task-force groups**, which usually focus on a specific issue, meet a few times, and then disband.

Characteristics of Groups Groups, in general, appear to have some common characteristics. Three of these characteristics are that groups set norms, instill conformity, and engender cohesiveness. If you think about it, we see groups form with these common characteristics in the workplace. We also see them in other group examples, such as professional organizations and even in our own family unit.

- *Norms.* A **norm** is a generally agreed-on standard of behavior that every member

© CORBIS

of the group is expected to follow. For example, a norm for a dance group might be the way they wear their hair at performances and their lively dance expression. Human nature compels most of us to gravitate toward groups of like-minded individuals with a strong identity, so these norms ordinarily do not offend group members. If being a member of a group is important to an individual, he or she will change personality, beliefs, and behavior to conform to the group.

- *Conformity.* Group pressure forces its members to conform, or comply, with the norms established by the group. Because nonconformity threatens the group's standards, stability, and longevity, the pressure placed on each member to conform is oftentimes intense. For the group to succeed, its members must show they are united in their efforts and that they uphold the standards of the group.

- *Cohesiveness.* Cohesiveness is an emotional closeness that exists among the group members, and its success depends on how well the group sticks together and acts as a single unit instead of as a group of individuals. As you may recall from a previous chapter, the middle level on Maslow's hierarchy states the need for social interaction—a feeling of belonging, to be identified with one or more groups, and to simply fit in somewhere. Few people like being alone or working in isolation for extended periods of time.

Motivation to Join Groups People become part of a group for one, or more, of the following reasons—affiliation, power, identity, and goal accomplishment.

People become part of a group for many reasons, such as affiliation, power, identity, or goal accomplishment.

- *Affiliation.* Group companionship provides feelings of security, belonging, and friendship.

- *Power.* There is strength in numbers. Being a member of a group provides reassurance and support, often giving its members the courage to take a stand on an important issue, which they might not do on their own. Unions are one example of strength in numbers.

- *Identity.* Along with membership in a group comes an increased awareness of personal identity—a sense of being somebody. Through membership in a group, an individual's self-esteem is positively reinforced.

- *Goal accomplishment.* In most situations, a group will accomplish goals more effectively than any individual effort, due in part to the variety of skills and knowledge that are collectively provided. Typically, the more brainpower used to solve a problem, the better the chance for a successful resolution.

In order for groups to function well, members must be aware of the presence of groupthink and hidden agenda issues.

Groupthink and Hidden Agenda Issues

Formal and informal groups are important to organizations and affect their performance and success in a variety of ways. The effect that groups have can be either positive or negative, and this effect often manifests itself in terms of groupthink and the hidden agendas of individual group members as discussed in the next sections.

Groupthink Issues

Groupthink is the tendency of highly cohesive groups to lose their critical evaluative abilities and, out of a desire for harmony, often overlook realistic, meaningful alternatives as attitudes are formed and decisions are made. At times, groupthink can contribute to unethical behavior in the workplace. Symptoms of groupthink are arrogance, over-commitment, and excessive loyalty to the group.

The more cohesive the group, the more likely the individual members tend to "agree not to disagree," especially when it comes to challenging the ideas of the group leader. Unfortunately, in that way, groupthink can undermine the analytical process, legitimize lack of knowledge, and reinforce biases because people do tend to be influenced by their peers. Instances of groupthink occur most often at meetings where decisions have been made *before* the meeting begins.

In other words, the other members of the group are there merely to rubber-stamp the leader's choice.

Although a certain amount of groupthink can be expected from any group situation, some techniques are available to leaders to minimize its occurrence. Leaders can, for example, diversify the group membership to get different perspectives as well as provide opportunities, encouragement, and permission for open debate on issues. An effective leader looks for ways to encourage participation.

Hidden Agendas

Another pitfall of any group interaction is the possibility that someone will be safeguarding a hidden agenda or personal goal. **Hidden agendas** are composed of attitudes and feelings that an individual brings to the group. While often planned, hidden agendas can also arise spontaneously as a result of a disagreement with some idea expressed or conflict with a member in the group.

When there is a hidden agenda present, goal orientation shifts from the group to the individual so that the person with the hidden agenda nearly always, either consciously or subconsciously, places obstacles in the path of the group's planned agenda. Hidden agendas represent what an individual or group want, instead of what they say they want.

While hidden agendas are neither better nor worse than planned agendas, they are important to understand. At the very least, administrative managers need to recognize their existence because they can profoundly interfere with the ability to focus on everything being said and can block the process of groups.

If not recognized and understood, hidden agendas can waste a great deal of a group's energy and the organization's resources.

Here are three ways you, as a leader, can help a group handle hidden agendas:

1. Realize that a hidden agenda is a natural part of the group process because individual members have individual goals and needs.
2. Recognize that a hidden agenda might be present when the group is having difficulty in reaching its goals.
3. Decide how to bring the hidden agenda to light.

Teamwork and Team-Building Elements

Teams exist in every organization, even if they are not formally recognized or named. They exist because you need teamwork to complete special projects and day-to-day activities—whether it's rolling up your sleeves and pitching in on a year-end report or asking a coworker to help you plan a meeting.

By combining the resources and skills of interdependent work-group members with the high energy and motivation created through effective teamwork, employees and supervisors can attain extraordinary levels of achievement through teams.

Effective teams have these characteristics:

- Members are loyal to one another and the leader.
- Members and leaders have a high degree of confidence and trust in each other.
- The group is eager to help members develop their full potential.

- The members communicate fully and frankly all information relative to the group's activities.
- Members feel secure in making decisions that seem appropriate to them.
- Activities of the group occur in a supportive atmosphere.

As shown in Figure 12.1, organizations must help build effective teams because team-building does not just happen. Team-building is one of many interventions used to create change in an organization. Its purpose is the creation of a work environment that enables and promotes achievement of organizational and individual goals. Modern team-building efforts usually include concentration on how team members relate to each other and how work is completed.

Here are some ways managers and employees can contribute to and help make a team effort more effective:

1. *Put the organization first.* Let your coworkers know that your concern is for the success of the company, not just successful fulfillment of your job responsibilities or career goals.
2. *Avoid arguing for your own viewpoint.* Instead, state your point as clearly and concisely as you can and listen to others.
3. *Remain committed.* Problems and frustrations will surely arise, but don't give up.

FIGURE 12.1 Effective team-building efforts concentrate on how team members relate to each other and how work is completed.

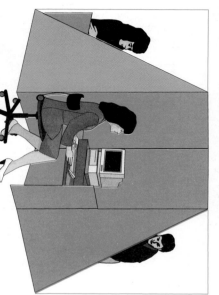

Support your colleagues. Remember, you need them as much as they need you. If the discussion reaches an impasse, do not assume that someone must win and someone must lose. Look for a new option that is the next best alternative for everyone. Encourage differences of opinion among team members.

4. *If an agreement comes too quickly, take another look at the issue.* Varied interpretations of what was agreed to may be hiding differences. Make sure that everyone fully understands the intent and content of the agreement. Do not give way to other viewpoints unless you feel they have reasonable merit in this particular situation.

5. *Avoid using conflict-reducing tricks to reach agreement.* For instance, using majority vote, calculating an average, flipping a coin, and bargaining are not recommended choices of actions.

6. *Welcome input from others.* Respect the ideas that others share, just as you would like them to respect your contributions. Make sure that every member of the group contributes.[2]

The secret of a company's overall success lies in asking everyone to commit to teamwork, even if they physically work away from the office on a virtual team.

Virtual Teams

As communication technologies improve, employees often exchange ideas and information with distant colleagues. But what happens when a project or task depends on the ongoing cooperation of employees who are miles apart? **Virtual teams**—usually formed when geographical separations can't be bridged—may be the answer. By definition, they are composed of members who rarely, if ever, meet physically. They do meet and work together electronically.

Companies may form virtual teams to serve a number of purposes. For example, virtual teams get employees out of the office and closer to customers, and they cut time and travel costs. Sometimes companies use virtual teamwork to integrate employees who were added through a merger or acquisition of another company and its employees.

Effective communication represents a tremendous problem for virtual teams. Managers can foster camaraderie between team members and keep them engaged by encouraging media-based "face-to-face" encounters and through communication via e-mails, telephone calls, and instant messages. Technology and cooperation can resolve many of these problems, but team members must work hard to overcome the gaps left by their inability to communicate face-to-face.

Virtual teams are a special challenge for managers. Besides having to think through and formalize almost every aspect of communicating, socializing, team-building, and productivity, managers must often change their management style. Many administrative managers, for example, initially feel discomfort when they can no longer keep tabs on an employee's progress with cubicle visits or by asking questions during a coffee break.[3]

Establishing trust and commitment, encouraging communication, and assessing team members pose tremendous challenges for virtual team managers. Here are a few tips to make the process easier:

- Establish times for group interaction.
- Set up firm rules for communication among members.
- Use visual forms of communication where possible.
- Agree on standard technology so all team members can work together easily (i.e., same software version like Word XP).

CONFLICT RESOLUTIONS

Managers are required to deal with diverse conflict situations almost routinely each day. The reason is because no two people are exactly alike. And this uniqueness guarantees at least one thing—there will always be conflict in the workplace. Since we all take our personal values, experiences, beliefs, and perceptions with us everywhere, the chance that our values will clash with those of someone else from time to time is very real. Conflict is an inevitable part of life, and the workplace is no exception. That is what makes effective conflict management an essential skill for any successful manager.

Conflict, itself, is not a bad thing. Disagreement can, in fact, be a healthy and creative exercise in the growth and development of an individual, team, or project. Further, conflict can ultimately strengthen work relationships. Trouble erupts, however, when conflict goes unmanaged and unresolved. Therefore, a manager's goal should not be to eliminate all conflict but to minimize and redirect disputes by seeking and applying constructive resolutions.

Whether the outcome of a conflict issue is positive or negative is almost totally determined by the way it is managed. One could ask, "Why not let individual 'flash fires' burn themselves out?" A thoughtful response is because ultimately, the physical,

© Getty Images/PhotoDisc

Understanding and Resolving Conflicts

Conflict of any sort in the workplace is often viewed as unwelcome—perhaps because many people associate it with a lack of harmony, emotional pain, or a serious type of destructive behavior. Though it is true that conflicts can have a devastating effect on productivity, morale, teamwork, and ultimately an organization's bottom line, there are some reasons why conflicts can actually be healthy for a business. Here's how:

1. *Conflict produces change.* Conflict often leads to the first step toward getting rid of outdated procedures, revising regulations, and fostering innovation and creativity.

2. *Conflict leads to unity.* Addressing, rather than suppressing, conflict opens the lines of communication, gets people talking to each other (instead of about each other), and makes people feel like they are part of a team that cares.

3. *Conflict promotes compromise.* People learn how to work harmoniously, come up with creative solutions, and reach outcomes that benefit everyone involved.

Where conflict is not acceptable in the workplace is when rudeness can spiral down into outright bullying. Included in this category are verbally harassing someone on a

psychological, emotional, and financial toll they take on an organization and its employees can be tremendous.

Difficult situations occur at work because people have different interests, goals, and priorities. It could also be because there are communication problems, power struggles, mistaken perceptions and assumptions, and personality clashes. Many people wince at the thought of having an argument or avoid confronting work colleagues. Everyone, regardless of their position at work, can learn how to handle conflict more effectively.

With conflicts, every situation is different and managers need a separate way of solving each one. One successful approach to conflict management is to demonstrate that you have heard the other person's deeper needs and feelings by making reference to them in your conversation. For example, try the following techniques:

- Clarify perspective. Example: "When did this happen?"
- Acknowledge differing viewpoints. Example: "I can see you really feel angry about that."
- Invite elaboration. Example: "Why is that important to you?"

Conflict resolution in process—making progress to solve a disagreement.

regular basis, withholding resources to guarantee another's failure, and spreading stories to undermine a person's reputation in the workplace. A study, conducted by researchers from Wayne State University, found that one in six workers in the sample group had suffered on the job through destructive bullying.[4]

In another study involving people who had been on the receiving end of incivility at work, a management professor at the University of North Carolina's graduate business school, found that conflict affected the bottom line. Of the 775 people surveyed:

- 53 percent lost work time worrying about the incident or future interactions.
- 46 percent thought about changing jobs to get away from the instigator.
- 37 percent reported a weakened sense of commitment to their organization.
- 28 percent lost work time trying to avoid the instigator.
- 12 percent did change jobs—to avoid the instigator.[5]

Conflict occurs when two parties perceive their interests as incompatible. These interests are basically differences in needs, goals, or values. To resolve a conflict, both persons need to discuss their concerns openly and honestly, but state the problem in a non-threatening way. Interacting with others in ways that resolve conflicts instead of intensifying them is vital to establishing healthy and lasting relationships in your work and home life.

Two key behaviors that resolve differences are to talk candidly about your needs and concerns with others and to focus on mutual interests. People frequently have pointless arguments because they fail to focus on the real needs and interests at stake. They don't understand what the other person wants and don't think through what they really want. Their focus instead is on their differences.[6] That approach doesn't lead to conflict resolution.

The goal in resolving conflicts is to come up with the best solution—the one most likely to satisfy the basic needs and interests of both sides. For example, suppose you want a raise. Your position might be, "I need a higher salary," while your boss's might be, "I can't increase wages without reducing benefits." You both have what appear to be opposing interests. But perhaps your boss may be willing to pay you a higher salary if you can increase production, which, in turn, can increase profits that could cover the cost of benefits.

When resolving a difference, you can argue in a way that is both productive and professional by being as diplomatic as possible. When you feel your temperature start to rise, your stomach start to knot up, and your voice start to quiver, regain control of your emotions and remember to show respect for your coworker or associate.

Rephrase what you want to say to take the harsh emotion out of your words. By stating flatly, "You're wrong," you are attacking your coworker on a personal level, disregarding his or her feelings, and putting yourself in adamant opposition. A more effective way to say you don't agree would be, "I see what you're saying, but I don't agree. Here's where I'm coming from—can we find a middle ground?"[7]

The Conflict Resolution Process

Adhere to these five steps when you need to resolve a conflict with another person.

1. *Identify the problem.* Sometimes the problem merely needs to be reframed. **Reframing** refers to looking for evidence of a more positive, less catastrophic, view of some problem. If, for example, you put a new frame on a picture, the picture looks different. In the same way, if you put a new meaning on a problem, the problem can look different, too, so it is easier to go to the next step.

2. *Look for solutions.* Good solutions come most often from random, nonjudgmental brainstorming. Identify as many alternatives to consider as you can. Remember, when brainstorming any suggestion may be a good one and is therefore not dismissed.

3. *Choose the best solution.* The best solution does three things—it solves the problem, does not hurt anyone or interfere with his or her rights, and satisfies both parties. There should be no winner or loser with a best solution; both sides should feel as if they have achieved something. It is important to acknowledge and preserve the value of the relationship.

4. *Act.* Follow through on one of the solutions.

5. *Evaluate.* If your approach turns out to be ineffective, do not look on it as a failure. It just means you have eliminated one approach and you are ready to try another. You may need to evaluate why it was ineffective before you move on. (Go back to step 1.)

At each step during the conflict resolution process, communication is important.

Communication does not mean just telling someone what you want. It means listening to what he or she wants. It means establishing eye contact and being sensitive to the other person's body language. It means not making demands or ultimatums but offering suggestions instead. It means wanting a workable solution, rather than just having your way.

When conflicts become heated, and they sometimes do, follow these hints to control your impulses:

1. *Be aware of your feelings.* Although some people are ashamed of their angry, sad, or jealous feelings, these feelings are real, and you are entitled to them. If you are angry, admit it to yourself and express your feelings using adult-like behaviors.

2. *Take a break if your feelings get too hot to handle.* Divert yourself. Do something else or go somewhere else.

3. *Count to ten slowly.* It will give you at least ten seconds to cool off and think about your approach.

4. *Consult with someone such as a close friend, relative, or coworker who has a calming effect on you, and whom you can trust in confidence.* Sometimes an objective third party can offer meaningful suggestions that benefit both sides.

There is one final point to mention about understanding organizational conflicts. Organizations by their very nature create unique problem-solving obstacles. Be aware of these workplace realities that do, in fact, hamper honest conflict resolution attempts:

- Employees are afraid to criticize their bosses. The superior-subordinate relationship creates this fear.

- People are protective of their positions and power. This is sometimes referred to as "protecting one's turf," such as one's job security.

- A person with technical expertise is intimidating to those with less knowledge. This expertise could come from either more education or more experience as perceived by the other person.

- People see problems from their own viewpoints. What is needed is to look at conflict or differences from the broader organizational perspective.

Managing and Negotiating Effective Solutions

Many managers prefer to not deal with conflict. However, conflict must be managed and not suppressed. If conflict is suppressed, it may slowly poison a company with employee anger and hostility.

It's critical that clear expectations for governing conflict exist. It's the job of management to establish the environment of an organization, which includes outlining expectations governing disagreements and how employees treat each other. To listen openly, to be respectful, and to appreciate the differences in individual style and perspective of others are all part of these expectations.

When managers spend a large amount of their time refereeing conflict, the result is a lot of time spent dealing with issues that retard progress, productivity, support, and cooperation. The goal of conflict resolution, therefore, is for parties involved to move from some form of compromise to ultimate collaboration marked by a shared success.

To be candid, even noble attempts to create a "win-win" resolution for all parties are unlikely to be successful. In many cases, one party actually obtains more (materially) than the other. The measure of success often lies in the degree to which all parties to the negotiation feel satisfied with the results they have achieved.

Negotiation is a psychological process requiring a give-and-take between the participants. Relative to conflict resolution, it is less likely that a negotiator will leave a session satisfied if she or he has not experienced the give-and-take during the negotiation process. Because conflict inherently occurs in each of our lives, over the years we've learned about the negotiation process by taking these six actions.

1. We describe what we want and how we feel.

2. We express why we feel as we do and the motives for our desires.

3. We acknowledge the other person's perspective.

4. We look for solutions.

5. We choose one solution, and

6. We put it into effect. [8]

When negotiating, if a coworker's point of view is more logical, recognize that fact and say, "I'm glad we explored all avenues, and at this point, I have to agree with you." While such an admission can be difficult, put your ego aside and concede your coworker's point gracefully, without sarcasm. Further, say something to show that you don't have any hard feelings. Make a comment like, "I'll back your plan 100 percent and help you in any way I can." This will ensure a productive working relationship and preserve your professional integrity.

There may be times, of course, when you may not be able to give in gracefully. In cases like these, try removing yourself from the conflict for a brief period of time to let things cool down a bit. Just tell your coworker that you have another pressing deadline to meet and that you'll get back to him or her in a day or two. Take the time to think the problem over objectively. Above all, remember that your priority is to find a feasible solution to the conflict—not to win an argument.

Conflict Management Styles

If you have a conflict with a colleague, be aware of how you respond. Your reaction may deescalate the situation or fan the fires. There are five generally accepted styles for dealing with conflict. Nothing is inherently right or wrong with any of these styles. In fact, each can be appropriate and most effective depending on the situation and issues to be resolved and the personalities involved. These conflict management styles are competing, accommodating, avoiding, collaborating, and compromising.

- **Competing** could mean "standing up for your rights," defending a position that you believe is correct, or demonstrating a win-at-all-costs attitude. If you compete, you're assertive in pursuing your own concerns. This style is useful when quick action is necessary or when you need to make an unpopular decision. This is a power-oriented mode in which a person uses whatever means that seems appropriate to win.

- **Accommodating** usually takes the form of selfless generosity or blind obedience by yielding completely to another's point of view. If you accommodate, you're cooperative, but unassertive. This style is useful when you realize that you're wrong or that the issue is more important to the other person.

- **Avoiding** might take the form of diplomatically sidestepping an issue, postponing an issue until a better time, or simply withdrawing from a threatening situation either emotionally, physically, or intellectually. If you avoid, you don't address the conflict. This reaction is useful when the issue is trivial, a confrontation could be damaging, or you need time to cool off or gather information. An avoider generally chooses to dodge conflict at all costs.

- **Collaborating** involves agreeing not to compete for resources or use confrontation to find creative solutions to mutually engaging problems. If you collaborate, both sides are assertive and cooperative. Rather than avoiding a problem, you attempt to work with another person to find a mutually satisfying solution.

- **Compromising** involves finding expedient, mutually acceptable solutions that partially satisfy both parties. If you compromise, you address rather than avoid an issue. Compromising means splitting the difference or agreeing on a middle ground. It might mean exchanging concessions or seeking quick, middle-ground solutions. Whatever the format, it means being tactful and acting responsibly.

When used appropriately, each of these styles can be an effective approach to conflict resolution. Recognize that any one style or a mixture of the five can be used during the course of a dispute to arrive at the collaboration and compromise required for ultimate agreement.

Remember, conflict may be unavoidable in organizations, but the anger, grudges, hurt, and blame that often ensue from it are not. Although negotiation involves conferring, discussing, or bargaining to reach agreements, most managers realize that in practice, negotiations involve conflict and, therefore, can result in a win-lose, lose-lose, or win-win situation.

Negotiating Strategies Managers spend a good portion of their time negotiating with employees, suppliers, customers, or other work groups. Unfortunately, when people bargain over positions, they tend to back themselves into corners defending their positions, which results in a number of either win-lose or lose-lose outcomes rather than a win-win result.

Win-Lose. The **win-lose negotiating strategy** assumes that one side will win by achieving its goals and the other side will lose. When engaging in a win-lose negotiation, the person with the most information is in the most powerful position. A win-lose approach to negotiations is sometimes obvious and appropriate, while at other times it is less apparent and destructive.

For example, groups often set themselves up for win-lose outcomes by following the principle of majority rule—if 51 percent of the group votes one way, then 49 percent

are losers. Another example of the win-lose approach occurs when the parties start the negotiation process by stating the specific outcomes they want to see.

When the issues involved in a conflict are trivial or when a speedy decision is required, this style may be appropriate. It is also appropriate when unpopular courses of action must be implemented—for instance, when implementing the strategies and policies formulated by higher-level managers. In general, use the win-lose style when:

- You have a clear conflict of interests.
- You are in a much more powerful position, or
- You are not concerned with promoting a long-term relationship.

Lose-Lose. The outcomes of the **lose-lose negotiating strategy** are common when one party attempts to win at the expense of the other. Lose-lose outcomes also occur when, for example, unreasonable union demands have forced companies into bankruptcy or when employers destroy the effectiveness of their workers by taking advantage of them. Mutually destructive outcomes can also surface from personal disputes among employees. Feuding co-workers may destroy their own careers by acquiring a reputation of being difficult to work with or not being team players.

Compromise can sometimes seem better than fighting a win-lose battle and risking a lose-lose outcome. When resources are scarce or limited, compromise may indeed be the best solution.

Win-Win. The **win-win negotiating strategy** assumes that a reasonable solution can be reached that will satisfy the needs of *all* parties. Instead of looking at their opponent as an adversary to be defeated, win-win negotiators see others as allies in the search for a satisfactory solution through collaborative means.

In most situations, the needs of the negotiating parties are not incompatible; they are just different. The four basic components of a win-win negotiation are as follows:

1. Focus on interests, not positions.
2. Separate the people from the problem.
3. Generate a variety of possibilities before deciding what to do.
4. Insist that the result be based on some objective standard.

There is a vast difference in results among the three styles. By focusing on the end result instead of the means of getting there, win-win solutions can frequently be found. Although this strategy may not always work, it's a good idea to strive toward its use. You will want to use the win-win style when:

- You have common interests.
- Power is approximately equal, or you are in a weak position.
- You want to maintain a continuing, harmonious relationship.

When you can bring the conflicting parties together to discuss the issues face-to-face, you are using a powerful conflict management technique known as integration. **Integration** is a win-win method, instead of a win-lose or lose-lose method. In a win-win situation, all parties walk away with something gained by using their imagination to work out a mutually satisfactory solution. The major advantage of integration is the shared commitment for all parties to find a solution. Having shared this commitment, a strong foundation exists for continued collaboration and opportunities to resolve future conflicts.

CONFLICT ISSUES IN ACTION

Other conflicts can arise on the job that demand a manager's attention. Increasingly, managing multiple projects, coping with job stress and burnout, and time management concerns become troublesome for workers and managers alike. An overview of these issues, therefore, is fitting at this time.

Managing Multiple Projects

Scenario: You already have your hands full. Often you're asked to do more with fewer resources. And the more you succeed, the more people expect of you. Your in-box overflows with memos, reports, publications, and more—and all of it needs your immediate attention. What do you do?

As customer demands continue to change and grow in today's highly competitive marketplace, so does the need for consistent, effective project management to meet them. With so many projects, both large and small, being implemented everyday, it is vital that they be well-planned and carefully managed. If not, the outcome could mean overrun budgets, missed deadlines, and dissatisfied customers.

An administrative manager today must be a master juggler, responsible for keeping several balls in the air even as new balls are randomly tossed in from all sides. To effectively manage multiple projects, you must draw on skills from time management, task completion, organizational psychology, and more. It requires this many-sided approach to provide a system for easily managing concurrent projects and guiding each to its successful completion.

It is not easy because as you can see, these skills are multidimensional unto themselves as well. Managing multiple projects successfully requires yet another skill called multitasking.

Multitasking is defined as the ability to execute more than one *task* at the same time. When should you consider using multitasking?

1. *When performing routine tasks.* If your brain is familiar with performing an activity, it takes less effort to do it and work on another task simultaneously.
2. *When the outcome isn't critical.* Deleting unwanted files from your hard drive, for example.
3. *During "time traps."* When standing in line or waiting for a meeting to begin, bring reading materials to fully occupy your time. Or, order supplies while photocopying a large document.

On the other hand, when is *multitasking* ill-advised?

1. *When you are in a hurry.* When you are rushing to complete a project, your stress hormones are already interfering with your brain's ability to process information and work efficiently. Multitasking makes the situation worse. (This is when you will spill coffee or soda on your final report!)
2. *When the task requires clear focus and concentration.* Preparing a cost-analysis spreadsheet demands your full attention.
3. *When you are on the telephone.* You may think it's simple to finish typing a memo while talking on the phone, but your caller can easily recognize your distraction as well as hear you keying. If the person on the other line is a customer, you could lose more than time by not giving him or her your full attention.

Today's workplace is often complex and unpredictable. As a manager today, you must be a master juggler, responsible for keeping several balls in the air even as new balls are randomly tossed in from all sides.[9] You know the feeling. You're trying to save time by doing two or three things at once — sending e-mail while on the phone with your boss, listening to a colleague while sorting junk mail, making a list during a meeting. A growing body of scientific research shows that one of a juggler's favorite time-saving techniques, multitasking, can actually make you less efficient. Trying to do two or three things at once or in quick succession can take longer overall than doing them one at a time. Multitasking may leave you with reduced brainpower to perform each task, thereby making you less efficient.

According to David Meyer, a psychology professor at the University of Michigan, there's scientific evidence that multitasking is extremely hard for somebody to do, and sometimes impossible. Further, Meyer puts forward that those who multitask are less efficient than those who focus on one project at a time. The reason appears to be that the time lost switching among tasks increases with the complexity of the tasks. People who are multitasking too much experience various warning signs—short-term-memory problems can be one. Intense multitasking can also induce a stress response, an adrenaline rush that when prolonged can damage cells that form new memory, Meyer says.[10]

Job Stress

Scenario: The phone is ringing off the hook. Your report on the new project is due in half an hour. Your boss asks to see you immediately. You have not had any time to eat lunch. And you cannot get the cap off the aspirin bottle. You are stressed.

Stress in the workplace is costing American businesses staggering amounts of money. **Stress** may be defined as any external stimulus that produces wear and tear on a person's psychological or physical well-being. A person under severe or prolonged stress cannot function as effectively as a person leading a more balanced life. Workplace stress costs businesses billions of dollars a year in absenteeism, staff turnover, errors, accidents, and theft to support drug or alcohol habits.

Workplace stressors affect everyone who works in organizations today. Politics on the job can be stressful when you deny or respond ineffectively to them. Interruptions, conflicting demands, procrastination, ineffective delegating, and poor organizational and time management skills also add pressure to the workday.

On-the-job stress isn't limited to workplace issues. Violent world events, the fear of terrorism and a faltering economy, and personal stressors, such as family and financial problems, can also negatively affect one's physical and mental health and work performance. Although the implication is that stress is negative, a certain amount of it can have quite positive effects. For example, improving one's health through athletic competition is considered a positive stressor.

A healthy body can normally handle a big jolt of stress now and then. But continued or frequent exposure to stressors weaken your immune cells and leave you more susceptible to illness. A near-constant increased heart rate raises your blood pressure, forcing your heart to work harder at pumping blood and oxygen throughout your body. This could possibly lead to a heart attack. Other physical negative effects include headaches and muscular aches, exhaustion, insomnia, and anxiety.

When you're under stress, it's very easy to lose perspective about things in your work and personal life. Relatively minor problems often appear large and difficult to handle. Naturally, this feeds your feelings of stress, which makes the problems seem even greater. One way to try to eliminate self-induced stress is to try to view problems as learning experiences. If, for example, a reprimand from the boss for not getting your reports in on time makes you better organized and more efficient, the reprimand that raised your stress level takes on a positive value in managing your work life.

Business organizations know that job-related stress can result in employee illness, turnover, job dissatisfaction, reduced productivity, and other workplace problems. The symptoms of stress are often invisible, but the effects are unmistakable. Going beyond productivity, the impact on the individual is substantial. Stress prevents people from feeling fulfilled, from feeling happy, and from feeling valued both on and off the job. We all need to be vigilant in managing stress and, from time to time, take back control of our lives.

When you're in control of your life, you can usually control the level of stress. Being in control of your life is largely about planning and investing a little of your free time in setting personal and professional goals. Planning also allows you to anticipate and be prepared to handle problems in advance, which, in turn, can reduce your stress levels. Although the level of stress in relationships is, in part, about personalities and compatibility, your attitude can significantly affect how others respond to you.

You can form harmonious relationships with others that diffuse stress if you take a positive approach. People enjoy working with and relating to happy, optimistic people. When things are getting difficult, a smile or positive approach to a problem can make the difference between success and failure of a project.

Being the target of someone else's bad behavior or negative attitude is stressful. But your own attitude toward the person will often determine the amount of stress you

experience. Consider the following techniques:

- *If someone is critical of or rude to you.* The probable cause is a fault in the person's character; he or she likely irritates and offends other people as well. However, think carefully about the person's comments; if they're unfair, reject them; if they're on the mark, learn from them.

- *If someone hurts you.* Don't bear grudges because you'll tend to churn them over in your mind. This creates negative thinking that can raise your stress levels. Forgiveness—as long as it's genuine—is important in maintaining relationships. But if you can't dismiss a hurt, it may be better to discuss it with the person; and avoid or circumvent people who are unnecessarily hurtful.

- *If others frustrate you.* Should coworkers, family members, or friends create difficult situations or are just plain annoying, relaxation techniques such as deep breathing, reading, or mild exercises can help you remain calm and neutral. This allows you to respond more clearly and effectively in stressful situations.[11]

As managers get their own stress under control, they can help employees handle theirs by doing the following:

1. *Encourage open communication.* Ask that employee with a chip on his or her shoulder what's causing the anger. Invite staff members to talk about their stress and really listen to them. But remember to show concern and promise confidentiality.

2. *Offer employee assistance.* Send your employees to a stress management seminar and provide a list of community mental health services that ensure confidential counseling and guidance.

3. *Lighten up.* Encourage a relaxed and casual atmosphere at your company. Humor can be a powerful antidote to stress, and people who have fun at work are less anxious and more productive.

4. *Be generous with benefits.* Offer a solid medical plan including preventive or alternative healthcare options, contribute to your employees' gym memberships and day care, and provide flextime and job sharing. Stock vending machines with healthful snacks.

5. *Provide boundaries, support, and trust.* Offer job predictability with written company policies, procedures, and job descriptions. Provide effective training, and show your appreciation with praise and motivational and incentive programs.

6. *Give appropriate responsibility.* Let employees have more say over what they do and how they perform their jobs. Invite suggestions on how they could add or eliminate certain duties, or make changes to how they contribute to your company.[12]

Stress is not based on what happens to you, but on *how you deal with what happens to you.* The key to stress is "choice" in how to deal with the stressors. Because you cannot build a life completely free from stress, it is important that you develop some ways of dealing with stress such as the following:

1. Work off stress with some physical activity.

2. Talk out your worries with someone you trust and respect.

3. Learn to accept what you cannot change.

4. Avoid self-medication like alcohol or other chemicals because, in the end, the ability to handle stress comes from within you, not from the outside.

5. Get enough sleep and rest.

6. Balance work and recreation by scheduling time for recreation to relax your mind.

7. Do something for others; this gets your mind off yourself.

Burnout

Although there are some positive aspects of stress, companies are primarily concerned with preventing the negative outcomes, most notably job burnout. Stress in the workplace, when successfully managed, can be a healthy motivator. Unmanaged, it can lead to a loss of motivation and eventual burnout. **Burnout** is essentially caused by a feeling of powerlessness on the job and is a stress-related affliction resulting when people invest most of their time and energy in a particular activity.

People use "stress" and "burnout" interchangeably, but they are quite different. You can be stressed and still be motivated. If you start to feel overwhelmed, take a quick break. Just getting away from the task at hand, even briefly, can clear your mind and rejuvenate you. If you notice these signs of burnout, discuss with your supervisor how you can take a different or more positive approach to your job.

Signs of burnout to look for are sleep loss, hair loss, chronic exhaustion, and feeling hopeless and overwhelmed. Other symptoms include poor concentration, general irritability, unprovoked anger, resentment toward others, prolonged bouts of insomnia, and a lack of, or marked increase in, appetite. If not addressed, these warning signals can hasten the deterioration of your emotional and physical health, and likewise contribute to additional workplace stress and lack of productivity.

Some strategies to combat burnout, offered by lifestyle coach Cheryl Richardson, include:

- *Eat well and exercise.* Take vitamins and seek help for any chronic physical or emotional discomfort.

- *Use technology to your advantage.* Don't let it take advantage of you. For example, turn your phone ringer off at home unless you are on call. Can that be an inconvenience for someone trying to reach you? Yes, but are you really willing to give up your peace to suit their schedule? Call back when it suits yours.

- *When in doubt, throw it out.* E-mail files, paper files, clippings, magazines, and catalogs—they pile up and we panic, thinking, "What if I trash something important?" Just do it.

- *Don't skip your breaks and vacation days.* Use this time to get away from work, whether for a few minutes or a couple of weeks. Spend your work breaks relaxing, meditating, or just laughing with coworkers. Don't take work with you on your vacations.

- *Get your rest.* Do your best to get a good night's sleep. Go to bed and get up at the same time every day.

- *Breathe again.* Slow, rhythmic deep breathing—taking air into your belly (diaphragm), not just your chest—is a great way to de-stress. Make a habit of breathing in through your nose and out through your mouth.

- *Before you over commit to others, take care of yourself.* If you are exhausted, sick, or stressed, you cannot really be at your best for yourself, your family, or your job.

- *Take it easy.* Make excellence, not perfection, your goal. Redefine success in terms of cooperative effort, not just individual competition. Strive to be effective and productive, but recognize that you cannot control other people and every circumstance. Knowing this may help you overcome stressful situations.[13]

Time Management Issues

Many of us are victims of our attitudes about time. We put things off, we complain about the lack of time, and we misuse the time we have. The purpose of time management is to help us overcome these problems. Time is an important element and resource that is often mismanaged. Creating workable time management strategies for ourselves, handling interruptions by others effectively, overcoming the tendency to procrastinate, and recognizing time wasters are four methods that work for many managers in today's workplace.

Time Management Strategies People who get things completed are those who prioritize their tasks, organize them, and recognize other ways they can use their time to the fullest.

1. *Prioritize.* People who believe they do not have enough time to accomplish everything they want to accomplish may be misusing time by not setting priorities. After thoroughly analyzing and eliminating unnecessary tasks, prioritize your work. Start by making a list of everything you have to do. Then assign each task a level of importance using the following three categories.

- *Important and urgent.* Only a few things actually fall into this category. Those items might include a major presentation your boss needs help with at the last minute or an urgent phone call with instructions that must be carried out immediately. Project deadlines are important and urgent.

- *Important, but not urgent.* These tasks generally are the major focus of your job, such as records management or project preparation. If you keep up with them, they're manageable. But if you leave them undone too long, they may become "important and urgent." An example might be a project with a future deadline. If you tackle a piece of the project each day, you'll easily manage the workload. If you procrastinate, you'll find yourself in a last-minute scramble to complete the entire project—at the expense of your other work.

- *Things that are nice to do.* These items are not important or urgent, but simply things to do if you have time.

Responding immediately to an e-mail inviting you to lunch next week or writing an unnecessary cover letter are nice to do. But put them low on your priority list because they rob you of time you need to accomplish the things that are important.

2. *Organize.* Now that you've assigned a priority to each task, create a to-do list that groups items according to their importance. For example, "important and urgent" tasks will naturally take priority. Even so, if you consistently manage your time well, you won't have a great number of these tasks. A good rule of thumb is to be in the "Urgent" mode for no more than 2 1/2 hours a day. Plan to spend about 3 1/2 hours on important (but not urgent) tasks. And devote only 1 to 1 1/2 hours to nonessential tasks.

Working from a list is a great way to organize yourself and gain control over your day. You may not cross off everything every day, but it will give you a plan. Allow yourself to remain flexible, so that if another "important and urgent" task comes up, you are ready for it. Then you can get right back to your list as soon as it's accomplished. You won't waste time trying to decide what to do next.[14]

3. *Other Strategies (in no particular order).*

- Examine every task you perform. The time you invest upfront in assessing your work will pay dividends later. What are you doing that isn't essential? Are you doing certain tasks just because you think they have to be done?

- Plan ahead. For example, as soon as you're assigned to do a project, first gather as much information about it as you can, then think through the steps that are needed to get it done, and finally "pencil in" each step or phase of the project in your appointment book. This way, your appointment book becomes a planning tool.

- List what you need to cover during telephone conversations before you dial. Doing this will help you remember everything you want to discuss.

- Aim to conclude every phone call in five minutes or less—except a customer or your supervisor.

- Drop low-priority tasks from your to-do list. You'll probably never get to them anyway.[15]

- Clear your desktop without losing track of current assignments by creating "action files" for work in progress.

- Make a decision or take action on each piece of paper you handle so that you handle it only once.

- Use sticky notes. When not overused, they can be a helpful addition to your appointment book because they can be added or removed easily.

- Replace e-mail with voice mail. It's not only faster to leave voice-mail messages than e-mail messages, but recipients can access and respond to voice mail faster. E-mail is best for nonurgent communications or when you must keep a detailed record of the information.[16]

Interruptions Interruptions during the day steal little bits of time. Whether it's a chatty coworker looking for a sympathetic ear or the company president who wants a budget update ASAP, interruptions impede your productivity and make it difficult to return to unfinished tasks. How can you protect your productivity from interruptions? First, accept business-related interruptions—as opposed to interruptions by chatty coworkers or chronic complainers—as normal occurrences that may also be beneficial.

Impromptu conversations with your colleagues—as long as they're business-related—can lead to relationships that help all of you succeed. The key is knowing how to handle the interruption. The following techniques are offered for handling business-related interruptions.

- *Develop control systems.* For example, request that people send routine questions to you by e-mail, written notes, or voice mail. That allows you to decide when you will deal with the questions to give them the time they deserve. Set aside a time to return phone calls. By grouping interruptions, you avoid the inefficiency of starting and stopping work in progress while still taking care of people's concerns.

- *Determine the nature of the interruption.* Stop what you're doing, listen attentively to the person, and ask: "How can I help you?" or "What do you need?" If the timing is bad, ask: "Would it be possible for us to discuss this later?" That approach conveys a willingness to help without permitting excessive demands on your time.

- *Set limits.* Tell the person how much time you can spare. For example: "I have about five minutes. How can I help you in that time?" or "I can spare two minutes on this. What can I do to help you?"

- *Complete short, easy tasks right away.* If you can fulfill a request in less than two minutes, do it while the person waits. That way, you're not wasting time, since it takes the average person five minutes or more to return to a task once he or she is interrupted. If the task requires more time, prioritize and put it on your to-do list.

  For handling interruptions that are not business-related, use these techniques tactfully. A smile can also help to make your tone more pleasing.

- *Assert your needs.* Tell the interrupter that you're working on an important project with a tight deadline. For example: "I'm very busy right now on a report that I must complete by noon." Or "I'm working on a project that my boss wants in a half-hour. Let's set an appointment to talk later."

- *Redirect the conversation.* Tell the interrupter that you would prefer to talk at another time. For example: "I really want to hear about your vacation. But right now, I need to finish this report. Can we meet for lunch?"

- *Watch the time.* If a conversation seems to last longer than expected, glance at your watch and announce: "Oh my! It's later than I thought. I have to get back to work now." Or "Excuse me; it's getting late. We'll have to continue this later."

- *Convey urgency.* Stand when someone enters your office. Besides allowing you to extend a polite greeting, standing sends the signal that the conversation should be short. Recognize that when you sit down, you convey that you have time to talk. Remember: Nothing beats honesty when an interruption runs too long. If you can't spare the time, let the interrupter know it—politely but firmly.[17]

Procrastination

Your boss just dropped a stack of files on your desk and asked you to update all the documents. The project could take hours—or even days. What do you do? Do you put aside your current work and dive right into the pile? Or do you procrastinate, like most people, pushing the files aside and maybe playing around with the new desktop publishing program with the probability of making mistakes.

Every task presents an opportunity for procrastination. Any task, assignment, or project that is not really compelling or urgent gives you ample opportunities not to do it. You may find yourself struggling with *when* to do it, *how* to do it, and even *whether* to do it.

Everyone puts things off from time to time. But professional procrastinators can be headed for trouble. By habitually putting things off, you risk wasting time, missing opportunities, performing poorly, feeling bad about yourself, and increasing your stress. Not only do you feel the fallout, but every-one around you does as well.

People become chronic procrastinators for many different reasons, but typically it is to avoid doing something they perceive as unpleasant. Most reasons stem from real-life experiences and situations. However, unrealistic or irrational expectations—which are no less powerful—may also be responsible. Some other reasons for procrastinating include fear of accepting responsibility, doing something wrong, being successful, or being asked to do more.

If you're in the habit of procrastinating, here's a step-by-step approach to break the pattern:

- *Identify what you need to do and then get organized.* Write down the tasks you must complete and rank them in order of priority. Then set out to tackle number one on your list. If you're overloaded, don't volunteer to take on any more tasks. Know your limits.

- *Recognize the benefits of completing the task.* Instead of resenting the fact that you have to complete the task, think of the satisfaction you'll receive and the relief you'll experience once it's done. Conversely, realize the consequences of delaying it. Will delaying a task be worth a missed deadline, poor-quality work, or loss of a customer?

- *Set aside a specific time to do it.* Make an appointment with yourself and keep it. The commitment to the time is half the battle.

- *Break the project into small, manageable tasks.* The overall project may seem to be overwhelming when viewed in its entirety. A series of smaller tasks will make the project more manageable. Get going with something easy and routine; then shift into the harder aspects of the task.

- *Set deadlines and promise results.* Self-imposed deadlines and the expectations of others are often enough to get us to act. No one wants to lose face.

- *Reward your efforts.* When you complete a portion of the project or meet a deadline you've set, reward yourself for the effort with a movie, a new book, an energizing break, or a favorite snack. This will be added incentive to keep working. But save the biggest reward for completing the task.

- *Stay on course.* Even if you've set aside time to perform the task, you'll likely run into unavoidable interruptions. Get yourself back on track and in control of the situation as soon as possible. The longer you wait to return to the task at hand, the harder it will be to pick up where you left off.[18]

Time Wasters Many people complain that they do not have enough time when the real problem is that they spend too much time on unimportant matters while spending too little time on what is important. While it is true that people with family and work responsibilities have many demands on their time, some people are able to get more done in the same amount of time than others. The truth is that each of us has the same 24 hours each day. How we use those hours is the critical factor. When asked for details of how they spent the day, most people cannot account for where their time goes. Unfortunately, the time for many of us is spent by doing insignificant tasks that merely take time and do not contribute to effective or efficient work habits.

The following list contains nine common time wasters in the workplace that most of us are guilty of occasionally and that can account for why it takes more time to finish a task than necessary.

1. Unnecessary phone conversations
2. Ineffective meetings
3. Unannounced visitors
4. Poor delegation
5. Excessive paperwork
6. Putting off making decisions
7. Stress
8. Personal disorganization and clutter
9. General distractions and interruptions

Not knowing how to politely, but firmly, turn down requests for your time is a sure productivity buster. Here are six ways to say "no," according to an October 2002 article that appeared in *Essential Assistant*.

1. "This project really lies outside my expertise. Copy me on meeting agendas and minutes, and I'll make any suggestions I can."

2. "I don't have time to write the cover letter, but I'll be happy to review and edit the draft."

3. "I can't help you figure out what you ought to be doing, but I can... refer you to someone else"; "serve as a reference"; "suggest a great resource."

4. "It sounds great, but I just can't fit it into my calendar right now!"

5. "I'm so under the gun, I won't be an enjoyable luncheon partner. How about next time?"

6. "I can't help you out this month, but if you give me more notice, perhaps I can contribute in December."[19]

Another way to look at time wasters is relative to the basic management functions. Put another way, is time being wasted by inadequacies in carrying out basic management functions?

- *Planning function.* Are there any objectives? Is crisis management the norm? If so, your time is being wasted.

- *Organizing function.* Do you have multiple bosses? Is there confusion over responsibility and authority?

- *Staffing function.* Is your office over- or under-staffed? Do you have untrained personnel?

- *Directing function.* Is there any coordination of teamwork? Do you look for ways to delegate?

- *Controlling function.* Are your measurements and controls in place and reasonable? Do you have effective methods for handling the telephone and drop-in visitors?

- *Communicating function.* Are directions, objectives, and missions clearly communicated and easily understood? Are you and your boss always in meetings? How much socializing is going on?

- *Decision-making function.* Are managers indecisive? Are snap decisions made frequently? Do committees make decisions? Clearing up any of the above may help you control your time better.

OFFICE MANUALS AND PROCEDURES

Establishing sound administrative work systems is essential in organizations and can reduce the incident of conflicting situations and allow workers to use their time more productively. One of those valuable, time-saving tools is an office manual.

Office manuals include procedures that specify a standard way for dealing with recurring situations or activities so that they will be handled uniformly throughout an organization. Examples of typical office procedures include how to format correspondence and reports, how to handle incoming mail, and how to answer the telephone. The list is endless.

A **procedure** is a written, step-by-step standardized pattern of behavior that is followed when completing a specific task or activity. Written procedures are especially helpful when training new workers or when retraining current workers in new methods. Procedures further add continuity to the organization by providing some consistency among workers in handling routine tasks.

Although all office tasks are not routine and predictable, the majority of them are and should have written procedures. If you are the one responsible for writing a procedure, how do you go about the task? Although the content of the procedure is most important, it is best for all procedures to be written in a consistent manner. You will be more successful if you keep these few simple ideas in mind.

1. Verify the sequence; then number each step in sequence.

2. Always start each numbered step with an action verb, such as sort, verify, key, or open.

3. Use simple words and easy-to-understand language.

Using an office manual can be advantageous. Namely, a manual can provide written information when training new employees, reduce the problem of repetitive training, and serve as an invaluable reference book. It eliminates confusion, inconsistencies, and inefficiencies when completing a task. As anyone who has moved from one company to another knows only too well, most companies do the same administrative tasks—only differently. Over time, however, a company will develop its own distinctive ways of accomplishing common tasks. Unfortunately, these rules of operation—almost invariably unwritten—are expected to be learned by new hires through a process that is often undefined.

Once employees learn the system, many go through the same motions in repeated production cycles without giving much thought to whether there's a better way. The staffer who comes across a shortcut method for handling a routine task may be so consumed by the need to meet deadlines that he or she never gets around to sharing the discovery with others. That is why creating office manuals is so important because it has the promise to clarify and simplify organizational tasks that save time, money, and stress.

At the outset, creating the manual appears to be an overwhelming task—and one that some on the staff view as hopelessly bureaucratic and dispiriting. But writing the manual can be a valuable team-building exercise that leads to the uniform adoption of best practices. It also results in the restructuring or elimination of outdated job duties and in some cases, the reassignment of responsibilities because it just makes sense to do so.

The benefits for management that a procedures manual brings is not only that it greatly simplifies the training process for new employees, but also it brings a measure of confidence that all staffers know precisely what is expected. Finally, if properly structured, the manual creates a mechanism for ongoing examination of functions and institutionalizes a method for making process improvements.[20]

MESSAGE FOR MANAGERS

Administrative managers can help group members learn that in group efforts, even though their ideas are disputed, their personal competence is not being questioned. Phrases like "we are all in this together," and "let's find a solution that is good for everyone" indicate the appropriate attitude for the group, rather than "I'm right and you're wrong." As an administrative manager, you will want to help group members look for shared successes and rewards—as well as shared responsibility for failures—not individual recognition.

This chapter introduced critical elements in handling job stress and managing projects and time. These work-related issues erode office productivity and steal valuable time. You should put into practice each day the task of breaking large projects down into small, manageable parts. Smaller tasks are attractive because they are short, easy, and produce an immediate sense of accomplishment. This technique makes it easier to delegate because it forces you to be clear and concise about the project boundaries. Remember also that all projects, no matter how massive, are only a series of small steps that taken in their whole become the finished project. Remember to make use of technology to help you stay organized. Store some paper documents on your computer; use a shredder to quickly dispose of excess and unwanted paperwork; and e-mail requests and responses when appropriate to cut down on excess paper flow.[21]

S U M M A R Y

1. When individuals associate on a fairly continuous basis, groups will form, with or without the approval of management. Informal groups evolve out of employees' needs for social interaction, friendship, communication, and status. Formal groups are deliberately created by management for the purpose of attaining organizational goals. People tend to join groups for affiliation, power, identity, and/or goal accomplishment.

2. Teams come together for a specific purpose. By combining the resources and skills of an interdependent work group, employees and supervisors can attain extraordinary levels of achievement through teams. Virtual teams are usually formed when geographical separations can't be bridged.

3. Conflict is an inevitable part of life and the workplace is no exception. It can ultimately strengthen work relations, but it must be managed. Conflict can produce change, lead to unity, and promote compromise in organizations.

4. The five steps to resolve a conflict are: identify the problem, look for solutions, choose the best solution, act, and evaluate the effectiveness of the solution.

5. Negotiation is a psychological process requiring give-and-take between participants and is used when resolving and negotiating effective solutions to conflicts. The conflict management styles are competing, accommodating, avoiding, collaborating, and compromising.

6. Three accepted negotiation strategies are those in which a) win-lose occurs when one side will win by achieving its goals and the other side will lose; b) lose-lose occurs when one party attempts to win at the expense of another; and c) win-win is the most reasonable solution because its goal is to satisfy the needs of all parties.

7. Multitasking is an aspect of managing multiple projects, and it is the ability to execute more than one task at a time. Multitask when performing routine tasks, when the outcome isn't critical, or during time traps.

8. Workplace stress costs businesses billions of dollars a year in absenteeism, staff turnover, errors, and accidents. Stress is any external stimulus that produces wear and tear on a person's psychological or physical well-being.

9. Creating good time management strategies, handling interruptions by others, overcoming the tendency to procrastinate, and recognizing time wasters are four methods that managers use to manage time.

10. Office manuals include procedures that specify a standard way of dealing with recurring situations and assist in time and stress management. A procedure is a written, step-by-step standardized pattern of behavior that is followed when completing a specific task or activity.

KEY TERMS

Acceptable-use policy

Accommodating

Avoiding

Burnout

Collaborating

Competing

Compromising

Formal groups

Groupthink

Hidden agendas

Informal groups

Integration

Lose-lose negotiating strategy

Multitasking

Negotiation

Norm

Office manuals

Problem-solving committees

Procedure

Reframing

Stress

Task-force groups

Virtual teams

Win-lose negotiating strategy

Win-win negotiating strategy

REVIEW

1. Describe the types of groups and explain their purposes. What are three common characteristics of groups and why do people join groups?

2. What are six ways managers and employees can help make a team effort more effective? Explain each by giving a clear example for action by a manager.

3. What does the term virtual team mean? What purposes may such a team serve?

4. What is the goal in resolving conflicts and what is the five-step process that is generally used?

5. Make a distinction among the following negotiating styles: competing, accommodating, avoiding, collaborating, and compromising.

6. Managing multiple projects and using multitasking skills are desirable goals, but what are some downside risks associated with doing so?

7. List five methods of dealing with stress when trying to achieve work/life balance.

8. Define burnout and some strategies managers and employees can use to combat this difficulty.

9. List three time management strategies.

10. How can you overcome the habit of procrastinating?

11. What is the purpose of an office manual?

12. Define procedure.

CRITICAL THINKING

1. Describe a workplace situation in which teams may not be the best method to use in solving problems.

2. Based on your experience, what percentage of the time have you tried following most of the five steps to conflict resolution when resolving personal conflicts? Was it effective?

3. Have you observed an individual who is very adept at getting lots of things done by managing multiple projects? Why do you think that person is successful doing that activity?

4. When you experience job stress, how does it affect you? In other words, what symptoms show up? How do you deal with stress, in general?

5. Are you a good time manager? If so, what techniques do you use that are effective for you? In your study of time management techniques covered in this textbook, what are two approaches you might try to manage time better?

6. Write a simple procedure describing how to change margins in a word processing software program.

CASE STUDY 12-1: "ME" COMMITTEE MEMBER

Assume you are a member of a strategic planning committee, and the goal is to review the correct wording and intent of the organization's mission statement. There is one member of the committee who exhibits the following behaviors and attitudes during discussions: "I must have everything my way. Everything has to be perfect."

Discussion Question

Using the chapter's five steps to resolve conflicts, describe how you and/or other committee members should approach and work with this member. After you have analyzed the situation, make notes for the class discussion as directed by your instructor.

CASE STUDY 12-2: STRESS SEMINAR

The comptroller's secretary came in on Monday morning and announced she had attended a seminar on stress management at the local university over the weekend. As a result, she announced that she's going to manage her stress better. One thing she will do is, to every stressor, she will ask, "What's the worst thing that can happen if I don't do this?" Her boss, the comptroller, is happy she is continuing her self-improvement and attending workshops but is unclear about how her new approach to getting things done will affect his position as comptroller of the organization.

Discussion Questions

1. Do you see any problem with the approach the secretary is taking?

2. Should the comptroller be concerned about his secretary's new attitude?

Think about the results and ramifications of her newfound attitude. Then write an analysis of the case which will include your answers to the questions. Be prepared to submit your analysis to the instructor if requested and to discuss the case in class.

INTERNET RESEARCH ACTIVITY

Learn about organizing and keeping your life in control by visiting several web sites of your choice. Go to the course web site http://odgers.swlearning.com to obtain information about sites you can access. Several sites can be accessed by using search words such as communication tips and tools; communication tips for home, office; communication in a computer organization.

Learning Activity:

Prepare a one-page report on your findings that you either present in class or hand in as a written assignment.

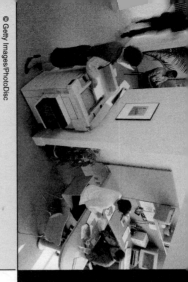

Part 4

Managing Essential Administrative Services

Workplace

NEAL E. JONES, AIA

President, Jones Studio, Inc.
Phoenix, Arizona

I have 23-years' experience in the design, production, and project management of various project types. In addition to handling all the administrative and marketing affairs of the firm, I am also responsible for directing the project team in the overall design and management of each project. Some of my tasks are to deal with the individual client on matters pertaining to overall project objectives, plan the delivery of services, and monitor the results as they relate to fulfilling the client's needs in a consistent way. In addition, I assist in the coordination of appropriate staffing, monitor and approve contract amounts, time commitments, and overall project control.

I received a B.S. degree in architectural studies and double masters' degrees in architecture as well as business administration.

QUESTION

What are some architectural issues and trends in office design and use of office space?

RESPONSE

Overall, I would have to say, "Good design sells." By that I mean that by paying attention to design excellence in an office environment, the payback is exponential in terms of increased worker productivity, less absenteeism, less office environ sickness, and less worker turnover. People are happy to come to work because the employer has created a stimulating environment and an inspiring place to work.

Though it is easy to mimic what everyone is doing, students should be aware of three important office design elements:

Modular Furniture. Although modular furniture is popular, it is a fact that having your office furniture custom designed and built is more economical.

Furthermore, it maximizes the use of office space because it utilizes space to its highest and best use.

Fresh Air. An operable window to let fresh air in is a concept America is just discovering. This is done in Europe all the time. A possible downside of this trend is it can play havoc with the balance of the heating and air conditioning systems if not properly designed and taken into account during the initial stages of design.

Office Lighting. Office lighting is moving more and more toward task lighting at the work surface in lieu of total overhead general illumination. Great strides have been made with the emergence and use of "lighting designers" who specialize in lighting and keep up with the newest trends and product development.

In my opinion, natural daylight is the single most important issue when designing office space. It works well in offices because it improves worker productivity and lessens sickness, resulting in lower absenteeism of workers.

Chapter 13

Office Design, Space, and Health Issues

After completing this chapter, you will be able to:

1. Discuss your understanding of several office design elements that include layout, work flow, space allocation, and office design trends.

2. Define ergonomics relative to the office and give examples of ergonomic tips for the office worker.

3. Describe the occupational risks of the following five primary sources of frequent physical problems in offices: air, lighting, noise, workstations, and chairs.

4. Identify ways of preventing repetitive stress injury and carpal tunnel syndrome while using an office computer.

5. Explain how computers can contribute to eyestrain and computer vision syndrome.

How an office is designed and laid out can affect health, comfort, and harmony, and results in increased energy and positive thinking in organizations.[1] Large and small companies alike use the design of their offices to convey a positive image, which they aim to communicate to their employees, stockholders, and customers. When designing office space, most companies want to impart a certain type of culture and corporate story.[2] The trend in office design is for spaces to have very specific uses, but yet be able to adapt as needed to a range of events and circumstances.[3]

Chapter 13 covers design and layout considerations for the office environment, and also describes occupational risks associated with office air, lighting, noise, workstations, chairs, and computers.

Simplicity is the ultimate sophistication.

—Leonardo da Vinci

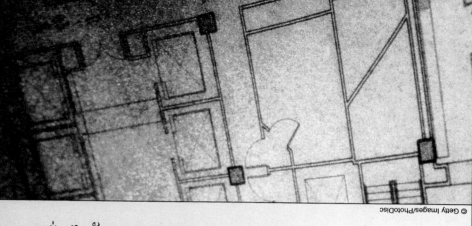

© Getty Images/PhotoDisc

TECHNOLOGY APPLICATIONS IN THE WORKPLACE

Technology and the Architect

According to progressive Chicago architect Doug Garafalo, architectural design is now moving away from singular autonomous objects and spaces with a single function or purpose, toward spaces that are more open to a variety of human interactions. Instead of an office as a place to house employees, he says, you have a well-connected, networked neighborhood.

The idea that design and architecture can serve multiple purposes is very exciting and liberating. Technology isn't something that started with the computer. For architects, it's a set of activities and tools rather than a separate discipline. Designers are simply in a position to take advantage of technology to effect meaningful structural change by producing things that are elegant, beautiful, and efficient, whether they're interiors or buildings or products.[4]

ISSUES TO THINK ABOUT:

1. How important is the design and layout of businesses that you frequent regularly?
2. What changes do you anticipate will happen in the workplace with the office environment, design, and layout ten years from now?

OFFICE DESIGN ISSUES

One of the most important aspects of an administrative manager's position is ensuring the office is set up and that it functions soundly for all employees. Although each organization has its own personality that adds character to the office environment, the basics of office layout, design, space allocation, workflow, and knowledge about office design trends need to be in place first.

Office Layout and Design

Effective office layout and design are based on the interaction among equipment, workflow, and employees. In general, **office layout** is thought of as the working arrangement of facilities and workstations. If space planning is inadequate, results such as reduced employee productivity, increased absenteeism, increased turnover, decreased physical comfort, and poor employee morale will probably surface.

Office design encompasses many trends, which change as business theories change.

© Getty Images/PhotoDisc

Office design is based on worker interaction and the needs of work flow and communication.

For example, office spaces are designed in some cases to encourage teamwork; in other cases, the design of the office spaces helps reinforce new corporate values with fewer status-laden private offices. Primarily, however, interior designers attempt to make the office space arrangement totally adaptable so that corporations can change work patterns as often as necessary to survive and prosper in fast-changing economies. For example, some AOMs use modular furniture to accommodate the changing office space needs in their corporations.

In practice, many companies provide employees with different workspace options. A design, for example, might include drop-in offices, conference rooms, and project rooms—all equipped with phones, computers, fax machines, copiers, or whatever equipment the employees who use a particular work space indicate they need. For example, individual tasks could be handled in the drop-in offices, while teams would use the project rooms for long-term jobs. Conventional office design wisdom, therefore, dictates that both individuals and teams have access to work areas that vary in size and are set up to meet different concentration needs. Administrative managers must consider the need for providing a balance when influencing office layout and design because no single design can be all things to all workers.

Layout Considerations An office environment is made up of several interdependent systems that include people, floor plans, furniture, equipment, lighting, air quality, and acoustics. These systems are constantly changing; and for that reason, offices should

© Rubberball Productions

be designed with the ability to adapt to changing needs. When planning layout, an AOM should keep these ideas in mind:

1. Become aware of the mandatory layout stipulations dictated by the Americans with Disabilities Act and design office space in keeping with the law. For example, aisles should be sufficiently wide to accommodate the rapid efficient movement of *all* current and future employees. That is to say a worker's wheelchair requires suitably wide corridors, doors, and aisles in the layout design to provide "reasonable accommodation" to workers with disabilities or injuries.

2. Consider communication relationships between individuals when planning layout and locate individuals or work groups performing similar or related duties near each other. Design and layout offices with the needs of how work passes from one workstation to another.

3. Position individuals or work groups with frequent public contact near the entrance to the premises; conversely, those individuals whose tasks require considerable concentration should be placed in a low-traffic, quiet area of the building.

4. Plan space so that everything in the office has a purpose. Eliminate—sell, trade, throw away, or put in storage—all unnecessary items. Reorganize the remaining items to enhance office productivity and worker comfort and efficiency.

With these layout considerations identified, an administrative manager can then move to a design that meets these identified needs.

Depending on identified needs, lighting can be adapted to how workers will use it.

Design Issues In designing an office, specific questions need to be asked and answered regarding lighting, décor, noise, and air control. Consider:

1. What are some characteristics and types of lighting systems appropriate for the office space? To what extent will natural lighting, fluorescent lighting, or incandescent lighting be used? Because natural lighting has to be controlled on overcast days, for example, fluorescent lighting is typically considered a popular and relatively inexpensive alternative. By comparison, **incandescent lighting** (filament bulbs, similar to that which is found in most homes), is often used in offices because of its cost-effectiveness. It produces the most amount of light in relation to the energy it consumes. Will task lighting and ambient lighting be used? **Task lighting** illuminates the work surface, while **ambient lighting** illuminates the areas surrounding a work surface.

© Digital Vision

Offices should support a variety of work processes, functions, and activities.

2. What are the most desirable color schemes for floors and wall coverings? In designing décor, is there a need or desire to consider and incorporate elements of the corporate culture into the design ideas?

3. How can office noise be controlled through proper construction and sound-absorbing materials? Are workers who need quiet as well as those who frequently collaborate considered when allocating how space settings will be used?

4. What are some air concerns that must be considered relative to temperature, humidity, ventilation, and cleanliness? Will plants be used and if so, in what ways?

Table 13.1 identifies some key concerns and offers some tips with possible solutions when working out design issues.

Use of Office Space

Students of architecture are taught to design facilities that are imaginative, cutting edge,

aesthetic, and exciting. The form should express the function. The interior layout can then be modified to fit the exterior design. When you study how most administrative and office workers really operate or function on a day-to-day basis, you find they spend a lot of time working in common spaces. Workers occupy their workstations or offices between 10 percent and 40 percent of the workday.[5]

With real estate representing a sizable portion of the assets of a large company, management is closely scrutinizing this investment and considering alternative methods to reduce costs and save space. Three different approaches are generally taken to use office space effectively. They are open plan areas, private offices, or a blend of the two called the hybrid approach. Those involved in planning the office layout should carefully examine each approach.

Open Plan Using Modular Design The open plan is designed to foster the free flow of information and is characterized by the lack of interior walls and the freestanding placement of desks, partitions, and other office furnishings. The main attraction of open plan areas is flexibility because of its efficiency when teamed with modular design. The downside is noise and inability to focus on work. Sometimes workers feel a loss of privacy in the open plan. This may well be the case if workers are used to being in private offices. Management attention is needed to ensure that it is getting the most value possible for each "space dollar" spent. An example of the type of users of the open plan is a sales and customer service group of

TABLE 13.1 Office Lighting, Color/Décor, Noise, and Air Control Systems

Office Systems	Key Concerns	Possible Solutions
Office Lighting	Glare Proper lighting systems that may include: • Task/ambient lighting • Natural light • Fluorescent lighting • Incandescent lighting	Adjust most office work areas for task illumination to 100 to 150 footcandles. Avoid overhead lighting that reflects on computer screens or off-white paper. Use adjustable window coverings. Use task lamps with at least two levels of adjustment to supplement overhead lighting.
Color/Décor	Color provides aesthetic value Color provides functional value Color tends to create moods	Use light colors to make a small room look larger. Paint low ceilings a lighter color than the walls to make them appear higher. Use cool colors (blue, green, violet) to create calm and retiring moods; in contrast, use warm colors (red, orange, yellow) to create warm and cheerful moods.
Noise	Hazards to the ears Annoyance to workers of loud sounds	Adjust the noise level in the average office to around 55 decibels (equivalent to average conversation at home with music in the background). Control sound problems with acoustical ceiling tile, panels with sound-absorbing materials, carpeting, and window coverings.
Air Control	Temperature control Air quality	Establish uniform levels of cooling, heating, and ventilation. Redirect excess heat away from the worker and recycle into the building heating, ventilating, and air-conditioning system. Add humidity into the air through humidifiers if static electricity is a problem.

workers who have no real need for privacy and at times need to openly collaborate regarding a particular customer issue or concern.

In an earlier chapter, we addressed the dramatic change in the workplace with regard to "absent employees" and an increase in personnel on the move.

For these reasons, organizations are turning to modular furniture that can be easily reconfigured to fit new space and that encourages communication and sharing as primary functions of employees. **Modular design** refers to the design of office furniture that facilitates the use of different components and variations in the way those components are arranged in the space provided. A modular unit is custom fit and may consist of such components as a desk or working space, storage space, file space, and shelf space.

To offset the loss of privacy, the open-plan design frequently incorporates conference rooms for confidential meetings or for working when deep concentration is required. In addition, soundproofing and privacy are achieved with free-standing padded separation panels.

Private Office The private office will probably always exist in most organizations, although it is decreasing in use. Several reasons frequently cited for doing away with private offices are difficulty in supervising

employees and communicating with others. In addition, built-in private offices create problems when making layout changes as organizations continually reconfigure their needs. This type of design also creates air-conditioning and heating problems within the building, with each office desiring to control the thermostat's temperature.

Typically, upper management and workers in the Human Resources Department prefer the private office option. Their work and interaction with others is often of a confidential and private nature.

Hybrid-Space Approach A hybrid approach encompasses both open and closed spaces with convertibility that is easy and economical. For example, through the use of floor-to-ceiling panels, private offices are created in an instant and can be moved into other arrangements that facilitate workflow.

Workflow Considerations

What organizations desperately need is to put knowledge in the hands of the right individual at the right time. Workflow is one way to help ensure this occurs. **Workflow** is the movement of information from person to person within an organization. Another way of describing workflow is as a tool set, which enables organizations to proactively analyze, compress, and automate business processes, and then to develop and manage these processes.

One of the first activities in workflow management is to examine *how* documents move and are managed. The process begins by examining how documents, business forms, and other information wind their way through an organization. This examination clearly pinpoints bottlenecks and outdated procedures that slow things down and add to paperwork costs.

Various physical arrangements are used to accomplish efficient office workflow. For example, workstations can be arranged in groups or clusters to facilitate communication and efficient office operations. A cluster arrangement might be in the form of a Y, an X, or a variation of a circle as shown in Figure 13.1. Regardless of the physical arrangement used, workflow should be promoted and unnecessary traffic patterns eliminated.

When planning efficient office workflow, an administrative manager should:

- Analyze the interrelationships among equipment, information, and personnel in the workflow. Determine who needs what information and when. How will a mixture of office equipment, telecommunications, and technology be blended to process that information?

- Move work in a circular pattern or in as straight a line as possible. Try to circulate workflow around major documents and processes. Avoid crisscrossing and backtracking because they are time consumers and energy wasters. Papers should move to workers only once.

- Take work to the employee; do not ask the employee to get up and get work to do. One way organizations do this is by incorporating the process of scanning, storing, and moving paper documents from workstation to workstation electronically instead of manually. Creating online forms and developing computerized templates for the most common office documents are two more ways organizations bring the work to the employee. Some examples of documents that can be used online and in template form include timesheets, expense claim forms, purchase orders and requisitions, and personnel evaluation forms.

FIGURE 13.1 Good workflow facilitates communication and efficient office operations.

Use These Workflow Patterns

Avoid the Criscrossing or Star Workflow Pattern

Office Design Trends

It wasn't too long ago that office spaces were pretty much the same—everyone had a space, a desk, or a cubicle in which to work. But the Internet, wireless technology, and cell phones have changed all that. Today, companies are considering all design options to determine what really suits their needs and the needs of their employees.

The conference-room congestion, coupled with a vast number of empty cubicles, symbolizes how technology is changing the way we work. Tools like instant messaging, file sharing, and wireless networking allow employees to easily collaborate and be on the move without negatively affecting productivity. As a result, managers are abandoning their long-cherished notion that a productive employee is an employee who can be seen.

Appearing on time and looking busy is becoming irrelevant. Technology and new patterns of office use are making companies judge people by what they do, not by where they spend their time. Producing results is more important than how or where those results were achieved. Two aspects of office design trends are alternative officing and the office of the future as envisioned by IBM Corp. and the Steelcase Co.

Alternative Officing

Alternative Officing Alternative officing or AO was a term coined in 1992. It is a way to describe ways of officing outside the mainstream—meaning, the concept of one body to one seat in a fixed location. **Alternative officing** describes flexible work arrangements and settings that support work processes, functions, or activities that can't be encompassed in one space. The expres-

sion is changing to *appropriate officing* to convey what is becoming the norm in office culture. Some experts predict that by the end of this decade, more than 20 percent of the nation's nonclerical staff may find themselves without a permanently assigned desk. Others estimate the percentage to be higher.[6]

Setting up alternative officing practices increases the collaborative power of teams and helps reduce the amount of square footage necessary for some companies to operate effectively. Making the office a fluid and fun place in which to work can be accomplished by setting up work spaces that can be "checked in" and "checked out," and by offering technology that empowers the employee. These steps are a successful combination for the future. New ideas for spaces include quiet rooms where people can work or think undisturbed, labs for meetings and brainstorming, and gardens or cafes where employees can meet and/or take a breather while at the work-site location. Before jumping on the AO bandwagon, managers should first determine whether it's right for them. In other words, alternative officing works with some types of businesses and some types of employees and not with others. IBM, for one example, allows its sales, marketing, and consulting staffs to log in to an entryway computer, be assigned an office, have their cell phones routed to the office, plug in their laptops, and then sign out when needed.

For alternative officing to be successful, two major issues must be in place: 1) should a company not have a system of trust factors in place, AO will struggle; 2) if it does not have the necessary technology infrastructure for remote access to servers, AO will not work. In other words, alternative officing is not a "one-size-fits-all" approach. The needs of the company and the employees must be evaluated in-depth.

To use an analogy and put it another way, a successful approach to alternative officing is like a three-legged stool. It requires the right balance of a physical space and setting, human resources processes and trust in place, and tools and technology. If you're not looking at all those elements equally, then the program will be less efficient, or it will be unsuccessful.

The Office of the Future Although many ideas are giving way to the office of the future, one in particular is interesting. It is a collaborative effort between Steelcase and IBM that seems to have evolved out of need and each company's individual success and reputation in the office. As work becomes more collaborative and office workers become increasingly dependent on technology and the ability to be more mobile, Steelcase and IBM are offering new ways to develop future office environments that provide highly effective, user-centered space. This includes the need to eliminate "distractions" through user control of the physical environment, to improve knowledge sharing and collaborative work through the ability to constantly display information, and to increase speed and access to information. These needs provided the basis for many of the elements developed and designed for Blue Space.7

Blue Space is an interactive and personalized office of the future. The joint project combines IBM's technology expertise with Steelcase's workplace knowledge to create a new office environment that integrates the physical work space with advanced computer, sensor, display, and wireless technologies.

With a combination of technology and design, Blue Space enriches the overall work environment by providing greater comfort and personalization through unmatched user control. For companies, Blue Space has been designed to enhance productivity, increase collaboration among employees, and improve space utilization.

Highlights of this fully Internet-enabled IBM-Steelcase *smart office* approach include the following elements:

- *Blue Screen:* This touch screen, which sits adjacent to the computer monitor, puts users in control of their physical and virtual environments. Interactive icons allow users to adjust with the touch of a finger—temperature, air flow, or lighting to suit their preference. Interactive icons help employees share projects, better communicate with their team members, and access real-time news feeds.

- *Monitor Rail:* This moving rail consists of a work surface that travels the length of the work space and a dual monitor arm that almost rotates to a complete circle, allowing the users to be positioned anywhere in the area. Currently, most office environments have stationary computer monitors that limit the position of users.

- *Everywhere Display:* A display projects information onto any surface, be it a wall, desktop, screen, or floor, transforming everyday objects into interactive displays, and untethering employees from their desktop computers. Wireless and computer processed sensing technologies enable touch sensitivity, allowing fingers to act as cursors, even on walls or desktops.

- *Threshold:* Designed in response to a need for increased privacy control and monitoring, this movable work surface, ceiling, and wall act as a "technology totem" that provides on-demand visual and territorial privacy to the user. An integrated front panel display on the threshold can visually communicate what each employee wants to share with colleagues, such as current projects and scheduling.

No doubt other leaders in office technologies and networking, such as Microsoft, Cisco Systems, and others will create, modify, and enhance how offices look and function in the future. In so doing, however, office ergonomics and health factors must always be incorporated into the designs and monitored as to their use.

OFFICE ERGONOMICS AND HEALTH FACTORS

Scenario: Your secretary is out for surgery related to carpal tunnel syndrome. Your switchboard operator is complaining her chair is too hard and her shoulder is stuck in the shrug position from cradling the telephone handset. Your best project manager can't make a meeting because of a prior engagement with his chiropractor. Given these situations, the organization's administrative manager may be in need of an office ergonomic makeover.

An increased concern for the health of employees is causing great interest in the area of office ergonomics. An ergonomically sound office is one solution to increasing efficiency, productivity, and contentment in offices. The Occupational Safety and Health Administration (OSHA) of the U.S. Department of Labor defines **ergonomics** as the science of designing the job to fit the worker, rather than physically forcing the worker's body to fit the job.[8]

In the office, the concept embraces the idea that machines and office products should fit people, not the reverse. These products include chairs, desks, keyboards, mouse devices, monitors, telephones, and a grab bag of accessories, all aimed at taking the physical stress and strain out of administrative tasks in the workplace.

Whether from true concern about their employees' well-being or as a defense against possible legal action, many companies recognize the value of an ergonomically designed, and peaceful workplace.[9] Some common ergonomic guidelines for the office worker are:

- Don't sit in one position all day long. Keep moving to eliminate static posture.
- Keep your mouse next to and on the same level as your keyboard.
- Minimize awkward postures and reaches, whether they involve your wrists, arms, or other body parts.
- Invest in adjustable work surface systems, such as keyboards and desktops with height adjustments.
- Put the keyboard in front of the monitor, not off to the side.
- Use a telephone headset if you're on the phone a lot.

• Pay attention each day to warning signs from your body that may be relieved with proper ergonomic practices you may incorporate or tools you may use.[10]

According to OSHA, businesses spend $170 billion a year on costs associated with occupational injuries and illnesses—expenditures that come straight out of company profits. But workplaces that establish safety and health management systems can reduce their injury and illness costs by 20 percent to 40 percent. In today's business environment, those cost encumbrances can be the difference between operating in the black and running in the red.[11]

Injuries and illnesses increase workers' compensation and retraining costs, absenteeism, faulty product returns, and customer complaints. They also decrease productivity, morale, and profits. Businesses operate more efficiently when they implement effective safety and health management systems. Safe environments improve employee morale, which often leads to increased productivity, better service, and greater profits.

Other than computers, according to occupational health experts, there appears to be five primary sources of frequent physical problems in offices. These sources are air, lighting, noise, workstations, and chairs. Though these health factors abound in offices, they are controlled in several ways by successful administrative managers.

Air

Air quality is a growing concern because of the steadily increasing number of sealed office structures. The so-called "sick-building syndrome" has been used to describe a range of complaints that encompass eye, nose, throat, and skin irritation, headache, fatigue, dizziness, difficulty in concentration, and shortness of breath.

This syndrome is considered to exist in a particular building when at least 20 percent of the employees complain of similar symptoms, but the symptoms tend to disappear after employees leave the premises. A good source for more information about the quality of air in offices today is at the U.S. Environmental Protection Agency's web site, http://www.epa.gov/air.

Although it is difficult to establish direct cause-and-effect relationships between office conditions and such illnesses, some serious ailments can be linked to a host of microorganisms born in air-conditioning or ventilation systems. Similarly, chemicals in carpets, drapes, and copying machines or the building materials themselves may induce physical reactions or illnesses.

A great idea is to use air purifiers if you need to control or alleviate workplace allergens, such as dust and mold. Air purifiers also control heavy odors that may linger in the air, such as perfume, smoke, and other odors. Unlike purifiers made even a few years ago, today's air purifiers are small, quiet, and can clean the air up to three times per hour in an office space as small as 9 by 12 feet.[12]

One easy, yet relatively inexpensive, way to improve air quality is to add plants. Some plants that require low light are especially effective in filtering certain chemicals from the air. Not only are plants used to improve air quality, they also serve as stress reducers. Researchers from Texas A&M University and Washington State University concluded that interior workplace plants signal stability and offer employees a touch of humanity in the workplace while stimulating a more productive environment.[13]

Lighting

Poor lighting may lead to headaches or fatigue. Natural lighting is easiest on your eyes; but, because natural light is not always available in offices, incandescent lighting, which *almost* replicates natural daylight, is often used. Most employees don't realize why lighting affects their moods, but the reasons are simple and physiological. When light enters the eye, the retina sends signals to the pineal gland to suppress production of melatonin, the sleep-inducing hormone, while increasing the production of energy-giving serotonin. Give people too much light, and they'll eventually become disoriented; take away light and they'll show signs of depression. You want something in the middle — right in the bright, cheery range.[14]

One of the more common lighting problems, a desktop in shadow, can be taken care of easily with a desk lamp. The recommended intensity range for office lighting is 100 to 150 foot-candles. A **foot-candle** describes the quantity of light. It is the

amount of light a distance of 1 foot from a standard candle. Put another way, 1 watt of light per square foot produces approximately 15 foot-candles. Eyestrain from dim lighting or harsh shadows should be corrected. Many vision problems office workers have today, however, are related to computers which will be discussed soon.

Noise

Open-plan space is the current fashion in office design, partly because people believe it is more cost-effective, but also because it is conducive to the team concept many organizations have adopted. Whatever the impetus, more and more of these open offices are being built, which means there are more and more distractions and potential health hazards keeping workers from producing at their most efficient level.

According to a Cornell University study, working in a moderately noisy office with ringing telephones, worker conversations, the sounds of office equipment whirring, and drawers opening and closing may lead to heart-damaging stress hormones to become elevated. Current trends in office design have relegated 25,000,000 Americans to open-plan office space, or "cube farms," where a sense of teamwork and camaraderie may flourish—but noise distractions and potential health hazards do so as well.[15]

In another study, conducted for the American Society of Interior Designers, conversational noise was the number one complaint of office workers. An overwhelming 70 percent said they would be more productive if there were no noise distractions. Similarly, in a study by Armstrong World

Industries, 52 percent of workers reported that the noise level in their workplace was stressful, and 81 percent said they could get more work accomplished if their workplace were quieter. [16]

So what is the answer? Since it is unlikely that the open-plan office will go away anytime soon—and since phones will continue to ring, people will continue to talk, machines will continue to beep, and drawers will continue to open and close—the next best thing is to mask the intrusive sound so that it is less distracting and stressful to the worker.

One solution is a portable and affordable system designed to mask intrusive sounds. It operates by blanketing an individual's work space with unobtrusive, natural sound that reduces the intelligibility, and therefore the distraction, of nearby conversations and various other sounds. The system uses two

tiny emitters that are used to create a gentle whooshing sound similar to air conditioning that fades into the background as it masks unwanted office noise.

Workstations

Working in awkward positions leads to injury because the muscles become strained and fatigued. Awkward positions can be cultivated by working in a cubicle that's too small or sitting on an uncomfortable chair. Many monitors are positioned too high, too low, or off to one side.

Placed on top of the desk, keyboards are often too high; but placed on your lap they are too low. Mice are often too far away to be reached without straining. A workstation designed for the employee's size helps the employee be more productive and feel less fatigue. Figure 13.2 shows an example of a well-designed computer workstation.

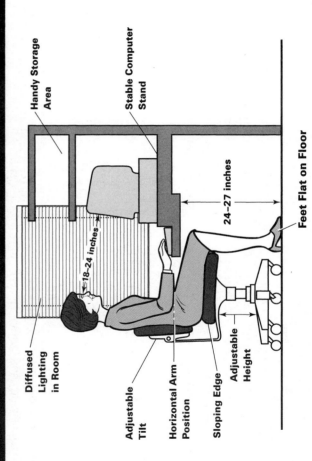

FIGURE 13.2 **Work and comfort do go together in an ergonomically designed workstation.**

Diffused Lighting in Room

Handy Storage Area

Stable Computer Stand

Adjustable Tilt

Horizontal Arm Position

Sloping Edge

Adjustable Height

18–24 inches

24–27 inches

Feet Flat on Floor

In an office environment, ergonomics is relative. People come in different shapes and sizes, and what works for one person may not easily work for another. As a worker, the most important rule for an ideal workstation is that you feel comfortable in your environment. To ergonomically fit a workstation to your needs, consider the seven steps that follow.

1. *Identify your workstation needs.* Is your computer used primarily for word processing? If so, make sure that you have a good keyboard setup.

2. *Get the right mouse device.* Are you mostly a web surfer? If so, make sure that you have a good mouse/pointing device configuration.

3. *Know your physical needs.* Adjust your workstation to best meet your specific needs and to minimize the amount of strain necessary to perform your most common tasks. For example, if your right wrist tends to throb after two hours of inputting data into a spreadsheet, then there is a problem. Try to obtain the best keyboard setup as soon as possible.

4. *Adjust your keyboard to work properly.* If you use a desktop keyboard or one that is placed on a conventional, articulating tray, position the keyboard tray either flat or at a downward slope (i.e. so that the row of keys beginning with the letters "QWERTY" is lower than the row of keys beginning with the letters "ZXCVBN." Center the keyboard so that the space bar is roughly the same height as your elbows, with the "B" key lined up with your belly button.

5. *Consider a wrist rest.* In the case of a desktop keyboard, you can also use a broad, flat wrist rest as a forearm support. The wrist rest should be approximately the same thickness as the bottom of your keyboard. Wrist rests should generally not be used as actual resting places for your wrists while typing, but instead they are best used as a place to rest your wrists between periods of typing.

6. *Keep your mouse close.* If you don't have a mouse tray, at least make sure that the mouse is close to the side of your body, so that your upper arm can remain relaxed and your posture can remain as neutral as possible.

7. *Accommodate different size-people.* Make sure that your feet are supported and the area behind the knees is not compressed. If you have a fixed height workstation and cannot purchase an adjustable keyboard tray, you can raise your chair and purchase a footstool. If you are a person of small stature, you can also use a foot rest so that your feet rest comfortably on the floor.

Chairs

Backaches and neck aches are related directly to the adaptability, design, and condition of the chair. Adjustability is a key characteristic in all ergonomic furniture and equipment, so invest in ergonomic furniture and equipment. One of the best ergonomic investments is an adjustable chair. What should you look for in a good chair?

Look for good lumbar support for the curve in the small of your back. Using height-adjustable lumbar support is critical for that part of the chair. Another characteristic to consider is depth of the seat pan; you don't want one that cuts into the back of your knees, possibly reducing circulation. Being able to raise and lower the chair is important, too, because dangling your legs and feet or bending them beneath your chair also could impair blood flow. Here are some additional tips for chair adjustments:

1. Chairs should be adjustable to fit your body height, giving your legs good circulation. Your feet should be able to rest flat on the floor with your knees bent at 90 degrees.

2. The seat and back should be contoured to the curves of your thighs and back.

3. Adjustable armrests should take some of the pressure off when you keyboard.

4. A chair should let you fidget—tilting, swiveling, and rocking as the spirit moves you.

Many workers either do not know how or do not bother to make the needed adjustments in their furniture. Know how to work the levers and knobs on your adjustable furniture and then train your employees in office ergonomics. Just having ergonomically correct furniture and equipment in the office (chairs, keyboards, and monitors, for example) isn't enough if you don't know how to make the furniture and equipment fit you and other workers in the workplace. Regardless of how your chair is designed, however, it is important to get up from your desk and walk every half hour. Otherwise, you will invite fatigue, muscle stiffness, and computer-related injuries.

RECOGNIZING AND PREVENTING COMPUTER INJURIES

The U.S. Bureau of Labor Statistics estimates that nearly 700,000 workdays are lost annually because of work-related computer disorders, costing employers $15 billion to $20 billion in workers' compensation annually.[17] Individuals employed in clerical and computer work are at high occupational risk for such disorders. The economics of ergonomics are simple. When employees use computers correctly to minimize strain or repetitive-motion injuries, productivity stays high and companies may stay out of court.[18]

Increased use of personal computers for word processing, data entry, personal organization, and other business tasks related to using the Internet and intranets has drawn new attention to workplace ailments that can reduce employee productivity and increase a company's costs for workers' compensation. Two office work musculoskeletal disorders are repetitive strain injury and carpal tunnel syndrome, which will be discussed in the sections that follow.

Musculoskeletal Disorders (MSDs)

Musculoskeletal disorders (MSDs), such as carpal tunnel syndrome and tendonitis, are potential physical outcomes for workers using poorly designed office equipment, furniture, and work spaces, or for employees who are inadequately trained in ergonomic practices. Other injuries or discomfort resulting from exposure to ergonomic risk factors, such as static postures and repetitive motions, include decreased blood circulation, visual problems, headaches, and fatigue.

The Bureau of Labor Statistics (BLS) reports that MSDs account for more than one-third of all lost work-time cases. Eliminating ergonomic risk factors, and thereby preventing repetitive strain injury and carpal tunnel syndrome, is vital to increasing office productivity and reducing downtime.[19]

Repetitive Strain Injury

Repetitive strain injury (RSI) is an injury or disorder of the muscles, nerves, tendons, ligaments, and joints. Some of the risk factors for repetitive strain injury are well-known, such as spending long hours working with a mouse or sitting in a poorly configured workstation. Others are not readily apparent. For example, having long fingernails leads you to type with flat rather than curved fingers.

Four major risk factors to RSI are listed below and workers must be aware of these risks in order to take preventive measures against each occurring.[20]

- *Sitting.* Sitting in one place for long periods is a risk because it slows blood

© Getty Images/PhotoDisc

circulation, which is needed to remove the waste products of simple muscle activity, such as keying and using the mouse. Continuously holding your elbows bent in the palms-down position strains the nerves and muscles of the arms and upper body. In addition, poor sitting habits compound the problem. For example, leaning on your elbow can compress the nerve, or sitting on one foot can impede circulation in your legs.

- *Repetitive movements.* Making the same movements again and again, such as keying numbers into a spreadsheet or circling a mouse or trackball, tires the muscles. Working for extended periods without breaks does not allow the muscles time to recover from the exertion.

- *Faulty keyboarding technique.* Faulty technique includes resting your wrists, forearms, or elbows on the desk or armrest as you key. Avoid movements such as pounding the keys, tightly gripping the mouse, or twisting your wrists from side to side or in an up-and-down action.

- *Awareness of discomfort.* People have varying degrees of awareness about their personal level of pain and comfort or how they move, sit, and stand. Some people concentrate so much on the task at hand while at the computer that they forget about their posture or movements. Becoming sensitive to these matters helps workers become aware of symptoms and avoid unnecessary injury.

If these risk factors resonate with you, take measures to prevent injury now before you start having problems. If you develop RSI, your ability to work will be greatly

It's important to do whatever it takes to reduce the risk of computer-related injuries.

diminished because by repeating the offending activity or merely performing daily tasks, you can reinjure yourself.

Good ways to decrease your risk of injury include: (1) reducing the amount of time you use a computer; (2) taking regular, frequent breaks (at least every 20 minutes); (3) avoiding sitting for long periods; and (4) stretching and strengthening the muscles of your upper body, especially the back, three to five times a week.[21]

Carpal Tunnel Syndrome Carpal tunnel syndrome (CTS) is a medical problem of the hands, specifically an inflammation of the nerve that connects the forearm to the palm of the wrist. The pinching of the large nerve that travels under the palm causes the problem. Normally, the nerve carries information about the sensation of touch from the hand to the brain, but when the nerve is pinched, the sensation of touch can be blocked. The use of highly repetitive wrist movements appears to be connected with the development of carpal tunnel syndrome.

The symptoms of CTS can include numbness, tingling, pain, and weakness in the thumb, index, middle, and ring fingers. Initially, the feelings may come and go, but the pain is often worse at night and can awaken you. Moreover, the symptoms may worsen when you are doing forceful or repetitive work with your hands, like driving, gardening, cleaning, or using a computer. The best prevention for workers who may be at risk for carpal tunnel syndrome is correct use of the keyboard and mouse.

Treat carpal tunnel syndrome early, because if treated correctly it can be reversed. If treatment is delayed, the condition is likely to worsen and surgery may be necessary. After a physical examination, a doctor with appropriate training can tell what the cause of the problem is and how to treat it.

Treatment for carpal tunnel syndrome can be surgical or non-surgical. Non-surgical treatment is usually the first choice and may include modifying the way you use your hands (at work and at home), wearing wrist splints at night, and injecting the carpal tunnel with steroid medication. These non-surgical treatments are especially valuable for people with mild symptoms or symptoms that tend to come and go. Surgical treatment for people with CTS should be considered when symptoms have failed to respond to the treatments just mentioned or if CTS is at a late stage and the symptoms are constant.

Computer Vision Syndrome and Eyestrain

The way that cathode ray tubes (CRTs) work creates a number of vision-related problems for users. In fact, some OSHA studies have found that a full 90 percent of CRT users suffer from **computer vision syndrome (CVS)**, which is characterized by eye fatigue, blurred vision, dry eyes, and headaches. Furthermore, since people with vision-related problems frequently hunch over to see better, CVS is often accompanied by neck, back, and shoulder pain.[22] Intensive computer use, inadequate or poor lighting, stress, poor posture, and any existing eye problems all can make CVS worse.

We all know that it's good to take breaks during prolonged periods of monitor use. But what's really happening when we overexert our eyes? Staring at your monitor can lead to a variety of ailments, including headaches, blurred vision, dry and irritated eyes, eyestrain, slow refocusing, neck and/or backache—all common symptoms of CVS.

Let's take a look at some of the symptoms of and solutions for computer vision syndrome in Table 13-2.

TABLE 13.2 Symptoms of Computer Vision Syndrome

Symptoms	Suggested Solutions/Remedies
Headaches. Headaches are the primary reason most people seek an eye exam.	Headaches can be caused by a variety of sources. A complete eye exam should be the first action to take on your list.
Dry or irritated eyes. Although blinking is a reflex, we tend to blink less often when looking at a computer than when reading or performing other tasks. This causes our eyes to become dry and uncomfortable.	Try to blink more often when using your computer. Artificial tears are helpful (and even essential) in some office environments and are also good for contact lens wearers.
Blurred vision (distance or near). In your work environment, blurred vision can be the result of something as simple as a dirty screen, poor viewing angle, reflected glare, or a poor quality or defective monitor.	Glasses are the most likely solution to a blurred vision problem. They may be worn for distance viewing or for near viewing, depending on the findings of the eye examination.
Eyestrain. In the computer environment, eyestrain can also be caused by different environmental (and visual) conditions.	Eyestrain usually results from a combination of poor ergonomics, improper work habits, or an undetected visual condition. A complete eye exam, an on-site ergonomic evaluation, and instruction on correct working habits should all be considered important to do if this problem exists.
Slow refocusing. When you focus on "close-up" objects (such as reading materials) for extended periods of time without taking breaks, your eye's muscles begin to "adapt" to that range of vision. This stresses the muscles, which then have difficulty relaxing.	Make sure you take adequate rest breaks. During the breaks, make sure not to do the same kind of work you were doing before. That is, look far away if doing near work, and do close-ups if doing far work.
Neck and/or backaches. If your visual system isn't seeing properly, you may assume awkward positions to compensate, which can lead to neck and back pain.	Correct your posture. However, people who wear glasses often sit in an awkward posture to see properly, so make sure that your eyesight isn't causing you to sit poorly.

Adapted from information on web sites that include: http://www.cvconsulting.com/, http://www.doctorergo.com/, http://www.healthycomputing.com/articles/computer_vision_syndrome.htm, 2003.

Visual ergonomics, a new and relatively novel concept, is the interaction of your vision with the task that you are performing. How does computer usage cause eyestrain? Visual fatigue is caused by staring at small letters and numerals on a screen for hours on end. The glare of an over-bright or badly placed light that reflects off a computer screen only complicates the problem.

Follow these basic work habits to reduce eyestrain in the workplace:

- *Keep your hard copy close to the screen.* Place the copy just below or on a keyboarding stand next to the screen.
- *Take breaks.* Follow the "20/20/20" rule for computer use: Every 20 minutes, take 20 seconds and look 20 feet away.
- *Blink regularly.* We tend to blink less often when viewing a computer screen. Remember to blink fully and often.

- *Move the monitor.* Be sure your monitor is at least 20 inches away. If you have difficulty seeing the image on the screen at this distance, enlarge it by adjusting the zoom setting that is available on most computer software programs.
- *Have your eyes checked.* Be sure to have an annual eye examination. Measure your viewing distances and take those numbers with you to the exam. If you wear multifocal lenses, avoid bobbing your head, tilting your head backward, or leaning forward to read the computer monitor screen. Consult your eye care professional about single lens correction eyeglasses with a longer focal length for the viewing distance that you sit from your computer monitor. This will help prevent neck, shoulder, and visual ergonomic issues.[23] Sometimes it helps if the doctor sees the type of work that you do.

MESSAGE FOR MANAGERS

Perhaps the most control an employer can exercise over health costs is control over the employee's work environment. Making an office environment human-friendly and ergonomically sound is easier to do when utilizing the advice and suggestions in this chapter. In the office, as in other areas of our lives,

little things can and do mean a lot. The results of planning ahead to ward off problematic injuries generally pay off in a substantial way over time.

Taking precautions to prevent office-related problems as they occur need not be complex or expensive. In relation to the workstation environment, for example,

just simply looking at how a person is using the workstation will probably tell you if he or she is comfortable.

Administrative managers play a critical role in keeping workers happy and healthy by assisting in the design, layout, and space utilization of workstations and the overall office environment.

Chapter **Thirteen**

S U M M A R Y

1. Effective office layout and design are based on the interrelationships among equipment, workflow, and employees. Because no single design can be all things to all workers, administrative managers must provide a balance when influencing office layout and design. Inadequate space planning can result in reduced employee productivity, increased absenteeism, increased turnover, decreased physical comfort, and poor emploee morale.

2. In designing an office, specific questions need to be asked regarding lighting, décor, noise, and air control.

3. Organizations need to put knowledge in the hands of the right individuals at the right times and this is best accomplished through studying workflow and how movement of information travels from person to person within the organization.

4. Alternative officing or AO describes flexible work arrangements and settings that support work processes, functions, or activities that cannot be encompassed in one space. Setting up AO practices increases the collaborative power of teams and helps reduce the amount of square footage necessary for some companies to operate effectively. For alternative officing to be successful trust factors should be in place and the necessary infrastructure for remote access to servers must be available.

5. Ergonomics is the science of designing the job to fit the worker, rather than physically forcing the worker's body to fit the job. In the office, the concept embraces the idea that

machines and office products should fit people, not the reverse. These products include chairs, desks, keyboards, mouse devices, monitors, telephones, and various accessories.

6. Injuries and illnesses increase workers' compensation and retraining costs, absenteeism, faulty product returns, and customer complaints. Businesses operate more efficiently when they implement effective safety and health management systems.

7. Other than computers, according to occupational health experts, there appears to be five primary sources of frequent physical problems in offices. These sources are air, lighting, noise, workstations, and chairs.

8. Work-related musculoskeletal disorders are potential physical outcomes for workers using poorly designed office equipment, furniture, and work spaces or those with inadequate employee training in ergonomic practices.

9. Repetitive strain injury (RSI) is an injury or disorder of the muscles, nerves, tendons, ligaments, and joints. Four major risk factors for RSI are sitting, repetitive movements, faulty keyboarding techniques, and an ongoing awareness of discomfort.

10. Carpal tunnel syndrome (CTS) is a medical problem of the hands, specifically an inflammation of the nerve that connects the forearm to the palm of the wrist. Symptoms of CTS can include numbness, tingling, pain, and weakness in the thumb, index, middle, and ring fingers.

KEY TERMS

Alternative officing
Ambient lighting
Carpal tunnel syndrome (CTS)
Computer vision syndrome (CVS)
Ergonomics
Foot-candle
Incandescent lighting
Modular design
Musculoskeletal disorders (MSDs)
Office environment
Office layout
Repetitive strain injury (RSI)
Task lighting
Visual ergonomics
Workflow

REVIEW

1. What should AMs keep in mind when planning office layout? Explain the reasons behind these ideas.
2. What are the key concerns when planning for office lighting, color/décor, noise, and air control?
3. Describe the appearance of an open plan that uses modular design.
4. Why is workflow an important concept to integrate when processing paperwork in offices today?
5. In what ways does alternative officing meet today's businesses needs?
6. What are some good operational aspects and benefits of the *Office of the Future* as conceived by Steelcase and IBM?
7. Monetarily speaking, why are businesses willing to consider and pay for equipment and furniture that is ergonomically correct?

8. Describe the features of a chair that is designed with ergonomics in mind.
9. Distinguish between the computer-related injuries of repetitive strain injury and carpal tunnel syndrome.
10. What are the most common symptoms of computer vision syndrome?

CRITICAL THINKING

1. Out of the design elements discussed in the chapter (layout, workflow, space allocation, and office design trends), which ones do you think are of most importance to an AOM when designing modern offices? Defend your selections.
2. If you were asked to present a workshop on office ergonomics, which tips (not to exceed 10 in number) would you include in your presentation? Rank the tips from most important to the least. How would you present your ideas to employees (PowerPoint, lecture, handouts, etc.)?
3. Describe the physical problems or effects in offices from negative environment elements that result from office air, lighting, noise, workstations, and chairs. How can these physical problems be prevented?
4. Describe the physical condition or symptoms of someone you know who has either repetitive strain injury or carpal tunnel syndrome as a result of using an office computer.
5. Do you know anyone who has experienced eyestrain from using a computer or has the effects of computer vision syndrome? Describe their experience with this computer-related health issue.

6. Schulte Inc., a multinational corporation, has its manufacturing plant and headquarters in New Orleans and overseas plants and sales offices in Rotterdam, Lyons, Munich, and Zurich. A new plant and sales office are being constructed in the suburbs of Linz, Austria.

Mitchell Swan, manager of administrative services, has responsibility for coordinating all phases of space management, forms design and control, and administrative systems in the home office and all overseas offices.

Mignn Garonne, the newly selected manager of the sales office in Linz, sent a layout of the new office to Swan. This layout, illustrated in Figure A, has been designed by Garonne for a staff of 12. The office expects, however, to employ 14 workers when the plant opens and to provide workstations for three more persons three months later. In her letter, she has asked Swan for his ideas on rearranging the present 12 workstations to provide for the additional five people. Garonne does not want the 17 workers to be overcrowded.

In earlier correspondence with Garonne, Swan had indicated that she should purchase office furniture with dimensions similar to the following:

Furniture:

Size in Centimeters (and inches)

L-shaped units consisting of a return 152.4x76.2x76.2 (60 x 30 x 30)

Desk measuring 152.4x76.2x76.2 (60 x 30 x 30)

1 round table 106.7x76.2 (42 x 30)

3 cabinets, 2-door 91.4x45.7x182.9 (36 x 18 x 72)

2 file cabinets 38.1x68.6x144.8 (15 x 27 x 57)

5 bookcases 91.4x38.1x106.7 (36 x 15 x 42)

Swan has recommended that Garonne observe the following guidelines regarding minimum space allocations:

• Space between desks facing in the same direction: 72 to 90 cm (28.4 to 35.4 inches)

• Space for the two main aisles: 1.22 to 1.83 cm (4 to 6 feet)

Based upon the information Swan has given Garonne and upon the layout she has submitted, prepare a revised layout of the Linz office showing how the 17 workstations may be provided without overcrowding. Additional desks and returns do not need to be purchased. Because of the permanent partitioning that encloses the conference room and the reference room, the arrangements of these two rooms must remain as shown in Figure A. Be prepared to discuss your layout features as a class discussion.

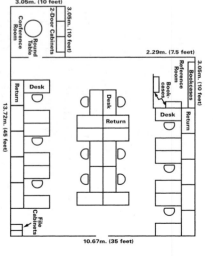

Figure A. Rough Layout of New Office Area

CASE STUDY 13-1: AN ERGONOMIC ENVIRONMENT FOR A HOME OFFICE

Bob Wilson plans to design a home office where he can write and illustrate books for preschool children. Wilson turns to you for advice on the basic ergonomic needs in his home office and asks for your thoughts about a desk and chair, lighting, floor covering, paint colors, and general decor.

Discussion Question

Prepare a list of requirements in terms of "essential," "useful," and "nice-to-have" categories. Present your ideas in a panel discussion as set up by your instructor.

CASE STUDY 13-2: HALF-MILLION-DOLLAR OFFICE COMPLEX

Helen Jackson, administrative assistant to the human resources director, has been assigned to a task force committee that has been charged with determining the basic considerations for the architects as they design and oversee the building of a new $500,000 office building complex, Hufford Advertising Agency in Atlanta, Georgia.

President Hufford met with Helen's group and identified some design pitfalls he wants the task force to specifically avoid; namely: failure to provide individual privacy, choosing a too-trendy look, cutting corners on lighting and comfort, too much or too little technology interfacing, and inadequate office ergonomics attention to office furniture and the office environment in general.

Discussion Question

If money were no object, and given the corporate culture of an advertising agency, what are five major considerations Helen should suggest at her first task force meeting? Of course, these considerations would take into consideration President Hufford's concerns.

Develop your list, incorporating these considerations and concerns. Be prepared to present and discuss your list as directed by your instructor.

INTERNET RESEARCH ACTIVITY

Carry out current research on ergonomic issues relative to an office environment and write a report for your instructor according to his or her direction.

To find information on ergonomic issues, access the course site

http://odgers.swlearning.com

You may also search the Internet using words/phrases such as ergonomics, sick-building syndrome, office health and safety, as well as other words/phrases you may identify from reading the chapter.

Learning Activity:

Develop a research study from the information you obtained that could be presented to a business organization, such as a local Chamber of Commerce. Prepare any slides or handouts needed as directed by your instructor for a presentation.

Chapter 14

Managing Workplace Safety

OBJECTIVES

After completing this chapter, you will be able to:

1. Identify the components of the crisis management program that deals with the four types of workplace violence.

2. Describe the major content areas of a workplace safety policy.

3. Defend the need for companies to use pre-employment background checks.

4. List steps that managers and employees can take to identify and prevent acts of workplace violence.

5. Discuss the need for plans that deal with the aftermath of workplace violence.

Changes in the American workplace have created a fertile breeding ground for discontent and potential violence. In virtually no other high-risk area is education, training, planning, and prevention as vital as in the case of managing and ensuring safety in the workplace.

Companies can help protect employees and keep them safe—and the firms free from lawsuits—if they face behavior problems directly, heed warning signs, train managers in violence prevention, intervene skillfully and quickly, and take all threats seriously.

Businesses should have clear, strong, fair, and consistent written policies against violence and harassment, along with effective grievance procedures, efficient security programs, a reasonably supportive work environment, open channels of communication, and employee training in resolving conflicts through team-building and negotiation skills.

The first step toward improvement is to look facts in the face. —Holmes

© Getty Images/PhotoDisc

TECHNOLOGY APPLICATIONS IN THE WORKPLACE

Online Electronic Background Checks

The Internet advertisement reads:

"Let us do your snooping for you. Our background-check searches return: possible aliases, current and previous addresses, phone numbers, relatives, roommates, family members, spouses and friends who may have shared an address; possible neighbors, deceased search (name, date of birth, date deceased), bankruptcies, civil judgments (lawsuits), tax liens, real property value (assessment), schools, banks and storage facilities in the area, and includes a county or statewide criminal history record search. You'll receive a comprehensive Background Profile Report that creates a virtual portrait of past relationships, addresses, family members, and criminal history. You're just a click away from finding out everything you want to know about anyone."

ISSUES TO THINK ABOUT:

1. In your opinion, is this type of advertisement on the Internet legal and in keeping with the need to protect an individual's privacy?
2. Do you think that the ease with which technology allows for personal information to be disclosed and shared is a concern for society in general?

SCOPE OF SAFETY MANAGEMENT

Business crises come in many forms and can occur anytime without notice. So, whether it is an accident, a scandal, an act of nature, or a malicious act, organizations recognize that they need to be prepared. Managers increasingly occupy a pivotal role in an organization's violence prevention program. They not only must know how to help create a safe work environment, but also must understand the ramifications of what can happen when a company doesn't live up to the law and to the federal Occupational Safety and Health Act (OSHA) requirements.

OSHA requires employers to provide their employees with a place to work that is "free from recognized hazards that are causing or likely to cause death or serious physical harm to... employees."[1] Designed to encourage companies to take steps to prevent violence in the workplace, criminal penalties may be imposed against an employer who is convicted of having willfully violated an OSHA standard or rule.

In its 1996 Guidelines for Preventing Workplace Violence, OSHA defines **workplace violence** as any physical assault, threatening behavior, or verbal abuse occurring in the work setting. According to the Occupational Safety and Health Administration, 2 million workers are victims of workplace violence each year.[2]

Basis for Safety Management

Stress seems to be a growing part of modern life and is often manifested in emotional and physical workplace outbursts. Besides road rage and air rage, in Corporate America, we have desk rage. **Desk rage** can take the form of yelling, verbal abuse, rudeness, destroying equipment, and overall negativity. In extreme cases, it could be a precursor to workplace violence. Downsizings, longer hours, greater workloads, higher productivity demands, lack of interpersonal communication, and the feeling that work is never-ending are all contributing factors to the need for managing safety in the workplace.[3]

According to Michael Mantell and Steve Albrecht in *Ticking Bombs: Defusing Violence in the Workplace*, the cost of workplace violence to American businesses runs more than $4 billion annually, including lost work time, employee medical benefits, and legal expenses. Additional costs of workplace violence include replacing lost employees and retraining new ones, decreased productivity, higher insurance premiums, raised security costs, bad publicity, lost business, and expensive litigation.[4]

The *Workplace Violence Prevention Reporter* states that the average out-of-court settlement for this kind of litigation is about $500,000. The average jury award is $3 million and can skyrocket from there.[5]

Types of Workplace Violence

Workplace violence is not easy to define but it can be categorized into four types. These four categories are easily described as violence by strangers, violence by customers or clients, violence by coworkers, and violence by personal relations. In each type, managers need to assess the company's security hazards and whether or not organizational liability is indicated, if steps to address the violence are not addressed in an appropriate and safe manner.

Type 1: Violence by Strangers This type of workplace violence involves verbal threats, threatening behavior, or physical assaults by an assailant who has no legitimate business relationship to the workplace. An example is a person who enters the workplace to commit a robbery or other criminal act. To limit violence by strangers, inspections for workplace security hazards include:

- Reviewing the need for security surveillance, such as mirrors or cameras.
- Posting highly visible signs notifying the public that limited cash is kept on the premises.
- Developing employee response procedures during a robbery or other criminal act.
- Creating procedures for employees to use to report suspicious persons or activities.
- Posting emergency telephone numbers for law enforcement, fire, and medical services where employees have access to a telephone with an outside line.
- Ensuring that staffing levels during evenings and at other high-risk times are sufficient for protection and safety purposes.
- Ensuring that doors are locked after hours and entry is possible only by those who have a reason to be in the building after hours.
- Escorting employees to their cars or to their mass transit stops at the end of the workday.
- Checking that lighting and security for designated parking lots or other work areas are adequate.

Since strangers could appear at any time, having these measures in place could save lives and/or property.

Type 2: Violence by Customers or Clients Type 2 workplace violence involves verbal threats, threatening behavior, or physical assaults by an assailant who either receives services from or is under the custodial supervision of the affected workplace or the victim. Assailants can be current or former customers. Clients can be patients, prisoners, students, or passengers. Inspections for workplace security hazards from violence by customers or clients include:

- Assessing the frequency and severity of threatening or hostile situations that may lead to violent acts by persons who are service recipients.
- Training employees on how to safely handle threatening or hostile customers or clients.
- Installing and using alarms or panic button systems to warn others of a security danger or to summon assistance.

Violence perpetrated by customers or clients could come at any time or place. Being prepared is an important step in prevention.

Type 3: Violence by Coworkers This type of workplace violence involves verbal threats, threatening behavior, or physical assaults by an assailant who maintains a form of job-related involvement with the workplace. This person could be a current or former employee, supervisor or manager, for example. In committing a threat or assault, the individual may be seeking revenge or a type of payback for what is perceived to be unfair treatment. Inspections for workplace security hazards from violence by coworkers include:

- Assessing how well the anti-violence policy has been communicated to employees and managers.
- Determining how well employees and managers have been trained to know the warning signs of potential workplace violence.
- Identifying the risks related to access to and freedom of movement within the workplace by non-employees, specifically recently discharged employees.
- Researching any prior violent acts, threats of physical violence, verbal abuse, property damage, or other signs of strain or pressure in the workplace.
- Re-evaluating the employee disciplinary and discharge procedures to ensure fairness in its application to all employees.

These security hazards may be eliminated or reduced if proper procedures are in place.

Type 4: Violence by Personal Relations

Personal relations may include a current or former spouse, lover, relative, friend, or acquaintance. Violence involves verbal threats, threatening behavior, or physical assaults by an assailant who, in the workplace, confronts an individual with whom he or she has or had a personal relationship outside of work.

The assailant's actions are motivated by perceived difficulties in the relationship or by psycho-social factors that are specific to the assailant. Here are actions to take to inspect workplace security hazards involving violence by personal relations:

- Assessing access to and freedom of movement within the workplace by non-employees, specifically personal relations with whom an employee is having a dispute. Pass cards and security guards can help prevent access to the property.
- Determining the frequency and severity of employee-reported threats of physical or verbal abuse which may lead to violent acts by a personal relation. Confidentiality is of utmost importance.
- Identifying incidents of any prior violent acts, threats of physical violence, verbal abuse, property damage or other signs.
- Training employees to seek police involvement to remove personal relations of employees from the work site as well as informing workers of the effectiveness of using restraining orders, as appropriate.

© Getty Images/PhotoDisc

Security should be visible in the workplace to discourage inappropriate behavior or violence.

When a person becomes alert to each of the four types of workplace violence, the workplace environment becomes safer. Learning about risk factors that may lead to violence is another way to ensure workplace safety.

Workplace Risk Factors

The four types of violence identified in the previous section illustrate different characteristics of workplace violence and some preventive safeguards to take to minimize each. The significance of these four types is that each one involves somewhat different *risk factors* and means to prevent or respond to the potential violent incident.

A **risk factor** is a condition or circumstance that may increase the likelihood of violence occurring in a particular setting. Each risk factor only represents a *potential* for an increased likelihood of violence. No risk factor, or combination of risk factors, guarantees that violence will occur or that its incidence will increase. However, the presence of the following risk factors, particularly of several in combination, increases the likelihood that violence *may* occur.

- Contact with the public.
- Exchange of money.
- Delivery of passengers or services.
- Working with unstable or volatile persons in health care, social services, or criminal justice settings.
- Working in isolation.
- Working late at night or during early morning hours.
- Working in high-crime areas.

Is it that employees should be frightened if they work in the presence of these risk factors? No, but to be aware is to be alert to potential problems that any crisis management program geared to the workplace seeks to avoid.

Crisis Management Program

If companies only view workplace violence as a security issue, they are unlikely to go beyond alarms, access control procedures, and emergency response. Instead, when companies look at violence as a safety issue, it compels them to set up employee counseling programs, violence prevention work groups, and training and awareness education.[6]

Companies should develop a crisis management program that addresses types of workplace violators and risk factors. The program should contain policies for preventing and managing crises with potentially violent visitors, customers, or employees. It should also train workers in recognizing and managing assaults, resolving conflicts, and maintaining hazard awareness.

A crisis management program, therefore, includes these major components: hazard assessment, hazard prevention and control, training and instruction, as well as a written reporting procedure. These aspects of the program will be discussed now.

Hazard Assessment The hazard assessment should examine vulnerability to the four categories of violence previously described—violence by strangers, violence by customers or clients, violence by co-workers, and violence by personal relations. It involves a step-by-step, common-sense look at the workplace to find existing or potential hazards for workplace violence. This can include analyzing and tracking records of violence at work, examining specific violence incidents carefully, surveying employees to gather their ideas and input, and conducting periodic inspections of the work site to identify risk factors that could contribute to injuries related to violence.

Hazard Prevention and Control Once existing or potential hazards are identified through the hazard assessment, then hazard prevention and control measures can be developed and implemented. These measures may include, but are not limited to:

- Using engineering controls, such as locks and alarms;
- Establishing consistently applied sign-in procedures for all visitors;
- Offering employee assistance program to workers;
- Providing adequate lighting to, from, and within the worksite;
- Marking exits clearly and making them easily accessible in the work place;
- Distributing the grievance policy and procedures employees must follow to all staff; these items should be discussed during orientation and periodically in department meetings, especially if procedures change;
- Posting applicable laws, such as those prohibiting assaults and stalking, in visible work site areas;
- Conducting pre-employment background checks;
- Informing employees and enforcing a policy of zero tolerance for violence;

- Limiting access to the company's property to those with a legitimate business interest;
- Providing initial counseling and support services to all employees and to their immediate family members in the event of a major workplace incident.

All employees should be informed of these procedures and understand their importance.

Training and Instruction Training and instruction on workplace violence ensures that all staff members are aware of potential hazards, warning signs of violence, and ways to protect themselves and their coworkers through established prevention and control measures. Courses covering communication, problem-solving, building effective working relationships, stress management, and related or similar course topics can be encouraged and supported by tuition reimbursement and onsite training classes.

Reporting Procedure A reporting procedure for violent incidents should be developed for all types of violent incidents, whether or not physical injury has occurred. Violence other than physical injury would include, for example, verbal abuse or threats of violence. This procedure should be in writing and should be easily understood by all employees. It should take into account issues of confidentiality because employees may otherwise be reluctant to come forward to report incidents of workplace violence. Furthermore, employees should not fear reprisal for bringing their concerns to management's attention.

SAFETY POLICIES

A written policy provides the foundation for every successful safety program and can help avoid the expense, inconvenience, and other consequences of workplace accidents by making sure that employees know what is expected of them. Although you can orally inform employees of safety standards and procedures, for lasting effect there is no substitute for a written policy to which an employee may refer. And if each employee acknowledges that he or she has read the policy, it can help protect companies when there is a workplace accident.

An example of a general safety policy is shown in Figure 14.1. A basic safety policy generally includes the following. It should be flexible and revised if circumstances change.

- Objectives of the safety program
- Persons responsible for various safety practices and for overseeing the wide-ranging safety program
- Consequences of not following established procedures
- Process for reporting unsafe conditions or accidents by using some type of critical incident report

FIGURE 14.1 Workplace Safety Policy

ABC Company is concerned and committed to our employees' safety and health. We refuse to tolerate violence in the workplace and will make every effort to prevent violent incidents from occurring by implementing a Workplace Violence Prevention Program. We will provide adequate authority and budgetary resources to responsible parties so that our goals and responsibilities can be met.

1. All managers and employees are responsible for implementing and maintaining our Workplace Violence Prevention Program. We encourage employee participation in designing and implementing our program.

2. Our program ensures that all employees adhere to work practices that are designed to make the workplace more secure, and do not engage in verbal threats or physical actions which create security hazards for others in the workplace.

3. All employees are responsible for using safe work practices, for following all directives, policies and procedures, and for assisting in maintaining a safe and secure work environment.

4. Managers are responsible for ensuring that all safety and health policies and procedures involving workplace security are clearly communicated and understood by all employees.

5. We require prompt and accurate reporting of all violent incidents whether or not physical injury has occurred.

6. We will not discriminate against victims of workplace violence.

7. Rules will be enforced fairly and uniformly.

- A listing of specific safety rules and guidelines

- A listing of safety hazards to look for and how to report them.

In addition to a basic safety policy, an explicit policy regarding domestic violence in the workplace can further help ensure workplace safety in three ways:

1. The fact that there is a policy at all sends a strong message to every employee.

2. The severity of the penalty for violent behavior (and it should be severe) should further reinforce the message.

3. The policy clearly informs employees exactly what conduct is prohibited in the workplace.

Domestic violence is abusive behavior that is physical, sexual, and/or psychological, and intended to establish and maintain control over a partner. Domestic violence is a serious problem that affects people from all walks of life. It can adversely affect the well-being and productivity of employees who are victims, as well as their coworkers. Other effects of domestic violence in the workplace include increased absenteeism, turnover, health care costs, and reduced productivity. Figure 14.2 illustrates an example of a Domestic Violence in the Workplace Policy. Employees should be advised on this policy during orientation or at departmental meetings as needed to reinforce the help provided by the company.

FIGURE 14.2 Domestic Violence in the Workplace Policy

ABC Company will not tolerate domestic violence including harassment of any employee or client while in our facilities, vehicles, on our property, or while conducting business. This includes the display of any violent or threatening behavior (verbal or physical) that may result in physical or emotional injury or otherwise places one's safety and productivity at risk.

- Any employee who threatens, harasses, or abuses someone at our workplace or from the workplace using any company resources such as work time, workplace phones, fax machines, mail, e-mail, or other means may be subject to corrective or disciplinary action, up to and including dismissal.

- Corrective or disciplinary action may also be taken against employees who are arrested, convicted, or issued a permanent injunction as a result of domestic violence when such action has a direct connection to the employee's duties in our company.

- ABC Company is committed to working with employees who are victims of domestic violence to prevent abuse and harassment from occurring in the workplace. No employees will be penalized or disciplined solely for being a victim of harassment in the workplace.

- Our company will provide appropriate support and assistance to employees who are victims of domestic violence. This includes confidential means for coming forward for help, resource and referral information, work schedule adjustments or leave as needed to obtain assistance, and workplace relocation as feasible.

© Digital Vision

PRE-EMPLOYMENT BACKGROUND CHECKS

As deceptively simple as it sounds, the best way to avoid workplace violence is not to hire violent workers. Ways to help ensure this include thorough application reviews and background checks, careful interviewing of prospective employees, and administering appropriate psychological screening measures as needed.

Because of increasing incidents of workplace violence, more and more governing bodies and courts in the United States have created laws or made rulings regarding employers' responsibility to know whom they are hiring before they put customers and employees at risk. By conducting a reasonable background check, employers should have the information needed to make better hiring decisions. By not conducting a check, the employer may be subject to lawsuits and crippling penalties and court awards if an unchecked employee commits a crime against a client or colleague.

An increase in employment screening has been spurred by workplace events such as the following:

- Terrorist acts of September 11, 2001, have resulted in heightened security and identity-verification strategies by employers.
- Corporate executives, officers, attorneys, and directors now face a degree of scrutiny in both their professional and private lives unknown before the Enron debacle and other corporate scandals of 2002.
- Federal and state laws require that background checks be conducted for certain

jobs. For example, most states require criminal background checks for anyone who works with children, the elderly, or the disabled.

An employer doesn't have to perform the same type of background investigation on every applicant or employee, on one condition: that any differentiation the employer makes is based on legitimate business interests. For example, if the company has a fleet of drivers to drive trucks on the road, it may need to conduct background checks on all of them to verify their driving records to see if they had any criminal convictions for driving under the influence. That would be a legitimate business interest.[7]

Background checking is not the last thing done after selecting a candidate. It should be one of the first considerations, and the centerpiece of how the hiring process is organized. A comprehensive check, including criminal, employment, education, plus a few other specific checks, typically ranges in price from $100 to $200. A basic criminal check could be as little as $25.[8] The result of

Be careful to contact a reputable company to conduct employee background checks.

ETHICS & CHOICES

Your brother, a police detective, casually mentions a case about the investigation of a person accused of "big time" workplace theft. You realize that he is talking about a new employee in your department. Do you go to your company's human resources department with this important information, even though your brother really should not have shared this confidential information with you?

Negligent hiring lawsuits are on the rise. If an employee's actions hurt someone, the employer may be liable. **Negligent hiring** is the failure on the part of the organization to use reasonable care in the selection process while hiring. And the key, of course, is the phrase "reasonable care" and the consequences for failing to use it. Generally speaking, **reasonable care** is the level of care that a reasonably prudent person would exercise under the circumstances.

What employers can do to show that reasonable care was used in the hiring process is to thoroughly check references and to verify all other pertinent information about each candidate before making a job offer. In general, negligent hiring occurs when a company knew or should have known that an applicant had a past record, and it did not check for it.

Negligent hiring is probable when an employee, or in some circumstances an ex-employee, harms someone where it would not have occurred except for the fact that this person was an employee. For example, if the employee has responsibility for accepting cash transactions from customers, and then money ends up missing in the money drawer, it may be negligent hiring if that employee had a criminal record that the company could have discovered with a background check.

not doing a background screening could be theft, embezzlement, a sexual assault, or a lawsuit.

The cost of checking is really quite low compared to the liability of not checking. A background check takes two to four days in most cases.

Although specific industries have some specialized search reports, the most common background reports that provide information to prevent negligent hiring lawsuits include the following:

- Prior employment verification
- Education verification
- Licensing verification
- Motor vehicle record
- Credit history
- Social Security numbers
- Reference checks
- County criminal records (i.e., felony only, felony and misdemeanor, misdemeanor only)

When conducting background checks, organizations must follow the edict of the Fair Credit Reporting Act.

Fair Credit Reporting Act

The **Fair Credit Reporting Act** (FCRA), enforced by the Federal Trade Commission, is designed to promote accuracy and ensure the privacy of the information used in consumer reports and background checks. The federal FCRA does not require employers to conduct employment background checks. The law does not set a national standard that employers must follow in employment screening. Under the FCRA, the employer must always obtain the applicant's written authorization before the background check is conducted.

Often a potential employer will contact an applicant's past employers. When completing the employment application, the applicant is often notified in a statement at the bottom of the form that he or she is authorizing a credit or background screening. When the applicant signs this, he or she has agreed to this. A former boss can say anything (truthful) about a person's performance. However, most employers have a policy to only confirm dates of employment, final salary, and other limited information about the former employee. When adverse employment action is taken (i.e., not hiring an applicant) based on adverse credit ratings contained in the credit report, the FCRA may require the employer to provide the applicant with a notice of the adverse action and the name and phone number of the agency that furnished the report containing the basis for this adverse action.

There are many companies that specialize in employment screening. This can range from individuals commonly known as "private investigators," to companies that do nothing but employment screening, and to online data brokers.

When an administrative manager is charged with this task, the first step is to find a reputable company that conducts background checks. Organizations should beware of companies advertising on the Internet when they state, for example, that they can "find everything about anyone."

Use caution with these companies because they may not stay in strict compliance with federal and state laws, especially the provisions that require accuracy of background check reports.

PREVENTING WORKPLACE VIOLENCE

At any time, employees may come face-to-face with a disgruntled former employee, a demanding person who wants to see the manager immediately, a mentally ill person, or even a life-threatening bomb call. And since the 9/11 terrorist attacks, employees who interact with the public may now need to be more vigilant than ever before.

Incumbent on ensuring a safe work environment is the need for employers to understand what acceptable employee behavior is, and what it is not. Managers specifically must know what constitutes harassment or a hostile work environment. A **hostile work environment** is one that unreasonably interferes with an individual's work performance or contains intimidating or offensive behavior. Such an environment can be manifested through comments, jokes, and any other conduct that makes it difficult for an employee to perform his or her job. Further, this behavior can be transmitted by spoken or written words, e-mails, faxes, Internet material, posters, and calendars.

Preventing workplace violence requires that the following steps be taken:

1. Identify prevention strategies;
2. Acknowledge the warning signs of potential violence; and
3. Offer training to all managers and staff.

© Digital Vision

Prevention Strategies

Numerous security devices may reduce the risk for assaults against workers and facilitate the identification and apprehension of perpetrators. These include closed-circuit cameras, alarms, two-way mirrors, card-key access systems, panic-bar doors locked from the outside only, and parking lot trouble lights.[9]

Violence is an increasing danger in the workplace as workloads and stress levels rise. In general, if you find yourself in a potentially violent situation, follow these tips:

- *Be an empathetic listener.* Convey a sense of interest by asking clarifying questions such as, "So you think that... Is that right?" or "I think we should do this... Do you have any other ideas?"

- *Observe personal space.* Stand at least 2 feet to 5 feet apart. Standing any closer will cause the person to feel threatened. And it could put you in more danger.

- *Make eye contact.* But be aware that staring—or glaring—can send a challenging message. You don't want to put the person on the defensive.

- *Pay attention to your tone of voice.* Keep frustration, anger, annoyance, and similar tones out of your voice. Maintaining a calm, soothing tone helps you defuse the person's anger and frustration.

- *Let the person vent.* Venting can help defuse a tense and potentially violent situation. Allow the person to release energy and frustration verbally instead of physically.

- *Avoid overreacting.* Remain as calm and rational as possible. That reinforces the person's feeling that his or her problems are important.[10]

Should you suspect that someone could turn violent in your office, take the threats seriously. About 15 percent of those who send threats will attempt a physical encounter with those they threaten. You can help prevent that from happening in your company by writing down the exact content of threatening messages and immediately informing your boss or security department about the threats. An investigation should be conducted promptly. Restraining orders and fast-track prosecutions are available in many jurisdictions to formally warn stalkers and others making threats that their actions will not be tolerated.[11]

If the company doesn't already have an emergency-response system in place, advocate for one. All employees should know whom to contact if they fear that someone is acting abnormally or could pose a threat to themselves or others. With that in mind, remember to share your fears. Find a backup

Become aware of the warning signs of potential workplace violence.

person who is willing to help you in an emergency. This person could be your boss, a security guard, a manager, a receptionist, or someone on the maintenance staff—a person whom you trust to handle a situation without making it worse.

Once you have designated someone, sit down with your backup and devise an action plan. The action plan should detail how you will respond in a critical situation, who should be contacted, and what steps you will take to bring the situation under control.

Remember to write down any information that might lead to a dangerous situation. For example, if you receive a bomb threat, find answers to the five "W" questions— who, when, where, what, and why. You may not be able to ask these questions of the person who called in the bomb threat, but you can pay close attention to what the caller says. Gather as many facts as you can as quickly as possible. This will help you to better explain the situation to company officials, who can then decide the best way to address the situation. An example of a bomb threat checklist is shown in Figure 14.3. Though you may not be able to respond to each one of the questions asked on the checklist, it is important to be as accurate as possible when completing it. Try to remain calm as you are asking questions or collecting information. You do not want to sound as if you are writing down the information being given. Clicking the top of a ballpoint pen in nervousness is a signal that you are writing in some cases.

Finally and most importantly, don't be a hero or heroine. That is the last thing you would want to do for your own safety. Instead, trust your gut feelings. There is a

fine line between job loyalty and personal security. Know when you should back off and let someone else step in. If no one is around or other company officials cannot bring the situation under control, call the police, who are trained to handle crises.[12]

Warning Signs

Sometimes, despite the best efforts at prevention, a dangerous situation begins to brew and a violent incident becomes a distinct possibility, or an incident just erupts explosively and personnel have to respond immediately. The nature and success of the response will depend on how thorough the pre-incident planning and training have been.

Warning signs may be observed for hours, days, or weeks before a violent incident, and may be preceded by a history of work-related problems. In all-too-many cases, the sparks of a potentially violent reaction have been fanned into flames by abusive discipline, clumsily executed termination, or failure of management to address employer-employee grievances, causing the worker to "take matters into his or her own hands." Table 14.1 identifies five warning signs employees and managers should look for that may indicate escalating violent behavior is brewing in the workplace.

Training

Training may be considered to be a function that's designed to enhance job skills, productivity, efficiency, and employee growth. While it certainly is all those things, it is also a valuable tool for protecting employees from workplace violence.[13] Employers are taking a closer look at how they can limit the risk of workplace violence. As with any important workplace issue, employers should have their managers undergo training about workplace violence. It's not enough to have a written program that is ready to go if managers aren't trained.

FIGURE 14.3 An Example of a Bomb Threat Checklist

Checklist Issue	Responses
Time and Date Incident was Reported	
How Threat was Reported	
Exact Words of Caller	
Questions to Ask • When is the bomb going to explode? • Where is the bomb right now? • What kind of bomb is it? What does it look like? • Where are you calling from? What is your name?	
Description of Caller's Voice • Accent? • Young, Middle Age, Old? • Male or Female?	
Description of Caller's Speech • Slow, Rapid, Normal, Broken, Excited, Loud, Disguised, Sincere? • Tone of Voice: Is voice familiar? If so, whom did it sound like? Was the message read?	
Description of Background Noises	
Time Caller Hung Up and Your Name	

T A B L E   1 4 . 1   Five Warning Signs of Escalating Behavior

Warning Signs	Possible Responses
Confusion: Behavior characterized by bewilderment or distraction. Unsure or uncertain of the next course of action.	• Listen to the concerns. • Ask clarifying questions. • Give the person factual information and be as clear as you can in your responses.
Frustration: Behavior characterized by reaction or resistance to information. Impatience. Feeling a sense of defeat in the attempt of accomplishment.	• Relocate to quiet location or setting. • Reassure the person. • Make a sincere attempt to clarify concerns.
Blame: Placing responsibility for problems on everyone else. Accusing or holding others responsible. Finding fault or error with the action of others. Crossing over to potentially hazardous behavior.	• Disengage and bring second party into the discussion • Use teamwork approach. • Try to draw the agitated person gently back to facts.
Anger (Judgment call required): Characterized by a visible change in body posture and disposition. Actions include pounding fists, pointing fingers, shouting, or screaming. This signals very risky behavior.	• Don't offer solutions or argue with comments made. • Prepare to evacuate or isolate. • Contact your supervisor and/or the security office.
Hostility (Judgment call required): Physical actions or threats which appear imminent. Acts of physical harm or property damage. Out-of-control behavior signals that the agitated person has crossed over the line.	• Disengage and evacuate. • Isolate person if it can be done safely. • Alert supervisor and contact security office immediately.

Source: Adapted from Coconino Community College's *Emergency Procedures Handbook*, 2003, Flagstaff, Arizona.

Workplace violence training helps managers learn how to prevent or limit violent situations, recognize how violence at work can occur, and actions to take (and not to take) when dealing with violence. To recap, therefore, managers should learn how to keep an unpleasant situation from becoming a violent situation and how to keep a violent situation from becoming worse.[14]

Legal protection begins with knowing what's going on in the workplace, recognizing and responding to problem behavior, and making every effort to provide employees with a safe work environment. Many of the most common legal liabilities are related to an employer turning a blind eye to repeated threats, intimidation, and other festering problems that eventually explode into violent acts. The worst thing to do legally is to see an escalation and not intervene.

All employees need to receive instruction and guidelines on general and job-specific workplace security practices. Some of this can be accomplished through issuing handbooks during the employee orientation process. General workplace violence security training and instruction includes, but is not limited to, the following:

- An explanation of the Workplace Violence Prevention Program (safety and workplace violence policies) including measures for reporting any violent acts or threats of violence.

- Recognition of workplace security hazards including the risk factors associated with the four types of violence and those likely to commit these acts of violence that were described earlier in the chapter.

- Measures to prevent workplace violence, including procedures for reporting workplace security hazards or threats to managers and supervisors.

- Suggested behaviors to defuse hostile or threatening situations.

- Measures to summon others for assistance or to notify law enforcement authorities when a criminal act may have occurred.

- Explanation of the pre-employment screening instruments used including background checks.

Training should not be regarded as the sole prevention strategy but as a component in a comprehensive approach to reducing workplace violence. To increase vigilance and compliance with stated violence prevention policies, training should emphasize the appropriate use and maintenance of protective equipment, adherence to administrative controls, and an increased knowledge and awareness of the risk of workplace violence.

Training employees in nonviolent response and conflict resolution can reduce the risk that volatile situations will escalate to physical violence. Plans and training for defusing violent episodes must be developed, put in place, and reviewed periodically.

Spelled out clearly are those initial actions a worker should take when a violent episode appears to be threatening. Clear instructions on how to summon for help and who should be contacted to handle emergencies of this nature are critical as well. Moreover, guidelines are needed to illustrate the appropriate use of verbal control tactics and body language, scene control and bystander containment, measures for dealing with weapons, and procedures for resolving hostage situations.[15]

Though there are many types of training that employees and managers should receive, the following are some of the more important topics.

1. How to look for signals that indicate the potential for violence. Training includes:

- Noting verbal expressions of anger or frustration.
- Spotting threatening gestures or other body language that suggest anger.
- Recognizing indications of drug or alcohol use.
- Looking for the presence of weapons or objects that individuals might use as weapons.

2. How to maintain behavior that helps defuse anger. Training includes these reminders:

- Exhibiting a calm and caring attitude.
- Not matching threats.
- Not giving orders.
- Acknowledging the person's feelings (e.g., "I know you have been waiting a long time.")
- Avoiding any behavior that individuals may interpret as aggressive (e.g., moving rapidly, reaching into a pocket, getting too close, glaring intently, touching, or speaking loudly).

3. How to reduce the risk of getting into a violent situation. This type of training includes the following key discussions:

- Evaluating each situation for potential violence when entering a room or

interacting with a client, visitor, or customer.
- Remaining vigilant throughout the encounter, looking for signals of escalating frustration.
- Being aware of the path a potentially violent person will have to take to exit the environment and making it a point to never stand between that person and the exit.

4. How managers and employees are to protect themselves from uncontrollable situations. Training calls for:

- Knowing when to remove themselves from the situation after looking for signals described in Step 1.
- Knowing the organization's procedures for calling for help and making sure that a reference book on the exact procedure to follow is available for ready reference in case of an emergency.
- Reporting any troubling incidents to safety and security staff, so they can accurately match safety controls and actions against the identified and described risk.

Unfortunately, even though the best efforts have gone into preventing incidents of workplace violence, it still may occur in the best of organizations and harm may come to employees and customers. With the chances for bad things to happen to good people, a company still must take the proper action following an incident of workplace violence. The next section covers the activities that must take place in the aftermath of workplace violence.

IN THE AFTERMATH OF WORKPLACE VIOLENCE

The crisis is not over when the police and TV crews leave. People may have been killed, others wounded, some held hostage, and many psychologically traumatized. Plans and policies for dealing with the aftermath of workplace violence are just as important as planning for the incident itself; and both may come under sharp scrutiny in later investigations, litigation, and corporate public relations.

Companies should proactively set up policies and procedures for responding to the aftermath of a workplace violence incident.

These policies and procedures should include among them: mobilization of mental health services, media and public relations responses, family interventions, collaboration with law enforcement, physical security and cleanup, legal measures, post-incident investigations, and plans for getting back to business as soon as possible. The objective is for an organization to resume normalcy as quickly as is reasonable to expect.

All incidents, including near misses, should be investigated as soon as possible. When conducting the investigation, remember to:

* Collect facts on who, what, when, where, and how the incident occurred.
* Get statements from witnesses.
* Photograph damage and injuries where appropriate.
* Identify contributing causes to the violence and situation.
* Recommend corrective action to be better prepared or to avoid having a similar situation take place in the future.
* Encourage appropriate follow-up by necessary departments and persons who are involved.
* Consider the possible need to make changes to controls, procedures, or existing company policies.

Careful observation and accurate descriptions of events and individuals in the early stages of an emergency situation can be extremely helpful to those investigating and/or managing the situation later. Law enforcement officers recommend that employees do the following from the time they become aware of an emergency until police arrive: observe what is occurring,

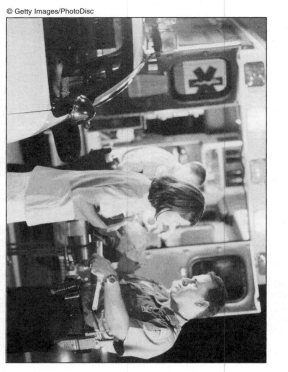

When violence erupts at a company and becomes public information, a proper company response is essential.

describe as many details as you can about what you are observing, and notify law enforcement as soon as you are able to do so safely.

Since violent situations often involve weapons and people in extreme emotional distress, utmost caution and calm behavior on the part of all people involved is essential. Police experts recommend that all employees put distance and/or barriers between themselves and the threat. Stay calm but alert during these situations.

MESSAGE FOR MANAGERS

Many people, even those who take every precaution to safeguard their lives and property at home, take their personal safety at work for granted. It is natural to be complacent while you're working: You are focused on accomplishing the tasks of the day and assume your employer will see to your protection. But your safety is something you cannot afford to take for granted.

Although most companies are very conscious of liability and risk management and their associated costs, not all of them have a formal security program. Things happen so fast during a crisis you do not have time to think. That is why it is important to plan ahead for emergencies and train employees to follow prescribed company procedures. When faced with danger at your desk, a cool head and common sense greatly increase your chances of survival. You can protect yourself and your coworkers by being prepared.

Bad things do happen to good companies—but they happen a lot less often than to bad ones. There will always be a few dangerously unstable people scattered among the work force. However, businesses that treat their employees honorably, take the time and concern to implement safety measures, use firm but fair disciplinary procedures, and make it clear that harassment of its employees—by customers, clients, personal relations, coworkers, or management—will not be tolerated, tend to have fewer violent incidents than less well-run companies.

SUMMARY

1. Whether it is an accident, a scandal, an act of nature, or a malicious act, organizations must be prepared to deal with workplace violence.

2. Workplace violence is defined as any physical assault, threatening behavior, or verbal abuse occurring in the work setting. The four types of workplace violence are violence by strangers, violence by customers or clients, violence by coworkers, and violence by friends, relatives, or acquaintances.

3. Risk factors are conditions or circumstances that may increase the likelihood of violence occurring in a particular setting. Factors such as public contact, exchange of money, delivery of people or services, working with unstable or volatile persons, working in isolation or at night or early morning, or working in high-crime areas can put a person at risk.

4. A crisis management program includes these major components: hazard assessment, hazard prevention and control, training and instruction, and a written reporting procedure.

5. A basic safety policy includes the following elements: objectives of the program, persons responsible for safety practices, consequences of not following procedures, process of reporting unsafe conditions or accidents, a listing of specific rules and guidelines, and a listing of safety hazards to look for in the workplace. The safety policy should have revisions made when circumstances change.

6. Domestic violence is defined as abusive behavior that is physical, sexual, and/or psychological, and intended to establish and to maintain control over a partner. Companies complement their basic safety policy when they include a policy that deals with domestic violence in the workplace.

7. The most common pre-employment background information that employers request are prior employment verification, education verification, licensing verification, motor vehicle record, credit history, Social Security number verification, reference checks, and criminal records.

8. Negligent hiring is the failure to use reasonable care in the employment selection process. Employers, therefore, ensure their hiring decision is a good one by conducting necessary background checks on job applicants who may become employees.

9. Prevention strategies to avoid workplace violence can include using security devices like cameras and alarms as well as training in techniques regarding how to identify potential violent situations, how to look for signals that indicate potential violence, how to defuse anger, and how to protect oneself and others from uncontrollable situations in the workplace. This training should be available to all employees on an ongoing basis.

10. There are five warning signs employees and managers should look for that may indicate escalating violent behavior in the workplace. These are confusion, frustration, blame, anger, and hostility.

KEY TERMS

Desk rage

Domestic violence

Fair Credit Reporting Act

Hostile work environment

Negligent hiring

Reasonable care

Risk factor

Workplace violence

REVIEW

1. What does desk rage mean and why is it important to understand relative to workplace violence and safety issues?

2. List five measures that employees and companies can take to prevent and control potential hazards to employees in the workplace.

3. What are the most common safety policies that companies put in writing? Why are policies important to have and communicate to employees?

4. How does negligent hiring relate to companies that conduct frequent background checks on prospective employees?

5. In what way does the Fair Credit Reporting Act protect potential employees and ultimately affect the way background checks are conducted?

6. If you find yourself in a potentially violent situation, what actions might you take? What actions would you want to avoid if you find yourself in a potentially dangerous situation?

7. Describe each of the warning signs of escalating violent behavior and possible responses that a worker might give.

8. When conducting a training class for employees on workplace violence, what are some topics that should be included? When should this training be conducted and how should it be presented?

9. When conducting an investigation following a workplace violence incident, what steps should you take? Should companies allow the police investigation to be the sole record and follow-up in the aftermath of an incident?

CRITICAL THINKING

1. In what way do the components of the crisis management program relate to managing the four types of workplace violence? Have you ever witnessed any of these four types of workplace violence? If so, describe how you and/or others reacted during the situation.

2. If you were asked to write a workplace safety policy, what items would you include?

3. Given that personal privacy is an important right, defend the need for companies to use pre-employment background checks. Do you feel that it is easy for a background check to intrude on an individual's personal privacy?

4. Assume you are responsible for conducting a training session on ways to identify and prevent acts of workplace violence. If you only had 10 minutes to present, what are five key points you would want to make during your training session? How would you present this information to the attendees? Would you use any scenarios or role-playing activities in which the attendees could participate?

Explain your methodology of presentation.

5. What employee and company issues are involved in the aftermath of workplace violence?

6. Do you consider desk rage to be a frivolous term and one that doesn't deserve concern in the workplace? Explain the reasons for your position. Have you experienced desk rage in your workplace? Give examples of any problems that you or your coworkers have had with desk rage. Why do you think desk rage occurs in the workplace in these situations?

CASE STUDY 14-1: THE SMOKING GUN

After an incident with a younger worker, your manager got angry and began ranting and raving to anyone who would listen that younger workers are the *smoking gun* for work-force violence. He was unyielding in stating that the emerging young work force is ill-equipped for the world of work, work culture, and required work ethic. He supported his statement with these ideas that current and future generations of workers will continue to have:

1. Less emotional maturity;
2. Greater feelings of unearned entitlement;
3. Poorer social skills;
4. Little experience in nonviolent conflict resolution;
5. Less respect for older generations;
6. A shorter attention span and less attention to details;
7. Inappropriate dress, image, and grooming habits;

8. Poorer self-discipline; and
9. Higher rates of violence.

Discussion Questions

1. If you were to be involved in a rationale discussion with your manager on this issue, what points would you make that would defend the generation of workers he is referring to?

2. In your opinion, is there any support you would give to your manager's arguments? If so, explain.

Research workplace violence on the Internet using various search terms such as workplace violence, youth in the workplace, violence in the workplace, or others you determine. Then analyze your research results. Prepare a two-page report to use in a class discussion or to submit as directed by your instructor.

CASE STUDY 14-2: DOMESTIC VIOLENCE ON THE JOB

Ruth Wimberly, administrative manager at Prescott Insurance Co., notices that Sylvia, an office worker, has been looking toward the front door and acting jumpy since arriving at work an hour ago. It appears also that Sylvia is not focused on getting her work done.

Ruth approaches Sylvia and asks if she can meet with her for a moment in the conference room. After closing the door, Ruth askes if Sylvia is all right. Sylvia says that she is really scared. She had separated from her husband last night after a violent argument and is afraid he will come to see her on the job today. She says that he threatened her last night, saying that if she left him, she'd be sorry.

Discussion Questions

1. In your opinion, is there reason for a safety concern on the AM's part? If so, why?

2. In your opinion, what are the initial steps an administrative manager should take in a situation like this? Be as specific as you can in your discussion of these steps.

Prepare an analysis of this situation; incorporating the answers to the questions. You may want to interview a human resources manager to get input on current information used in your city or town in such situations. In addition, you may be able to contact your local police department or local woman's shelter to get some ideas as to how extensive a problem domestic violence is in your community. Your classmates may have input that will be helpful in your analysis for a brief report.

INTERNET RESEARCH ACTIVITY

Safety policies are written differently for each company. However, there are certain elements that are similar. Research three different security or safety policies online. This can be done easily by typing in the keywords "Safety Policies" in your favorite search engine. You may also key such words as violence in the workplace, workplace safety procedures, and/or workplace accidents or deaths. Analyze your research to get a picture of the similarities and differences in the information you found.

Learning Activity:

Write a brief paper to present in class that includes a discussion of the similarities among the three safety policies you found and the differences among them. In addition, draft in your own words a safety policy for a fictitious company of your choosing and submit it to your instructor, as directed.

Chapter 15

Other Workplace
Productivity Systems

OBJECTIVES

After completing this chapter, you will be able to:

1. Describe document management systems—in both paper and electronic forms.

2. Identify features of digital copiers that make them multifunction device systems.

3. Describe the growth of business telephone systems relative to services and types of devices used.

4. Cite some safety concerns relative to managing mailing systems in the workplace.

5. Distinguish between the purpose of a balance sheet and that of an income statement.

6. Discuss features that businesses prefer when purchasing facsimiles and shredders.

Corporate America is faced with a problem unlike anything it has experienced since the Great Depression—a customer crisis. This stems from the fact that we are a better-educated and more affluent, discerning, and demanding society in terms of product quality and service responsiveness. Traditional allegiance to a brand, an institution, or even a party line is almost a thing of the past.

Whether a customer remains loyal could depend on how efficiently office productivity systems (other than computers) are managed to meet or even surpass, customer needs. These other office productivity systems include document management, copier, telephone, mail, and accounting systems.

It's the little things that make the big things possible. —J. Willard Marriott

TECHNOLOGY APPLICATIONS IN THE WORKPLACE

© Getty Images/PhotoDisc

Voice Mail Systems Can Be Attacked

The evolution of voice networks from closed, stand-alone systems to open, network-integrated platforms has produced new management problems. As home systems become integrated into corporate networks, issues of security and privacy are compounded. Hardware vendors have moved away from older, proprietary systems to those such as Windows NT, whose publicized vulnerabilities are often a target of attack. Security issues such as viruses and denial-of-service attacks, and even message privacy, have now migrated into the voice domain.

Next-generation communication systems are vulnerable to both external and internal attacks. External threats, arising from outside the intranet, typically result from holes in hardware configuration or lax operational policies that leave systems vulnerable. The majority of breaches, however, are still the result of overlooked or unenforced internal operational procedures.

ISSUES TO THINK ABOUT:

1. Do you think that hacking into voice mail systems will be as devastating to the business world as hacking into computerized databases is now?
2. Why would a person (hacker) choose to attack a major company's voice mail system?

DOCUMENT MANAGEMENT SYSTEMS

We live in an information-based society. The longer an organization remains in business, the greater the accumulation of information and records or documents. As a result, the amount of misfiled paperwork increases, a number of old records cannot be located, and pieces of a file may become scattered among several locations or on various computer media, and eventually misplaced or lost.

Document Management

In an organization, **document management** deals with the control, retention, and security of records and files whether in paper form or on electronic magnetic storage devices. The pace of business today demands that information be made available in a matter of seconds, rather than hours. This demand requires that organizations develop effective document management guidelines which provide safeguards to protect organizations from the loss of records vital to the operation of the business.

Protecting records is one of the most important tasks for any organization. References to business records are in the news media virtually every day. Corporations find themselves defending in the press or explaining in court various statements made in documents written many years ago or on e-mail messages written more recently. The irony is that establishing an effective corporate-document management program could prevent most of these problems.

These realities make it imperative to have a program that addresses records retention,

inactive records storage, and active records management. Whether this is achieved through traditional filing storage cabinets or with electronic systems using document management software and other technologies, responsible companies must do this.

Document Management Guidelines

Figure 15.1 illustrates the consequences of a poor document-management system. Improper records maintenance and destruction can create severe legal problems for a business. Organizations must, therefore, establish procedures to follow and guidelines to keep in mind when making decisions. These decisions should include: which records are inactive and should be kept; which ones are inactive and should be transferred; and which documents should be destroyed. The costs associated with records maintenance include:

- Filing and retrieval time;
- Equipment and supplies for housing records;
- In-house storage space; and
- Out-of-house storage of old or inactive records, as well as computer software and various storage devices and media.

The time necessary to file or retrieve a record in organizations increases in proportion to the growth of those records. Many companies either keep records forever or, because of high costs and lack of space, indiscriminately destroy old ones. At best, maintenance decisions often are based on educated guesses or the basics of the "seven-year rule," which typically applies to something needing to be completed within seven years. When an organization sets up a solid,

Can some records management systems give you this feeling?

HELP!!

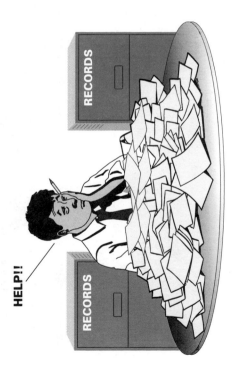

well-managed records system, specific guidelines are clearly established for legal as well as efficiency purposes. Table 15.1 describes what an administrative manager must develop and plan for when setting up an effective document management system.

Document Classification

One of the most important skills in document management is classifying documents and records correctly. Generally, the four classifications used are records that are vital, important, useful, and nonessential, as discussed below.

- *Vital Records* are irreplaceable documents, such as property deeds, copyrights, leases, contracts, and other legal documents. These documents are typically kept permanently.

- *Important Records* are documents that contribute to the smooth operation of the business but can usually be replaced, such as financial documents, inventory, and tax records. These documents are kept for a longer period of time but are eventually destroyed.

- *Useful Records* are documents reflective of everyday business operations, such as correspondence and reports. They are kept relative to retention schedules based on various acts, statutes of limitations, or company regulations.

- *Nonessential Records* are documents such as internal memos, letters, or progress reports. These documents can be destroyed when their purpose is accomplished.

TABLE 15.1 Document Management Guidelines

An Effective Document Management System Should Detail

- How to locate and organize document for easy access.

- How to identify inactive records, when to retire records to storage, and how to maintain these records in accordance with established document management procedures, as well as what the statute of limitations is for retention purposes.

- How office personnel will be trained in the use and function of established document management procedures.

- When and who evaluates current records programs for possible conversion to computer-based storage or microimaging applications.

- Who is assigned to supervise the microimaging production process and document retrieval systems.

Once documents have been analyzed and classified correctly, the next step is to determine which technology to use to save and archive them. The numerous technologies available are discussed in the next section.

Document Management Technologies

Before archiving files electronically, most company records were kept in paper form. Filing cabinets held hard copies of documents, while microfiche (microform on a sheet of film) stored document images long term. Those storage methods required staff members to search through the filing cabinets to find the appropriate paperwork and then search through each document to find the information they needed. It could easily take 15 minutes to 30 minutes to find a single piece of information. Moreover, documents that were stored on microfiche took an even longer period of time to access.

Workers spend a lot of time duplicating, distributing, filing, and searching for documents to meet company needs. This can change when the organization is rolling out an electronic archiving system that allows personnel to retrieve documents using their desktop computers.

The infiltration of electronic computers, magnetic tape, and disk storage in the workplace has not replaced paper documents or the need for an effective way to store them. However, recent technology provides companies with many more options for paper storage, including document micrographic and imaging systems.

Microimage Technology Microimage technology takes the form of both microfilm and microfiche. **Microfilm,** which generally comes as a 35 mm or 16 mm roll of film, is a proven economical archival medium for long-term storage with low equipment costs and comparatively fast retrieval. This medium is used extensively for storage of newspapers and other full-text documents. After processing, the original paper records can be destroyed or recycled.

Microfiche, on the other hand, consists of index-card-sized film that can be read on a variety of microfiche readers or printed out in the form of paper enlargements, usually 8 1/2 x 11 inches. Microfiche is also easy to copy and mail in a regular envelope. Reader-printers can be operated manually or electrically, and are fairly inexpensive, easy to use, and constantly undergoing improvement. These printers provide users with cost-effective access to and paper copies of data stored on either microfiche or microfilm. They record both text and numbers in an inexpensive and durable format. When companies use micrographic technology, they decrease storage space, reduce retrieval time, and eliminate file duplication. These actions result in a more cost-effective and efficient document management system.

Document Imaging and Management

Every organization generates large amounts of paper and electronic documents. As files grow in number, the time and effort required to manage them also increases. Electronic document imaging revolutionizes the archiving of information and provides the means to rapidly find, retrieve, and share all documents in a company.

Document imaging is the conversion of paper documents into electronic images on your computer. These images then can be organized easily and retrieved quickly. Document imaging builds on the strengths

of paper, meaning that files are scanned or electronically converted and a high-resolution digital copy is stored on a hard drive or optical disk. Electronic "index cards" can attach information to a document such as author, reference number, or date created. Files can be viewed, printed, shared, and stored.

A complete document imaging system is composed of three elements—bringing in documents, storing documents, and indexing and retrieving documents.

1. *Bringing in Documents.* This action brings documents into the system. Major advancements in scanning technology make paper document conversion fast, inexpensive, and easy. A good scanner makes it easy to put paper files into your computer.

2. *Storing Documents.* The storage system provides long-term and reliable storage for documents. A good storage system will accommodate changing documents, growing volumes, and advancing technology.

3. *Indexing and Retrieving Documents.* The index system creates an organized document filing system and makes retrieval simple and efficient. A good indexing system makes existing procedures and systems more effective. The retrieval system uses information about the documents, including index and text, to find images stored in the system. A good retrieval system uses the right search tools and makes finding documents fast and easy. It also lets authorized personnel—whether in the office, at different locations, or over the Internet—access papers quickly and with security safeguards.

Which documents people can read, and what actions they can perform on these documents, depends on their level of security, which is controlled by the document imaging system. Therefore, how to bring documents into the system, how to store them, and how to index these documents are three basic considerations when choosing a system.

1. *Bringing in Documents.* There are three primary methods of getting files into an electronic document imaging system: scanning, conversion, and importing.

• *Scanning.* **Scanning** a document produces a picture image that can be stored on a computer. When choosing a scanner, it is important to consider overall budget and the size and volume of paper to be scanned. The ability to use a wide range of scanners is one of the defining characteristics of a good imaging system. A document imaging scanner should have an **automatic document feeder** (ADF). This device allows stacks of paper to be placed into a tray and automatically fed one page at a time into the scanner, speeding up the scanning process. The speed of the document scanner is another consideration. Document imaging scanners can handle between 10 to 200 pages per minute. These are available in both duplex mode and simplex mode. **Duplex scanning** allows both sides of a two-sided document to be scanned in a single pass; whereas, **simplex scanning** scans one side of a document only. Similar to other options, high-speed scanning and duplex scanning will increase the price of the scanner.

• *Conversion.* Converting documents is the process of transforming electronic word processor or spreadsheet documents, for example, into a permanent image format for storage within an imaging system. Windows applications, such as Microsoft Word or Excel, can "print" existing files into an unalterable image of the document. These images are usually stored as archival-quality TIFF (Tagged Image File Format). Converting electronic documents eliminates the need to scan; thereby, it saves paper and printing resources, and produces a cleaner image than if the document were scanned.

• *Importing.* Importation is the third method for bringing in electronic files, such as office suite documents, graphics, audio clips or video files, into a document imaging system. Files can be "dragged and dropped" into an imaging system and remain in their native formats. These files can be viewed in their original format by either launching the originating application (i.e., MS Word, PowerPoint, etc.) or by using a file viewer from within the imaging system.

2. *Storing Documents.* Once documents have been brought into the system, they must be stored in a reliable form. Document imaging storage systems must accommodate not only changing technologies and increasing numbers of documents, but also withstand the test of

time. The needs and budget for image storage are best determined by the individual organization involved. A good document imaging system, however, should be compatible with any storage device currently available—as well as those on the horizon—to provide long-term document storage. Some popular storage devices include magnetic media (hard drives), magneto-optical storage, compact discs, and DVDs. The advantages and drawbacks of each storage medium are described below.

- *Magnetic Media (Hard Drives).* Increasingly fast response times (the time it takes to store and retrieve a document) and dramatic reductions in storage prices make magnetic media such as hard drives a popular choice when storing documents. The main drawback for magnetic media is that while inexpensive, they still contain moving parts, which are subject to mechanical failure. Data files can also be completely erased. Computer personnel should perform regular backups of hard drives; should data be erased or damaged, it can be more easily restored.

- *Magneto-Optical (MO) Storage.* An MO system achieves its high data density by using a laser and a magnetic read/write head in combination. Both the laser and the magnet are used to write data onto the diskette. The laser heats up the diskette surface so it can be easily magnetized, and also to allow the region of magnetization to be precisely located and confined.

Then a less intense laser is used to read data from the diskette. Data can be erased and/or overwritten an unlimited number of times, as with a conventional 3.5-inch diskette. The main benefits of using MO drives are convenience, modest cost, and reliability. The chief limitation of MO drives is that they are slower than hard disk drives and still subject to mechanical failure, although they are usually faster than conventional 3.5-inch diskette drives. Data files can also be completely erased.

- *Compact Discs (CDs).* **Compact discs** are small plastic discs used to store information digitally. Digital information is recorded on a CD as a series of microscopic pits on the reflective surface of an aluminum disc. The disc is covered with a transparent plastic coating and is played on a machine that uses an infrared laser to read the pattern of pitted and unpitted areas on the surface of the disc. Since nothing touches the encoded portion, the CD is not worn out by the playing process. Three standard CD formats include: (a) CD-ROM or Compact Disc-Read Only Memory, a preprinted media format; (b) CD-R or CD Recordable, a single-use recordable disc; and (c) CD-RW or CD Rewritable, a multi-use recordable compact disc which offers a safe and reliable media that can provide long-term storage for images, in some cases for up to 100 years. Furthermore, CD-ROMs do not require specialized hardware or software to retrieve information since most computers come with CD drives as a standard feature. CDs use ISO-9600 specifications, which means the data can be read on many computer platforms (i.e. PCs, Macs, NT servers, Novell servers) unlike magneto-optical disks. The primary drawback of compact disc media is its limited storage capacity of only 650 MB. A **megabyte** is one million characters, or bytes of data.

- *DVDs.* **DVD**, which stands for Digital Video Disc or Digital Versatile Disc, is the newest generation of optical disc storage technology. It is essentially a faster CD that can hold more information, and video, as well as audio and computer data. DVD aims to encompass home entertainment, computers, and business information within a single digital format, eventually replacing audio CD, videotape, LaserDisc, CD-ROM, and even video game cartridges. DVD has unprecedented widespread support from all major electronics companies and all major computer hardware companies, which says much for its chances of success. Never before has one new technology changed so many aspects of data storage and retrieval. DVD achieves its huge capacity by packing more data into the same physical space as a CD. The disc is played by a beam of laser light, so there is no wear and tear even if you keep reading the same data. Moreover, the tough plastic surface is forgiving of fingerprints, dust, and dirt. This means a DVD can be accessed thousands of times and

3. *Indexing and Retrieving Documents.* When paper documents are received in an office, they must be organized to be useful. They are usually labeled, sorted, indexed, stapled, placed in folders, and filed in a cabinet, either in the office or in some centralized filing center. Without these important steps, nothing could be found in a busy workplace. Electronic documents are no different. A document management system provides several different methods of organizing information for future use (i.e., date created, keywords used, file name, etc.). Whatever the combination of indexing methodologies, it needs to be easily used and understood by the people who retrieve the documents, as well as those who file them.

Every day thousands of organizations around the world use document imaging instead of paper filing systems. Table 15.2 shows how document imaging offers a number of benefits over paper and microfilm.

COPIER AND MULTI-FUNCTION DEVICE SYSTEMS

A staple in offices for decades, the photocopier has come a long way since Xerox introduced the first fully automated plain-paper version in 1959. Today's models have more in common with computers than they do with those first Xerox 914 units that were introduced and used at that time.

continue to represent the best long-term option for reliable document imaging storage.

TABLE 15.2 **Benefits of Document Imaging**

Retrieves files quickly	Imaging lets you find documents quickly without leaving your desk. Paper and microfiche are slower because users must go to files and search manually.
Offers flexible indexing	Imaging can index documents in several different ways simultaneously. Indexing paper and microfilm in more than one way is awkward, costly, and time-consuming.
Can search full text	Imaging systems can retrieve files by any word or phrase in the document, a capability that is impossible with paper or microfiche.
Protects files	Imaged documents remain in their folders when being viewed, so none are lost or misplaced. Plus, index template and full-text searches can find documents if they are accidentally moved. Lost paper documents are expensive and time-consuming to replace.
Saves space	Imaging will help recover valuable office space that was previously taken up by storing bulky paper files.
Archives digitally	The risk of loss or damage to paper or electronic files is reduced with a document imaging system.
Shares files easily	Imaging makes it easy to share documents electronically with colleagues and clients over a network, on CD, or through the Web. Paper documents usually require photocopying to be shared and microfilm requires conversion to paper.
Improves security	Imaging can provide better, more flexible control over sensitive documents. Imaging controls security for different groups and individuals through the assignment of access rights. In contrast, all paper documents in a filing cabinet or filing room have the same level of security.
Provides disaster recovery	Imaging provides an easy way to back up documents for offsite storage and disaster recovery. Paper is a bulky and expensive way to back up records and is vulnerable to fire, flood, and theft.

Machines that have traditionally been called photocopiers (copiers) are so multifunctional that the word "photocopier" is becoming outdated. Instead, you'll hear phrases such as "digital imaging system," "multifunctional device," and "digital copyprinter" to describe all classes of copiers that do far more than just make photocopies.

In order to determine what business functions you would like your copier to perform beyond making photocopies, ask yourself these three questions:

1. *What is my budget?* Copier speed is measured in copies per minute (CPM, also known as pages per minute or PPM). Copiers can produce from four to more than 100 copies per minute. The slowest machines begin at around $300 and the fastest, digitally connected, multifunctional machines can cost over $100,000. Copiers that cost more than a couple thousand dollars are most often rented or leased, but they can also be bought. Leases for copiers typically extend for three to five years.

2. *Do I want color?* Color copiers use digital laser technology and start at a few thousand dollars. They can cost as much as $100,000 at the highest end. Many digital color copiers can duplicate in black and white as well and can also be configured to act as a color printer.

3. *Do I want it to fax and/or print as well?* Today's trend is toward **multifunctionality**, with one machine performing two or even three different functions. Whether you are short on space or you're looking to replace your fax machine or printer, it's worth keeping your options open when you shop for a copier. Multifunctional devices with a copying platen—the glass upon which you place the original—are known as **digital copiers** or digital imaging systems. Many copiers can also tell the user when paper or toner is required as well as where a jam may be.

Once you know what kind of copier you're looking for, you'll have to consider a few other factors before you select the model that best suits you. The speed and strength of the copier you choose should depend upon the number of copies you make in a month and other needs. For example, does your office need to make two-sided copies (called **duplexing**), copying on to larger sheets, or use automatic feeding or sorting? If you will be doing these types of copying, make sure you anticipate and plan for the slower speed of your copier system.

How you plan to use your copier will determine which of the following features you need. General features for most types of copiers include feeders, sorters and staplers, duplexers, and paper supply trays.

- *Feeders.* A **document feeder** allows you to copy multipage documents without having to lift and lower the platen cover for every sheet you copy. A platen is the glass upon which an original is placed for copying. Instead, you drop a stack of originals (anywhere from one to 50 sheets) into the feeder, press start, and the copier automatically pulls each sheet through.

- *Sorters and staplers.* You may want a sorter if you're frequently going to copy and collate many sets of multipage documents. **Collating** is the process of organizing copies of documents in the proper reading order. Sorters consist of a set of 10, 15, or 20 bins attached to the side of the copier. Some sorters are equipped with automatic staplers as well, so your sets of copies can be stapled together. More advanced stapler/sorters are often called **finishers** and can three-hole punch or even fold your finished copies.

- *Duplexers.* A copier with a duplexer can make two-sided copies with the press of a button. To reduce paper costs, companies often opt to order copiers with this feature.

- *Paper supply trays.* A copier's paper supply refers to the sets of trays and holders that hold paper inside the copier. Depending on which paper source you select, you can copy onto different sizes or types of paper. The number of paper trays (or sources) available is important if you want to be able to frequently copy onto different paper stocks such as letterhead, colored paper, legal-sized paper, or plastic transparencies.

One of the most important questions to ask when determining what copier to order is: Should you buy a digital copier or analog machine? The answer is probably a digital copier. Particularly because the difference in price between analog and digital copiers is minimal, it makes little sense these days to buy analog. Most manufacturers are no longer introducing new analog models into the market.

Digital copiers have been available since 1987, and almost every copier manufacturer (Xerox, Minolta, etc.) has one model on the market by now. When exploring digital copiers as an option, it's worth taking a look at their distinctions because digital copiers do have some advantages over analog models.

- *Fewer moving parts and less noise.* Digital copiers have far fewer moving parts than analog copiers, but the unmentioned downside is that the parts are more expensive. So if something does break,

you'll likely end up paying more to replace it or have a maintenance contract that is more costly. Digital copying makes far less noise than analog copying. Many new owners of digital copiers find this quieter copying to be a welcome surprise.

- *Slightly better quality.* Although the quality of output of any copier manufactured today can be exceptional—no matter if it's digital or analog—digitals do stand out in certain situations. Fine lines like those in graphs or blueprints are more accurately reproduced on digital machines, as are photographs. Additionally, where output from an analog copier can differ slightly in density across copies, each reproduction from a digital copier is a duplicate of the same scan, so it is absolutely identical to the copy before and after it. A digital copier can even be smart about how it makes copies of originals that combine text and graphics. In other words, a good digital copier will copy the graphics in photo mode and the text in text mode.

- *Multifunctionality.* If space is at a premium or you intend to buy a new printer or fax machine anyway, digital copiers can fill two or even three document management needs. Today's digital copiers are called digital imaging systems, digital copier/printers (or copy-printers), or even digital multifunction products. (Digital copiers restricted to copying only are slowly becoming extinct.) Many digital copiers can be upgraded with modules that equip them to perform different functions such as printing, faxing, or both. Digital copiers can even be

© CORBIS

Office copier systems can be either centralized or decentralized.

networked into a computer's internal operating system so staff can print, copy, or send faxes from their desks.

Centralized and Decentralized Copying

Office copier systems can be set up either as a centralized copy center where copier specialists perform all copying or as several decentralized copiers available to employees on an "on demand" basis. Many organizations end up having a combination of both in the copying system they offer employees.

Centralized Copying Centralized copy centers can save organizations money by limiting the number of individual copiers needed and by reducing per-copy costs. Upfront costs may be high due to the cost of large machines designed to handle high-volume photocopying, but the benefits of centralized copying are many. Besides cost issues, advantages include increased security via access codes and the opportunity to review printing quantities for a specific

department or organization. Issues to consider when installing a centralized copy center include convenience, storage and work-space requirements, and location. A user evaluation of the copy center's continued effectiveness should be conducted by the administrative manager on a regular basis.

Decentralized Copying In a decentralized copying environment, copiers are strategically and conveniently located throughout a company. As copies become less expensive and equipment more sophisticated and multifunctional, many offices are choosing to purchase additional individual copiers. Employees do not have to walk far to reach the machines and they can make copies whenever they need them. This kind of "on-demand" system works well in small offices where the volume of copies does not justify a centralized system. The significant advantage of the decentralized approach is convenience, while the major disadvantage is lack of control over who is making copies and how

many copies are being made.

Regardless of whether a copier system is centralized or decentralized, the use of copier controls is on the rise as companies struggle to keep costs down and reduce waste. Several methods of copier control have been developed to help eliminate copier abuse and misuse. One method is to assign numbers to users so that every time an employee uses the copier, a pre-assigned number (example: 2470) is entered that serves to track usage. Another method is to ask employees to use a magnetic-strip or swipe card, much like a credit card, that will authorize use and activate the copier.

Although copiers may seem all the same at first, keep in mind the wide range of capabilities and options that are available to you today. You also need to consider special new technology by certain manufacturers, security concerns, and with networking in mind, compatibility issues with other machines you already own and the software available for your company's future expansion.[1]

Network Copiers and Connectivity

When users and equipment are connected throughout an organization, it is often referred to as a networked or "connected" system. If enough users demand connectivity, more office equipment dealers will try to fulfill that need. Once a user fully understands the benefits of connectivity, there's no choice but to have workers fully connected.

Here's a closer look at some of the key advantages that connectivity offers.

1. *Copying and printing from the desktop.* By having the copier connected to the network, users can now program copy jobs, from the simplest to the most complex, from their desktop computers.

2. *Access to a wide range of finishing capabilities from the desktop.* Related to the benefit of copying and printing from the desktop, users can program the device to staple, sort, make two-sided copies, and anything else they would typically program at the copier.

3. *Faxing from the desktop.* If the copier/printer also offers fax functionality, users can send and receive faxes via the device, initiating fax transmissions from their computers.

4. *Scanning to the network.* Users can walk up to the copier, scan in a document, and have that document stored magnetically on the network, so it becomes immediately accessible to other users within the networked system.

5. *Enhanced productivity.* Ultimately, connectivity is a productivity enhancer. Although employees will still need to make trips to the device to pick up their copies or printouts, they'll usually be notified by an on-screen prompt when their print jobs are completed. This reduces the amount of time spent waiting at the copier to access the device or waiting for a walk-up job to be copied.

Making the most of connectivity involves some additional considerations. Once you've made the decision to connect, it's a good thing to reflect upon your existing work flow and how to integrate the connected device into that work flow or adapt that work flow to leverage the benefits of connectivity. Printing and copying from the desktop on a single device means changing the office work flow and the way people are accustomed to working. Old habits are hard to break, but if you want to reap the most rewards from your digital copier, breaking old habits is a must.[2] Additionally, workers can e-mail print jobs to office supply stores that will print and deliver the finished product.

TELEPHONE SYSTEMS

After payroll, telecommunication costs are the highest business expenditure for most U.S. companies, according to Mass Tel Communications Inc., headquartered in San Francisco. From toll-free calls made by customers, supply orders placed over the Internet, and network connections to satellite offices, the telephone is an essential workplace productivity tool.[3]

Many persons, if asked, would say that the telephone is perhaps *the* most important piece of business equipment. Businesses use telephones to make first impressions, sell products, provide customer service, and negotiate contracts. The telephone can be a painful interruption to the business at hand, or it can be a vital tool for getting things done. The difference, of course, is determined by how you use it. When properly used, communication tools that make an organization's telephone system more efficient greatly improve customer service.

Telephone Services and Features

Today's organizations are providing their workers with state-of-the-art telephone communication devices that offer multiple features. Table 15.3 provides a brief explanation of several of the more optional calling services.

Voice Mail and Security Issues

At a time when qualified, skilled employees are harder than ever to find, eliminating the need to hire extra telephone receptionists to handle routine calls—from vendors, employees, and/or salespeople—makes good economic sense. **Voice mail** is a computerized telephone system that allows callers to leave messages. This technology permits a higher volume of phone traffic to be handled quickly, without having to add extra employees to the payroll. An automated phone system relieves the constant pressure and wear on an already busy staff, while virtually eliminating inaccurate messages.

Supporters of voice mail say a well-designed voice mail system cuts down on missed phone calls, eliminates long waits on hold, delivers clear messages, and ends infuriating bouts of "telephone tag." In addition, modern systems can field routine calls quickly and automatically, freeing operators for calls that require a personal response.

Voice mail systems include automated attendant, sophisticated messaging services, and call processing—all available through the wonder of computer chips. Should offices install voice mail? Consultants advise that if you answer "yes" to two or more of the following questions, you probably should consider installing voice mail:

1. Do you spend a lot of time providing the same information to many callers?

2. Are most of your callers in different time zones?

3. Do you want to add services but lack the personnel to handle the phones?

4. Do callers complain that they frequently get busy signals?

5. Could your customers order your product or service after hearing an informational message without speaking to you personally?

6. Do you often work on a number of projects at the same time?

T A B L E   1 5 . 3   Business Telephone Services

800/888 service. This service is free to callers. Long-distance charges for calls are paid at a volume discount rate by the company you are calling.

Anonymous call rejection. This feature blocks anonymous or private phone calls unless the calling party reveals his or her phone number.

Automatic or continuous callback. When you call a busy number, the automatic callback feature "remembers" the number and dials it for you automatically after you hang up.

Call forwarding—busy line—don't answer. This feature reroutes calls to a designated answering station.

Call waiting. This feature allows the caller to reach you even when your line is busy. A gentle signal alerts you to an incoming call while you are talking.

Caller ID. Caller ID shows you the name and number of the person who is calling and keeps a log of recent calls.

Distinctive ring. This ring signals the source of an incoming call. One ring means it is an inside call; two rings mean it is an outside call.

Priority call. With priority call, you can tell by a distinctive ring when designated people are calling.

Speed calling. Speed calling saves time and avoids wrong numbers by dialing frequently called numbers with a fast one- or two-digit code that you have programmed into the phone system.

Voice messaging service. This service records your incoming calls when you cannot answer or when your line is busy.

After determining if you need voice mail, the next step is to understand the choices for the various systems that are available. Table 15.4 provides information on different voice mail systems and how they can be acquired.

For small businesses or home-based workers, using a service offered by the local phone company or outside service bureau is probably the simplest, most effective, and least expensive option, at least in the short

run. For a small monthly charge, you get voice messaging and answering options, depending on the number of mailboxes and other options you require.

Typically, a voice messaging system works this way. When you pick up your phone, a beeping tone notifies you that you have a message waiting, which you retrieve by dialing a special number. Or you might see a blinking or steady red light signaling

TABLE 15.4 Voice Mail Systems

What Can Voice Mail Systems Do for the Business Office?

- Voice mail systems can answer and route calls, direct inquiries, record messages, provide information, and take sales orders.

What Types of Voice Mail Systems Are Available to a Business?

- You can buy and install a voice mail board in your computer. The voice mail software runs in the background while you work in another program. You record a greeting or series of greetings and callers leave voice messages stored on your computer system. You receive an on-screen notification that you have a message. One possible drawback to voice mail is that you have to leave the computer on to keep voice mail active. The main advantage of voice mail boards is their low cost. They start at around $170.

- You can purchase a stand-alone system. This stand-alone system includes its own computer. All you do is plug it into your power and phone lines, record your outgoing messages, and you are in business. However, the stand-alone voice mail systems are expensive, starting at around $3,000, so they make the most sense for a large business with several phone lines and many workers.

- You can use a service offered by your local telephone company or an outside service bureau.

that a message is waiting. Another advantage of this option is that you can also pick up messages from any other touch-tone phone by dialing a special message number assigned to your account. Most hotels also have voice mail services on room phones.

Voice mail is not without its concerns. It is true that among the more frustrating technological developments of recent years are the automated phone-answering systems that imprison callers in loops, sentencing them to listen to endless recorded messages. Potential customers often are left yearning for a human voice or just want to go back to the previous menu, but they are afraid if they do, the cycle will start over again.

The way to avoid trapping your callers has more to do with *how* you set up your system than with *which* system you choose. Use these suggestions:

- Decide whose phones should and should not be answered by voice mail. For instance, it's a good idea that people should answer lines directed to receptionists, customer service representatives, and top managers.

- Make sure callers get clear instructions on how to reach a "live" person again after they have been routed to an individual voice mailbox. Keep recorded instructions brief, clearly worded, and informational.

- Change your outgoing message whenever you plan to be out of the office or tied up in meetings. Ideally, you should change your message every day.

Voice mail systems usually have less security than other sensitive communication systems at companies and, unfortunately, the four-digit personal identification numbers used to guard access to users' messages can be easily discovered. Companies do not always protect the confidentiality of their voice mail systems with the same critical security that they would with the networks. The bottom line is, ever since we started digitizing voice mail, it is just another file sitting on a server and can be accessed by a knowledgeable hacker.[4]

Cell Phones and Unified Messaging Systems

Offices are undergoing tremendous changes in the way workers communicate because the era of wireless data and telecommunications has arrived. You can, for instance, connect to the Internet with a cell phone, download and play games and music, store, send, or receive color photos, and send and receive e-mail—with attachments that can include text or picture files.

At the end of 2002, some 22.5 million mobile-phone subscribers said they use their phones to connect to the Net, up from 9 million in 2001, according to researcher eMarketer. The most popular wireless feature has been messaging. Sending text, photos, and sound bites has caught on. Already, 13.5 million wireless users—10 percent of the total—regularly tap short messages into their cell phones.[5]

The cell phone messages don't need to be short either. A secure connection between mobile phones and companies' corporate e-mail systems allows workers to exchange e-mails with files attached.

Many communication systems today are expanding into unified systems. **Unified messaging systems** give users a convenient way to retrieve their e-mail, voice mail, and fax messages. They also offer conferencing capabilities, call forwarding, call routing, and a service typically referred to as Find Me Follow Me, a number portability function that allows subscribers to be reached no matter which of their phones they happen to be using.

While unified messaging and telecommunications allow number portability, they also streamline communications by providing a universal inbox where all of a user's messages can go. In this way, they are never far away from the information that requires their attention.[6]

MAILING SYSTEMS

Efficient mail systems are designed to ensure organizational cost-effectiveness and efficiency, resulting in better service to customers. For that reason, administrative managers need to advise others in the organization about how to get the maximum benefits from mail services. Workers, for example, need to know what postal and

---

MANAGEMENT TIP

Remember to exercise good and safe judgment when using your cell phone in the company of customers, in restaurants, and while in your automobile.

delivery services are available for their use. They also need to know the correct procedures to follow when safely processing and routing incoming and outgoing mail, given recent terrorist threats.

Mail Services and Procedures

Although fax machines are cost-effective and quick when used to send information immediately, the U.S. Postal Service (USPS) offers several delivery services to corporate customers that can be more effective than other methods. These types of services include special delivery, certificates of mailing, certified mail, collect on delivery, return receipts, insurance, registered mail, express overnight, two- to three-day delivery, and many forms of international mail service. In addition to the USPS, commercial delivery services such as Federal Express and United Parcel Service are used.

For companies to process mail accurately and efficiently, employees should understand incoming and outgoing mail procedures. Typical procedures for processing mail are reviewed in Table 15.5.

Safety Concerns and Precautions

Mail center managers throughout the U.S. are scampering to respond to new safety and environmental hazards. Energized by troubling news reports, countless numbers of otherwise unaffected mail centers now ask: "What can we do to protect ourselves and our employees? Are there any simple and

practical steps that we can take to reduce the incidence or the impact of a terrorist act?"

Mail handlers must be aware of emergency procedures associated with the detection and handling of suspected mail and sufficiently understand those procedures. These practices and procedures, those things the average mail center in the United States can do to improve its position relating to an unforeseen event, include:

- *Post emergency information.* Telephone numbers for the following individuals and organizations should be posted in a prominent location within your mail center: the local fire department; the local security personnel; the next two levels of management; emergency health officials for the local community, the city, the county, and the state; and the postmaster of the U.S. Postal Service facility that delivers or receives mail to and from your offices. The posted information should be located near a telephone.

- *Remove personal belongings.* All personal items belonging to the mail center staff and supervisors should be totally removed from the mail center. Storage space for personal items should be made available nearby but elsewhere. This includes individual desks, coats and coat racks, lockers and file cabinets for storing personal items such as lunch boxes, family pictures, and trinkets. Given the downside risks associated with cluttered mail centers, this routine practice is more important than ever. The objective is to create an environment where the mail being processed is absolutely visible, without obstruction or opportunity to be lost, misplaced, left behind, or confused with personal belongings.

TABLE 15.5 Basic Procedures for Processing Incoming and Outgoing Mail

Incoming Mail

1. Sort the mail.

2. Open the mail.

3. Date and time stamp the mail.

4. Read and annotate (write notes on) the mail.

5. Prioritize and arrange the mail.

6. Perform other activities such as attaching related material, using action-requested slips, saving advertisements, and keeping a mail register.

7. Distribute the mail.

Outgoing Mail

1. Assemble the mail in proper order if there is more than one page.

2. Make sure the letter has been signed.

3. Check that any enclosures have been included with the letter.

4. Verify that the address on the letter and on the envelope is the same.

5. Select the appropriate mail classification from among first class, second class, third class, fourth class, or express mail.

- *Use dump tables.* In those mail centers where mail arrives loose in bags or tubs or returns from mail runs in loosely filled containers, use a dump table as the first step in rough sorting. A **mail dump table** is a large, flat table with a small lip around three or four sides. By using a dump table, you can dump and spread loose mail for visual inspection before individual handling. The lip prevents the mail from sliding onto the floor. If, for some reason, a piece of mail is deemed suspicious, there's a good chance that it can be spotted while it's still on the dump table, without the need for individual handling. As well as assisting in the sorting process, a dump table offers added security for mail handlers.[7]

  In addition, the U.S. Postal Service urges people to report suspicious letters or packages such as mail with:

  - Excessive postage, no postage, or non-canceled postage.
  - No return address or a fictitious return address.

Mail rooms are responding to new safety and environmental concerns.

- An improper spelling of addressee names, titles, or locations.
- Lumpy or a lopsided appearance to the letter or package; any stain, powder, wetness, or noise should be suspicious.
- Excessive amounts of tape used for sealing.
- A foreign country address or mail that is unexpected from anywhere.
- A postmark showing a different location from the return address.
- Distorted handwriting or cut-and-paste lettering.

If you receive a suspicious letter or package, remember these warnings: a) do not open it; b) do not shake, bump, or sniff it; c) do cover it or place it in a plastic bag; d) wash your hands thoroughly with soap and water, even though you may be wearing gloves for protection; and e) contact your supervisor before calling the sheriff/police non-emergency number.[8]

© CORBIS

ACCOUNTING SYSTEMS

Business organizations of all types must keep financial records and establish accounting systems either electronically through the use of computers or manually on paper. One reason the government requires businesses to keep records is that certain information must be reported to the Internal Revenue Service on a periodic basis. Another reason is that accurate records are the basis for sound business decisions.

Businesses thrive, in part, as a result of maintaining accurate, up-to-date records in usable form. This is because competition in business rewards maximum efficiency. Inaccurate accounting records can contribute to business failure and bankruptcy. As business owners and managers strive for economic success, sound decisions and plans require the use of complete and accurately prepared accounting cycle information. The **accounting cycle** involves recording, classifying, and summarizing financial information for owners, managers, and other interested parties. Summaries of financial information are reported for a specific period of time in the form of financial statements.

Financial statements permit owners, managers, and accountants to analyze business activities and interpret their effectiveness. Analyzing financial statements provides answers to questions such as, "How do sales and profits from this year compare with sales and profits from the last two years?" or "What was our cash flow this month?" All businesses should prepare financial statements on a regular basis so that any changes or trends can be noted immediately.

Although administrative managers do not prepare financial statements per se, they should understand their importance and be able to interpret critical data from them that indicate trends or changes affecting office administration. Getting further training in popular accounting software packages, such as QuickBooks and Peachtree, is always a good idea for administrative managers. Learning how to interpret financial statements is another.

In most organizations, usually the accounting department or business manager is available to assist in these financial areas. The two most common financial statements used to answer these types of questions or track financial activities are the balance sheet and the income statement.

Balance Sheet

The **balance sheet** shows the financial condition of a business at a particular time—for example, on December 31 or June 30. In reality, the details of a company's financial condition change constantly. Every day, a company pays bills and receives payments. Every day, some inventory is used and must be replaced. All balance sheets, however, must satisfy this basic accounting equation: Assets = Liabilities + Capital.

Figure 15.2 shows an example of a simple balance sheet.

Income Statement

An **income statement** is a summary of all income and expenses for a certain time frame, such as a month or year. It is probably the most frequently studied of all financial statements. Owners study an income statement to determine how much

profit they are making. Bankers study income statements to decide whether to approve a business loan. Unlike a balance sheet, which represents a stationary financial picture, an income statement reflects a business's profitability over a given time period. The accounting formula for income statements is as follows:

Net Income = Revenue − Expenses.

Figure 15.3 shows an example of a simple income statement.

OTHER AUTOMATED OFFICE EQUIPMENT SYSTEMS

Because so much is written about computers today, at times it is easy to forget that other automated systems are just as vital in helping an office run smoothly. When processing office information, you can expect to use equipment other than computers to get a job done. In the office, for example, you will use a fax to quickly send a letter to a customer in another city, a paper shredder to safeguard personnel and financial records, perhaps an electronic typewriter to fill in preprinted forms, and dictation machines or voice recognition software to speak your thoughts when processing business letters and reports. Each of these office devices will be briefly discussed now.

Facsimiles

With the speed and convenience of a phone call, fax machines deliver business communications in a fast and relatively inexpensive way. A **facsimile (fax)** machine translates copies of text or graphics documents into electronic signals, which are then transmitted over telephone lines or by satellite.

FIGURE 15.2   The Balance Sheet formula is Assets = Liabilities + Capital

	Assets	=	**Liabilities**	+	**Owner's Equity**

	Assets	+	Supplies	+	Prepaid Insurance	=	Accts. Pay.,— Ling Music Supplies	+	Barbara Treviño, Capital
Balances	$5,863		$4,297		$1,200		$1,360		$10,000

Encore Music
Balance Sheet
August 11, 20—

Assets		Liabilities	
Cash	5863 00	A/P—Ling Music Supplies	1360 00
Supplies	4297 00	Owner's Equity	
Prepaid Insurance	1200 00	Barbara Treviño, Capital	10000 00
Total Assets	11360 00	Total Liab. and Owner's Eq.	11360 00

FIGURE 15.3   The Income Statement is Net Income = Revenue – Expenses

Encore Music
Income Statement
For Month Ended August 31, 20—

			% OF SALES
Revenue:			
Sales		4411 00	100.0
Expenses:			
Advertising Expense	273 00		
Insurance Expense	100 00		
Miscellaneous Expense	10 00		
Rent Expense	250 00		
Supplies Expense	2564 00		
Utilities Expense	115 00		
Total Expenses		3312 00	75.1
Net Income		1099 00	24.9

There is no doubt that facsimile machines are permanently changing the way customers place orders and how corporate offices acquire data from field offices—altering the very nature of business. Today, an office without a fax machine is about as rare as one without a computer or copier. Fax users are becoming aware of some concerns, however, such as proliferation in the use of the fax and security issues.

- *Proliferation.* As businesses and institutions rely more on faxes, concerns over product speed and quality, training and usage, and cost containment have taken on a new urgency. Fax machines provide speed and convenience, to be sure; yet, most offices currently lack the organization or discipline to control this powerful technology. By establishing clear, simple guidelines for using the fax, unnecessary transmission is reduced, thereby saving time and money. In addition, under new Federal Communication Commission rules, you must give written consent to receive product information, advertisements, and promotions via facsimile from a fax sender.[9]

- *Security.* Relative to fax usage, security is an increasingly worrisome issue. The sheer number of fax machines in use increases the possibility of sending confidential information to a wrong number. Additionally, as more fax machines are connected to computerized networks, the chances of unauthorized tapping are growing. Cellular phones are particularly vulnerable to eavesdropping, making mobile faxing risky, as well.

Fax documents promote an increase in paper copy. A popular means to address any security issues surrounding confidential paper in organizations is to investigate the use of a shredder device.

Shredders

One of the simplest security measures for any office continues to be the regular use of shredders. With computers, fax machines, and copiers spewing out seemingly limitless amounts of paper, virtually every business produces huge volumes of documents. But one result is a wealth of information—from financial data to confidential reports—that can cause problems in the wrong hands. Shredding provides a simple way to protect such data.[10]

Office paper **shredders** provide document security and, at the same time, help the environment. Most companies use shredders to destroy sensitive material to ensure that it stays confidential. Shredded paper is easier to recycle and more biodegradable when placed in a landfill. Paper shredders, which are experiencing marked growth each year, vary greatly in productivity and price.

Although some models fit over waste bins, larger shredder machines placed in central locations are generally more powerful and accept more paper. When purchasing

ETHICS & CHOICES

You decide to work late one evening to catch up on some work at the office before the state tax auditors arrive the next day. A vice president, whom you do not report to, has asked you to shred a 4-inch pile of papers before you go home and also to make some monetary changes to ten expense claims that have already been paid to the vice president. Your initial feeling is not to do it. How would you handle this situation?

paper shredders, buyers should consider the materials they will be destroying and the overall capacity in terms of their current and future needs. Paper shredders range from over-the-trash-can models costing less than $50, to heavy-duty models costing several thousand dollars.

It is interesting to note that paper shredders used to be considered expensive, but now some companies are paying for them by selling the shreds to recycling centers and to animal breeders who use the shreds for bedding. Also, many companies now reuse shreds as packing material for fragile items. Shredders have several features and options that affect performance and price. Understanding each of these is the key to finding the right shredder for the business office.

- *Throat Size.* Sometimes called throat width or entry width, this is the easiest feature to understand. It is simply the width of the cutting mechanism. This determines what size paper the shredder will handle. Most office paper is 8 1/2 x 11 inches so many shredders have throats 8 3/4 inches to 9 1/2 inches. You want it a little bigger than the paper so the paper doesn't have to be fed in straight. When one side is no longer clearing the throat, it may crumple up and sometimes cause the shredder to jam.

- *Sheet capacity.* This refers to how many pages can be fed into the shredder at one time. If you shred a lot of large-size reports, this will be important to you.

- *Speed.* This is usually listed in feet per minute or FPM. A desk-side unit may only have 10 FPM. In other words, within

one minute, the unit can shred up to 10 feet of paper. It's more common, however to see numbers from 20 to 60 FPM or higher in today's offices.

- *Staples.* Small models like desk-side ones can't handle these (or paper clips) so just plan on removing them first. A larger office model should be able to eat staples with no problem.

- *Shred Size & Cut Type.* Since these both relate to security, they are presented together. The cut type is usually listed as "strip" or "cross." Strip cut means the paper comes out in long thin strips. It is cut once along its length as it passes through the shredder. The strip size is how small those strips are. Obviously, the smaller they are, the harder it would be for someone to put them back together or glean information from them. Cross cut means it is cut a second time, perpendicular or diagonal to the first cut. The paper in this case comes out more like confetti than strips and affords greater security. It is, therefore, infinitely harder to decipher than even the thinnest strips.

Typewriters and Dictation Machines

There is no question about the effect that increased use of computers among managers has had on the use of typewriters and dictation machines in the office. Increasingly, offices use neither of these devices, which were so prevalent a decade ago. Nevertheless, they are still found in many offices and used by office support workers.

- *Typewriters.* Some users of office electronic typewriters often prefer these machines to personal computers for tasks such as printing mailing labels, addressing envelopes, and filling in multipart forms and index cards.

• *Dictation Machines.* A dictation machine is a device used to capture thoughts on magnetic voice media. The use of dictation machines, however, has shrunk in recent years. The reduced use of dictation machines can be directly attributed to the advent of portable computers and a lack of trained transcriptionists. Dictation machines are still used by doctors and attorneys to dictate notes to be transcribed for the patient's or client's records.

Voice recognition software is becoming increasingly popular as a dictation method for professionals. Mobile units can be used that connect later to the computer. Doctors often use these devices at patient bedside to dictate progress reports.

A professional is capable of using tools and gaining the know-how to perform tasks in a professional manner. It doesn't matter if it is a computer, a typewriter, a fax or a shredder; the important thing is to select the most appropriate office equipment tool for the task at hand.

MESSAGE FOR MANAGERS

The 21st century will see changes at a faster and faster pace. The one thing we know is that tomorrow's business will be very different from today's business. However, some things do not or should not change, even as we become more technologically advanced. Customers still expect their needs to be met by office staff in a timely, consistent fashion.

In other words, customers have grown to expect a company they do business with to serve them in a stellar manner. An administrative manager needs to monitor the office systems on a daily basis. There is no doubt technology will make these systems easier to handle by office staff; however, trained workers are a critical issue when ensuring the efficiency of the systems and the effect they have on overall customer satisfaction and therefore on company revenues.

S U M M A R Y

1. Document management deals with the control, retention, and security of records and files, whether in paper form or on electronic magnetic storage devices. Protecting records is one of the most important tasks for any organization. References to business records are in the news media virtually every day. Statements made in documents written many years ago or on e-mail messages written recently have become the object of court cases or the media. Establishing an effective corporate-document management program could prevent most problems.

2. Recent technology provides companies with many options for paper storage, including micrographic (microfilm and microfiche) and document imaging and management through a conversion of paper documents into electronic images on a computer.

3. Today's trend in copiers is toward multifunctionality, with one machine performing two or even three different functions. Digital copiers can be upgraded with modules that equip them to perform different functions: printing, faxing, or both. They can even be networked into a computer's internal operating system so staff can print, copy, or send faxes from their desks.

4. Several optional telephone services that businesses can request are anonymous call rejection, automatic callback, call forwarding, call waiting, caller ID, distinctive ring, priority call, speed calling, and voice messaging service.

5. Offices are undergoing tremendous changes in the way workers communicate

because the era of wireless data has arrived, ushering in unified messaging systems that give users a convenient way to retrieve their e-mail, voice mail, and fax messages.

6. Efficient mail systems are designed and set up in organizations to ensure cost-effectiveness and efficiency, as well as safety through new practices and procedures recommended and implemented as a result of terrorist threats.

7. The accounting cycle involves recording, classifying, and summarizing financial information for owners, managers, and other interested parties. Two financial statements used in businesses are the balance sheet (which shows the financial condition of a business at a particular time) and an income statement (which summarizes all income and expenses for a business during a certain time period).

8. A facsimile (fax) is a machine that translates copies of text or graphics documents into electronic signals, which are then transmitted over telephone lines or by satellite. Fax users are becoming aware of proliferation in the use of the fax and security issues.

9. A simple security measure for any office is the regular use of shredders. Shredders come in all sizes and with various features but their primary function is to destroy sensitive material to ensure that it stays confidential.

10. Though the use of typewriters and dictation machines has diminished, they are still found in many offices and used by office support workers.

KEY TERMS

Accounting cycle
Automatic document feeder
Balance sheet
Collating
Compact discs
Digital copiers
Document feeder
Document imaging
Document management
Duplex scanning
Duplexing
DVD
Facsimile (fax)
Finishers
Income statement
Mail dump table
Megabyte
Microfiche
Microfilm
Multifunctionality
Scanning
Shredders
Simplex scanning
Unified messaging systems
Voice mail

REVIEW

1. What are the four classifications for records and how do they differ from each other?

2. Briefly describe the purpose of the three elements in a business's document imaging system. What are the basic considerations of these when choosing a system?

3. In making a copier-buying decision, what are three questions you should ask yourself?

4. Why would a company want to centralize the copying system versus decentralizing it throughout the organization?

5. What are some advantages when companies network multifunctional copiers and provide connectivity throughout departments?

6. What are some suggestions you might make to create a voice mail system that is especially user-friendly to customers?

7. What steps should be taken to ensure that safe procedures are followed by employees in mail rooms of organizations across the U.S. (according to the U.S. Postal Service)?

8. Why is the accounting function in companies such as an important system? In other words, what is the purpose of accounting to the world of business?

9. What are some features AOMs should consider when buying a shredder for a busy office?

CRITICAL THINKING

1. Why would a company choose to convert to an electronic document management system? What are the advantages of doing so?

2. If you were in charge of making the copier-buying decision for your company, what factors would you consider before placing that copier order?

3. Where do you think the use of cell phones and voice mail systems will be in the next decade? As you forecast this scenario, imagine what they will look like and function as in the world of business.

4. In your opinion, are we as a nation overreacting relative to mail safety and environmental hazards? Defend your stand.

5. If you were president of an organization, would you be more interested in the information provided by a balance sheet or information from an income statement? Why?

6. In your opinion, what features are "must haves" when businesses purchase facsimiles and shredders? How can you justify these features if cost is an issue?

CASE STUDY 15-1: THE DISPLACED RECEPTIONIST

A new chief executive officer (CEO) has just been brought in to run Accessories Unlimited, a well-established company with more than 170 employees. Mr. Guy Pfefferman, the new CEO, is so different from Mr. Raul Jimenez (the former CEO) in his approach to innovative systems that it has many employees just a little bit nervous.

For example, Mr. Pfefferman wants to change Hilda's job. Hilda has been the only receptionist at the company for more than 15 years. Some workers refer to her as the "heart and soul of the organization."

Mr. Pfefferman says that within three weeks Accessories Unlimited will have a fully automated voice mail system installed, and Hilda will become a part of the new customer service team. (No one knows what that is yet.) Mr. Pfefferman also informed staff that customer service training will start next month. There also is a rumor that some managers may go back into their old positions. For now, morale is very low at Accessories Unlimited.

Discussion Questions

1. If you were an employee at Accessories Unlimited, how would you feel right about now?

2. Is there cause for alarm in the organization, or is what is happening at Accessories Unlimited a natural development as companies become more competitive in a world-class economy and managers change? Discuss your ideas.

3. If you were to advise your closest friends at work on what their response to this new CEO should be, what would you say?

Study the case, making notes that will help you develop an overall view of the situation and where the company may be heading. Review the literature on companies that have experienced a change in leadership. You may find these by searching the Internet for organizational changes, new CEOs, new ideas for management change, or others you can think of to get you the information you need. A management textbook may also provide some examples or search clues.

Analyze your research and write a two-page report based on your research. Incorporate the answers to the questions in your report. Be prepared to discuss your findings in a class project discussion or to submit your report.

CASE STUDY 15-2: A HODGEPODGE SYSTEM

Consolidated Steelcase Products in Savannah, Georgia, has been manufacturing filing cabinets and other products for 17 years. It has 35 employees and enjoys $2 million in sales annually.

Recently, however, it has become apparent that there is a problem in their current computerized and manual record-keeping procedures. The departments—sales, accounting, production, and shipping—realize they are making frequent errors because of information they cannot find and are wasting time and supplies having to redo a form or other documents in the course of each day's work.

Discussion Questions

1. What effect would the following suggestions have on providing a solution to the problems Consolidated Steelcase Products is facing?

- Install a computer network with document management software for each worker in the organization.
- Assign a person to be responsible for records management throughout the company.

2. Which of the two suggestions would you implement first and why?

Analyze the facts presented in the case. Is there other information you need? If so, what is it and where would you locate it?

Search the Internet by using words such as records management systems, inventory systems, and others that you think may help you with the information needed. Then after you have analyzed the information to get a good idea of the types of systems available, interview one or two inventory managers or shipping managers in your area. Ask what they would do in this situation. Record their answers to incorporate into your two-page report. Be prepared to report to the class your findings.

INTERNET RESEARCH ACTIVITY

Assume you are doing an oral report on usage, trends, and current features in cell phones. Make a comparison study by going to the web sites of several cell phone service providers, such as Sprint, AT&T, Verizon, or others. To find information on this issue, access the course site http://odgers.swlearning.com

Learning Activity:
Write a brief paper to present in class that includes a discussion of the usage, trends and current features in cell phones today.

Endnotes

Chapter 1

1. Nan Bauroth, "Digital Workplace Styles," *Office Solutions*, May 2001, p. 28.
2. Frederick W. Taylor, *The Principles of Scientific Management* (New York: Harper & Bros., 1911).
3. W. Edwards Deming, *Out of the Crisis*, MIT, Cambridge, 1986.
4. Andrew S. Grove, "Knowing When—and How—To Assert Your Authority," *Working Woman*, April 1993, p. 24.
5. Tess Kirby, "Delegating: How to Let Go and Keep Control," *Working Woman*, February 1990, p. 32.
6. Nancy Miller, "Administration 2000," *The Secretary*, February 1997, p. 19.
7. Helen Wilkie, "Managing your own Career," Association of Administrative Professionals, *The Executive Secretary*, June 2003.

Chapter 2

1. American Management Association, http://www.amanet.org (©2003).
2. "Street Smarts," *Inc.*, January 1, 2001, p. 25.
3. Kenneth Blanchard and Norman Vincent Peale, *The Power of Ethical Management*, 1988, William Morrow Publishers.
4. Ibid.
5. Denis Waitley, *Empires of the Mind*, Quill Publishers, 1995. Reprinted by permission of HarperCollins Publishers Inc.
6. Eric Krell, "Recruiting Outlook: Creative HR for 2003," *Workforce*, December 2002, p. 45.
7. Eric Allenbaugh, "The Eyes Have It," *HR Magazine*, April 2003, pp. 101–102.
8. Michelle Conlin, "The Big Squeeze on Workers," *Business Week*, May 13, 2002, p. 96.
9. "Workloads are Getting Heavy," *Essential Assistant*, September 2002, p. 11.
10. Conlin, Loc. cit.
11. "Work/Personal Boundaries Shifting," *Office Solutions*, February 2001, p. 8.
12. www.ama.org (©2003)
13. Monte Enbysk, "Should you Monitor Your Employees' Web Use?" *SmallTech*, June 2003.
14. Sharlene A. McEvey, "E-Mail and Internet Monitoring and the Workplace: Do Employees Have a Right to Privacy?" *Communication and the Law*, June 2002, p. 70.
15. "Help Employees Take Charge of their Careers," *Workforce*, January 2002, p. 62.
16. "Certification Provides Proof of Continuing Education," *OfficePro*, January/February 2002, p. 11.
17. Gene Sharratt and Eldene Wall, "Falling to the Top," *OfficePro*, August-September 2002, p. 9.

Chapter 3

1. Anya Martin, "What's Next," *Office Pro*, January/February 2002, p. 8.
2. "AAs Make Up One of the Nation's Largest Occupations," *Essential Assistant*, May 2002, p. 3.
3. *AMA Research*, "AMA Fall 2002, Administrative Professionals Survey," http://www.amanet.org/research/index.htm.

4. U.S. Department of Labor, Bureau of Labor Statistics, *Occupational Outlook Handbook*, 2003 http://www.bls.gov/oco/oco/ocos002.htm.

5. Anya Martin, "Management Skills that Matter," *OfficePro*, April 2002, p. 10.

6. U.S. Department of Labor, loc. cit.

7. Ibid.

8. Anya Martin, op. cit., pp. 10-11.

9. Dana H. Shultz, "Effective Information Management," 2003 www.ds-a.com.

10. Robert Rosen, "Developing Globally Literate Leaders," *Training & Development*, May 2001, p. 80.

11. Kathryn Tyler, "Sink-or-Swim Attitude Strands New Managers," *HR Magazine*, February 2003, p. 10.

12. Leslie A. Weatherly, "Human Capital—the Elusive Asset," *HR Magazine*, April 2003, p. 125.

13. Anya Martin, "Management Skills that Matter," *OfficePro*, April 2002, pp. 8–9.

14. Ibid., p. 9.

Chapter 4

1. "Cell Phones Increasing Personal Calls at Work," *Essential Assistant*, September 2002, p. 8.

2. Marvin J. Cetron and Owen Davies, "Trends Now Changing the World: Technology, The Workplace, Management, and Institutions," *The Futurist*, March 2001, pp. 27-29.

3. Gary B. Shelly, Thomas J. Cashman, and Misty E. Vermaat, *Discovering Computers 2003 Complete*, Course Technology, Boston, MA, pp. 11.32.

4. Marvin J. Cetron and Owen Davies, "Trends Now Changing the World: Technology, The Workplace, Management, and Institutions," *The Futurist*, March 2001, pp. 30-32.

5. John A. Challenger, "The Transformed Workplace: How You Can Survive," *The Futurist*, November 2001, p. 24.

6. Jim Clemmer, *Pathways to Performance: A Guide to Transforming Yourself, Your Team, and Your Organization*, Prima Publishing, 1995.

7. Pattie Odgers, *The World of Customer Service*, Thomson/South-Western, 2004.

8. Lauri J. Bassi, George Benson, and Scott Cheney, "The Top 10 Career Trends," *The Secretary*, May 1997, p. 22.

9. U.S. Small Business Administration Web Page http://www.sba.gov/manage/change.html 2003.

10. Ibid.

11. Anya Martin, "The Digital," *OfficePro*, August/September 2001, p. 12.

12. Sarah Fister Gale, "Formalized Flextime: The Perk that Brings Productivity," *Workforce*, June 2003, p. 22.

13. Fast Forward: 25 Trends That Will Change the Way You Do Business, *Workforce*, June 2003, pp. 43–56.

14. Roberta Chinsky Matuson, "How to Manage a Contingent Workforce," www.monster.com 2003.

15. "Fast Forward: 25 Trends That Will Change the Way You Do Business," *Workforce*, June 2003, pp. 43–56.

16. JoAnn Davy, "Outsourcing Human Resources Headaches," *Managing Office Technology*, September 1998, pp. 6–7.

17. Rick Maurer and Nancy Mobley, "Outsourcing: Is it the HR Department of the Future?" *HR Focus*, November 1998, pp. 9–10.

Chapter 5

1. Judy Voss, "Etiquette Tips for Modern Mobile Workers," *Office Solutions*, April 2001, p. 12.
2. Michael Bartlett, "Workers Can't Wait to Go Mobile," *Newsbytes News Network*, March 18, 2002.
3. Deena C. Knight, "Employee Mobility is Changing the Face of Today's Workplace," *Office Solutions*, September 2001, p. 13.
4. Kinetic Workplace Web site, 2003 http://www.kineticworkplace.com/
5. "The Virtual Workplace of the 21st Century: Is Your Organization Ready For It?" An Interview with Magid Igbaria and Margaret Tan, authors of *The Virtual Workplace*, Idea Group, Inc. © 1998, http://www.brint.com/igp/virtual.html.
6. Jeanne L. Allert, "You're Hired, Now Go Home," *Training & Development*, March 2001, p. 43.
7. Deena C. Knight, "Employee Mobility is Changing the Face of Today's Workplace," *Office Solutions*, September 2001, p. 15.
8. International Association of Virtual Office Assistants Web site, 2003, http://www.iavoa.com/va.html
9. Mary Ann Donovan, "E-mail Exposes the Literacy Gap," *Workforce*, November 2002, p. 15.
10. http://www.sba.gov.
11. Kevin Dobbs, "Developing Workplace Training Programs," *Workforce*, November 2002, p. 54.
12. "Where Do Training Dollars Go?" *HR Focus*®, May 2003, p. 8.
13. Jill Vitiello, "New Roles for Corporate Universities," *ComputerWorld*, April 9, 2001, p. 42.
14. Richard Greenberg, "Corporate U. Takes the Job Training Field," *Techniques*, October 1998, pp. 36–38. See also http://www.motorolacareers.com/university (© 2003).
15. "Eight Common E-Learning Mistakes to Avoid," *HR Focus*, March 2003, p. 10.

Chapter 6

1. Tom Starne, "No Limitations for the Disabled: Workplace-Related Assistive Technologies," *Risk & Insurance*, April 1, 2002, p. 22.
2. Janet Wiscombe, "Workplace Bias Claims Rise," *Workforce*, May 2002, p. 16.
3. Brenda Paik Sunoo, "Accommodating Workers with Disabilities," *Workforce*, February 2001, p. 86.

Chapter 7

1. "Research Demonstrates the Success of Internet Recruiting," *HR Focus*, April 2003, p. 7.
2. Dave Patel, "Testing, Testing, Testing," *HR Magazine*, February 2002, p. 30.
3. Nancy S. Ahlrichs, "Day One: A Manager's Checklist," www.monster.com, 2003.
4. William J. Rothwell, *The Worker Learner*, Amacom Publishing, 2002, p. 222.
5. Anya Martin, "Training Day," *OfficePro*, October 2002, p. 8.
6. Iris Randall, "Realizing the Dream Deferred," *Black Enterprise*, February 1998, p. 196.
7. Seminar materials from "Criticism & Discipline Skills for Managers," CareerTrack, 2003.
8. Todd Raphael, "Meet HR's New Best Friend: Turnover," *Workforce*, January 2003, p. 72.
9. "Employee Turnover Continues To Dive; Telecoms Boost Job Cuts," *HR Focus*, August 2002, p. 8.

Chapter 8

1. "The Cost of Spam: $874 Annually Per Employee," *Newsline*, July 2, 2003.
2. "Salary Budget Survey Results Released," *Newsline*, June 6, 2003.

3. Steve Bates, "Benefit Packages Nearing 40 Percent of Payroll," *HR Magazine*, March 2003, p. 37.

4. Joseph McCafferty, "Cost of Perks Piling Up," *CFO, Magazine for Senior Financial Executives*, March 2003, p. 15.

5. "Phased Retirement," *Training & Development*, January 2000, p. 11.

6. Donna G. Albrecht, "Getting Ready for Older Workers," *Workforce*, February 2001, p. 25.

7. *Developing a High-Performance Workforce*, Lawrence Ragan Communications, Inc., 1999, pp. 40–41.

8. Carol Hymowitz, "In the Lead: Baby Boomers Seek New Ways to Escape Career Claustrophobia," *Wall Street Journal*, June 4, 2003, p. B1.

9. "Employee Handbooks May Have Hidden Legal Ramifications," *Knight Ridder/Tribune Business News*, July 8, 2003.

10. Gillian Flynn, "Have Good Reasons for Large-Scale Layoffs," *Workforce*, March 2002.

11. Web site www.aflcio.org, 2003.

Chapter 9

1. Samuel Greengard, "Dealing with Addiction," *Workforce*, February 2003, p. 8.

2. Jim Halloran, "Is There Drug Abuse In Your Shop?" *Motor Age*, May 2003, p. 22.

3. Deena C. Knight, "Substance Abuse in the Workplace," *Office Solutions*, March 2002, pp. 18–19.

4. *Merriam Webster's Collegiate Dictionary*, Merriam-Webster, Inc., Springfield, Massachusetts, 2001, p. 311.

5. "Depression on the Rise," *HR Magazine*, May 2002, p. 32.

6. Duane Lawrence, "Depression Prolific, Very Costly, Studies Say," *The Columbus Dispatch*, June 18, 2003, p. A2.

7. Ibid.

8. Janet Gemignani, "Can Your Health Plan Handle Depression?" *Business & Health*, June 2001, p. 47.

9. "Depression on the Rise," *HR Magazine*, May, 2002, p. 19.

10. Kathryn Tyler, "Happiness from a Bottle?" *HR Magazine*, May 2002, p. 27.

11. Steve Villano, "HIV/AIDS Is Diversity Issue," *Multichannel News*, September 23, 2002.

12. Carrie Morantz and Brian Torrey, "Guidelines for Employees with HIV, AIDS," *American Family Physician*, September 15, 2002, p. 110.

13. "Assessing The Evidence Submitted In The Development Of A Workplace Smoking Regulation," *Public Health Reports*, May–June 2002, pp. 291–293.

14. Paula C. Morrow and Teresa Leedle, "A Comparison of Job Performance and Disciplinary Records of Smokers and Nonsmokers," *The Journal of Psychology*, May 2002, p. 339.

15. Gillian Flynn, "Gray Areas in Controlling Employee Lifestyles," *Workforce*, February 2003, p. 35.

16. *Merriam Webster's Collegiate Dictionary*, Merriam-Webster, Inc., Springfield, Massachusetts, 2001, p. 779.

17. "Elle and MSNBC.Com's 'Office Sex and Romance' Survey," *PR Newswire*, May 13, 2002, pp. 28–29.

Chapter 10

1. John W. Zimmerman, "Is Your Company At Risk? Lessons from Enron," *USA Today* (*Magazine*), November 2002, p. 27.

2. Carroll Lachnit, "Why Ethics Is HR's Issue," *Workforce*, March 2002, p. 12.

3. Jennifer J. Salopek, "Right Thing," *Training & Development*, July 2001, p. 23.

4. Patrick M. Lencioni, "Make Your Values Mean Something," *Harvard Business Review*, July 2002. pp. 113–115.

5. "Manpower Inc. International Survey Confirms Employee Loyalty Is Alive And Growing, But Reveals Surprising Differences Across Demographic Groups," *Business Wire*, May 27, 2002, p. NA.

6. Chuck Martin, "Employee Loyalty Just Isn't What It Used to Be," *Darwin Magazine*, March 2003, p. 18.

7. "Workplace Rudeness Is Common and Costly," *USA Today* (*Magazine*), May 2002, p. 9.

8. Paula Gamonal, "Business Etiquette - More Than Just Eating with the Right Fork," http://www.ravenwerks.com/practices/etiquette.htm, 2003.

9. "Proper Introductions Are Still In Style," *Essential Assistant*, May 2002, p. 10.

10. "I'm Good with Faces, But Not with Names," *Essential Assistant*, May 2002, p. 9.

11. Sharon Massen, *Telephone & Voice Mail*, South-Western, Thomson Learning, 2002, pp. 22–28.

12. Nichole L. Torres, "Mind Over Manners: What You Need To Know To Make A Great Impression At Your Next Business Meal," *Entrepreneur*, May 2003, pp. 119–120.

13. "Bad Lunch Behavior Can Help Lose Clients," *USA Today* (*Magazine*), July 2003, p. 7.

14. "Dawn Waldrop, "Fear Factor Corporate Style," *Newsletter from best-impressions.com*," July 2003, p. NA.

15. John Fetto, "Dress Code," *American Demographics*, May 1, 2002, p. 45.

16. Kim Johnson Gross and Jeff Stone, *Dress Smart™ Men*, Warner Books, 2002.

17. Gillian Flynn, "Gray Areas In Controlling Employee Lifestyles," *Workforce*, February 2003, p. 11.

18. Lisa Grimaldi, "What To Wear," *Meetings & Conventions*, July 2001, p. NA.

19. Thomas Tennant, "The Art of Protocol," *Association Meetings*, June 1, 2003, p. NA.

20. Letitia Baldridge, *Letitia Baldridge's Complete Guide to Executive Manners*, Scribner Publisher, 1993.

Chapter 11

1. Ronald Roach, "Digital Workforce Study Released," *Black Issues in Higher Education*, August 1, 2002, p. 22.

2. "Leadership Styles, from Elvis to Rosa Parks," *Workforce*, March 2003, p. 52.

3. Craig R. Hickman, *Mind of a Manager, Soul of a Leader* (New York: John Wiley and Sons, 1990).

4. Shari Caudron, "Where Have All the Leaders Gone? And How Can HR Get Them Back?" *Workforce*, December 2002, pp. 29–30.

5. Ed Rose, "Your Best Leader—an ACTOR," *Workforce*, October 2002, pp. 32–34.

6. Stephen R. Covey, *The 7 Habits of Highly Effective People*, (New York: Simon & Schuster). © 1999 Franklin Covey Co. The 7 Habits are Registered Trademarks of Franklin Covey. Reprinted with permission. All rights reserved.

7. Douglas McGregor, *The Human Side of Enterprise*, (Illinois: McGraw-Hill, 1985).

8. William Ouchi, *Theory Z*, (New York: Avon Publishing, 1993).

9. A.L. Evans and V. Evans, "Leadership Workshop," *Education*, Fall 2002, pp. 18–21.

10. Johnnetta B. Cole, "Six Steps to Effective Leadership," *Black Issues in Higher Education*, October 24, 2002, p. 146.

11. Janet Wiscombe, "Rewards Get Results: Put Away Your Cash," *Workforce*, April 2002, pp. 42–44.

12. Claire Sykes, "Ready... Set...Motivate: How to Get Your Employees Going," *Office Solutions*, December 2001, p. 32.

13. Leslie Gross Klaff, "Getting Happy with the Rewards King," *Workforce*, April 2003, p. 47.

14. Phaedra Brotherton., "Retire This! For Baby Boomers, Retirement Doesn't Mean the End; It's Simply the Start of Something New," *Black Enterprise*, May 2002, p. 89.

15. Cynthia G. Wagner, "Keeping Older Workers On The Job," *The Futurist*, July-August 2003, pp. 10–11.

16. Carroll Lachnit, "Brave Old World," *Workforce*, March 2003, p. 8.

17. Adapted from Gregory P. Smith, "Baby Boomer Versus Generation X: Managing the New Workforce," President, Chart Your Course International, ©1999-2003, Attard Communications, Inc. and Gregory P. Smith, www.businessknowhow.com.

18. Joanne Sujansky, "The Critical Care And Feeding Of Generation Y," *Workforce*, May 2002, p. 15.

19. "Five Ways To Tame Tough Decisions," *Essential Assistant*, March 2003, p. 2.

20. "Zero-Defect Decision Making," *Inc.*, March 1, 2002, p. NA.

Chapter 12

1. Brad Patten, "Organization Can Cut Tech Expenditures," *Business First*, August 22, 2003, p. A27.

2. "Powerful Teamwork Gets the Job Done," *Essential Assistant*, April 2003, p. 1.

3. Carla Joinson, "Managing Virtual Teams," *HR Magazine*, June, 2002, p. 8.

4. "Tom Terez, "The Power of Nice," *Workforce*, January 2003, p. 22.

5. Ibid.

6. "Get PeopleSmart—A Surefire Eay to Resolve Conflict," *Essential Assistant*, February 2002, p. 3.

7. "Don't Let Office Disputes Get Out of Hand," *Essential Assistant*, September 2002, p. 6.

8. Franky D'Oosterlinck and Eric Broekaert, "Integrating School-Based and Therapeutic Conflict Management Models at Schools," *Journal of School Health*, August 2003, pp. 222–224.

9. Irene Tobis and Michael Tobis, *Managing Multiple Projects*, McGraw-Hill Publishing Company, 2002.

10. Sue Shellenbarger, "Multitasking Makes You Stupid, Studies Say," *Star Telegram*, March 1, 2003. pg. NA.

11. "How Well Do You Manage Stress?" *Essential Assistant*, May 2002, p. 11.

12. Claire Sykes, "Say Yes to Less Stress," *Office Solutions*, July-August 2003, p. 26.

13. Caroline V. Clarke, "Guarding Against the Stress of Success: Recognize the Early Signs of Burnout—and Take Proactive Steps to Prevent It," *Black Enterprise*, February 2003, p. 150.

14. "Swim—Don't Sink—When Swamped," *Essential Assistant*, May 2003, p. 1.

15. "Time Management for the Hopeless," *Essential Assistant*, June 2003, p. 7.

16. "Need More Time in your Workday? Here's How to Get It," *Essential Assistant*, June 2002, p. 6.

17. "How To Handle Those Interruptions," *Essential Assistant*, October 2002, p. 1.

18. "Eight Ways to Kick The Procrastination Habit," *Essential Assistant*, December 2002, p. 4.

19. "How to Handle Those Interruptions," *Essential Assistant*, October 2002, p. 1.

Chapter 13

1. "Office Color and Design Influence Health, Comfort, and Harmony," *Office Solutions*, August 2001, p. 10.

2. Matthew B. Jarmel, "How Corporate Identity Influences Design," *Brandweek*, January 27, 2003, p. 20.

3. Jen Renzi, "Time for a Change," *Interior Design*, May 15, 2003, p. 201.

4. Cindy Coleman, "What Makes Progressive Chicago Architect Doug Garofalo Run?" *Interior Design*, May 2002, p. 307.

5. Robert B. Footlik, "Sizing up Sites," *IIE Solutions*, March 2002, pp. 27–29.

6. Deena C. Knight, "Alternative Officing: Thinking Outside of the Cube," *Office Solutions*, May 2002, pp. 31–32.

7. "IBM and Steelcase Announce Global Initiative to Design Office of the Future," *Business Wire*, January 14, 2002, p. NA.

8. Web site www.osha.gov, 2003.

9. Jim Seymour, "The Civil Workplace," *PC Magazine*, January 29, 2002, p. 59.

10. Karen Fritscher-Porter, "Ergonomic Advice: How Ergonomically Friendly Is Your Workspace?" *Office Solutions*, January-February 2003, pp. 21–22.

11. Web site www.osha.gov, 2003.

12. "Purifiers Can Clear Office Air," *Essential Assistant*, May 2002, p. 7.

13. "Workplace Greenery Reduces Stress," *Office Solutions*, May 2002, pp. 8–9.

14. Nadine Heintz, "The Light Idea," *Inc.*, April 2003, p. NA.

15. "Noise May Endanger Employees' Health," *USA Today (Magazine)*, April 2002, p. 7.

16. Ibid.

17. Adam Burke and Erik Peper, "Cumulative Trauma Disorder Risk for Children Using Computer Products," *Public Health Reports*, July-August 2002, pp. 351–352.

18. Amanda C. Kooser, "Health, Wealthy and Wise," *Entrepreneur*, September 2002, p. 48.

19. Karen Fritscher-Porter, "Ergonomic Advice: How Ergonomically Friendly Is Your Workspace?" *Office Solutions*, January-February 2003, p. 24.

20. http://www.iwh.on.ca/products/atwork2003/Summer03/in_33a.3.htm, 2003.

21. From information received at an In-service Professional Development Conference through Flagstaff Medical Center, Flagstaff, Arizona, November 2003.

22. Irene Korn, "Flat Panel Monitors Are Here and They Offer Us the Opportunity to Revolutionize Office Design," *Architecture*, June 2003, pp. 82–83.

23. Karen Fritscher-Porter, "Ergonomic Advice: How Ergonomically Friendly Is Your Workspace?" *Office Solutions*, January-February 2003, p. 23.

20. Miles Maguire, "Writing the Unwritten Rules," *Folio: The Magazine for Magazine Management*, December 15, 2000, p. 15.

21. Janet L. Hall, "Stay Organized-Schedule Priority Tasks, Stay Late, and Automate," *Essential Assistant*, August 2002, p. 10.

Chapter 14

1. Web site www.osha.gov, 2003.

2. "The Occupational Safety and Health Administration," *Journal of Environmental Health*, January-February 2003, p. 17.

3. "Will 'Desk Rage' Be The Next Workplace Epidemic?" *HR Focus*, September 2003, p. 9.

4. Laurence Miller, "How Safe Is Your Job? The Threat of Workplace Violence," *USA Today (Magazine)*, March 2002, p. 52.

5. "Vigilance Stops Violence—And Lawsuits: Behavior That Can Escalate To Violence Is Increasing," *Workforce*, October 2002, pp. 38-40.

6. "Have You Considered These Safety Management Challenges?" *HR Focus*, January 2003, p. 11.

7. Lawrence Chambers, "Security Blankets for Your Office," *Office Solutions*, March 2002, pp. 12-13.

8. "Protecting People and Profits With Background Checks," *Workforce*, February 2002, pp. 51-52.

9. "Is Your Lobby Ripe For Violence?" *HR Focus*, September 2003, p. 5.

10. "Prevent Workplace Violence," *Essential Assistant*, January 2003, p. 7.

11. "Help Prevent Workplace Violence," *Essential Assistant*, November 2002, p. 7.

12. "Receptionists Must Be More Vigilant Than Ever," *Essential Assistant*, August 2002, p. 1.

13. "The Most Effective Tool against Workplace Violence," *HR Focus*, February 2003, p. 11.

14. D. Lewis Clark, Jr., "Guns & Workplace Violence: Are your Employees Packing Heat?" *Columbus CEO*, July 2003, p. 64.

15. Gillian Flynn, "Know the Background of Background Checks," *Workforce*, September 2002, p. 96.

Chapter 15

1. Scott Cullen, "Copier Buyers Guide," *Office Solutions*, July-August 2003, pp. 13-14.

2. Scott Cullen, "Hook It Up: Why Your Copier Should Be Connected to A Network," *Office Solutions*, May-June 2003, pp. 16-17.

3. "Make Your Phone Your Friend: Slashing Business Telecom Costs," *Office Solutions*, May-June 2003, p. 29.

4. "Voice-Mail Systems Easy Prey for Hackers: Fiorina Incident Is 'Wake-Up Call' About Lack of Security for Phone Messages," *Computerworld*, April 15, 2002, p. 6.

5. Roger Crockett, "Web Phones Take Wing," *Business Week*, March 3, 2003, p. 122.

6. Michael Cohn, "Messages from Anywhere: Unified Messaging Systems Let Businesses Access Voice Mail, E-Mail, and Faxes Over the Phone or the Web," *Internet World*, April 2002, p. 50.

7. Richard W. Pavely, "New Concerns For Mail Center Managers: Guidelines For Keeping Your Mailroom Safe Amidst A New World Of Hazards," *Office Solutions*, December 2001, p. 25.

8. Web site http://www.usps.gov, 2003.

9. Web site http://www.faxpermission.com, 2003.

10. Mark Rowh, "Office Security," *Office Solutions*, May-June 2003, p. 43.

Glossary

A

Acceptable-use policy prohibits employees from installing software, downloading programs from the Internet, passing pornography around the office, and the like (p. 283)

Accommodating usually takes the form of selfless generosity or blind obedience by yielding completely to another's point of view (p. 294)

Accountability involves judging the extent to which employees fulfill their responsibilities (p. 21)

Accounting cycle involves recording, classifying, and summarizing financial information for owners, managers, and other interested parties (p. 382)

Administrative office manager the person responsible for planning, organizing, and controlling the information-processing activities and for leading people in attaining the organization's objectives (p. 7)

Affirmative Action Program provides guidelines to eliminate discrimination in the employment selection process (p. 161)

Alternative officing flexible work arrangements and settings that support work processes, functions, or activities that can't be encompassed in one space (p. 322)

Ambient lighting illuminates the areas surrounding a work surface (p. 317)

Ambiguity uncertainty (p. 87)

Americans with Disabilities Act (ADA) prohibits private employers, state and local governments, employment agencies, and labor unions from discriminating against qualified individuals with disabilities in job

application procedures, hiring, firing, advancement, compensation, job training, and other terms, conditions, and privileges of employment (p. 134)

Anti-virus program protects computers against viruses by identifying, removing, or quarantining any computer viruses found in memory, on storage media, or on incoming files; also know as *antivirus software* (p. 75)

Artificial intelligence application of human intelligence to computers (p. 36)

At-will employment the employer can fire the employee for no reason or any reason (p. 197)

Authority the right to do something, to tell someone else to do it, or to make decisions that affect the reaching of organizational objectives (p. 20)

Autocratic (authoritarian) leader one who makes most of the decisions alone instead of allowing followers to participate in the decision-making process (p. 261)

Automatic document feeder (ADF) a device that allows stacks of paper to be placed into a tray and automatically fed one page at a time into the scanner, speeding up the scanning process (p. 368)

Avoiding might take the form of diplomatically sidestepping an issue, postponing an issue until a better time, or simply withdrawing from a threatening situation either emotionally, physically, or intellectually (p. 383)

B

Balance sheet a statement that shows the financial condition of a business at a particular time

application procedures, hiring, and ethical principles that guide decision-making behavior (p. 230)

Basic beliefs deeply felt moral and ethical principles that guide decision-making behavior (p. 230)

Behavior science approach the modern approach to worker behavior; cuts across the fields of psychology, anthropology, and sociology to emphasize interpersonal relations and democratic actions on the part of workers (p. 10)

Behavioral interview questions questions that elicit a response detailing how the applicant did a job in the past or performed a particular task (pp. 159–161)

Bereavement leave offered by companies to provide eligible employees paid time off in the event of a death in the employee's immediate family (p. 188)

Brainstorming the process of providing or recording as many solutions as possible without sorting or evaluating them (p. 277)

Buddy system matches a new employee with an experienced employee who maintains close contact with the new employee and lends support by answering routine questions (p. 166)

Budget financial plan for a certain period of time—a fiscal year, an academic year, or a calendar year (p. 19)

Bureaucracy a form of organization, which is formal, impersonal, and governed by rules rather than by people (pp. 8–9)

Burnout essentially caused by a feeling of powerlessness on the job and is a stress-related affliction resulting when people invest most of their time and energy in a particular activity (p. 300)

C

Cafeteria benefit plan allows an employee to contribute a certain amount of pre-tax dollars to a plan to avoid income taxes on the amount allocated to these qualified benefit plans (p. 190)

Carpal tunnel syndrome (CTS) a medical problem of the hands, specifically an inflammation of the nerve that connects the forearm to the palm of the wrist (p. 331)

Centralized authority concentration of power and authority is near the top of an organization (p. 20)

Certification a way for employees to ensure a level of competency, skill, or quality in a particular area (p. 54)

Chain of command defines the organizational and reporting structure of a company (p. 14)

Change management involves managing the changes organizations are experiencing (p. 94)

Coaching an ongoing, collaborative process intended to clarify performance targets, reinforce strengths, and encourage individuals to stretch to even higher levels of performance (p. 43)

Collaborating involves agreeing not to compete for resources or use confrontation to find creative solutions to mutually engaging problems (p. 294)

Collating the process of organizing copies of documents in the proper reading order (p. 372)

Communication media cables, telephone lines, cellular radio, and satellites (p. 110)

Communication process by which messages, information, and human attitudes are exchanged with others (p. 74)

Compact discs small plastic discs used to store information digitally (p. 369)

Comparable worth implies that jobs with comparable levels of knowledge, skill, and ability should be paid similarly even if actual duties differ significantly (p. 130)

Compensatory damages pay for actual monetary losses, for future losses, for mental anguish and inconvenience (p. 140)

Competing could mean "standing up for your rights," defending a position that you believe is correct; or demonstrating a win-at-all-costs attitude (p. 294)

Compressed workweek condenses the hours worked each week into fewer days (p. 98)

Compromising involves finding expedient, mutually acceptable solutions that partially satisfy both parties (p. 294)

Computer addiction occurs when computer use consumes someone's entire social life (p. 84)

Computer monitoring involves using computers to observe, record, and review an individual's use of the computer, including communications such as e-mail, keyboard activity (to measure activity), and Internet sites visited (p. 45)

Computer security risk any event or action that could cause a loss of or damage to computer hardware, software, data, information, or processing capability (p. 75)

Computer system group of computer devices that are connected, coordinated, and linked in such a way that they work as one to complete a task (p. 110)

Computer vision syndrome (CVS) characterized by eye fatigue, blurred vision, dry eyes, and headaches (p. 331)

Controlling management function of devising ways and means of ensuring that planned performance is actually achieved (p. 23)

Core activities an organization's operations, including the creation, selling, and support of the products and services that the company produces (p. 73)

Core competencies primary functions of a business that directly make money for the company (p. 102)

Corporate culture invisible driving force that reflects the collective values and behaviors of those associated with the organization (p. 40)

Corporate universities centralized, proactive entities that are responsible for all training and education at a given company (p. 119)

Cross-functional team a group staffed with a mix of specialists focused on a common objective, problem, or goal (p. 91)

Cultural literacy understanding and being sensitive to race, religion, global etiquette; helping people feel comfortable in the workplace; and understanding other cultures (p. 70)

D

De facto policies policies embedded in the everyday work of the organization (pp. 193–194)

Decentralized authority power and decision-making are dispersed to successively lower levels of the organization (p. 21)

Defensive reaction a way of thinking that cushions the blow resulting from an immediate inability to overcome an obstacle or barrier that has been placed in your path (p. 270)

Delegation process by which managers distribute and entrust activities and related authority to subordinates in the organization (p. 20)

Depression state of being sad, or a psychoneurotic or psychotic disorder marked especially by sadness, inactivity, difficulty in thinking and concentration, a significant increase or decrease in appetite and time spent sleeping, feelings of dejection and hopelessness, and sometimes suicidal tendencies (p. 213)

Desk rage can take the form of yelling, verbal abuse, rudeness, destroying equipment, and overall negativity; could be a precursor to workplace violence (p. 255)

Digital copiers digital imaging systems; multifunctional devices with a copying platen (p. 372)

Digital divide describes the idea that people of the world can be divided into those who have access to technology with the ability to use it and those who do not (p. 23)

Direct compensation an employee's base pay as well as any incentive pay programs (p. 186)

Document feeder allows the user to copy multi-page documents without having to lift and lower the platen cover for every sheet copied (p. 372)

Document imaging conversion of paper documents into electronic images on your computer (p. 367)

Document management deals with the control, retention, and security of records and files whether in paper form or on electronic magnetic storage devices (p. 364)

Domestic violence abusive behavior that is physical, sexual, and/or psychological, and intended to establish and maintain control over a partner (p. 346)

Drug-Free Workplace Act of 1988 ensures the employers who have contracts with the U.S. government maintain a drug-free

environment for their workers (p. 212)

Duplex scanning allows both sides of a two-sided document to be scanned in a single pass (p. 368)

Duplexing two-sided copies (p. 372)

DVD (Digital Video Disc or **Digital Versatile Disc)** the newest generation of optical disc storage technology (p. 370)

E

E-commerce a financial business transaction that occurs over an electronic network; also known as *electronic commerce* (p. 89)

Effectiveness ability to get the "right things" accomplished by selecting the most suitable goals and the proper steps, people, and physical resources to achieve them (p. 23)

Efficiency ability to "get things right" in a reasonable and timely manner with a minimum expenditure of resources (p. 23)

E-learning a person learns at his or her own pace using computers and telecommunication devices (p. 120)

Employee handbooks commonly used manuals that communicate to workers numerous company policies, ranging from time off to insurance coverage to drug testing (p. 195)

Employee recruitment process of generating a pool of qualified applicants for organizational job vacancies (p. 152)

Employee selection process of choosing individuals who have relevant qualifications to fill jobs in an organization (p. 154)

Employment application form serves as the basis for initial screening of minimum qualifications and becomes the basis for any subsequent interviews (p. 154)

Empowerment a set of practices designed to authorize, drive, and enable day-to-day decision-making at lower levels within an organization (p. 90)

Entrenched bureaucracy a company where workers are more concerned with their bosses rather than with customers; can be seen in the typical vertical organization (p. 91)

Equal Employment Act forbids discrimination on the basis of race, color, sex, religion, or national origin (p. 131)

Equal Employment Opportunity Commission (EEOC) agency that handles complaints relative to race, sex, color, religion, and national origin, plus age and disability discrimination and compensation charges (p. 130)

Equal Pay Act of 1963 prohibits discrimination on the basis of sex in the payment of wages or benefits, where men and women perform work of similar skill, effort, and responsibility for the same employer under similar working conditions (p. 130)

Ergonomics an applied science devoted to incorporating comfort, efficiency, and safety into the design of items in the workplace; designing the job environment to fit a worker's physical and psychological needs (p. 75, 324)

Ethics moral guidelines involving right versus wrong; behaviors that tell people how to act in ways that meet the standard that our values set for us (pp. 38, 230)

Exempt employees employees who are not paid overtime and usually are classified as being in professional or administrative positions (p. 184)

Exit interview to obtain information from departing employees concerning their experiences with various aspects of their employment (p. 198)

F

Facsimile (fax) a machine that can transmit and receive documents by translating copies of text or graphic documents into electronic signals, which are then transmitted over regular telephone lines or by satellite (p. 383)

Fair Credit Reporting Act (FCRA) designed to promote accuracy and ensure the privacy of the information used in consumer reports and background checks (p. 348)

Fair Labor Standards Act (FLSA) major law affecting compensation administration (p. 184)

Family and Medical Leave Act (FMLA) entitles eligible employees to take up to twelve weeks of unpaid, job-protected leave in a twelve-month period for specified family and medical reasons (p. 137)

Finishers advanced staple/sorters that can three-hole punch or even fold the finished copies (p. 372)

Flextime workers are required to report for work on each working day and work a given number of hours (p. 97)

Foot-candle describes the quality of light (p. 326)

Formal groups groups that are deliberately formed and created by management to attain organizational goals and objectives (p. 284)

Free-rein (laissez-faire) leader focuses on the welfare and feelings of followers, and has self-confidence and a strong need to develop and fully empower team members (p. 262)

G

Generation X people born between 1965 and 1976 (p. 268)

Generation Y people born after the year 1977 (p. 269)

Globally literate seeing, thinking, and acting in culturally mindful ways (p. 69)

Grievance procedure provides the mechanism whereby employee and union grievances can be aired and judged according to prescribed and agreed-upon steps (p. 201)

Groups two or more freely interacting individuals who have a common identity and purpose (p. 74)

Groupthink the tendency of highly cohesive groups to lose their critical evaluative abilities and, out of a desire for harmony, often overlook realistic, meaningful alternatives as attitudes are formed and decisions are made (p. 286)

H

Hawthorne Experiments studies that found that changes in the work environment had little long-term effect upon worker productivity (p. 10)

Hidden agendas composed of attitudes and feelings that an individual brings to the group (p. 286)

Horizontal organizations managing "across" has become more critical than managing "up and down" in a top-heavy hierarchy (p. 91)

Hostile work environment occurs when supervisors or coworkers do things that make the work atmosphere more difficult for people based on their gender; it interferes with an individual's work performance or contains intimidating or offensive behavior (pp. 134, 349)

Human capital collective sum of the attributes, life experience, knowledge, inventiveness, energy, and enthusiasm that the company's people choose to invest in work (p. 72)

Human relations approach the early approach to worker behavior; calls attention to the importance of the individual within the organization (p. 10)

Hygienic (or maintenance) factors factors that are related to productivity on the job but usually based on set criteria established by the employer (p. 186)

I

Incandescent lighting achieved with filament bulbs; similar to lighting found in most homes (p. 317)

Incentive plans direct compensation that is optional but usually based on set criteria established by the employer (p. 186)

Income statement a summary of all income and expenses for a certain time frame, such as a month or year (p. 383)

Indirect compensation includes the whole array of benefits (p. 186)

Informal groups arise spontaneously throughout all levels of the company (p. 284)

Information literacy the ability to use computers and technology to find, analyze, and use information in a meaningful way (p. 68)

Information technology consists primarily of computing, combined with telecommunications and networking; also known as *Infotech* (p. 44)

Injunction a court order requiring a person or corporation to do or to refrain from doing a particular act (p. 130)

Insider trading use of information unavailable to the public (p. 38)

Integration a powerful management technique that brings conflicting parties together to discuss the issues face-to-face (p. 296)

Internet addiction disorder the condition of being addicted to the Internet (p. 84)

Internet world's largest network system used to send messages to others, obtain information, shop for business-related goods and services, and meet or converse with people around the world (p. 76)

Intranet a company's internal network that uses Internet technology to make company information accessible electronically to employees using an assigned username and password (p. 77)

Inverted pyramid organizational model that charts the "who, what, and how" of management in an opposite way to the traditional upright pyramid chart (p. 28)

J

Job analysis process of collecting and organizing information about jobs performed in the organization and the principle elements involved in performing them (p. 140)

Job description defines in written form the tasks, duties, and responsibilities of a particular job (p. 142)

Job posting positions are announced on bulletin boards or in company publications as openings occur (p. 191)

Job sharing allows two people to share the duties—and prorate salaries and benefits—of one full-time position (p. 98)

Job specification clarifies the knowledge, degree, skills, and abilities a worker needs in order to do the job competently (p. 142)

L

Labor unions associations of employees formed to represent work force concerns and interests (p. 142)

during negotiations with management (p. 201)

Leadership the art of influencing people to work willingly and enthusiastically to attain organizational objectives by embracing a vision or goal as their own (pp. 74, 256)

Leading management function of motivating individuals and influencing group activities to accomplish objectives (p. 22)

Learning organization encourages training as essential to actual work; learning is emerging as a byproduct of work rather than something done in isolation (p. 92)

Lose-lose negotiating strategy common when one party attempts to win at the expense of the other (p. 295)

M

Mail dump table a large, flat table with a small lip around three or four sides that allows users to dump and spread loose mail for visual inspection before individual handling (p. 381)

Management the process of working with and through others to blend together people, materials, money, methods, machines, and morale in an effort to set and to achieve the goals of the organization (p. 6)

Management by objectives (MBO) objectives set forth for every area where performance and results directly and vitally affect the survival and prosperity of the organizations (pp. 11–12)

Management science makes use of engineering and mathematical skills to solve complex decision-making problems; also known as *quantitative business methods* (p. 12)

Management theory principles that are classified and grouped into a managerial framework (p. 24)

Mediation an impartial third party tries to bring both sides to a point of common agreement (p. 135)

Megabyte one million characters, or bytes of data (p. 370)

Mentor an adviser, teacher, sounding board, cheerleader, and critic, all rolled into one (p. 54)

Merit pay based on established criteria or performance at an exemplary level as usually reflected in an employee's performance appraisal (p. 186)

Microfiche index-sized film that can be read on a variety of microfiche readers or printed out in the form of paper enlargements (p. 367)

Microfilm economical archival medium for long-term storage with low equipment costs and comparatively fast retrieval (pp. 366–367)

Modem enables computers to communicate, usually via telephone lines or cable (p. 110)

Modular design refers to the design of office furniture that facilitates the use of different components and variations in the way those components are arranged in the space provided (p. 320)

Motivation-hygiene theory theory that states we work in environments where two kinds of factors are present: motivators and hygienic (or maintenance) factors (p. 11)

Motivators factors that result from experiences that create positive attitudes toward work and arise from the job content itself (p. 11)

Multifunctionality one machine performing two or even three different functions (p. 372)

Multitasking the ability to execute more than one task at the same time (p. 297)

Musculoskeletal disorders (MSDs) potential physical outcomes for workers using poorly designed office equipment, furniture, and work spaces, or for employees who are inadequately trained in ergonomic practices; includes carpal tunnel syndrome and tendonitis (p. 329)

N

Negligent hiring the failure on the part of the organization to use reasonable care in the selection process while hiring (p. 348)

Negotiation a psychological process requiring give-and-take between the participants (p. 293)

Nepotism favoritism shown to a relative on the basis of relationship (p. 218)

Network a collection of computers and devices connected by communications channels that facilitate communication among workers and allow users to share resources with other users (p. 76)

Network administrator an individual who provides upgrades and assistance with networking difficulties (p. 111)

Noncore functions security, information technology, and human resources (p. 102)

Nonexempt employees employees who are paid overtime and are usually paid an hourly wage (p. 184)

Norm a generally agreed-on standard of behavior that every member of the group is expected to follow (pp. 284–285)

O

Objectives measurable end results; the goals or targets that an organization, department, or individual seeks to attain (p. 16)

Office environment made up of several interdependent systems that include people, floor plans, furniture, equipment, lighting, air quality, and acoustics (p. 316)

Office layout the working arrangement of facilities and workstations (p. 316)

Office manuals procedures that specify a standard way for dealing with recurring situations or activities so that they will be handled uniformly throughout an organization (p. 307)

Office politics leveraging, positioning, and building alliances (p. 272)

Organizing multifaceted management function that gets things done (p. 20)

Orientation a meeting or formal activity that specifically prepares employees for working in a particular organization and working environment (p. 163)

Outsourcing management strategy by which an organization utilizes specialized, efficient service providers to perform major, noncore functions (p. 102)

P

Paradigm a set of assumptions or a frame of reference (p. 89)

Paradigm shift a fundamental change in the assumptions we make about a certain body of knowledge (p. 89)

Participative (democratic) leader involves followers heavily in the decision-making process by using group involvement to set basic objectives, establish strategies, and determine job assignments (pp. 261–262)

Patience ability to be able to wait for results without complaint or anxiety (p. 39)

Pension plans retirement benefits established and funded by employers and employees (p. 188)

Performance appraisals a management tool where supervisors notice employees' attitudes, performances, and their work habits (p. 172)

Permatemps long-term temporary employees (p. 101)

Persistence continuing steadfastly and being committed (p. 39)

Personal power informal power that is manifested by the extent to which followers are willing to *follow* a leader (p. 272)

Personal space the flow and shift of distance between people as they interact and communicate (p. 247)

Personality disorders excessive absenteeism, tardiness, withdrawal, and personality conflicts are behaviors motivated by the need to survive (p. 270)

Perspective broad view of an event or idea (p. 39)

Piggybacking the process of revising and expanding on suggested solutions (p. 277)

Planning management function of choosing or generating organizational objectives and then determining the courses of action needed to achieve those objectives (p. 16)

Policy a plan or course of action adopted by a business organization that is designed to influence and determine decisions, actions, and other matters (p. 193)

Portable skills an individual is able to transfer what he or she already knows to slightly new situations (p. 116)

Portfolio contains a collection of items in book form that documents and chronicles the accomplishments that can give an individual's career a boost (pp. 49–50)

Position approval form identifies the position title and related classification information; essential functions of the position; and the duties, experience, education, and training needed to perform the duties (p. 154)

Position power formal authority to tell others what to do that is granted by the organization (p. 272)

Posting the process of prioritizing the ideas from most important to least or vice versa (p. 277)

Power not an attempt to influence but the *ability* to influence others (p. 132)

Pregnancy Discrimination Act states that an employer cannot refuse to hire a woman because of her pregnancy-related condition as long as she is able to perform the major functions of her job (p. 132)

Principles broad, general statements that are considered to be true and that accurately reflect real-world conditions in all walks of life (p. 24)

Privacy policy articulates the reason for monitoring; specifies when, where, and how employees will be monitored; and outlines how any surveillance data will be used (p. 45)

Problem-solving committees groups that meet on an as-needed basis and are relatively permanent (p. 284)

Procedure a written, step-by-step standardized method of handling a task or action; it outlines the steps to be performed when completing a specific task or activity (pp. 193, 307)

Project organizations use a project planning process to achieve objectives (p. 19)

Punitive damages may be available if an employer acted with malice or reckless indifference (p. 140)

Pyramid traditional management organizational model (p. 14)

Q

Quality management both a philosophy and a set of principles used to guide the entire organization in continuous improvement; also known as *total quality management* (TQM) (p. 12)

R

Reasonable accommodation employer requirement to make accommodations to the known disability of a qualified applicant or employee if it would not impose an "undue hardship" on the operation of the employer's business (pp. 135–136)

Reasonable care the level of care that a reasonably prudent person would exercise under the circumstances (p. 348)

Reframing refers to looking for evidence of a more positive, less catastrophic view of some problem or change (pp. 87, 292)

Repetitive strain injury (RSI) an injury or disorder of the muscles, nerves, tendons, ligaments, and joints (p. 330)

Reputation what people think of the way you do business and how they assess your character as a business person (p. 38)

Responsibility obligation and accountability for properly performing work that is assigned (p. 21)

Retention strategy techniques to retain workers (p. 48)

Risk factor a condition or circumstance that may increase the likelihood of violence occurring in a particular setting (p. 343)

Rule an authoritative directive for conduct; an established standard or habit of behavior (p. 193)

S

Scanning a document produces a picture that can be stored on a computer (p. 368)

Serious health condition an illness, injury, impairment, or physical or mental condition that involves a period of incapacity or treatment connected with inpatient care or continuing treatment by a health-care provider that includes any period of incapacity (p. 138)

Sexual harassment unwelcome sexual advances, requests for sexual favors, and other verbal or physical conduct of a sexual nature that creates an intimidating, offensive, hostile work environment (p. 133)

Shredder machine that cuts paper documents into small pieces; provide document security and, at the same time, help the environment (p. 385)

Simplex scanning scans one side of a document only (p. 368)

Single-use plan plans that are developed and used for a certain period of time (p. 19)

Situational interview questions questions related to the job requirements and knowledge, training, and education needed for the position that is being advertised (p. 159)

Social Security includes old age benefits, survivor benefits, disability benefits, and medical benefits; also known as the *Old Age and Survivors Insurance (OASI) Program* (p. 187)

Spam an unsolicited e-mail message sent to many recipients at once; commonly known as Internet junk mail (p. 183)

Span of control refers to the number of employees who are directly supervised by one person (p. 27)

Specialist a person who masters or becomes expert at doing a certain type of work (p. 26)

Spyware software that is used for the sole purpose of tracking and recording computer actions (p. 47)

Standing plans rules, policies, and procedures that remain in effect within the organization (p. 19)

Strategic planning process involves defining an organization's mission, setting its objectives, and developing strategies that will enable it to operate successfully in its internal and external environment (p. 17)

Strategy detailed plan (p. 48)

Stress any external stimulus that produces wear and tear on a person's psychological or physical well-being (p. 298)

Structured interview questions questions that ask job applicants to tell about themselves and their experiences that qualify them for the job (p. 159)

System a group of parts that are interrelated in such a manner that they form a unified whole and work together to meet a defined need (p. 110)

Systems approach to training emphasis on formulating instructional objectives, developing learning activities to meet those objectives, establishing performance criteria to be met, and evaluating the results of training (p. 168)

T

Task lighting illuminates the work surface (p. 317)

Task-force groups groups that usually focus on a specific issue, meet a few times, and then disband (p. 284)

Technology an aid to making a task easier by using equipment and procedures to create, process, and output information (p. 115)

Telecommuting a work arrangement in which employees work away from a company's standard workplace, and often communicate with the office using telecommunications and computer technology (p. 98)

Termination a request for an employee to leave a job (p. 196)

Theory created when sets of principles are grouped into a general framework that explains the basic relationship among them (p. 24)

Theory X includes assumptions that people generally dislike work, lack ambition, and work primarily because they need to have money to live (p. 260)

Theory Y assumes that work is as natural as rest or play, and that workers will accept responsibility when self-direction and self-control can be used to pursue valued objectives (p. 261)

Theory Z emphasizes on long-range planning, consensus decision-making, and strong mutual worker-employer loyalty (p. 261)

Theory Z management the attitude of Japanese management toward work and workers (p. 12)

Total compensation package includes direct compensation and indirect compensation (p. 186)

Training intended to improve individual work performance by equipping people with the knowledge, skills, and attitudes they must possess to be successful in their work (p. 167)

Train-the-trainer workshops teach peer experts how to teach using interactive and instructional skills; can be conducted by trainers within the organization or by contracting with an outside training source (pp. 169–170)

Transactional employment employees continuously develop their skills to allow them to move from one employer to another (p. 102)

Turnover workers leaving their jobs in the business world (p. 176)

U

Undue hardship an action requiring significant difficulty or expense when considered in light

of factors such as an employer's size, financial resources, and the nature and structure of its operations (p. 136)

Unemployment compensation unemployment insurance; provides unemployed workers with benefits from a fund of payroll taxes imposed on employers (pp. 187–188)

Union contract usually specifies wages, benefits, work rules, and other workplace procedures (p. 201)

Unity of command reporting to one supervisor (p. 26)

V

Value-driven company one that consistently produces a high-quality product or service, treats employees with respect, and has demonstrated ways in which it incorporates the values it holds into the fabric and culture of its business (p. 230)

Values fundamental beliefs or principles that are important to an individual (pp. 48, 230)

Virtual assistant an independent entrepreneur who offers business support services in a virtual environment (p. 114)

Virtual company (workplace) where work is performed outside of a defined place (p. 112)

Virtual coordinator (VC) someone who can adapt quickly and without hesitation, step in when needed, and be able to access information immediately—whether it's electronically retrieved from the company's data storage system or researched on the Internet (p. 66)

Virtual organizations collaborative networks that make it possible to draw on vital resources as needed, regardless of *where* they are located physically and regardless of *who* "owns" them—supplier, worker, or customer (p. 112)

Virtual teams usually formed when geographical separations can't be bridged (p. 288)

Virtual work primarily the manufacture, retail, and distribution of *intellectual* property, or work that is produced with the mind (p. 112)

Virtual work force a work force where work is performed outside of a defined place (p. 113)

Visual ergonomics the interaction of your vision with the task that you are performing (p. 333)

Voice mail a sophisticated, computerized telephone answering system that digitizes incoming spoken messages, stores them in the recipient's voice mailbox, and then reconverts them into spoken form when retrieved; also known as *voice messaging* (p. 376)

W

Wage survey first step in a salary compensation policy where internal and external data is gathered and analyzed (p. 185)

Win-lose negotiating strategy assumes that one side will win by achieving its goals and the other side will lose (p. 295)

Win-win negotiating strategy assumes that a reasonable solution can be reached that will satisfy the needs of all parties (p. 296)

Work/life boundaries the goal of workers to perfectly balance responsibilities on the job with responsibilities at home (p. 215)

Workaholic a compulsive worker (p. 215)

Worker Adjustment and Retraining Notification Act (WARN) offers protection to workers, their families, and communities by requiring employers to provide notice 60 days in advance of plant closings and mass layoffs (p. 198)

Workers' compensation laws that protect employees and their families from permanent loss of income and high medical payments as a consequence of accidental injury, illness, or death on the job (p. 188)

Workflow the movement of information from person to person within an organization (p. 320)

Workplace literacy involves the ability to use words clearly and communicate with brevity and accuracy as those actions relate to employability and skill requirements for a particular job (pp. 69, 116)

Workplace violence any physical assault, threatening behavior, or verbal abuse occurring in the work setting (p. 340)

Wrongful termination refers to a person being fired when he or she shouldn't have been (p. 197)

Index